'Not a single formal publication exists in the area of Islamic Business Administration. This book fills that gap, suitable for use in classrooms and in practice and policy areas.'

– Professor Tariqullah Khan, Hamad Bin Khalifa University, Qatar Foundation, Qatar

'*Islamic Business Administration* opens the doors for learning about business administration from an Islamic perspective. This book takes a holistic perspective and offers a global focus, practical orientation and comprehensive coverage … A must read not only for business students, but also for business leaders and a general readership.'

– Omar Mustafa Ansari, Secretary General, Accounting and Auditing Organization for Islamic Financial Institutions, Bahrain

'This is the most comprehensive book on business administration from an Islamic perspective that I have found. It covers all areas of Islamic belief, norms and values, entrepreneurship, ethics and social responsibility including the latest issues of change and innovation, marketing, decision making and finance, all from an Islamic perspective … a valuable book.'

– Associate Prof Rifki Ismal, University of Indonesia and Tazkia Institute, Indonesia

'A comprehensive and well-researched Islamic business administration book for both academics and industry players.'

– Professor Dr Rosylin Mohd Yusof, Othman Yeop Abdullah Graduate School of Business, Malaysia

'Given the diversity of topics covered – from principles of Islamic business to Islamic management and governance issues – the book serves as a good textbook for students and a comprehensive reference for researchers and others interested in understanding the principles that must be upheld while running an Islamic business.'

– Dr Humayon Dar, Director General, Cambridge Institute of Islamic Finance, UK

'The first comprehensive textbook to cover all facets of Islamic Business … particularly relevant in the context of the rising influence of Gulf economies in the world economy. This is a book for both scholars from the West and those from the MENA region.'

– Dr Vivien Exartier, Royal University for Women, Bahrain

T0295929

ISLAMIC BUSINESS ADMINISTRATION

CONCEPTS AND STRATEGIES

MINWIR AL-SHAMMARI

MOHAMMAD OMAR FAROOQ

HATEM MASRI

BLOOMSBURY ACADEMIC
LONDON • NEW YORK • OXFORD • NEW DELHI • SYDNEY

BLOOMSBURY ACADEMIC
Bloomsbury Publishing Plc
50 Bedford Square, London, WC1B 3DP, UK
1385 Broadway, New York, NY 10018, USA
29 Earlsfort Terrace, Dublin 2, Ireland

BLOOMSBURY, BLOOMSBURY ACADEMIC and the Diana logo
are trademarks of Bloomsbury Publishing Plc

First Published 2020 by
RED GLOBE PRESS

Reprinted by Bloomsbury Academic

A catalogue record for this book is available from the British Library.

A catalog record for this book is available from the Library of Congress.

ISBN: PB: 978-1-3520-0947-7
ePDF: 978-1-3520-0948-4
ePub: 978-1-3503-0518-2

To find out more about our authors and books visit
www.bloomsbury.com and sign up for our newsletters.

To the teacher of mankind

CONTENTS

Part 1 Islamic Business Environment

Part 4   Finance and Accounting

LIST OF FIGURES

LIST OF TABLES

PREFACE

Business administration and practices vary in cross-cultural and globalized business environments according to many factors, such as national cultural values and ethics, and national and international institutions, such as labor laws, educational systems, and international, political, and socioeconomic settings.

Since the second half of the twentieth century, discourse about Islamic economics and finance and the development of Islamic banking and finance have received critical attention inside and beyond the Muslim world. Islamic finance is not a multitrillion-dollar global industry, but it is experiencing steady growth. During the last two decades, robust academic and pedagogical resources have emerged. However, similar development has not been seen in the area of business-related academic resources. Thus, one struggles to find an Islamic alternative to the "Introduction to Business" type of undergraduate courses.

In Islam, all business activities are governed by obedience to the moral order of Allah (God) and empathy and mercy to other humans. Islamic values, ethics, and principles determine a way of life that touches all aspects of daily human behavior and motivation, including commercial, social, and spiritual activities. Islamic teachings cover all aspects of business activities including marketing, financing, accounting, and contracts.

Islam has laid down many rules and regulations for administering business activity that have been used implicitly and for a long time by Islamic managers. Hence, with the emergence of Islamic finance, Islamic marketing, and Islamic accounting, managers started discovering the main Islamic rules and their impact on business administration. Islamic rules and laws are important not only for Muslim managers who would like to earn "Halal Rizq" (which means lawful or permissible earnings according to Islamic teachings) but can also be used by non-Muslim managers to better understand business situations and practices and enhance the performance of their organizations.

Although the Islamic perspective on business practices has been largely ignored in business-related academic resources, recent years have witnessed rising interest in exploring the influence of Islamic values and principles on business practices. While no specific books explicitly address the link between Islam and modern business activities, recent interest in exploring the influence of Islam on various business practices has grown.

This book seeks to offer to business or Islamic studies academics and practitioners a reinvigorated and enhanced view on practical ideas in Islamic business administration. The reader need not have any specific previous knowledge of Islam or business administration to grasp this book's contents.

This book represents the first attempt to provide a solid foundation for essential topics in business administration from an Islamic perspective and to make managers aware of Islamic rules and practices and how they can help managers understand and manage their business. It also seeks to establish a connection between the literature on Islamic studies and business practices, thereby creating added value to a new way of managing business operations according to Islamic rules.

It is hoped that the book will play a valuable role in developing and supporting courses, such as introductions to Islamic business or Islamic business administration. Experts from pertinent fields have contributed various chapters to make the book possible, and Macmillan, a leading publisher of college textbooks, will surely enhance the value and relevance of this trailblazing work.

We would like to thank all the contributors and reviewers whose valuable contributions and patient engagement have allowed this work, several years in the making, to come to fruition. All relevant feedback that would serve to improve this work is welcomed.

Minwir Al-Shammari
Mohammad Omar Farooq
Hatem Masri
University of Bahrain, Manama, Kingdom of Bahrain

PART
1

ISLAMIC BUSINESS ENVIRONMENT

ISLAM AND BUSINESS: BELIEFS, VALUES, AND NORMS

1

Mohammad Omar Farooq and Fareed Hadi

University of Bahrain, Bahrain

Learning Outcomes

LO1: Explain the role of business and resources used for it.

LO2: Describe the business environment, key stakeholders, and major types of decision making.

LO3: Understand the core beliefs and values of Islam pertaining to business and commerce

LO4: Recognize the emphasis of the Qur'an, as exemplified in the life of the Prophet (p), on trade and prosperity in human-centered, sustainable development

LO5: Explain the role trade has played in the history of Islamic civilization and the contemporary aspirations and initiatives to bring Islamic values to business and the economy

Contents

INSIGHT: Shared Prosperity

Chobani is a Greek yogurt maker, a privately owned multibillion-dollar company in the USA. Its CEO and founder is Hamdi Ulukaya, a Turkish immigrant to the USA.

On April 27, 2016, he declared that his company will offer shares to its 2000 full-time employees that are 10 percent of the company's future value in the event of a sale or an IPO. This will make many of its employees millionaires.

This is commonly known as an employee stock ownership plan (ESOP), and the underlying value is called shared prosperity – a highly relevant approach to profit sharing.

From an Islamic viewpoint, what the owner of Chobani did is not a matter of law or legalistic exercise. Rather, this is Islam beyond the realm of law or mere legal considerations. In it there is vision, values, ethics, and, most importantly, care reflecting Islam. We may wonder what the world would look like if those who have the power, wealth, and privilege to embrace, promote, and practice the value of "shared prosperity."

The Qur'an teaches that wealth should not circulate among the wealthy few [59/al-Hashr/7]! Beyond legality, this is a value-oriented approach.

Source: Chobani's vision in the owner's words: https://www.chobani.com/about/.

1.1   Introduction

An economy is a system that seeks to balance the resources of a country against the wants and needs of its people. The main activities in an economy consist of:

- Production (supply)
- Consumption (demand)
- Distribution (linking demand and supply).

Businesses participate in the economy to produce and supply what consumers demand. Businesses in a market economy serve as the growth drivers in a number of interrelated ways:

- Creating employment and income-earning opportunities for the working population
- Purchasing resources
- Supplying goods and services
- Fostering innovation
- Generating savings and capital
- Fulfilling the needs and wants of society.

In the Muslim world, businesses play roles similar to those played by businesses in the rest of the world where Muslims live and have businesses. Though businesses share certain features, Islam as a way of life brings certain beliefs, values, and norms in shaping and conducting business. A synopsis of these beliefs, values, and norms are explored in this chapter, which also presents the basics of business. Further, these beliefs, values, and norms underlie all aspects of business covered in this book.

Muslim societies throughout history have led, fostered, and facilitated trade and business around the world. That changed as the Western world embarked upon its colonizing enterprise throughout the world, including the Muslim world as the Ottoman Empire disintegrated. After the breakup of the Ottoman (Turkish) Empire (1299–1924 AD), the Muslim world emerged from the postcolonial period as nation-states. The Organization of Islamic Cooperation (OIC), an international organization established in 1969, consists of 57 member states and represents more than 1.6 billion people, with a combined GDP (at purchasing power parity, or PPP) $18.6 trillion (Euro zone: $12.39 trillion, NAFTA $20.1 trillion). These countries vary in area, demographics, stage of development, resources, and so forth. However, during the postcolonial era, only a few countries, among which are Malaysia and Turkey, have made significant progress in their industrial development.

1.2   Beyond Islamic banking and finance

During the postcolonial period, one of the key developments and contributions of the Muslim world that has gone mainstream and attracted significant attention from around the world is Islamic banking and finance (IBF). This niche industry is based on the avoidance of certain religious prohibitions, the most important of which is *riba* (traditionally equated with interest).

While there is no national economy that can be identified as an Islamic economy where business activities are conducted based on Islamic values and parameters, according to Islamic Finance Outlook 2018 by S&P Global Rating, the Islamic banking and finance industry has been growing at a robust pace and reached $2 trillion in assets. The development of this field has led to the establishment of:

- financial institutions (e.g. Al Baraka and Kuwait Finance House banks)

- standard-setting and other support institutions (e.g. Islamic Financial Services Board [IFSB], Accounting and Auditing Organization for Islamic Financial Institutions [AAOIFI])

- academic and professional research institutions (e.g. International Centre for Education in Islamic Finance [INCEIF], Islamic Shariah Research Academy [ISRA])[1]

- regulatory bodies as part of central banks.

However, there is little focus or emphasis on business in general or nonfinancial businesses in particular for which financial institutions and markets exist.

With the growth and expansion of the IBF industry, and for its sustainability and relevance, the focus needs to shift to the real world of business and help develop relevant knowledge, infrastructure, and competencies.

Whether it pertains to banking, finance, or economics, considering any of these from Islamic perspectives requires making explicit the underlying foundation of beliefs, values, and principles. The same is true of business from Islamic perspectives.

1.3   Essential Islamic beliefs pertaining to business

Islam as a practical, balanced, wholesome and comprehensive way of life (*deen*) is based on three core beliefs: *tawhid* (monotheism), *risalah* (prophethood, messengership), and *aakhirah* (afterlife). These beliefs constitute the foundation of every aspect of Muslim life, including business.

1.3.1   *Tawhid* (Monotheism)

Tawhid entails that there is a God, the one and only God, who created human beings as part of the universe. Even though humans share this universe with their fellow creations, God made human beings distinct as thinking and discerning creatures that are able to reason and make choices. Muslims are expected to acknowledge God in their lives by searching for and affirming his guidance and upholding it to the best of their ability.

1.3.2 *Risalah* (Prophethood, Messengership)

As part of our natural disposition, we human beings search for explanations of our life and existence, and if there is a Creator or God, it makes sense that mankind should receive communication from the Creator. God has sent divine revelations throughout history, and the last and final revelation is the Qur'an, received verbatim via the Prophet Muhammad (p).[2] The Qur'an is the fountain of the beliefs, principles, and values of Islam. The life of the Prophet (p) exemplifies the normative best practices of Islam, which is known as *sunnah* and preserved through *hadith*, but this source is not in the same category as the Qur'an.

1.3.3 *Aakhira* (Afterlife)

There is a life after death, which includes a Day of Judgment, when God will hold human beings accountable. Those who find favor with God in light of his guidance in this world will go to paradise and enjoy eternal bliss. In contrast, those who find disfavor with God will be doomed. Thus, the afterlife is based on the concept of accountability in this life, but more importantly in the life hereafter, which should shape all the transactions, pursuits, decisions, and choices, whether those relate to commercial or noncommercial activities.

The Islamic way of life (*deen*) is based on comprehensive guidance from the Qur'an and the exemplary life of the Prophet Muhammad (p). However, over time, Muslim societies have put disproportionately more emphasis on laws and codes, known as *fiqh* or Islamic law.[3]

1.4 Essential aspects of Islamic law

All activities in life are driven by certain values and conducted within a framework of legal precepts. But contemporary Islamic practices and norms are heavily legalistic, creating a fundamental gap between laws and values. We discuss values in the next section.

> **[Q 45:18]**
> Then We put you, [O Muhammad], on an ordained way [*Shariah*] concerning the matter [of religion]; so follow it and do not follow the inclinations of those who do not know.

The legal aspects of Islam can be understood in the framework of *Shariah* and *fiqh*. *Shariah* is the divine path that consists of broader and general guidance as well as a set of specific injunctions (*fardh*, obligation) and prohibitions (*haram*). Muslims are required to practice the *fardh*, avoid the *haram*, and conduct themselves only within the limits of what is permissible (*halal*). Both the domains of injunctions and prohibitions consist of a small list, leaving the overwhelmingly larger domain to human judgment and interpretation. When it comes to details about these injunctions and prohibitions, there are differences among various groups of Muslims. The domain of *fiqh* is the conscientious and dedicated effort of Muslim scholars and experts throughout the ages to interpret the *Shariah* to deduce rulings and solutions as needed in different contexts of life.

Islamic law is based on a number of sources, including the primary sources – the Qur'an and *sunnah/hadith* – and secondary sources – *ijma'* (consensus) and *qiyas* (analogical reasoning). *Urf* or custom that does not conflict with the Qur'an or *sunnah* is also regarded as an additional source.

The specialized part of *fiqh* that relates to business is *Islamic commercial jurisprudence*, which also covers various types of business contracts. Since all such interpretations are fallible, Muslims are to exercise their discretion in adopting and applying the principles in a harmonious and problem-solving way.

1.5 Essential values of Islam

As a comprehensive way of life, Islam offers as guidance to humanity a set of essential values that also applies to business. The distinction between laws and values is fundamentally important. For example, it is not legally required of a Muslim to feed a hungry person. But from a value-oriented perspective, Islam teaches, as the Prophet Muhammad (p) said, "A man is not a believer who fills his stomach while his neighbour is hungry."[4] While a more comprehensive framework can be contemplated, in the context of business and economy, the following main values are presented here.

Q 3:110
"O believers, you are created for mankind …"

1.5.1   Humanity orientation

Islam teaches its adherents that they are to serve humanity. It is a message and imperative for believers to serve as a model for humanity both at the individual and collective level. Indeed, one of the primary factors that facilitated the spread of Islam since the post-Prophetic era has been the merchants and traders, who through their exemplary conduct reflect strong ethics and deep empathy.

In practical terms, this means recognizing the importance of a high ethical standard (benchmark principles that, when followed, foster the higher values of fairness, trust, care, and transparency), best practices, and good governance for modern businesses at all levels. Such businesses pursue profit with relevant human sensitivity while fulfilling their social responsibility as well.

Q 4:58
"Indeed, God commands you to render trust to whom it is due and when you judge between people to judge with justice …"

Social responsibility is an ethically driven perspective where various entities, individuals or organizations, are considered duty-bound to fulfill their civic duty for the benefit of the broader society. Such a perspective seeks a balance between the pursuit of profit and economic growth on the one hand and the welfare of society and a sustainable environment on the other.

1.5.2   Integrity and delivering on promises

Makkah and Madinah, two of the holiest cities of Islam, were major centers of trade even during pre-Muhammad (p) ages. Muhammad (p) was born in Makkah in 570 AD and chose business as his profession. Before he became the Prophet, Muhammad (p) was honored by his community as *al-Amin* (the Trustworthy) through his role as a successful and trustworthy businessperson and a social activist. A core value he imparted to his followers is *amanah* (trust), which means that they should have the highest level of integrity and keep promises at all levels, individual, institutional, national, and international.

Q 49:13
"… the most honourable of you with God is that (believer) who has *taqwa*."

A related value is *taqwa* (God-consciousness; Q 49:13), or being aware of God as the most important reference in making any choice or decision. He is constantly cognizant of our actions and thoughts and will hold human beings accountable.

Furthermore, Islam ennobles business as a profession, as long as it is done with integrity and care while avoiding what is prohibited in Islam and what is harmful to others.

The Prophet (p) said: "The truthful, trustworthy merchant is with the Prophets, the truthful, and the martyrs." [*Jami al-Tirmidhi*, Kitab al-Buyu, #1209]

1.5.3   Shared prosperity and Islamic economy

Because Muslims believe in the life hereafter, they aspire to true and lasting gains in the form of rewards of eternal peace and happiness in the life hereafter. Thus, in this life, while they devote themselves to the full demands of life, or live fully, they

Q 59:7
"… let not wealth circulate among a few …"

should not give in to greed or miserliness. They embrace the notion or value of shared prosperity. Indeed, to believe otherwise would be inconsistent with Islam.

Thus, the business arena can and is expected to be competitive in a way that enhances the common good, but from an Islamic viewpoint it cannot be predatory.

Because Muslims seek prosperity, they have an inclusive attitude based on empathy, where the notion of shared prosperity is highly relevant. The Prophet's teaching is categorical: "A person is not a believer who fills his stomach while his neighbor is hungry."[5]

The issue of an Islamic economy or an economy that reflects the values and parameters of Islam is relevant in this context. While many academic definitions of an Islamic economy have been proposed, one holistic way to describe such an economy can be that an Islamic economy is based on "sustainable, shared prosperity, subject to a few Islamic prohibitions." Others have emphasized the following four ethical axioms for an Islamic economy: (a) _tawheed_ (unity); (b) _al'adl wal ihsan_ (equilibrium); (c) _ikhtiar_ (free will); and (d) _fardh_ (social responsibility).[6] Islamic businesses flourish in an economic system that reflects and upholds the core Islamic values and parameters.

1.5.4 Fairness

Fairness, in Arabic _adalah_ or _qist_, is one of the central values of Islam. The standard set by Islam for fairness is rather higher than in any other faith or ideology.

The Islamic conception of fairness requires a higher level of conscience and consciousness, where a person is expected to know and recognize what is unfair and is supposed to stand for fairness, _even if it goes against oneself_. When it comes to fairness, all religions consider it important, but Islam sets a much higher standard by asking people to stand for justice and fairness in a self-critical manner. Such a self-critical and self-reflective perspective can have major, positive implications for the choices and decisions people make, especially when others' lives and interests are affected. Upholding fairness makes people more sensitive to the potential impacts of their decisions, policies, and conduct.

Thus, a stakeholder-oriented approach to business considerations is more relevant from an Islamic viewpoint than a narrow, shareholder-focused approach. A stakeholder is any party that is affected by or can affect an entity. Thus, the shareholders of a business are among key stakeholders, but in a stakeholder-oriented approach, employees, customers, suppliers, communities, regulators, and government are all given due considerations in a company's decision making.

1.5.5 Stewardship and sustainability

God created man as his _khalifa_ (vicegerent) on the Earth. The notion of _khalifa_ embodies the role of stewardship as well. God also reminds us in the Qur'an of the balance he has created and calls upon mankind not to upset that natural balance. This is central to our understanding of the modern concept of sustainability and environmental/ecological balance.

All people, whether producers or consumers, businessmen or regulators, as stakeholders on this Earth have a responsibility as a steward, and their decision making and choice should be geared toward shared prosperity from both intragenerational and intergenerational perspectives.

1.5.6   Real economy and earned income and wealth

Islam teaches the value of labor and earning of wealth through work and contributions to value creation. That is why *riba*, commonly equated with interest or unjust unearned income, is prohibited.

A real economy consists of the domain of production and consumption, where there must also be due emphasis on savings and the production of capital goods. Technology is an important factor in real economic growth and development. Another relevant factor in this context is **institutions,** established ways of behaving or established procedures, as embodied in organizations and their structure.

Modern business as part of the industrial age requires proper emphasis on the real economy, avoiding excessive financialization.

Islam emphasizes avoidance of excessive uncertainty and speculation, commonly associated with financialization, and a focus on the real economy promotes real value creation, instead of merely making money from financial activities.

1.5.7   Success orientation

Islam encourages its adherents to pursue success and achieve things in both lives, this one and the hereafter. The call to ritual prayer from mosques includes the statement, "Come to *falah*" (success, prosperity; salvation), where success is ultimately linked with salvation in the hereafter.

Whether for the hereafter or in this world, human aspirations should push people and businesses to pursue success within an ethical framework.

This requires vision, knowledge, competence, experience, determination, and sincerity. Vision is what guides any entity toward specific goals or destinations. The journey toward success requires knowledge and competence. In a modern society, knowledge and competence are gained through education and training. Success in any endeavor also requires determination and perseverance. As Jack Welch, former CEO of General Electric (1981–2001), affirmed: "Good business leaders create a vision, articulate the vision, passionately own the vision, and relentlessly drive it to completion."

1.5.8   Teamwork and collaboration

Business is a collective enterprise, where teamwork and collaboration in every aspect are important. The concepts of *jama'ah* (organization) and *ta'awun* (cooperation/collaboration) are relevant in this context.

Effective teamwork and collaboration require skilled, motivated, and empowered **human resources.** The input of all stakeholders is duly sought, valued, and utilized, whenever appropriate.

While Islam motivates people to work in teams and to collaborate, it also instills a spirit of avoiding collaboration in unethical matters. Moreover, it inspires people to play a constructive role in preempting or preventing wrongdoings. This value has highly positive implications for the creation of a symbiotic organizational culture and environment, contributing to effective management of change and innovation.

The contemporary business world is highly dynamic, and the pace of change is often fast owing to many disruptive factors. Successful businesses must be adept at change management, where, along with individuals and teams, they are prepared to reallocate resources, revise business processes, adjust budget allocations, or change modes of operation, which may lead to reshaping the business. Organizational

---

[Q 2:275]
" … But God has permitted trade and has forbidden Riba …"

Financialization:
A process whereby the economy is dominated by financial capital, marginalizing the real economy, with rising vulnerability to asset price bubbles.

Resource: Thomas Palley (2013). *Financialization: The Economics of Finance Capital Domination*, Palgrave Macmillan, 2013.

[Q 3:104]
And let there be [arising] from you a community inviting to [all that is] good, enjoining what is right and forbidding what is wrong, and those will be the successful (*muflihun*).

[Q 5:2]
… And cooperate in righteousness and piety, but do not cooperate in sin and aggression.

Q: 42:38
And those … whose affair is [determined by] consultation (*shura*)

[Q 2:148]
… hasten towards all that is good.

change management (OCM) considers organizations in their entirety and determines what needs to change.[1] OCM principles and practices include CM as a tool for change focused solely on the individual. Management of change and innovation requires businesses to focus on how people and teams are affected by transitions and positioning employees effectively.

1.5.9   Continuous improvement

The dynamics of human progress and development depends on continuous improvement. In business, especially in a competitive environment, this is fundamentally important.

A relevant Islamic concept is *islah,* which has a broad range of meanings: improvement, amelioration, correction, reconstruction, renovation, remedying, establishment of peace, happiness, order, reformation, restoration, and redressing.

It is a comprehensive concept with broad implications. The very spirit of it is to approach a problem with a solution-oriented mindset to seek ways to make good things better and to transform conflicts into cooperation. People have the God-endowed power to change themselves individually and collectively. *Islah* provides a positive framework with a higher purpose. It begins at the individual level with emphasis on good and positive thought, which steadily leads to a positive attitude and, in turn, positive actions and outcomes for the society.

1.5.10   Accountability

Islamic belief in *aakhirah* inculcates a firm and deep sense of accountability (*hisab*), where it is believed that every action is recorded and acknowledged by God, and whatever happens in this world, there will be accountability in the hereafter.

This belief leads to *taqwa* (God-consciousness) that makes believers act and make decisions/choices that guide people, individually and organizationally, toward what is good and beneficial. A person or entity with *taqwa* upholds a high ethical standard with an inner sense of accountability.

1.6   Functional norms

Based on the aforementioned beliefs and values, Islamic civilization developed a robust, sophisticated, and vibrant business environment and culture. Islamic civilization was multiethnic, multicultural, and multifaith, and this was further facilitated by international and intercivilizational interactions, where Muslim societies enthusiastically embraced the language, knowledge, and experiences of other societies. This experiential factor enriched Muslim societies and civilization deeply, and it was the gradual disconnect in the same context in Muslim societies that led to their decadence, which is reflected in its position in global business and economy.

The development of the modern world in the past few centuries is now indispensable for businesses to develop from an Islamic perspective. The experience and rich history of modern business is a relevant treasure. Human experience crystallizes into customs and norms. Indeed, appreciating the accumulated human experience and benefiting in the form of customs (*urf*) is also a functional norm in Islam. With the exception of anything that contradicts the injunctions and prohibitions in Islam, Muslims can and should benefit from such experience, in light of some of the widely recognized norms that are also consistent with and valued by Islam.

[Q 4:124]
If any do deeds of righteousness (*amali salihat*), – be they male or female, – and have faith, they will enter Paradise, and not the least injustice will be done to them.

The Prophet Muhammad (p) said:
"Shall I not inform you of something more excellent in degree than fasting, prayer, and *sadaqah* (charity)?" The people replied: "Yes, Prophet of God!" He said: "It is *islah* – **putting things right between people**; spoiling them is the shaver (destructive)."
[*Sunan Abu Dawood*; vol. 3, #4901]

Q 88: 25–26
Verily, to Us will be their return: Then verily, for Us will be their Reckoning."

• Simplicity, Instead of Complexity

One modern business that has become iconic is based on the philosophy of "simplicity": Apple. Its founder, Steve Jobs, was passionate about innovation and value, but always keeping "simplicity" in focus as well.[7]

Islam inculcates the value of simplicity in life while pursuing effectiveness and desired outcomes. Normally, for any destination, we should seek the straight or simplest route, *sirat al-mustaqim* (the Straight Path).

• Emulation, Best Practices

General Electric is one of the largest and best managed conglomerates; its slogan is "We bring good things to life." Between 1981 and 2001, under the leadership of CEO Jack Welch, the company's stock value appreciated 4000 percent. Using a circumplex model consisting of 12 styles of thinking and behavior, Welch helped ensure "best practice in leadership development."[8]

The Prophet Muhammad (p) is presented in the Qur'an as exemplary (*uswatun hasana*). [Q 33:21]

Both from religious and competitive business perspectives, establishing or upholding best practices is an important part of Islamic business models.

• Self-Supervision

Google is a leader in the information technology revolution. A key aspect of the company's management model is to avoid micromanagement and promote self-supervision. The company promotes the idea throughout the firm that it "Empowers the Team and does not micromanage."[9]

The concept of *taqwa* is to value self-supervision. Inculcating *taqwa* among people enhances the culture and environment of self-supervision and helps avoid micromanagement. In the book *Managing by Values* (Dolan, et al.) it is underscored that "the best work arises from conditions of self-supervision rather than external control" (p. 102).

• Transparency

Transparency is not among the greatest virtues of most businesses. However, some companies embrace the principle and value of transparency as part of their commitment to best practices. MOZ is a small, emerging tech company that from its inception has treated transparency as a core value. According to its CEO Rand Fishkin, "Transparency for us isn't a question of business value or marketing strategy – it's one of our core values. That means we'd be transparent (and have been) even when it's harmful to the business."[10]

Islam also places a fundamental emphasis on transparency. Consider that before God, we are all transparent and nothing is hidden. Good governance requires transparency along with a sense of accountability. Businesses that care about Islamic norms value transparency in dealing with all stakeholders, where God should also be treated or acknowledged as the most important stakeholder.

• Self-Criticism and Self-Improvement

Microsoft, one of the leading global companies of modern times, incorporates self-criticism into its process of self-improvement.[11] Successful businesses have a well-established culture of self-criticism and self-improvement. Like self-supervision, it is internally driven by an entity's core values and norms.

In Islam this value of self-criticism is related to the principle of fairness. As mentioned earlier, the Qur'an teaches its adherents to "stand for justice … even if it goes against yourselves." [Q 4:135]

- ## Excellence as a Way of Life

IBM is another global business icon that embraces excellence in a special and focused way. According to IBM, "Excellence must be a way of life."[12]

The pursuit of excellence is a core norm for success in any field, including business. Islam teaches its adherents that whatever they do, they should do it in an excellent manner. This is the underlying spirit of being the follower of the *Uswatun Hasana*, the exemplary, Prophet Muhammad (p).

- ## Diversity as Enrichment and Enabling

Most successful businesses do not seek to form a monolithic group. Rather, they appreciate diversity as a form of enrichment. Ernst & Young is a multinational professional services company and one of the four leading accounting firms. It is also ranked third among the top 50 companies for diversity. The company articulates its commitment to diversity: "At EY, we believe that only the highest-performing teams, which maximize the power of different opinions, perspectives and cultural references, will succeed in the global marketplace. Our focus on diversity and inclusiveness is integral to how we serve our clients, develop our people and play a leadership role in our communities."[13]

Islam does not view diversity as something negative. God created mankind with diversity in terms of ethnicity, language, gender, age, habits, aptitude, interests, and so on. The dynamics of improvement, or positive change, is facilitated by an appropriate degree of diversity.

The preceding sections discussed beliefs, values, and norms from an Islamic perspective. The following sections will discuss the essential aspects of business that must be guided by those beliefs, values, and norms.

1.7   Islamic business environment

Environment is a key determinant of the success of any business. A business starts, exists, and evolves in a dynamic environment. Functionally, there can be a social/cultural environment, an industry environment, and an economic environment, while scopewise there are regional, national, and global environments.

A business must always be cognizant of changing environments, including the regulatory environment. Effective businesses not only monitor the various environments, but also play their own role to shape those environments in a positive manner.

Whether operating under normal conditions or during times of change, businesses that wish to pursue goals from an Islamic perspective are expected to strive to foster an environment that is consistent with the beliefs, values, and norms explained earlier. These are important not just from a religious perspective; rather these are beliefs, values, and norms essential for establishing and running profitable businesses.

1.7.1   Goal of business

A business is a commercial enterprise (**firm: *shirka***) or legal entity that earns income or **profit** (***rib'h***) by supplying products or services desired by consumers. All aspects of a business, from launch to operations to expansion, as well as the beliefs, values, and norms presented earlier in the chapter, need to be taken into consideration. While business-related topics are explored in this book, specific Islamic dimensions are identified when relevant.

Choosing to start a business is what **entrepreneurship** is all about. With a deep aversion to unearned or unjust income, commonly from enterprises that do not take appropriate risk, Islam emphasizes work and earning a livelihood, especially through entrepreneurial undertakings. At the macro level, an economy needs to promote and facilitate entrepreneurship and create opportunities through small and medium-sized enterprises, while at the micro level, it constitutes a major decision for an entrepreneur that entails a set of interrelated decisions in the following areas:

- the purpose and value of starting the business;
- the demand and stakeholders the business is trying to satisfy;
- the **resources (factors of production)** needed;
- key **management** functions this business will entail;
- the environment (economic, social, cultural, political) within which the business must operate.

Conventionally, the goal of any business is to earn a profit. A new business starts by identifying unmet demand that can be served by the entrepreneur. A demand may exist due to a gap in the market or competitive advantage based on quality, cost, innovation, or technology.

Profits or earnings are the difference between the revenues a firm takes in and the costs it incurs. In accounting terms, this is shown on an *income statement* as the *net profit* or the *bottom line*. The gross sales or revenues are known as the *top line* of a business. Increasing the bottom line requires either increasing the top line or reducing the costs of achieving efficiency (more output from fewer resources). It is only natural that businesses would like to increase profits as much as possible. However, contrary to the narrow economic concept of profit maximization, a business can achieve certain target profits as part of a broader set of goals that relate to key stakeholders.

Businesses usually thrive in an environment where entrepreneurs are free to choose what enterprises they want to get into and where they also have the freedom to enjoy the rewards of their efforts. However, businesses operate in organized societies, where government regulations are in place to ensure the proper functioning of the system, to enforce property rights, and to protect the rights of all participants in the economic system. These aspects are relevant from an Islamic perspective as well.

Nonprofit organizations also pursue specific goals, but profit is not their motive. They may make a profit, but instead of benefiting the owners or any shareholders, the profits are reinvested in the entity. Many hospitals and universities, for example, are nonprofit institutions, and they are regulated differently compared to commercial firms.

Also, the concept of social business is important in an Islamic context. Popularized by the founder of Grameen Bank and Nobel Laureate Muhammad Yunus, a social business is a cause-driven business whose purpose is to solve major socioeconomic problems in a "financially sustainable way." In a social business, the investors/owners are entitled to gradually recoup their capital invested, but they cannot earn any return or dividend.[14]

1.7.2   Resource needs of a business

A business needs resources or inputs to produce its products or services. These resources are also known as **factors of production**. From the perspective of modern economics, all resources are categorized into four factors of production:

a. Land: all natural resources unaltered by other factors of production.

b. Labor or human resources: all human exertions, physical or mental.

c. Capital: artificial resources used to produce something else, such as buildings, machinery, or equipment, for example.

d. Entrepreneur: a person who undertakes the initiative to organize and manage business activity and assumes risk.

From the viewpoint of Islamic economics, capital is not regarded as an independent category. Rather, the reward from capital must be based on some entrepreneurial activities. While conventional economies are based on interest as a reward of capital ownership, from a traditional Islamic perspective, instead of interest, profit is the reward of capital and entrepreneurship as a combined factor.

Also, from a financial viewpoint, a business needs funds, which is known as financial capital. The business may acquire financial capital from personal or institutional sources. For institutional sources, there are financial institutions, such as banks as financial intermediaries, that bring together savers and borrowers, as well as capital markets.

Though technology is not regarded as a resource, it does affect all factors of production. Technology can affect how various resources are combined in production, which in turn determines which resource earns what share of the pie. In modern business practice, in addition to technology in general, **information technology** (a specialized area of technology that facilitates the use of information to produce products) and **e-commerce** (business based on electronic communications, such as the Internet) have become pivotal.

1.7.3   Business decisions

Running a business involves a broad range of tasks and decisions. There are many aspects of decision making for which, depending on the size of the business, there are different functional responsibilities.

Setting up a business requires that the entrepreneur select a suitable location, employ effective human resources, establish relevant facilities, acquire the necessary raw materials, and produce, market, and supply the product or service.

Thus, businesses have a number of functional areas, including the following:

• **Management**, whose role involves planning, organizing, leading, and controlling the firm's resources to achieve the firm's mission. This area also involves identifying and managing risk and uncertainty. In the complex modern environment, a business needs to be familiar with various qualitative and quantitative tools for effective decision making.

• **Operation**, which refers to the processes by which a business utilizes and converts its resources into products or services. Modern technology and institutional frameworks have a major impact on business. Thus, depending on its nature and size, a business must cope with managing human resources to motivate employees using a number of strategies, from augmenting productivity to maintaining efficient distribution and supply chain management.

- **Finance**, which involves planning, securing, and utilizing funds. In particular, in this regard from an Islamic perspective, there are some key prohibitions, including *riba* (commonly equated with interest), *gharar* (excessive uncertainties), and *maysir* (gambling, speculation).

- **Marketing**, which involves activities connected with identifying customers' needs and designing products or services to meet those needs.

- **Accounting**, upon which managers base their decisions; thus, there is a need for relevant financial and business-related information that is accurate and timely. Accounting professionals gather, organize, and present relevant information to enable managers to analyze and make decisions. While much of conventional accounting presents no issues from an Islamic viewpoint, specific areas of accounting require adaptation to harmonize conventional standards. The AAOIFI and IFSB have made valuable contributions in this regard, with a particular focus on Islamic financial institutions.

1.7.4   The stakeholders

A broad range of parties have an interest or stake in a business. These parties are known as stakeholders, and they include owners (shareholders), employees, customers, creditors, and suppliers.

From an Islamic perspective, in addition to the stakeholders recognized in conventional businesses, there should be one more focal point in all our decision making: God, to whom we will all return and be accountable. Not recognizing or acknowledging God in our decision making and choices is the primary reason behind unethical and unfair decisions and choices made by people in their respective spheres. When leaders, managers, supervisors, or workers act or decide as if they were outside the purview of God (or as if they won't be held accountable for their choices and decisions), they create an environment in which unethical decisions are more likely. The Islamic business environment is discussed in further detail in Chapter 2.

Chapter Highlights

The world of business is competitive, sometimes brutal or even predatory. However, a good, successful business does not have to depend on or cater to the negative aspects of human behavior or aspirations.

In the contemporary context, most businesses worship profit and shareholders, the consequences of which are reflected in reoccurring crises that are often crises of ethics and poor corporate governance.

Businesses that embrace Islamic imperatives can play a vital role in the human community by setting examples that draw on the best of human experience while at the same time being guided by the beliefs, values, and norms enshrined in the Qur'an and exemplified in the life of the Prophet Muhammad (p). With a spirit of serving humanity in its quest to be successful in this world and in the hereafter, people need to harness their potentials to raise the standards of business in the Muslim world and beyond.

This opening chapter lays out a core set of beliefs, values, and norms that should serve as the foundation for the development of a robust and vibrant business environment and culture in this globally competitive world. Businesses inspired by these beliefs, values, and norms can offer a better model, contributing to human-centered progress and development based on shared prosperity and ethical conduct.

Key Terms

Accounting	*Fardh* (obligatory)	Nonprofit organization
Aakhira (afterlife)	Finance	Profit
Bottom line	Financial intermediaries	Real economy
Capital	Financialization	*Risalah* (prophethood/
Creditors	*Fiqh* (Islamic law)	messengership)
Dividend	Firm	Shareholder
E-commerce	*Halal* (permissible)	*Shariah*-compliant
Efficiency	*Haram* (prohibited)	Social business
Entrepreneur	Human resources	Stakeholder,
Entrepreneurship	Information technology	*Taqwa*
Factor of production	Institutions	(God-consciousness)
(Resources)	Management	*Tawhid* (monotheism)
Falah (success;	Marketing	Top line
prosperity)	Natural resources	

Discussion Questions

1. What are the three key beliefs of Islam? How do these beliefs relate to business?

2. What is the difference between *Shariah* and *fiqh*?

3. How does Islam view business as an occupation? How does the life of the Prophet Muhammad (p) relate to business?

4. Islamic civilization has been known for its robust and vibrant commerce. What factors facilitated the role of business in Islamic civilization?

5. What does Islam have to offer in terms of the development of world-class businesses?

6. What are the factors of production from conventional and Islamic viewpoints?

7. What are the functional decision areas for a business?

8. Who are the key stakeholders in a business? Who is the most important stakeholder for decision making from an Islamic perspective?

9. What are some differences in laws and values? Beyond legal aspects, how can embracing the values of Islam facilitate the development of better businesses in the Muslim world?

Selected Bibliography

Al-Jayyousi, O.R. (2012). *Islam and Sustainable Development: New Worldviews*. London: Routledge.

Becker, K. (Ed.). (2004). *Islam and Business: Cross-Cultural and Cross-National Perspectives*. London: Routledge.

Dolan, S., Garcia, S. and Richley, B. (2006). *Managing by Values: A Corporate Guide to Living, Being Alive, and Making a Living in the 21st Century*. Basingstoke, Palgrave Macmillan.

Farooq, M.O. (2011). *Toward Our Reformation: From Legalism to Value-Oriented Islamic Law and Jurisprudence*. IIIT: Herndon.

Helble, M. (2006). On the Influence of World Religions on International Trade. *Journal of Public and International Affairs*, 17(11), 279–288.

Naqvi, S.N.H. (2003). *Perspectives on Morality and Human Well-Being: A Contribution to Islamic Economics*. Leicester: The Islamic Foundation.

Wilson, R. (2006). Islam and Business. *Thunderbird International Business Review*, 48(1), 109–123.

Yusoff, N.M. (2002). *Islam and Business*. Selangor: Pelanduk.

Notes

1. Albaraka.com; kfh.com; aaoifi.com; ifsb.org; inceif.org; isra.my.
2. Whenever the Prophet Muhammad (p) is mentioned, Muslims send salutation to him in the form "Peace be upon him," which, as a reminder, is abbreviated throughout this book as (p).
3. Farooq (2011).
4. *Al-Adab Al-Mufrad*, https://sunnah.com/adab/6/12.
5. *Al-Adab al-Mufrad*, Book of Neighbors, #112.
6. Naqvi, Syed Nawab Haider (1997). "The Dimensions of an Islamic Economic Model," *Islamic Economic Studies*, Vol. 4, No. 2, 1–23.
7. Sarah White (November 11, 2015). "7 tech giants share their core values," cio.com, http://www.cio.com/article/3004381/careers-staffing/7-tech-giants-share-their-core-values.html#slide2.
8. Human Synergistics International (2011) "Best Practice Case Study," https://www.humansynergistics.com/docs/default-source/case-studies-and-white-papers/gecasestudy_v-1-0.pdf?sfvrsn=2.
9. D. Garvin (December 2013). "How Google sold its engineers on management," *Harvard Business Review*, https://hbr.org/2013/12/how-google-sold-its-engineers-on-management.
10. J. McGill (March 28, 2015). "Why these 9 companies choose transparency," *Entrepreneur*, https://thenextweb.com/entrepreneur/2015/03/28/why-these-9-companies-choose-transparency/#.tnw_N9B3lgls.
11. M. Cusumano and R. Selby (1995). *Microsoft Secrets*, New York, Free Press. Also, see Sarah White, op. cit.
12. IBM.com. "IBM Management Principles and Practices," http://www-03.ibm.com/ibm/history/documents/pdf/management.pdf. Also, see Sarah White, op. cit.
13. Ernst & Young, http://www.ey.com/us/en/about-us/our-people-and-culture/diversity-and-inclusiveness.
14. Yunus, Muhammad (2010). *Building Social Business: The New Kind of Capitalism That Serves Humanity's Most Pressing Needs*, Readhowyouwant.com.

ISLAM AND THE GLOBALIZED BUSINESS ENVIRONMENT

2

Muhammad Mansoor Khan

University of South Australia, Australia

Learning Outcomes

LO1: Understand the business environment from global and national perspectives.

LO2: Recognize the forces that shape the globalized business environment.

LO3: Understand the challenges faced by Muslim-majority countries in a twenty-first century competitive business environment and the skills and competencies needed by businesses.

LO4: Apply the Islamic values and norms that can be standard-setting for the development of business in an open economy environment.

Contents

2.1   Introduction

The globalized business environment has been driven by Western countries, who appear to be the primary beneficiaries of worldwide free trade, investment, and wealth creation in recent decades. Western economies have been facing a growing crisis over human and natural resources. There is also increasing competition among global countries to acquire a greater share of natural resources, which will further complicate the gross distribution of wealth and socioeconomic inequalities among nations. It is extremely important for Muslim-majority countries to understand the rapidly changing dimensions of the globalized world in order to deal with the challenges, threats, and opportunities arising from globalization. The Islamic vision of a globalized economy envisages the socioeconomic and political order of human polities with universal justice, brotherhood, peace, and prosperity.

2.2   The national business environment

The micro and national business environment strongly impacts business performance and sustainability. The domestic business environment differs among countries despite the increasing trends of deregulation and globalization in recent years. Figure 2.1 captures the key factors that strongly impact the national business environment and economy.

2.2.1   Political leadership

Progressive political leadership promotes strong business and economic growth in the country. It extends full support to boost investor confidence, capital formation, and healthy growth of trade and commerce at national and international levels. It takes effective measures to control unhealthy competition, monopolies, and other harmful practices in the marketplace. In contrast, autocratic political leadership largely leads to strikes, mass movements, and deteriorating law and order situations, causing losses to businesses and property damage. Western countries with old democratic norms and political legacies serve as the main hubs of international business and investment. Thus, democratic political leadership is indispensable for healthy business and economic growth.

Figure 2.1   Key forces affecting the national business environment

2.2.2   Macroeconomic measures

Key macroeconomic factors such as employment, income and savings, per capita income, inflation, interest rates, and market size strongly impact the growth of national economies. Favorable macroeconomic conditions strongly support high rates of growth and expansion of businesses and markets in developed countries. Poor macroeconomic indicators in the less developed countries seriously undermine healthy growth of national economies. Spiraling inflation and interest rates drastically increase the costs of doing business, which seriously limits profit margins, savings and investment, and overall economic growth in a country. It is highly desirable for developing countries to undertake comprehensive structural measures to promote a highly deregulated, innovative, and competitive business and market environment.

2.2.3   Demographic factors

There are core population characteristics such as age, gender, marital status, life expectancy, literacy, employment, income and occupation, life style, family size, religious, and ethical and social norms that strongly influence the national economy. Business enterprises take into account these demographic variables to sort out the economic behavior of individual community groups. Key socioeconomic factors, such as higher levels of literacy, employment, income and spending, standard of living, and social and family interactions, have stronger impacts on business growth and success. Larger family size, higher marital and birth rate, and longer-life expectancy promote higher growth in national markets and economies. Developing countries have larger family and population sizes and a cheaper supply of labor to promote robust business and economic growth. Developed countries face an aging problem and a shortage of workers in their saturated economies and markets. International business enterprises have been establishing and relocating their production plants to developing countries to take full advantage of their cheaper materials and labor. In sum, demographic factors strongly impact the business and market environment.

2.2.4   Legal framework

Business enterprises rely on a full-fledged legal framework in relation to their formation, structure, property acquisition, human resources, and dealings with customers, suppliers, and other parties. Business and market conditions have become increasingly complex and globalized in recent decades. The rapid growth of online business and market activities such as e-commerce, online sales, outsourcing of jobs, and consultancies have added new dimensions to worldwide business and finance. Domestic legal systems need to be very efficient and flexible to become integrated into international streams. Developing countries have been gradually adopting more flexible and universal legal traditions and practices in order to promote market deregulation and foreign business and investment in their economies. Several international business enterprises have shifted their operations to countries that have adopted internationally compatible legal systems and procedures. There is a wide scope to develop international legal standards and practices that promote the globalization of business and finance.

2.2.5   Customers

Business enterprises aim to offer a wide range of competitive products and services to their customers. They distinguish themselves in the market by offering either high-quality or cheaper products and services to their customers. They conduct regular surveys to obtain customer feedback, competitors' strategies, and underlying demographic and macroeconomic factors affecting the business environment. They try to improve their customer service, shorten response times, quickly respond to customer feedback, and quickly address complaints to maximize customer value, satisfaction, and loyalty. Business and financial markets have become increasingly competitive and dynamic due to advanced technologies and globalization. Online business, e-commerce, and Internet banking have greatly revolutionized global markets in recent years. Thus, customers have strong impacts on business sustainability and environment.

2.2.6   Employees

Business enterprises attract talented people with diverse backgrounds, experiences, values, and skills by offering them very competitive compensation packages. A country's quality and supply of human capital resources are based on a number of demographic factors, such as the general level of education, skills and training, income, savings and per capita income, unemployment, labor migration, and cultural and legal infrastructures. Large business enterprises have human resource departments that provide professional education, training, and career development opportunities and a safe, healthy, and multicultural working environment for their employees. International business enterprises play a very crucial role in the globalization of human resources and employment. Online workforces, IT jobs, and consultants are expanding worldwide. Thus, employees are one of the most important key drivers of the competitive business environment.

2.2.7   Communities

Business enterprises rely on community resources for their success and sustainability. They are expected to contribute to the socioeconomic and political development of their communities. Business enterprises offer people better quality products and services and career opportunities. They play a key role in improving community health, education, standards of living, and environment. They provide special support to women, the underprivileged, disabled, and other disadvantaged segments of society. They ensure community groups' engagement and consult with them to develop their corporate strategies and operations. International business enterprises increasingly provide humanitarian aid and socioeconomic support to weaker and poorer nations worldwide. If any business enterprise fails to meet community expectations, then its legitimacy and existence can be seriously jeopardized. Thus, business enterprises need to comply with community norms and expectations to survive and thrive in the contemporary business environment.

2.2.8   Suppliers

Supply chains create risks and opportunities for business entities in current global markets. The process of value creation and cost savings is largely based on the management control measures of supply chains and suppliers. Business enterprises integrate supply chain management into their strategies to cut costs of operations, products, and services. They aim to develop efficient resource management networks to secure a competitive advantage and promote sustainability. They maximize their competitive advantages and returns by drawing on suppliers' resources and credit facilities. They adopt proper procurement policies and choose suppliers with good financial, social, and environmental performance. They make critical decisions about insourcing, outsourcing, special orders, and capital investment largely by relying on their strengths in managing their supply chains and suppliers. Thus, an efficient supply chain improves business sustainability and success.

2.3   The globalized business environment

Business enterprises need to deal with the forces of the globalized business environment to survive and succeed. The following discussion explores the key factors affecting the global business environment (Figure 2.2).

2.3.1   Global population and diminishing natural resources

The global population is increasing at a galloping rate. In July 2015, the global population was 7.3 billion, and it has been growing by 1.18 percent annually and is set to reach 8.5 billion in 2030, 9.7 billion in 2050, and 11.2 billion in 2100. The average worldwide life expectancy is about 68 years but is estimated to rise to 75–82

Figure 2.2   Key forces in the global business environment

years by 2050 due to the constant decline in the fertility rate and improvements in the overall standard of living.[1] Around 48 developing countries in the world are overpopulated. Western countries also face a growing aging problem. The increasing population puts tremendous pressures on resources such as food, water, housing, employment, health, education, and other basic life necessities. The state of diminishing natural resources and increasing population have very strong impacts on international politics and the business environment. Business enterprises in developing countries face a serious challenge in meeting the demand for goods and services of a rapidly growing population, whereas business enterprises in Western countries face greater challenges in managing product development, workforces, marketing, and overall corporate strategies to serve their aging populations. There is increasing competition among global economies to acquire ever greater shares of resources, and such competition will further intensify with time. Powerful nations will become more desperate to gain control over the natural and human resources of weaker countries. However, there is an increasing awareness among global businesses and communities that their survival is largely based on making truly sustainable and equitable use of existing resources on Earth.

2.3.2   Global competition

Competitiveness is a key driver of worldwide economic and business growth. It is a powerful tool for directing global resources to the most efficient business and investment outlets. Business enterprises rely on key factors such as high quality, lower prices, diversity and standardization, ultrashort delivery times, and personalized customer service to establish the dependence and loyalty of their customers. They regularly conduct market research and surveys and undertake extensive research and development (R&D) to improve and innovate their product designs, production processes, and other features of value and supply chain systems. Business enterprises that fail to maintain their competitive edge lose market share to competitors offering better substitute products and services to customers. Global competition has intensified among market players from developed and developing countries.

Western multinational corporations (MNCs) have used their global experience, networks, and brand names to capture greater market share in developing countries. Similarly, the growing number of MNCs from emerging economies have entered developed markets to compete with local businesses based on cost and economies of scale. There has been a major paradigm shift in worldwide market competitiveness in recent years. The USA, Europe, and Japan, the main beneficiaries of globalization, have been losing their competitive advantage to Russia, China, India, and Brazil. These developments will radically change the dynamics of global business and market competitiveness in the coming years. Western countries need to use market competitiveness to ensure the general socioeconomic development and welfare of their people.

2.3.3   Globalization of business and finance

Globalization has greatly stimulated the socioeconomic, cultural, and political interdependence of people around the world. The increasing integration of global business and finance has acted as a catalyst in accelerating the holistic process of globalization. Recent developments in information technology (IT), mass communication, and transportation have played a key role in evolving borderless business, investment, and employment opportunities. There have been fast and free movements of capital, goods and services, and human resources worldwide. Business enterprises are experiencing unprecedented growth and expansion around the world. The volume of regional trade and commerce has increased tremendously due to regional trade agreements such as the Association of Southeast Asian Nations (ASEAN), the East African Community (EAC), European Free Trade Association (EFTA), and the North American Free Trade Agreement (NAFTA). Globalization promotes efficient and sustainable use of the planet's resources, which have been diminishing due to the worldwide population explosion. However, developing countries feel more threatened by the prospect of the powerful countries using globalization as a tool to acquire more control over the resources of weaker nations. Globalization may solve the problem of poverty and raise the overall standard of living for people around the globe.

2.3.4   Global warming

There are alarming signs of global warming such as rising sea levels, excessive rain, floods, droughts and high temperatures, and other thermal and hydrological changes. Human activities such as deforestation and the use of fossil fuels to meet energy requirements have increased emissions of CO_2 and other greenhouse gases in the atmosphere, which seriously disturb the ecological balance in the atmosphere and aggravate the shortage of food and agriculture produced around the globe.[2] Global political and business leaders must manage their respective countries' climate footprints and reduce their consumption of fossil fuels and waste. Worldwide business and social organizations such as Boosting Initiatives for Collaborative Emission-reduction with the Power of Shippers (BICEPS), the International Energy Agency (IEA), Institutional Investors Group on Climate Change (IIGCC), and UN Climate Change have been working with governments, businesses, and societies to devise a global climate policy. They aim to achieve the international environmental agenda of a 2 °C temperature rise to manage climate change and global warming.[3] Global business communities have duly incorporated key environmental dimensions in their corporate operations, procurement, and product development strategies. They have started offering more sustainable and environmentally friendly products and services to promote a low-carbon economy. Climate change and global warming challenges could have far-reaching impacts on business and market environments.

2.3.5   Modern technologies and innovations

Recent technological developments have revolutionized contemporary businesses and societies. Business enterprises have radically changed their corporate structure, operations, and culture by increasingly relying on modern technologies. They use innovative technologies to create the most effective value and supply chain processes ranging from R&D, design, production, distribution, and customer service to marketing and community engagements. They apply advanced marketing and R&D methods to develop highly cost-effective and innovative products and services to meet ever-changing customer needs and market conditions. Modern technologies have played a key role in promoting unprecedented efficiency, competitiveness, and integration of business and financial markets worldwide. There has been tremendous growth in digital intermediation and e-business across the global markets. In 2014, e-commerce sales amounted to US$1.089 billion, with the top ten e-commerce business markets being China, the USA, the UK, Japan, Germany, France, South

Korea, Canada, Russia, and Brazil. World-renowned e-businesses such as Alibaba, Amazon, Rakuten, Odigeo, and Coupang have invaded global markets with an infinite range of products and services.[4] The business world spends huge resources every year to upgrade its operations with advanced technologies.

2.3.6   Global connectivity and social media

Recent developments in mass communication and digital social networks have turned the entire globe into a small village. The tremendous exposure of the global community to networking platforms and social media tools has connected and created numerous groups in business and society across the globe. There were more than 2.2 billion social network users, representing 30 percent of the global population, in 2017. This year about 1.76 billion (80.1 percent) social network users around the globe will use their mobile phones to access social networks. In 2016, over 1.86 billion people used Facebook, 1.74 billion used mobile technology, and 319 million people used Twitter at least once a month.[5] Business enterprises are increasingly relying on social media tools for communication, competitiveness, marketing, customer service, strategic partnering, and building strong relationships with stakeholders. Business and community groups use social media networks to convey feedback, expectations, and needs to business firms. Social media networks have increasingly compelled business enterprises to provide timely, accurate, and transparent information about their economic, social, and environmental performance to external parties. Thus, business enterprises have faced increasing challenges and risks in this hyperconnected global environment.

2.3.7   Corporate governance and corporate social responsibility

Corporate governance and corporate social responsibility (CSR) are very popular trends in the globalization of business and markets. Globalization is rapidly changing interdependencies among regulators, business groups, and community groups. The demands for businesses enterprises to fulfill economic, social, and environmental responsibilities are increasing and becoming more complex due to the ever-changing dimensions of global business and markets. Major corporate failures and scandals such as AIG, HIH Insurance, One.Tel, Enron, Northern Rock, Tyson, and WorldCom in recent years have highlighted the need to bring more professional and ethical discipline to the contemporary business world. International businesses increasingly observe high standards of governance and CSR to secure market growth, transparency, competitiveness, and sustainability in globally integrated markets.

The best corporate governance model lays out guidelines in relation to the rights and responsibilities of the board and management in serving the best interests of shareholders and other stakeholders. CSR refers to a "social contract" that exists between business enterprises and communities. Business enterprises rely on community resources for their success and in return are expected to contribute to the socioeconomic and political developments of their community. Corporate governance and CSR standards are determined by key demographic factors such as socioeconomic and political conditions, religious and professional ethics, unions and community groups, media, and government and regulatory bodies in the host country. There exists greater scope to develop universal standards for the best corporate governance and CSR practices for business managers and policymakers in government and regulatory bodies.

2.3.8   Professional ethics and integrity

Business ethics are rooted in divine religions and other ethical codes of humanity. The worldly ethical philosophies, including teleological and deontological theories, are driven by ethos-religious doctrines of justice, benevolence, fairness, equity, and universal brotherhood. International enterprises have developed their own ethical codes to guide the professional behaviors and decision-making of their boards and managers. Business managers are more conscious about taking into account all ethical and social dimensions in their decision making. The underlying professional ethical codes have greatly promoted a culture of moral and social accountability and responsibility in business managers and market environments.

2.3.9   International accounting standards and practices

International accounting standards and practices have strong impacts on the globalization of business and market environments. About 150 countries and profiled jurisdictions have adopted the International Financial Reporting Standards (IFRS) issued by the International Accounting Standards Board (IASB) to report on their business and market operations.[6] The IFRS promotes universal, transparent, efficient, and consistent accounting practices in the business world. International business enterprises also use the Global Reporting Initiative (GRI) framework for reporting their social and environmental targets and outcomes. Advanced accounting information systems help global businesses to develop best models of corporate governance, decision-making, and reporting.

2.4   Challenges faced by Muslim-majority countries in the twenty-first century globalized world

The globalized world has increasing impacts on the socioeconomic and political dimensions of Muslim polities. Western countries are the key players of the twenty-first-century globalized world. A large number of Muslim-majority countries are very reluctant to open their doors to multinational enterprises, which could expose their structural market imbalances and take away a major share of their economic resources and wealth. Figure 2.3 shows the forces in the globalized business world and society that are challenging the socioeconomic and political order of Muslim-majority countries.

2.4.1   Muslim-majority government

A Muslim-majority government promotes fair and efficient market operations to ensure the optimal utilization of resources in the best interests of people. The increasing trends of globalization have rapidly changed economies, markets, governments, businesses, and communities around the globe. The globalization of business and finance carries far-reaching political and social implications for Muslim-majority countries that cannot remain isolated from the mainstreams of the world. Muslim-majority countries are feeling increasing pressures to open their economies to international trade, business, and finance. They cannot effectively use their traditional regulatory tools to regulate their national economies in the globalized world. Globalization largely promotes a laissez-faire market environment, which strongly favors powerful market players to serve their vested interests.

Figure 2.3   Challenges faced by Muslim-majority countries

The unfettered role of Western players in developing and Muslim markets may give them significant control over the national resources of the latter. The increasing trends of mergers and acquisitions in multinational enterprises may gradually transfer the wealth of Muslim-majority countries to Western countries. Muslim-majority countries face a serious challenge in connection with using globalization to address domestic socioeconomic and political imbalances.

2.4.2   Political autonomy of Muslim-majority countries

Powerful Western countries have been striving to establish their political and economic supremacy over Muslim-majority countries. Hundreds of thousands of Muslims in Middle Eastern countries, such as Egypt, Jordan, Lebanon, Iraq, and Syria, have lost their lives, families, property, and political freedom owing to mutual infighting instigated by Western countries for political and economic gain in this oil-rich region. Thus, globalization has posed serious challenges and threats to the life and political autonomy of Muslim-majority countries.

2.4.3   Muslim-majority countries and Western financial institutions

Western financial institutions such as the International Monetary Fund and World Bank largely operate against the economic, social, and political interests of developing and Muslim-majority countries. These institutions, overwhelmingly staffed and controlled by citizens of Western countries, provide financial assistance to developing and poor countries under the conditions of introducing radical structural changes to their economies. These market deregulations make it easier for Western MNCs to enter developing countries and exploit their resources and wealth. Muslim-majority countries may seek maximum financial and technical support from Western financial institutions without compromising their socioeconomic and political freedom, and they may urge Western market players to use globalization to eliminate poverty and gross socioeconomic inequalities among the nations of the world.

2.4.4   Muslim-majority countries' economies and financial markets

Muslim-majority countries face inherent structural imbalances in their economies and financial markets. Any unplanned or unfettered exposure of their economies at global levels may leave them vulnerable to a serious financial and currency crisis. The well-known currency and economic crisis of East Asian Muslim-majority countries in 1997–1999 was largely triggered and exploited by powerful Western market power brokers. Many people lost their jobs, businesses, and wealth in the region during the currency crisis. Consequently, these countries were pushed to the verge of financial, social, and political crisis. In the current context, Muslim-majority countries are very reluctant to allow the free integration and globalization of their markets and economies. However, they need to gradually expand the size of their economies to ensure optimal utilization of national resources and wider economic growth. They may follow the examples of China and India in using globalization as a tool to overhaul their economies.

2.4.5   Western and Islamic MNCs

Globalization opens the doors to Western MNCs to operate in developing countries to increase their market share and profitability. Western MNCs have entered Muslim-majority countries' markets to phase out local businesses that cannot compete with them on cost and quality bases due to their limited resources and size. The closure of local businesses could trigger an economic crisis, unemployment, and other socioeconomic complications within Muslim-majority countries. Western MNCs may acquire the lion's share of business and finance in Muslim-majority countries. They may transfer their profits and wealth to their countries of origin, so that they will remain the leading global economies. Muslim-majority countries offer great opportunities for MNCs to establish production units, which benefit from the cheaper labor and natural resources in those regions. However, they may also take full advantage of rich Western financial resources and expertise to enhance their business and market efficiency, growth, and sustainability. Like China and India, Muslim-majority countries may develop their own MNCs to counter the influence of Western MNCs in their economies. Such MNCs may enter into joint ventures with Western MNCs to enhance the market performance and competitiveness of Muslim-majority countries.

2.4.6   Muslim-majority countries and world politics

There have been increasing trends toward economic slowdown, recession, unemployment, aging population, and rising costs of living in Europe, the UK, and the USA. The growing economies of China, India, Brazil, and Russia are gradually winning a larger global market share from Western countries. A large number of Muslim-majority countries enjoy a very strong strategic position on the world political stage. Middle Eastern Muslim countries hold huge oil wealth, which has been largely exploited by Western countries for economic and political gain. Similarly, Pakistan, Iran, Turkey, and Afghanistan are well positioned to maximize their economic cooperation in the wake of China-Pakistan Economic Corridor (CPEC) developments in the region. China may lead several emerging subcontinent markets to become the greatest global business and financial hubs in the near future. Southeast Asian and African Muslim-majority countries have their own socioeconomic and political dimensions to ensure their participation and share in globalization. Muslim-majority countries may develop a joint strategy to deal with challenges arising from the globalization of business and finance. They may develop mutual trade initiatives similar to ASEAN, the General Agreement on Trade and Tariffs (GATT), and NAFTA to promote bilateral trade and commerce. Further, they may develop regional and global business participation models to address the challenges and opportunities presented by globalization. The increasing geopolitical and economic cooperation seen among Muslim-majority countries may gradually improve their performance and competitiveness in globalized business and finance.

2.4.7   Human resource crisis in Muslim-majority countries

Human resources are the most critical part of global business and finance. Developing countries have been facing the serious challenge of losing talented professionals to developed countries in the face of the globalization of economies and jobs. Western countries manage their acute shortage of human resources by offering opportunities to migrants worldwide who possess desirable skills. Muslim-majority countries devote huge portions of their national wealth to nurturing the skills of their people, only to see the top brass migrate to Western countries to seek better fortunes. The governments of those countries could effectively address this human resource crisis by offering globally competitive remuneration packages and better standards of living for their people.

2.4.8   Western culture and the Muslim polity

Islamic teachings guide Muslims to lead very spiritual and modest lives. However, globalization has allowed Western culture to undermine the religious, spiritual, and cultural values of Muslim polities. Muslims use the Internet, smartphones, social media, and satellite dishes, which have given them unlimited access to Western entertainment, movies, music, and magazines. Western norms, life styles, and holidays, such as Mother's Day, Father's Day, fashion trends, celebrations, New Year's Day, and Valentine's Day, are becoming part and parcel of life in Muslim-majority countries. It is extremely important for Islamic political and religious leaders to develop enlightened strategies to safeguard the religious and cultural traditions and values of Muslim people.

2.4.9 Global extremism and the Muslim polity

Islamic teachings nurture love, peace, care for one's fellow humans, justice, kindness, and universal brotherhood in the larger human community. The nations of the world are today more exposed than ever before to extremism, violence, and other injustices committed by a few individuals or groups. Certain radical Islamic groups promote violence and extremism across the globe. The tragic events they cause seriously affect the personal, social, and professional lives of Muslims living abroad. Consequently, Westerners and their institutions feel insecure about engaging with Muslims in social and business activities. This represents a serious challenge to Muslims in terms of becoming active agents of the globalized business community and economy.

2.4.10 Enlightened Muslim world

Muslim-majority countries face a real challenge in connection with adopting modern knowledge, skills, and technologies in their lives to derive maximum benefits from the opportunities offered by the globalized business environment. The Muslim intelligentsia may work on nurturing a very modern and enlightened outlook of the Islamic world. The Muslim polity may assume a crucial role in promoting universal brotherhood, justice, peace, and prosperity among nations.

2.5 Islamic values and principles for developing the open economy environment

Islamic teachings reflect serious concerns over the growing disparities among people around the globe. Islamic fundamental values and principles as they relate to evolving the open economy based on market efficiency, distributive justice, and universal brotherhood are thoroughly explored in Chapter 1.

Islam promotes a number of positive teachings and shuns a number of unethical economic elements that enable the evolution of a truly efficient and equitable economic system. Islam promotes private ownership and laws of inheritance to foster risk sharing and joint ventures in business and society. It supports voluntary consent, mutual trust, and cooperation to ensure the optimal level of business activity and economic growth. Islamic standards of honesty, fairness, and integrity support the fair and efficient use of resources, which creates greater value for shareholders, consumers, and communities. Islam promotes principles of justice and benevolence to nurture a deeper sense of professional accountability and excellence among business agents. It promotes altruistic economic and social behaviors through *zakah*, charities, and donations that fight poverty and deprivation and foster economic growth and human welfare at the grassroots level. Islamic teachings strictly condemn hoarding, black marketeering, monopolies, bribery, fraud, unfair gains, and extravagant and stingy economic behaviors. These unethical and antisocial tools are used by a handful of people to exert control over global wealth and resources. Islamic teachings prohibit the charging of interest, gambling, and speculation, which lead to the concentration of wealth, poverty, inflationary pressures, budget deficits, unemployment, debt, and global economic recession. Islam promotes business and financial dealings on the basis of zero-interest financing, equity and risk sharing, a shared economy, pooled funds, and venture capital leading to optimal economic growth and sustainability with distributive justice.

Chapter Highlights

The present business environment holds very dynamic complexities of economic, social, geopolitical, and environmental forces that largely determine business and market outcomes. Certain key forces and elements strongly impact the shaping of the business environment at national and international levels. Business enterprises need to address these internal and external forces to survive and thrive in the modern world. Globalization trends have been growing at an accelerated pace since the 1980s, and Western countries appear to be the main beneficiaries of worldwide trade and commerce. The globalized business environment has led to gross socioeconomic inequalities and deprivations among nations. A handful of advanced countries are enjoying enormous economic and political power at the expense of others. Muslim countries face formidable challenges and tremendous opportunities in their socioeconomic, political, and cultural arenas as a result of globalization. It is high time for the Muslim intelligentsia to come up with universal solutions to the underlying socioeconomic and political problems of the human polity. The Islamic model of a global economy relies on principles such as universal justice and benevolence, brotherhood, cooperation, honesty and fairness, charity, equity and risk sharing, and a ban on interest, gambling, and speculation to develop the most efficient, ethical, and sustainable use of global resources with a view to universal peace and prosperity for all the people of the Earth.

Key Terms

Business environment	Global business	Population explosion
Business ethics	Global connectivity	Professional ethics
Capital formation	Global finance	Regulatory bodies
Clean environment	Global warming	R&D initiatives
Climate change	GRI	Social accountability
Community engagement	Human resources	Social activism
Community welfare	Human resource crisis	Social consciousness
Corporate governance	IASB	Social media tools
Corporate structure	IFRS	Social responsibility
Customer satisfaction	International trade	Supply chain
Demographic factors	Legal framework	Sustainable communities
Development markets	Market competitiveness	Technological
E-commerce	Mergers and acquisitions	innovations
EFTA, NAFTA	Muslim-majority country	Universal brotherhood
Ethical codes	Online workforce	Western MNCs

Discussion Questions

1. What are four key micro factors of the national business environment? What impacts could they have on the national environment of a country?

2. What are the key determinants of the global business environment?

3. What is global warming and how does it pose a serious threat to human life on Earth?

4. How can Muslim business enterprises use modern technologies and innovations to improve their market sustainability and success?

5. What are the core challenges faced by Muslim-majority countries in a twenty-first-century globalized world?

6. How can religious beliefs and norms of managers help them achieve professional excellence in the business world?

7. Why should Muslim-majority countries promote bilateral trade and commerce in the global business environment?

8. What are the serious threats posed by Western culture to the religious and moral identity of Muslims?

9. What are the social responsibilities of Islamic business and financial institutions?

10. How can Islamic principles ensure the most efficient and ethical use of global resources?

Selected Bibliography

Adam, K. (2011). Government Debt and Optimal Monetary and Fiscal Policy. *European Economic Review*, 55(1), 57–74.

Benn, S. and Dunphy, D.C. (2007). *Corporate Governance and Sustainability: Challenges for Theory and Practice*. New York: Ebrary Inc.

Cruz-Cunha, M.M., Cortes, B.C. and Putnik, G. (2007). *Adaptive Technologies and Business Integration Social, Managerial, and Organizational Dimensions*. Hershey: IGI Global.

Dahan, N., Doh, J. and Raelin, J. (2015). Pivoting the Role of Government in the Business and Society Interface: A Stakeholder Perspective. *Journal of Business Ethics Journal of Business Ethics*, 131(3), 665–680.

Khan, M.M. and Bhatti, M.I. (2008). *Developments in Interest-Free Banking* (Palgrave Macmillan Studies in Banking and Financial Institutions). London: Palgrave Macmillan.

Madura, J. (2007). *Introduction to Business* (4th ed.). Canada: Thomson South-Western.

Morrison, J. (2011). *International Business Environment* (3rd ed.). New York: Palgrave Macmillan.

Narayanan, M. et al. (2012). Social Media and Business. *Journal for Decision Makers*, 37(4), 69–112.

Ritzer, G. (2011). *Globalization: The Essentials*. New York: John Wiley & Sons.

Singh, D. (2012). Emerging Economies and Multinational Corporations: An Institutional Approach to Subsidiary Management. *International Journal of Emerging Markets*, 7(4), 397–410.

Notes

1. UN World Population Division, 2015.
2. IPCC Climate Change Report, 2014.
3. The UNEP Emissions Gap Report, 2016.
4. www.emarketer.com.
5. The E-marketer Forecast 2017; www.statista.com.
6. www.globalreporting.org; www.ifrs.org.

ENTREPRENEURSHIP AND SMALL BUSINESS OWNERSHIP

3

Rasem Kayed

Arab American University, Palestine

Learning Outcomes

LO1: Explain entrepreneurship from an Islamic perspective.

LO2: Identify and analyze entrepreneurial opportunities.

LO3: Describe the advantages and disadvantages of owning-operating a small business and financing options available to entrepreneurs using Islamic principles.

LO4: Explain factors that enable or inhibit entrepreneurial development.

Contents

Box 3.1 Entrepreneurs Read Between the Lines

Bata Shoe purportedly sent two salesmen to Africa to open new territories. The first salesman went down the West Coast and reported back to the head office that it was pointless for him to be there since no one wore shoes. The second salesman covered the East Coast and made the same observation. He concluded however that this was an excellent territory for him; since no one wore shoes, everyone was a potential customer. (cited in Lenko, 1995, p. 20)

> The two salesmen, despite having identical information, access to the same resources, and being subjected to the same circumstances, had vastly differing outlooks and interpretations of the same findings.

Introduction

Regardless of how entrepreneurship is defined, and regardless of what motivates entrepreneurs to start their own businesses, entrepreneurship stands out as a symbol of business tenacity and achievement and affirms its presence as an integral part of any developmental equation. The main objective of this chapter is to introduce the entrepreneurial phenomenon from an Islamic perspective. The chapter therefore starts by presenting a summary of the entrepreneurial process and an account of the most common characteristics associated with successful entrepreneurs as background information necessary to the understanding of the entrepreneurial phenomenon.

Section 3.2 explores the basic tenets of Islamic entrepreneurship and discusses the spirit of Islamic entrepreneurial activity. Discussions will also be extended to survey Islamic attitudes toward private property ownership since the rights of individuals to property ownership is a central issue in entrepreneurship development. Similarities as well as differences between Muslim entrepreneurs and Islamic enterprises and their Western counterparts will be examined in order to gain a better understanding of both systems.

Section 3.3 focuses on the entrepreneurial opportunity as a key element in the entrepreneurial process. Entrepreneurial opportunities originate from creative business ideas, ideas that have been subjected to a strict screening process to determine their viability and marketability, then converted into tangible business entities, most likely in the form of small businesses. Discussions in this section will cover various topics, including opportunity screening, opportunity identification, three views of entrepreneurial opportunity, and some guidelines on where to find potential business ideas.

Section 3.4 establishes the relationship as well as the distinction between *entrepreneurship* and *small business* and attempts to explain whether a business is "small" or "big" utilizing quantitative and qualitative approaches. Furthermore, the section examines the advantages and disadvantages of owning small business enterprises and the factors contributing to their failure and success. New business ventures are often held back due to a lack of capital. Financial constraints become more acute in an Islamic business environment where Muslim entrepreneurs are banned from dealing with conventional banking. Section 3.5 looks into three modes of Islamic business finance most appropriate to the needs of small business start-ups; *al-qard al-hasan*, *mudarabah*, and *musharakah*.

The chapter concludes with a thorough investigation of the factors that influence the emergence and development of entrepreneurship: personality factors, sociocultural factors, institutional/environmental factors, and other external factors. These factors may have positive (enabling) and negative (inhibiting) influences on the emergence and development of entrepreneurship in a given society.

Being your own boss: An overview

Many people dream of owning their own business. The opportunity to earn substantial profits while contributing to society and the opportunity to map one's own future while making a difference in people's lives are but a few benefits of being an entrepreneur. Yet the majority never go beyond their dreams. In reality, not everyone is potentially capable of venturing into business, and not all those who are capable will necessarily take the challenge to swim in uncharted waters. Likewise, there is no guarantee of success for those who actually attempt to start a new business enterprise.

Recognizing business opportunities and creating sustainable, profitable, and yet ethical and socially responsible business entities that contribute to the wellbeing of society is an enormous task, one that only motivated, vigilant, committed, and visionary individuals can undertake; that is, entrepreneurs. Entrepreneurs, regardless of their location, background, faith, culture, age, and gender, share common unique characteristics, mainly, their ability to identify and exploit entrepreneurial opportunities, their know-how in mobilizing resources and their zeal to venture into unknown.

Activities driven by inspired and dedicated entrepreneurs are crucial to the socio-economic development of all countries. Small businesses, the tangible manifestation of entrepreneurship, are championed as engines for growth, not only for creating employment opportunities and being sources of innovation, but also for their indispensable contribution to the wellbeing of individuals and communities alike.

As much as starting a business is exciting and potentially fulfilling, it is mentally, physically and financially demanding, especially during the first few months, and probably few years of the life of the business venture. Anxiety and financial insecurity continually burden the entrepreneur until the business starts generating income, becomes profitable, and survives the critical stage of its life cycle.

Entrepreneurship is a universal phenomenon that is not restricted to any particular ideology, faith, social order, or economic-political system. It is a country-specific experience that flourishes in a conducive culture and thrives where enabling institutions exist.

Islam is an entrepreneurial religion, started by changing the way people think rather than the way they live. It goes far beyond extending passive endorsement of entrepreneurs and their enterprises to profoundly attaching a religious significance to entrepreneurial activity and providing the means for the emergence of a vibrant small business sector. Islam deems the engagement in lawful, ethical, and productive entrepreneurial activities to be a collective duty (*fard kefayah*) bestowed upon Muslims. This obligation must be met by an adequate number of Muslim entrepreneurs to cater to the basic needs of Muslim nations (*ummah*) as an indicator of self-sufficiency and a symbol of national independence.

It is sufficient to know that our beloved Prophet peace be upon him (PBUH) and some of his closest companions were successful entrepreneurs who contributed immensely to the cause of Islam and the wellbeing of the Muslim *ummah*.

3.1   The entrepreneurial process

Entrepreneurship is a process with the creation of new business ventures being its end product. Three major steps need to be carried out by competent entrepreneurs while endeavoring to create new businesses: (1) idea identification, (2) opportunity evaluation, and (3) resource mobilization.

A precondition for the entrepreneurial process is the existence of highly motivated and exceptionally competent entrepreneurs with the following skills:

1. Ability to identify creative business ideas that meet market demand and generate profits. The ideas must be practical so they can be transformed into business opportunities.

2. Ability to evaluate entrepreneurial opportunities by subjecting identified ideas to a screening process to determine their viability and marketability as genuine entrepreneurial opportunities.

3. Capacity to turn opportunities into tangible business entities, primarily to create *halal* wealth and socioeconomic value through the mobilization of needed resources such as the supply of talented human capital, access to financing, and fulfilling legal obligations, all under condition of risk.

The implementation phase of the entrepreneurial process involves one of the following: (a) introducing new products or services, (b) introducing a new method of production (new technology), (c) the opening of a new market, (d) utilizing a new source of supply, or (e) creating new (business) organizations of any industry (Schumpeter, 1934).

Entrepreneurship is largely defined as a process of socioeconomic change by which individuals identify ideas, transform these ideas into business opportunities, and turn business opportunities into business entities, primarily to create wealth and economic value through the mobilization of diverse resources, under condition of risk.

Entrepreneurs, therefore, are the people who identify new entrepreneurial opportunities, mobilize needed resources and take associated risks to convert such opportunities into marketable products or services. Entrepreneurs are recognized for being agents of change in society.

3.1.1   Who is an entrepreneur?

Who is an entrepreneur and what makes an entrepreneur an entrepreneur? The word *entrepreneur* is derived from the French verb *entreprendre* and the German *unternehmen*, both of which translate to "undertake" (Herbert and Link, 1988). The word first appeared in the writings of Richard Cantillon in 1730, where he used the term to describe the risk associated with a business decision due to uncertainty.

Two basic schools of thought attempted to define who is an entrepreneur: economists and social scientists.

3.1.1.1   *The economists*

Economists consider entrepreneurship to originate from the science of economics alone and the entrepreneur to be an agent who assumes certain roles—innovator, creative imitator, arbitrager, risk taker, risk manager, organizer, and coordinator. He is also an opportunity exploiter, "gap filler," and resource mobilizer. Cantillon, usually regarded as a pioneer in the field, defined the entrepreneur in economic terms and viewed economic development as a result of venture creation. More recently, a group of prominent scholars in the field defined entrepreneurship as "the creation of new organizations" (Meeks and Meyer, 2001; Bygrave, 1993; Gartner and Starr, 1993; Katz and Gartner, 1988; Gartner, 1988; Low and MacMillan, 1988).

3.1.1.2   *The social scientists*

Social scientists, on the other hand, pay considerable attention to the traits and characteristics that make a person act entrepreneurially. The attempt to construct a portrait of the typical entrepreneur based on personal characteristics prompted social scientists to study the behavioral characteristics of entrepreneurs.

While Kao (1991) identified 11 characteristics shared by the majority of entrepreneurs, Timmons (1994) reviewed more than 50 studies on the general characteristics of entrepreneurs and formulated a list of six entrepreneurial characteristics common to the vast majority of these studies:

- commitment and resolve;

- ability to lead and manage;

- opportunity keenness;

- tolerance of risk and uncertainty;

- creativity and adaptation; and

- high motivation to achieve.

The list could continue almost indefinitely recounting the characteristics and attributes of successful entrepreneurs. John Hornady (1982) examined various research findings and assembled a list of 42 characteristics associated with the entrepreneur. Other frequently mentioned characteristics include the following:

- high level of energy and willingness to work hard;

- confidence in one's ability to succeed;

- inclination toward autonomy and high sense of responsibility;

- taking initiative and personal responsibility;

- internal locus of control; and

- integrity and reliability.

3.2   An Islamic perspective of entrepreneurship

Islam fully recognizes the importance of ownership of private property for human welfare; the inclination to own is deeply embedded in human nature. Upholding the right of ownership is also a condition for entrepreneurship. Would-be entrepreneurs and investors in general are encouraged to engage in entrepreneurial activities in a stable and safe environment that protects their rights, rewards their hard work, and offers potential for success.

Islam views entrepreneurship as a two-dimensional activity intended to reward Muslim entrepreneurs in this life and in the hereafter (Kayed, 2006). Entrepreneurship is a means by which Muslim entrepreneurs earn *halal* in this life while advancing the goals and ensuring the wellbeing of society as a whole. Caring for the wellbeing of others through the entrepreneurial act is a good deed that pleases the Almighty Allah and thus brings Muslim entrepreneurs closer to salvation (*falah*) in this life and in the hereafter.

3.2.1   Ownership in Islam

The right of individuals to own property is a fundamental right that is recognized and protected under Islamic jurisprudence and is best understood within the unique *tawhidic* (God's Oneness) worldview. Allah is the creator and the real and ultimate owner of the Earth and its resources. He, the Almighty, entrusted humankind with the Earth and gave humans temporary and conditional rights to rule over it and benefit from its treasures. Ownership in Islam encompasses both private and common ownership.

3.2.1.1   *Property rights and private ownership*

Communism and, to a greater extent, capitalism are currently the two globally prevailing economic paradigms. They mainly differ from each other by the degree of freedom an individual has in the possession of private property and by the role of

> **Q 2:188**
> "and do not eat up your property among yourselves, for vanities"

Q 9:104
"Take from their property charity."

Q 4:02
"And give to orphans their property, and don't substitute the worthless (things) for good ones."

Q 6:20
"To Allah belongs the dominion of the heavens and the earth, and all that is therein, and it is He Who has power over all things."

Q 53:31
"To Allah belongs all that is in the Heavens and on earth: So that he rewards those who do evil, according to their deeds, and He rewards those who do good, with what is best."

Q 2:30
"Behold, your Lord said to the angels: 'I will create a vicegerent on earth.'"

Q 57:7
"Believe in Allah and His Messenger and spend (in charity) out of the (substance) whereof He has made you the heirs. For those of you who believe and spend (in charity), for them is a great reward."

Q 4:32
"And for men is the benefit of what they earn. And for women is the benefit of what they earn."

Q 3:195
"And their Lord has accepted of them, and answered them: Never will I suffer to be lost the work of any of you, be he male or female."

Q 7:56
"Do no mischief on the earth, after it hath been set in order, but call on Him with fear and longing [in your hearts]: for the mercy of Allah is [always] near to those who do good."

Q 8:27
"O you who believe! Betray not the trust of Allah and the Messenger, nor misappropriate knowingly things entrusted to you."

the state in the ownership and control of the means of production. The rights of individuals to property ownership have been explicitly endorsed in Islam. Islam affirms the sanctity of private property, but this sanctity is framed within the wider concept of the oneness of God and man's position of being Allah's vicegerent.[1]

The use of the words *your* and *their* reflects an explicit recognition of the individual's right to property ownership. The stipulation on private ownership in Islamic law is that property must be acquired legitimately and used in such a way that will not cause harm or inconvenience to others. The foundations of private ownership in Islam are as follows:

1. Everything in this universe belongs to Allah the Almighty. He is the creator, thus the real owner, the rightful governor, and the sustainer of the earth, its inhabitants, and its resources.

   Allah has the just and supreme authority to determine the mode of utilization of all forms of property, and human beings must act and conduct themselves accordingly.

2. Man is Allah's vicegerent (*khalifah*), who has been entrusted with earth and its resources and granted the right to own property acquired by lawful means.

   To ensure proper use of these resources, the *Shariah* has recognized the right to own property as legitimate and authentic. This right was conceived in the overall framework of Allah's sovereignty.

3. To carry out his responsibilities, man has been endowed with necessary faculties. These faculties are only a trust with him and are strictly meant to be utilized for the purpose for which they have been granted. It is imperative that "God-given resources" be properly employed to provide all human beings with an honest and decent life without waste, extravagance, and ostentation.

4. The socioeconomic wellbeing of all is affected by how scarce resources are being utilized and distributed among all. Therefore, man is to be held accountable and will be asked at the Day of Judgment how he honored this trust. Trust is neither to be misused nor abused.

3.2.1.2   Public ownership

Islam also recognizes a right of common ownership in certain resources. The prophet Mohammad PBUH stated, "People are full partners in three things: water, pastures and fire." Muslim scholars and jurists have built on this tradition and likewise maintained that key public utilities, such as streets, rivers, telecommunication, public transit, postal services, electricity generation and retailing, and national reserves are for the common good and cannot be owned individually, including by the state. The ownership of utilities is shared by the entire community, and the state, as a trustee, may manage them on its behalf and administer generated revenues for the benefit of all citizens. Public wealth belongs to the Muslim *ummah,* so it should be utilized in projects that serve the common need and the common interest of society.

3.2.2 Islam and entrepreneurship

At the heart of the Islamic faith is the question of why human beings exist. Allah created mankind for a sole purpose, and that purpose is worshipping Him, The Almighty.

> **Q 51:56**
> "I have only created Jinns and men, that they may worship Me."

The act of worship (*ibadah*) manifests itself in the actions of individuals while they perform their daily activities. Islam considers work to be *ibadah* when performed with sincerity and in accordance with the *Shariah* guiding principles. Working to make a lawful, *halal* living to support one's self and to attend to one's family's needs is work for the sake of the Almighty Allah, so it is *ibadah.*

Creating productive and ethical business enterprises (Box 3.2), where entrepreneurs aim at simultaneously benefiting themselves and society at large is an act of *ibadah*. Entrepreneurship in Islam is the source and the origin of sustenance (*rizq),* while employment is a recent invention that came about to fill the administrative needs of the (modern) state (Kayed, 2006). Muslim entrepreneurs have played a pivotal role in advancing the cause of Islam and the construction and expansion of Islamic civilization from the time of the Prophet (PBUH) and thereafter. Prophet Muhammad (PBUH) and many of his close companions were trustworthy and successful entrepreneurs. Abdul Rahman ibn Awf and Uthman ibn Affan, to name just two, are examples of early Muslim role models who started businesses from scratch and used Islamic business principles and business ethics to succeed as entrepreneurs. The Prophet (PBUH) explicitly emphasized the importance of entrepreneurship and encouraged Muslims to actively participate in business enterprises. It is told that the Prophet (PBUH) said, "9 out of 10 sources of sustenance (*rizq*) are derived from trade (business ventures)."

> **Q 62:10**
> "And when prayer is over, disperse in the world and search for the bounty of Allah."

Islam expects Muslims to be productive and self-reliant. It teaches them the dignity of engaging in business and labor to support oneself, provide for one's family, and contribute to the wellbeing of the larger Muslim community. It is narrated in (Sahih Al-Bukhari, Vol. 2) that the Prophet PBUH said, "It is better for any one of you to take a rope and cut the wood [from the forest] and carry it over his back and sell it [as a means of earning a living] rather than to ask others for something and that they may give him or not."

Islam furthermore urges and encourages Muslims to be proactive and take the initiative to be entrepreneurs, as evidenced by the following verses from the Holy Qur'an:

> **Q 67:15**
> "It is He Who made the earth manageable for you, so traverse ye through its tracts and enjoy of the sustenance which He furnishes: But unto Him is the Resurrection."

Searching and navigating over the earth goes beyond simply finding employment opportunities or even engaging in basic entrepreneurial activities. The search implies the exploration of the unknown in order to discover new possibilities and uncover new opportunities for the benefit of humankind. Such active searching involves taking risks and requires innovative thinking, and to Sadeq (1993), that is entrepreneurship. Likewise, the transaction of buying and selling for profit (*bai*) implies the existence of an entrepreneur.

> **Q2: 275**
> "But Allah hath permitted trade (*bai*) and forbidden usury (*riba*)."

Box 3.2 Productive and Ethical Entrepreneurship

Islam is a way of life, so Muslim entrepreneurs are expected to abide by the rules of *Shariah* and act in compliance with the Islamic code of business ethics in their business activities. The ultimate goal of Muslim entrepreneurs is to please the Almighty Allah through the act of entrepreneurship. They endeavor to ensure prosperity by helping the entire community and, in doing so, ultimately helping themselves.

Muslims are free to engage in business activities. However, this freedom is bounded and does not give entrepreneurs the right to undertake any business activity unchecked. Islam subjects every activity to moral and ethical standards and measures every business activity against a well-defined set of principles and guidelines. Consequently, some business activities and practices that are deemed lawful and socially acceptable by a Western entrepreneur may be excluded from the business portfolio of the Muslim entrepreneur. This exclusion is designed to protect society from the physical and mental harm that these transactions inflict on individual entrepreneurs, their communities, and the wellbeing of the Muslim *ummah* at large. However, the very few imposed limitations by no means would affect the ability or the drive of Muslim entrepreneurs to engage in productive and socially desirable business activities. On the contrary, it has been argued that the rationale for the imposed limitations is the preservation of "a moral, stable, and just economy" (Hassan and Hippler, 2014).

An entrepreneurial activity can be innovative but unproductive, economically viable but destructive when it is directed toward immoral, socially offensive, or harmful avenues. Islam, for instance, holds drug trafficking, alcohol production and promotion, prostitution, and gambling to be unethical and destructive (entrepreneurial) activities, so they are declared unlawful and forbidden, despite the fact that they might be economically viable. The integration of legality, morality, and social acceptability are the core components that determine the authenticity of a business undertaking.

Prohibited practices and transactions include the following:

- selling and purchasing intoxicating beverages, tobacco products, pork products, pornography, and illegal drugs;
- any transaction that involves paying or charging interest (*riba*);
- wealth hoarding;
- price fixing and monopolistic business activities;
- gambling, speculation, and taking excessive risk;
- any transaction deemed unethical, immoral, and socially objectionable such as fraud, dishonesty, exploitation, falsification, and misrepresentation;
- selling and purchasing of usurped property; and
- abusing and exploiting the environment and its resources.

3.2.3   The Muslim entrepreneur

The views of the two schools of thought (economists and social scientists) on the characteristics of the successful entrepreneur and his role as an agent of change apply also to the Muslim entrepreneur, but with some basic qualifications.

The Muslim entrepreneur understands entrepreneurship to be a religious, as well as an economic, activity. As *khalifah*, a Muslim entrepreneur starts his business with the ultimate aim of pleasing the Almighty Allah and rendering socioeconomic services to the wider community. Therefore, starting a business to him is an act of *ibadah* that provides him with (satisfactory) *halal* income in this temporary life and endows him with rewards for a better life in the everlasting hereafter.

The Muslim entrepreneur, as any typical faithful Muslim, is a just and truthful business player who is involved only in productive *halal* and socially desirable business activities. He is a socially responsible individual, dedicated to serving his community, and yet fair to all business stakeholders. He is sensitive to the wellbeing of the environment and is accountable for the sustainability of its natural resources for the sake of the welfare of future generations. Therefore, he is expected to constantly display high standards of ethical behavior while carrying out his productive *halal* entrepreneurial activities. Qualities such as honesty, truthfulness, straightforwardness, adherence to contracts, trustworthiness, and keeping promises are an integral part of his character and are obligations that he has no choice but to espouse and abide by. Through his good deeds and honest dealings, the Muslim entrepreneur is in an ideal position to represent true Islam and spread the word of Allah.

Islamic entrepreneurship and conventional entrepreneurship share many common features. Nevertheless, they differ in the following ways:

- **Goal:** Starting a business, to Muslim entrepreneurs, is a way of performing *ibadah* and a means to ensure prosperity by fulfilling obligations to the larger community, and in doing so, they, in due course, help themselves.

- **Success:** Income and wealth are not the sole means by which success is judged. Business owners may start an enterprise to create jobs for unemployed youth or to empower a neglected group in the community. Success is measured by the degree of compliance with Islamic rules while pursuing entrepreneurial opportunities.

- **Opportunity and business activity:** It is not up to the individual preferences or personal ethical standards of Muslim entrepreneurs to engage in or refrain from certain business activities. Muslim entrepreneurs must conform to the rules and guidelines of *Shariah*, so they are only allowed to participate in *halal,* moral, and socially acceptable business dealings.

- **Risk:** Muslim entrepreneurs avoid excessive risk taking, gambling, and speculation.

- **Finance:** It is unlawful for Muslim entrepreneurs to be associated with conventional interest-based banking. Conversely, Islam identifies contracts based on profit and loss sharing (PLS), *mudarabah* and *musharakah*, to be the legitimate means of financing new business start-ups through Islamic financial institutions.

In addition to the illegality of dealing with conventional banking as borrowers or investors, Muslim entrepreneurs must distance themselves from all businesses that are identified as participating in activities deemed illegal by Islam, be it financial or otherwise. Table 3.1 summarizes key differences between Islamic and Western perspectives on entrepreneurship.

Table 3.1 Key differences between Islamic and Western entrepreneurship

Factor	Western entrepreneurship	Islamic entrepreneurship
Motive	Entrepreneur's self-interest and desire for individual profit	Fulfilling religious obligation to please the Almighty Allah without failing to benefit from material rewards
Ultimate goal	Profit maximization; entrepreneur's self-interest comes first, other goals follow	Achieving prosperity and attaining wellbeing in this life and in the hereafter; self-interest will eventually be realized as a result of helping larger community
Rewards/ measure of success	Ultimate goal is material gain (wealth)	Adhering to rules of *Shariah* in pursuit of goals; success measured not only by personal financial success, but also by how well religious goals are achieved
Opportunity	Marketable and profitable product or service	Marketable and profitable and yet productive product or service that contributes to the real economy; opportunity must be *halal* and not cause mental, physical, or spiritual harm or offense to others
Risk	Entrepreneur bears all risks associated with business venture	Protection against risk and uncertainty by spreading risk between entrepreneur and investor (*rabb al-mal*) through partnership arrangements
Financing small business start-ups	Debt-based financing through conventional banking and financial institutions; borrowed loans must be repaid with interest regardless of outcome of business venture	Islam prohibits all forms of interest-based financial transactions (*riba*) regardless of terms; start-up businesses financed through application of PLS contracts; entrepreneurs enter into partnership contracts with financers utilizing PLS instruments, namely *mudarabah* and *musharakah*

3.3   Entrepreneurial opportunities

Definitions of entrepreneurs have increasingly focused on opportunity as a key element in the entrepreneurship process. The ability to recognize, discover, create, and exploit entrepreneurial opportunities is a top priority for the would-be entrepreneur. No business opportunity translates into no business venture.

3.3.1   From creative ideas to entrepreneurial opportunities

Entrepreneurial opportunities are creative new business ideas that have been assessed and proven to represent entrepreneurial opportunities that meet market demand and generate profit. Islam imposes certain stipulations on what can be considered a business opportunity. In addition to creating value for both target customers and the entrepreneur, the emerging venture has to be based on moral and ethical grounds and must conform to the principles and rules of Islamic *Shariah* in all its details (see Box 3.2 on p. 42).

3.3.2 Screening opportunities

Having a business opportunity does not necessarily mean that a good business opportunity is at hand. Business opportunities need further screening to establish them as real (product feasibility), viable (market feasibility), and profitable (economic feasibility) business opportunities (Day, 2007). Therefore, a business opportunity with high product and market feasibility does not justify starting a business venture if its economic feasibility is in question. Likewise, an entrepreneur may have a sound and economically feasible business idea but the good idea is not worth pursuing due to a lack of potential buyers.

The objective of the screening process is to inform entrepreneurs which opportunities are good entrepreneurial opportunities with the potential to be transformed into business ventures. At this stage, the entrepreneur has to determine whether a particular opportunity is worth developing further into a business form that creates value for both customers and the entrepreneur.

The screening process should address the following issues critical to the success of new entrepreneurial ventures:

1. Is there a real demand for the product or service? Will the product or service fulfill an unmet need or solve a problem for customers who are willing and able to purchase the product or the service? Are there enough customers willing to buy the product or service to justify investing in the solution?

2. Are the resources needed to create and operate the new business venture available? Does the entrepreneur have, or have access to, talented human capital, physical and financial resources, and legal counsel necessary to start the business venture and then run it?

3. How does the product or service compare against comparable competing solutions? Will the product or service serve customers in a different and better way at a reasonable price while generating profits?

4. Does the product or service meet other objectives of the entrepreneur that might go beyond achieving an acceptable return on investment? This is especially valid for the Muslim entrepreneur, because to him entrepreneurship is a religious as well as an economic activity.

3.3.3 The identification of entrepreneurial opportunities

The debate on the occurrence of entrepreneurial opportunities is frequently framed in terms of discovery vs. creation. Discovery theory of entrepreneurship assumes that opportunities exist and are waiting to be discovered and exploited by alert would-be entrepreneurs. On the other hand, creation theory of entrepreneurship works under the assumption that opportunities do not exist in a clear manner but emerge as a result of the active search and actions of would-be entrepreneurs to create them. Thus, while many scholars argue that entrepreneurial opportunities are discovered, others maintain that opportunities are created (Schaper, Volery, Weber and Gibson, 2014).

3.3.4   Three views of entrepreneurial opportunity

Sarasvathy et al. (2003) introduced a third view of opportunities based on their own so-called allocative theory of entrepreneurship. This view affirms that entrepreneurial opportunities do exist, and the opportunity for bringing them together has to be recognized. They apply the entrepreneur's level of knowledge regarding the market forces of supply and demand to determine whether an entrepreneurial opportunity was discovered, created, or recognized.

The three views of entrepreneurial opportunity are as follows:

1. Opportunities are discovered: (a) accidentally when an entrepreneur discovers an opportunity without intentionally searching for it. Opportunity is discovered purely by chance as a result of being at the right place at the right time; or (b) as a result of searching for a solution to either the supply of or demand for a product or service. The discovery is linked to the traits of the entrepreneur and his role and ability to gather, analyze, and interpret information. The entrepreneur is an alert person and very proactive in seeking opportunities.

2. Opportunities are created because two variables of the market, supply and demand, are not precisely known, enticing would-be entrepreneurs to engage in a discovering process to create a product/service to fulfill the supply variable of the market, create demand for a product/service, or both. Opportunity creation is linked to the action of the entrepreneur and his ability to act creatively.

3. Opportunities are waiting to be recognized by an alert entrepreneur since both the product/service (supply) and the market (demand) do exist. Opportunity recognition is linked to the traits of the entrepreneur (trait) and other considerations relating to his entrepreneurial role.

It can be strongly argued that the three perspectives of entrepreneurial opportunity have a complementary relationship, meaning that some opportunities are created, some are discovered, and still others arise from opportunity recognition.

Opportunities arise either through internal or external stimulation (Barringer and Ireland, 2008). Internal stimulation occurs when an entrepreneur decides to start a firm, searches for and recognizes an opportunity, then starts a business. Internal stimulation is connected to the creation of opportunities. External stimulation, on the other hand, takes place when an entrepreneur recognizes a problem or an opportunity gap (external environment) and creates a business to fill it. External stimulation is connected to recognizing an opportunity.

3.3.5   Where to look for promising business ideas

Generating business ideas is the starting point in the entrepreneurial process. Good ideas come from a variety of sources and when implemented can lead to full-fledged businesses. Great ways to generate promising business ideas include the following:

1. **Current and potential customers:**
   Listen to your current customers and talk to potential customers who might be interested in your product or service. Customer feedback helps entrepreneurs understand what, where, how, when, and at what price they want your product or service and, thus, helps in identifying potential business opportunities to pursue. Customers' complaints about existing, or the absence of, certain products or services are the best signals that a new product or service is needed.

2. **Inefficiency in the market:**
   Identify an inefficiency in the market, then envisage an idea on how to correct that inefficiency, ensure that there is a real opportunity embedded in the idea, mobilize needed resources, and turn that opportunity into a new business venture.

3. **Industry trends and insights:**
   Observe and analyze industry trends and insights for clues to potential opportunities. A business idea in a growing sector or industry is more likely to present a better business opportunity than investing in a stagnant sector or industry. Detecting a trend early on and creating a business to benefit from the trend puts the entrepreneur at an advantageous position over rivals.

4. **Market gaps (niche):**
   Find a gap in the market and take the initiative to fill that gap. An alert Muslim entrepreneur living in a Western society, for instance, sees a good business opportunity to start a *halal* business to fulfill unmet needs of the local Muslim community.

5. **Successful products or services in other markets:**
   Recognize a product or service being successfully sold in a certain market while it is not available in your market. Assess the feasibility of starting your own business to market the product or service in your home country. Be aware that, due to differences in taste, preference, culture, and religious convictions, one size does not necessarily fit all. Some tailoring or adaptation may be needed to make the product or service fit the new market.

6. **Listening to what colleagues, employees, and businesspeople say:**
   A business idea can also emerge through listening to and reading other people's thoughts. Stay vigilant and listen to colleagues, people in business, and employees. Refine generated ideas, subject them to strict evaluation processes, and pursue the one with the highest potential to be turned into a good business opportunity and, eventually, transformed into a new business entity.

7. **Strengths and special skills of an individual:**
   Many ideas for successful businesses come from people who have special skills and rich work experiences. They search for innovative ways to turn their strengths, special skills, and rich work experience in a particular market or industry into a business venture.

Source: https://www.inc.com/murray-newlands/7-awesome-opportunities-for-entrepreneurs.html

3.4 Small business start-ups

Small businesses account for 99.7 percent of all private US businesses, 99.3 percent of all businesses in EU countries; 93.9 percent in Pakistan, 98 percent in Kenya, more than 98 percent in Malaysia, and 97.4 percent in Australia.[2]

Harper (1984) explains that small businesses are, in reality, "an extension of the personality of their owners." The diversity of small business owners is not limited to differences in character or the purpose for starting their new businesses. It also extends to include their demographic backgrounds: small business owners are males and females, old and young, highly educated and illiterate, rich and poor, urban and rural, Muslims and non-Muslims. Each contributes to the common good in his own unique way.

3.4.1   What is a small business?

Although small businesses are the most prevalent form of business worldwide, there is no agreed upon definition that covers the highly heterogeneous small business landscape. Definitions differ from country to country and also according to the industry and the purpose of the business. There are two broad approaches commonly used to define whether a business is small or big.

3.4.1.1   Quantitative approach

Small businesses are identified by common quantitative variables including monetary value of assets owned by the business, total sales revenues the business generates, annual wages and salaries of employees, value of business owners' equity, and total number of people the business employs.

A definition based on the total number of employees remains the most common criterion used to differentiate between big and small businesses. While in some countries a business is labeled small if it employs less than 5 people, the US Department of Commerce considers a business small if it has fewer than 500 employees.

3.4.1.2   Qualitative approach

This approach uses certain qualitative characteristics to define whether a business is small. A business is considered small if it has the following attributes:

- The business is independently owned and operated (it is not totally or partially owned or controlled by another, larger, firm).

- It has a small market share and thus is not in a position to dominate or influence its industry.

- The owner is actively involved in running and managing the business, and the crucial decisions are made exclusively by the owner(s).

In the absence of a generally accepted criterion to define and categorize a small business, the literature tends to use a combination of both quantitative and qualitative measures; a business is considered small if it is independently owned and operated and typically has a small number of employees (as determined by the industry in various countries).

3.4.2   Small businesses and entrepreneurship

Figure 3.1 shows that small businesses are the tangible manifestation of the entrepreneurial process. New business enterprises generally start as small businesses and later may change their legal structure. Microsoft, Apple, Wal-Mart, Toyota, General Motors, and the vast majority of conglomerates started out as small businesses, but their founders had the entrepreneurial vision, drive, and appetite for success and growth.

Although the terms *small business ownership* and *entrepreneurship* are sometimes used interchangeably, they differ in the following ways:

- **Means of ownership**: While a small business owner opts to purchase an existing business, an entrepreneur faces the many challenges of building his/her business from scratch.

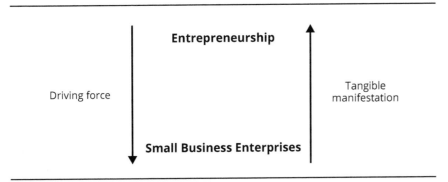

Figure 3.1   Small business enterprises and entrepreneurship

- **Product and innovation**: A small business is usually linked with an established product/service, whereas an entrepreneurial venture is identified with an innovative new product/service.

- **Motivation and growth**: The motives behind starting a business and the desired level of growth for the business venture may differ.

- **Nature and level of risk**: A small business owner is most likely to deal with known risk, while unknown risk is a defining aspect of the entrepreneurial process.

- **Impact and domain**: This refers to the level of impact that a business has on its field, other business sectors, economies, and communities.

- **Business operation**: A small business owner and an entrepreneur differ in their adopted approaches to running their businesses (Seth, 2014).

3.4.3   Popular sectors for small business enterprises

Since the early 1980s much attention has been focused on entrepreneurship and the small business sector. This interest has been motivated largely by the shift from manufacturing to service industries, the strategic downsizing of large corporations, and the flexibility of small firms and their ability to adjust and respond to emerging configurations.

Small business enterprises are found in all business sectors. Although the majority of small businesses are concentrated in the service and retail sectors, they virtually thrive in every industry, mainly services, retailing, construction, wholesaling, finance and insurance, transportation, and manufacturing. The service sector remains by far the largest and fastest-growing segment of small business.

3.4.4   Advantages of owning a small business

The Bolton Report (1971, p. 344) unequivocally concluded that "If small firms did not exist it would be necessary to invent them." Small businesses promise highly valued rewards to the entrepreneur and extend indispensable benefits to the welfare of society.

3.4.4.1   Benefits to the entrepreneur

Some benefits of owning a small business to the individual entrepreneur include the following:

- **"Being my own boss"** is an answer frequently given by entrepreneurs when asked about the incentives for starting their businesses. Many entrepreneurs are driven to launch new businesses by the goal of gaining independence from working for somebody else. Owning a business gives entrepreneurs the good feeling of being independent and in charge and provides them the opportunity to pursue and achieve what is important to them. Unlike being employees in larger corporations with limited authority to enact their ideas, owning their businesses enables entrepreneurs to do business their own way. In addition, it gives them a free hand to try out innovative ideas and steer their businesses into the future, guided by their own vision and skills.

- **Opportunity to fulfill religious duty and serve the community.** Muslim entrepreneurs in particular have much to gain from engaging in entrepreneurial activities. The foremost benefit is the fulfillment of a religious duty, thereby pleasing the Almighty Allah. Through entrepreneurship, Muslim entrepreneurs extend help to their Muslim brothers and sisters and contribute to the development of their communities, thereby gaining more rewards in the hereafter and achieving a state of spiritual satisfaction in this worldly life.

- **Opportunity to achieve rewarding profits.** Regardless of the motives driving entrepreneurs to venture into their own businesses, earning profits and securing a financial future for themselves remain important and legitimate incentives for entrepreneurs. Studies have shown that the majority of small business owners believe that they are financially much better off as business owners than working for a company in the same industry (Wall Street, 2010).

- **Opportunity to make a difference.** Entrepreneurs start their businesses motivated by a cause that is important to them, such as protecting the environment or helping a marginalized group in society. In due course they achieve multiple goals by making a difference in the lives of those they intended to help while, at the same time, earning a good living for themselves.

- **Opportunity to contribute to society and be recognized.** Small business owners in most countries are highly respected and trusted by members of their communities. Their efforts and contributions are recognized, and in many instances their success is celebrated. Research findings have shown that small businesses by and large are viewed much more favorably than large corporations (Hoover, 2014; Public Affairs PULSE Survey, 2015).

3.4.4.2   Benefits to the economy

In addition to the benefits businesses provide their owners, a strong and profitable small business sector benefits the broader economy and community. Small businesses are a source of:

- **Job creation.** Small businesses are the largest employers with lower investment per job than larger companies.[3] They contribute substantially to the fight against poverty by putting more people to work, either through self-employment or being employed in small firms. Statistics indicate that the trend in the last few decades has been marked by a shift from employment in large firms to self-employment or employment in small firms (Yildirmaz, 2015).

- **Training.** Small businesses provide training for unskilled workers, upgrading the skills of less-skilled, and sharpening the skills of skilled workers, thus contributing to the process of building a stock of human capital capable of leading future industrial expansion of the country.

- **Innovation.** The basic features of small firms, such as competitiveness, dynamism, simplicity in structure, and flexibility and responsiveness in the way they operate, place them in an ideal position to be a source of innovation in products, services, and technologies.

- **Networking.** Small business owners usually build informal, and sometimes personal, relationships with their customers, giving them the opportunity to have a thorough understanding of the problems their customers face. Being totally in charge allows small business owners to experiment with new ideas and try different innovative approaches to produce needed products or solve problems faced by customers.

- **Contributions to big business.** A symbiotic, complementary, and mutually beneficial relationship exists between big and small businesses. Most products made by big businesses are sold to consumers by small ones due to the efficiency in their distribution and the flexibility in their operations. On the other hand, a variety of products manufactured by small business are purchased by big businesses and incorporated into their final products.

- **Autonomy and economic independence.** Small businesses are owned and operated by indigenous people who come from within their communities. Being free from foreign domination and exploitation, small firms contribute significantly to preserving and safeguarding the national identity, and thus are seen as symbols of economic independence, particularly in developing countries.

3.4.5   Challenges of owning a small business

Although owning small business enterprises has many benefits and provides their owners with ample opportunities, would-be entrepreneurs need to be aware of the potential drawbacks associated with owning a small business, including the following:

- **Uncertainty of income.** Even if entrepreneurs have done their homework and prepared thoroughly for their new business ventures, the fact remains that there are no guaranteed outcomes. Being in business is marked by uncertainty, evidenced by fluctuations in sales and profitability, changes in government regulations, and the dynamics of the market. External forces are hard to predict and almost impossible to control.

- **Risks associated with being an entrepreneur.** Entrepreneurs put their financial security, careers, health, family, and social life at stake by taking multiple risks when they embark on business ventures with uncertain outcomes.

- **Risk of losing entire invested capital.** Entrepreneurs risk losing their entire investment and more (personal assets) if their business fails. A failing business can have economically, as well as emotionally, devastating effects and place immense burdens on entrepreneurs and their families.

- **High level of stress.** "It's hard to get a good night's sleep when you run a small business," commented a young entrepreneur. Business owners work hard and long days that, at times, exceed 10 hours a day, up to 7 days a week, especially during the early stages of launching their small businesses. It is not only sales and cash flow issues that cause most small business owners to endure anxiety and stress; recruiting reliable staff, ensuring product quality, not spending enough time with their family, complying with government laws and regulations, and dealing with economic slowdowns are all major issues causing stress for entrepreneurs.

- **Complete responsibility.** The small business owner/manager assumes total responsibility for the business. He makes decisions about all aspects of the business: hiring and firing, financial control of the enterprise, purchasing, marketing and sales, day-to-day problems, and compliance with government rules and regulations. Such responsibilities undoubtedly are very hard for one person to shoulder.

3.4.6   Small business: Factors leading to failure and success

While a single factor could lead to failure, "success must be the result of all factors working together and it is hard to distinguish the most significant" (Cusworth and Frank, 1993, p. 11).

3.4.6.1   Small business failure

The reality is that not all new business ventures succeed. The causes of failure are usually emphasized more in discussions of small business failure or success. Factors contributing to failure can be divided into two groups: internal factors and external factors.

3.4.6.1.1   Internal factors

Internal factors refer to the problems that are inherent in the organization itself and have to do with management and resources. Internal factors are broadly the primary causes of business failure despite the fact that business owners have considerable control over them. Internal factors of failure include the following:

- **Managerial incompetence or inexperience** in the areas of management, marketing, production, and personnel. The majority of small business owners lack managerial experience, formal business training, and familiarity with an institutional environment.

- **Neglecting the business** by not devoting adequate time or energy to attending to its demanding needs and requirements.

- **A weak control system** is a serious drawback affecting the majority of small business enterprises. Unlike large corporations, with their abundant resources that can be employed to protect assets and ensure proper functioning of internal systems and procedures, small businesses are usually limited in their human and financial resources, limiting their ability to effectively manage valuable resources and enhance performance. This reality puts more pressure on small business owners to assume additional responsibilities toward the success of their business ventures.

- An internal control system is a set of methods or procedures adopted in a business to:
  - protect its assets;
  - ensure the accuracy and reliability of financial information;
  - ensure compliance with all financial and operational requirements; and
  - generally, assist in achieving the business's objectives (Campbell and Hartcher, 2007).

- **Insufficient start-up capital** and difficulties in securing new capital. A lack of financial capital to start new or expand existing small businesses remains a major obstacle facing existing and potential entrepreneurs. Thus far, in practice, Islamic banking has not been conducive to the start-up of innovative business firms. Moreover, entrepreneurs tend to underestimate the cost involved in launching a business. They often overlook the need to account for intangible expenses that can arise over time and fail to set aside sufficient funds to cover their families' living expenses during the first 6 months of the life of the business while the business is being established and building up its customer base. New entrepreneurs often imagine that once the business opens its doors, sales and profits will start pouring in. As a "rule of thumb," would-be entrepreneurs are advised to have available on hand (or have access to) double the estimated amount needed for their business start-up.

- **Failing to prepare a practical strategic business plan** that clearly describes the business concept, the mission of the business, and the philosophy of the business owner. A professionally prepared business plan should lay out personal and business goals and set out specific timelines and strategies to achieve them.

- **Reputation risk** is more relevant to Islamic enterprises and is most likely to arise if an Islamic enterprise, for example, participates in unlawful business activity such as charging interest or selling alcoholic products. The certain outcome would be the loss of customers' confidence in the business, paving the way to its inevitable failure.

3.4.6.1.2 External factors

While small business owners might be able to rectify certain deficiencies in an internal business environment, they are usually helpless when faced with external challenges. They can do little to avoid external forces or minimize their negative impact on their business. Leading external causes to business failure are as follows:

- **inability of the business to compete** due to price, quality, or customer service disadvantage;
- **economic environment** in times of recessions or crises and the consequences for affordability and purchasing power;
- **changes in government policies and regulations** that might negatively impact certain industries or sectors; and
- **new technologies** that render current technology inefficient or outdated and the failure of the would-be entrepreneur to spot looming changes.

3.4.6.2 Small business success

Success in business is planned and does not happen accidentally. The following key factors working together contribute to the success of small business ventures:

- hard work, drive, and dedication of the business owner-operator;

- meeting market demand by offering the right product/service to the right audience at the right price at the right time;

- competent and experienced business owner-operator; and

- external factors that may play to the advantage of the business (good luck).

3.5 Starting and financing small business enterprises using Islamic principles

Entrepreneurship is often linked with the creation of new business enterprises, where entrepreneurs assume responsibility for mobilizing needed resources. Securing start-up capital and having access to financing facilities are major obstacles that continue to challenge the majority of entrepreneurs.

Islam prohibits all forms of interest-based financial transactions regardless of what terms accompany them. Hence, an alternative financial arrangement that is consistent with the religious convictions of Muslims and in harmony with their cultural values is sought to fulfill their business as well as personal financial needs.

3.5.1 Forms of business start-up enterprises and available financing options in an Islamic economy

Once a Muslim entrepreneur envisions a business idea and turns the idea into a business opportunity, decisions must be made regarding the: (a) most appropriate form of business ownership to engage in; and (b) the best available financing option that suits the chosen form of business start-up.

Sole proprietorship, *mudarabah* partnership, and *musharakah* partnership (*shirkah*) are the most common forms of business enterprise that Muslim entrepreneurs can choose from to start their business venture (Sheikh An-Nabhani, 2008). Correspondingly, the most common Islamic modes of business finance are *al-qard al-hassan* (interest-free, benevolent loan), *mudharabah* (silent partnership/trust financing), and *musharakah* (partnership contract).

3.5.1.1 *Sole proprietorship and* Al-Qard Al-Hasan

Sole proprietorship is a business owned and operated by a single individual. All the norms of Islamic economics relevant to sole proprietorship businesses are similar to those of classical economics.[4] The individual owner contributes his or her own capital, takes out a loan[5] if needed, makes his/her own decisions regarding the business, hires employees, buys raw materials, and sells finished products. The business owner receives all profits generated by the business as individual assets and, likewise, bears sole responsibility for any losses. If the business goes bankrupt, creditors have the right to target the business owner's private assets to recover their debts.

Al-qard al-hasan is an interest-free loan where the borrower only repays the principal. Islamic financial institutions, being socially responsible, extend their credit facilities to rural areas and provide the poor with short-term loans (*qard hasan*) to enable them to set up or develop microbusinesses. Interest-free loans are not conducive to establishing business relationships between lenders and borrowers.

3.5.1.2 Mudharabah *(Silent partnership)*

Mudarabah is a contract between two parties: the financer (*rabb al-mal*), which may be a financial institution, a bank, or an individual, and the entrepreneur (*mudarib*). *Rabb al-mal* acts as financer by providing needed capital, and the entrepreneur devotes his/her ideas, skills, expertise, and time to investing the funds in a productive and socially accepted (*halal*) business venture. The contract is based on the principles of PLS; profit when realized is shared by both parties according to pre-negotiated mutually accepted terms based on the actual profit generated by the business. In the case of losses, the provider of capital (financer) bears the entire financial burden and may lose all invested capital, whereas the entrepreneur's loss is limited to his/her invested time, effort, and livelihood.

Under *mudarabah*, the entrepreneur (*mudarib*) assumes total management of the business, rendering the financer (*rabb al-mal*) a passive (silent) partner with little or no real authority to influence the management of the business venture. The financer (*rabb al-mal*) has to have faith, trust, and confidence in the entrepreneur, who is expected to abide by Islamic business ethics. The entrepreneur ought to have a convincing argument for the economic feasibility of the proposed business undertaking in order to win the support of the *rabb al-mal*. Both parties have an equal right to terminate the partnership contract at any time, provided notice is given to the other party within a reasonable time prior to the effective date of termination.

There are two types of *mudarabah* transactions, discussed briefly in what follows: restricted and unrestricted *mudarabah*.

3.5.1.2.1 Restricted *mudarabah*

A restricted *mudarabah* is defined by the Accounting and Auditing Organization for Islamic Financial Institutions (AAOIFI) as "a contract in which the capital provider [*rabb al-mal*] restricts the actions of the *mudarib* to a particular location or to a particular type of investment as the capital provider considers appropriate, but not in a manner that would unduly constrain the *mudarib* in his operations." According to this definition, the power of the *mudarib* is restricted by the terms of the contract where the *rabb al-mal* has the right to specify what, where, and when he/she wants the *mudarib* to invest funds in. The financer usually has legitimate and justifiable motives for imposing such restrictions. However, such restrictions are not meant to tie the hands of the *mudarib* and prevent him from performing normal business functions.

3.5.1.2.2 Unrestricted *mudarabah*

Under unrestricted *mudarabah*, the *mudarib* is under no restrictions to trade or not to trade in any specific business or within a certain geographic location. The entrepreneur is left to his expertise, knowledge, and good judgment to invest in any type of permissible business at any location he deems appropriate and in accordance with the principles of *Shariah*.

3.5.1.3 Musharakah *(Partnership financing)*

Musharakah in Arabic literally means sharing (partnership). It is a contract between the entrepreneur and the financer (*rabb al-mal*), and in Islamic contracts there must be an offer and acceptance between partners over the subject matter of the contract. While *musharakah* is a form of partnership between two or more parties, it is managed and run by one, two, or more of its partners on behalf of other "sleeping partners" in line with the PLS mechanism. *Musharakah* is similar to *mudarabah*, except that all partners in *musharakah* contribute starting capital and all have the right to participate in the management of the business and work for it. Contrary to the lending arrangements extended by conventional banking, financing through *musharakah* does not mean advancing money to the borrower, who is held accountable for the repayment of the borrowed amount plus interest regardless of the outcome of the business investment. Rather, it means participation in the business and the formation of a partnership between the investor and the entrepreneur where both parties share the assets of the business to the extent of the ratio of financing. The *musharakah* certificate represents the direct pro rata ownership of the holder in the assets of the project. Thus, the two instruments differ in the sense that *musharakah* gives both the entrepreneur and *rabb al-mal* the opportunity to share the finances (assets or working capital), as well as the management and the operation of the business. Consequently, the entrepreneur will be exposed to capital loss.

Profit is shared according to predetermined proportions such as (partners' percentage contribution to start-up capital after deducting the entrepreneur's management compensation). Losses are also borne accordingly in line with the partners' proportion of capital contribution.

Musharakah is the option most likely to be favored by financers because it exposes entrepreneurs to the real risk of losing a portion of their investment and so motivates them to adopt a more cautious approach to managing the business and to put forth extra effort to ensure its success. *Musharakah* contracts also provide *rabb al-mal* with the opportunity to be an active participant in the entrepreneurial endeavor and to oversee the operation of the business.

3.6   Factors that enable or inhibit entrepreneurship development

Entrepreneurship development is an ongoing and inclusive process that requires the existence of harmonious relationships and positive interactions between all factors. The development of an effective entrepreneurship sector is influenced by a variety of factors working together to ensure the success of the entrepreneurial venture and, consequently, promote entrepreneurship development. Leading factors that influence the emergence and development of entrepreneurship are the entrepreneur, sociocultural factors, institutional/environmental factors, and other external factors. These distinct factors may have positive (enabling) and negative (inhibiting) influences on the emergence of entrepreneurship. They collectively shape the entrepreneurial process and determine the level and quality of entrepreneurship development in any given society. Positive influences facilitate and create conditions conducive to the emergence and development of entrepreneurship, whereas negative influences not only inhibit the emergence of new entrepreneurial ventures but also work against already existing ones.

3.6.1   Personality factors: The entrepreneur

Bygrave and Hofer (1991) consider entrepreneurs to be the "the essence of entrepreneurship. It is entrepreneurs with their high need for achievement who create enterprises. Entrepreneurs are the backbone and the driving force behind the entrepreneurial process. The level of entrepreneurial activity in any country is linked to the ability of its potential entrepreneurs to generate creative business ideas and identify potential opportunities (through recognition, discovery, and creation) and their ability to turn such opportunities into business entities. This entails the existence of highly motivated, confident, and skilled enterprising individuals willing and able to mobilize needed resources and take the risk associated with starting a business.

3.6.2   Sociocultural factors

Culture is broadly defined as a distinct set of values, beliefs, attitudes, norms, customs, and symbols shared, accepted, and practiced as lawful and moral by the members of a certain group or society. Variations in the level of entrepreneurial activities between countries have a sociocultural dimension and could be explained, among other factors, by cultural differences. Some cultures value entrepreneurial activity more than others. While entrepreneurs are highly regarded in some societies, they are negatively perceived in others. Entrepreneurship thrives in societies known for their flexibility and openness toward various types of work, where people are free and encouraged to pursue entrepreneurial dreams. On the other hand, entrepreneurship is unlikely to take off in a society where the dreams of youth are focused on having executive offices in large corporations or being employed by the government because government employees enjoy considerable respect in the eyes of the public.

Decisions of potential entrepreneurs to pursue or hold back on their entrepreneurial aspirations are affected by:

- how people perceive entrepreneurship and how they regard entrepreneurs;

- the level of public awareness of the opportunities and benefits of entrepreneurship: a higher level of public awareness will drive more people into entrepreneurship;

- general attitudes toward entrepreneurship: a society with favorable attitudes toward entrepreneurship motivates people to start new businesses;

- real-life stories about successful entrepreneurs signifying what it is like and what it means to be an entrepreneur;

- how a society recognizes its entrepreneurs as role models and celebrates their success, whether the prevailing reward structure portrays entrepreneurship as an attractive business alternative to being a white-, blue-, or pink-collar worker.[6]

Religion, family, education, and the media are four powerful sociocultural institutions that have a profound influence on fostering entrepreneurial tendencies and shaping attitudes toward entrepreneurship emergence and development (Kayed and Hassan, 2011).

3.6.2.1   *Religion*

There are several hypotheses attempting to explain the relationship between religion and entrepreneurship. They range from portraying religions as being entrepreneurial to being barriers to the emergence and development of entrepreneurship. The fact that Islam is an entrepreneurial religion—as we established earlier in the chapter—presents Muslims with remarkable opportunities to raise awareness of and promote Islamic entrepreneurship. The educational system, the Mosque, Friday sermons, religious schools, public speeches, study circles, and other religious activities can play a crucial role in promoting entrepreneurship as a religious and a socioeconomic activity.

3.6.2.2 Family

Being one of the most, if not the most, influential social institution, family has a profound role to play in entrepreneurship development. Family offers a range of very important resources to entrepreneurs during every stage of the entrepreneurial process (Anderson et al., 2005). First, family has the means to encourage the entrepreneurial concept and, consequently, influence decisions to pursue the path of entrepreneurship by fostering entrepreneurial tendencies, nurturing entrepreneurial qualities, and shaping positive attitudes toward entrepreneurship. Family members can also pass on their experiences, help in identifying business opportunities, and act as inspirational role models to would-be entrepreneurs, considering that many would-be entrepreneurs come from families associated with entrepreneurship. Second, family involvement at the start-up phase continues and takes several forms, ranging from extending moral support to providing financial and physical support. Family members also provide specialist as well as general advice to young entrepreneurs and provide them with access to their social and professional networks in order to promote the new business. Third, a family's involvement continues after the start-up phase where family members extend their help with everyday business tasks and offer advice when needed.

3.6.2.3 Education

Education as a cultural trait and policy instrument has a significant role to play in fostering entrepreneurial values and preparing students to deal with day-to-day problems under uncertain circumstances. Education in general and entrepreneurship education in particular have a crucial, twofold role to play in the entrepreneurial process: (a) creating and spreading awareness, changing/affirming attitudes, and motivating and stimulating individuals to consider entrepreneurship as a worthy career option; it is therefore an effective means by which cultural values regarding entrepreneurship are nurtured, developed, and expressed; and (b) disseminating knowledge, providing training, developing and enhancing skills, and preparing enterprising individuals.

3.6.2.4 Media

Media has created heroes, champions, and idols from among musicians, sports icons, and movie stars that the majority of the population, especially younger generations, look up to and emulate. The same media is in a unique position to play a similarly influential role in creating entrepreneurial role models who are worthy of respect and admiration, not only from the business community but also from ordinary citizens.

Featuring successful and socially responsible entrepreneurs and profiling their hard work, dedication, and commitment to achieve will motivate and encourage potential entrepreneurs to pursue their dreams of owning their own businesses. Positive portrayals of entrepreneurs also bring about favorable reactions from various stakeholders such as investors, bankers, suppliers, customers, and the general public toward entrepreneurs and their entrepreneurial activities. Media, therefore, can be a constructive force in creating entrepreneurial culture and, consequently, an enabling factor in entrepreneurship development.

3.6.3   Environmental/institutional factors

Variations in the level of entrepreneurial activity across cultures are also affected by the level of institutional support and incentives extended to the development of entrepreneurship in a specific country. Even an entrepreneurial culture needs a friendly business environment and enabling institutions in order for entrepreneurship to emerge and develop.

Entrepreneurial success or failure depends largely on the prevailing legal, economic, political, and technological forces combined and supported by functional institutions. A friendly business climate and enabling institutions can create opportunities; otherwise, the environment will serve as an impediment to entrepreneurship development and promotion.

3.6.3.1   *Legal environment*

Governmental regulations affect entrepreneurial ventures in a variety of ways. A legal environment is considered pro-entrepreneurial if and where: (1) its legal system upholds the right of ownership and affirms the sanctity of private property, (2) its institutions are efficient and uncorrupted, and (3) its rules and regulations are characterized by simplicity and ease regarding:

- obtaining permits and good services from government agencies;

- registering and licensing new business enterprises;

- the volume of paperwork and reporting to various governmental departments and agencies;

- the cost and time of setting up a new business;

- laws related to products, patents, and resources; and

- laws to protect labor rights and the environment.

3.6.3.2   *Economic environment*

Entrepreneurship thrives in prosperous economies that are endowed with efficient infrastructural facilities, stable macroeconomic policies, and the availability of and access to appropriate financial institutions that respond to the needs of entrepreneurs and their enterprises in a timely manner. Economic factors that affect the development of entrepreneurship include the following:

- **Capital:** Needless to say, capital is one of the most, if not the most, pressing needs to a new enterprise. The availability of capital enables an entrepreneur to acquire and mobilize other factors of production, such as land, labor, raw materials, and machinery, facilitating the transformation of ideas and opportunities into actions. There exists a positive relationship between the availability of an adequate supply of capital and the level of entrepreneurial activity. Therefore, it is imperative for Islamic banks operating in Islamic environments to assume their entrepreneurial role through the honest application of PLS contracts and form genuine partnerships with Muslim entrepreneurs to promote entrepreneurship development.

- **Labor:** The availability of a mobile and flexible labor force is essential for the emergence and development of entrepreneurship. No enterprise succeeds without a skilled and committed workforce.

- **Raw materials:** A raw material is a must-have factor for any production process. No business or industry can function without an adequate supply of raw materials. The availability of quality raw materials at sensible prices is an enabling economic force for the emergence and development of healthy entrepreneurship.

- **Markets:** Earning profits remains a priority for the majority of entrepreneurs starting their own businesses, so they must have a product to sell or a service to offer that satisfies customers' needs in a better way than competitors and at a price that is greater than all costs involved in its production and marketing. Entrepreneurs need competitive markets to secure raw materials needed for the production of their goods and they need vibrant markets to sell their finished goods and services. The availability of active markets and the sound knowledge about market and marketing mechanisms are very important for the development and growth of entrepreneurship.

- **Infrastructure:** Entrepreneurial activities grow and prosper where reliable physical infrastructure and utilities are in place. Modern transport networks and steady power generation, coupled with reliable distribution facilities and unfailing communication services, for instance, drive the cost of doing business down and facilitate the proper functioning of businesses.

3.6.3.3 Political environment

Governments set up rules and regulations that guide the formation and operation of business. Incumbent as well as potential business owners must comply with these regulations. Therefore, establishing favorable laws and regulations and implementing policies, incentives, and support initiatives are essential for creating a thriving entrepreneurship sector.

3.6.3.3.1 Political stability

A stable political system enhances the ability of the government to preserve law and maintain order and so is most likely to have a positive effect on the business environment. Stable political conditions induce government to make business-friendly decisions and encourage the formation of new businesses and the expansion of existing ones, as investors feel that their investments are safe. On the other hand, uncertain political conditions, where government policies are subject to frequent change, discourage business, as investors fear for the safety of their investments.

3.6.3.3.2 Government policies and initiatives

Understanding the institutional and cultural realities of entrepreneurship in a country enables policymakers to map appropriate policies aimed at promoting entrepreneurship development, both directly and indirectly. First, the government can directly influence entrepreneurship by embracing policies focused on addressing specific needs for entrepreneurship development such as simplifying entry procedures and cutting down on rules to enable potential entrepreneurs to start their businesses with ease; initiating various programs to raise awareness and motivate and inspire individuals to consider becoming entrepreneurs; and carrying out different entrepreneurship capacity-building programs to equip potential entrepreneurs with the necessary training and appropriate skills for success.

Second, the government can also indirectly influence the level of entrepreneurial activity by targeting the general macroeconomic framework with the aim of creating a friendly environment conducive to entrepreneurship. The government, through general policies, can invest in sound infrastructure and make available basic utilities such as roads, power, and communication facilities, which are necessary for entrepreneurship development; create an enterprise culture that enables firms to take reasonable and calculated risks; and increase business opportunities to elevate the motivation of potential entrepreneurs to start their own businesses.

Furthermore, the state can embark on selective interventionist policies that favor, protect, promote, and support the small business sector. Financial aid, incentives, credit, counseling, training, and research are some areas where direct government assistance could be extended to small enterprises.

Government actions in favor of entrepreneurship or failure to act can, to an extent, mark the difference between having a promising entrepreneurship sector and a failing one.

3.6.3.4 *Technological environment*

The use of technology in business is becoming a necessity that no business, big or small, can do without and still be competitive and lucrative. Small business owners utilize computers, the Internet, smartphones, social media, information, and communication technology for various reasons, including to reduce costs, develop a competitive advantage, increase productivity, improve communication, and reach new markets, new consumers, and new suppliers.

The availability and accessibility of technology to small business owners and the familiarity of small business owners with technology and their ability to benefit from it are conditions for having successful business enterprises and, ultimately, having a promising entrepreneurship sector.

3.6.4 Other factors

External forces occasionally do find their way into the entrepreneurial equation and influence the sociocultural or institutional setting of the entrepreneurial process in certain societies. External factors, such as imposed ideological beliefs (communism in the former Soviet Union), the discovery of natural resources (Saudi Arabia), colonization (India), or a sudden influx of immigrants or expatriates, could affect the cultural and institutional balance of a country and subsequently enhance or obstruct the pace, level, and quality of its entrepreneurship development.

Chapter Highlights

Entrepreneurship is the process by which entrepreneurs identify new business opportunities, mobilize needed resources, and assume the risk of converting opportunities into marketable products or services. The entrepreneurship process therefore involves the following factors working together to create new value: (1) the individual entrepreneur; (2) sources of opportunities (ideas); (3) opportunity identification (recognition, discovery, creation), evaluation, and exploitation; (4) resource mobilization; (5) business organization; and (6) an environment in which culture and institutions complement each other. The entrepreneur is the core of the entrepreneurial process. Economists consider the entrepreneur an agent who assumes certain roles, including those of innovator, creative imitator, arbitrager, risk taker, risk manager, organizer, and coordinator. He is an opportunity exploiter, a gap filler, and a resource mobilizer. Behavioralists, on the other hand, have assembled a long list of traits of the successful entrepreneur and identified the need for achievement, tolerance of risk and uncertainty, and internal locus of control as the most important of these.

Islam holds entrepreneurial activity in high regard and expects Muslims to be productive and self-reliant. This positive attitude toward entrepreneurship is enforced by attaching religious significance to entrepreneurial activity. Entrepreneurship in Islam is the source and origin of sustenance (*rizq*). Islam views entrepreneurship as a two-dimensional activity intended to reward Muslim entrepreneurs in this life and in the hereafter. The creation of productive and ethical business enterprises by Muslim entrepreneurs is an act of *ibadah*. Muslim entrepreneurs seek to fulfill religious obligations to please the Almighty Allah without failing to benefit from the material incentives. They reap benefits for themselves while benefiting society at large.

While Islamic and Western entrepreneurship share many features, they differ in many others, including the motives, goals, definition, and measure of success, the definition and nature of entrepreneurial opportunity, and the sources for start-up financing. Islam subjects every activity to moral and ethical standards and measures every business activity against a well-defined set of principles and *guidelines* to ensure its compliance with the rules of *Shariah*.

Much emphasis has been placed on opportunity as a key element in the entrepreneurial process. An absence of business opportunities translates to an absence of business ventures. Ways to generate business ideas include current and potential customers, identifying current inefficiencies in the market, industry trends, market gaps, and listening to what colleagues, employees, and businesspeople say. New business ideas are assessed to determine whether they constitute entrepreneurial opportunities that will meet market demand and generate profit. Consequently, business opportunities would be subjected to a strict screening process to establish their authenticity as being real, viable, and profitable in order to be considered good business opportunities.

The three views of entrepreneurial opportunity identification are as follows. The first view is that opportunities are discovered either accidentally or as a result of a search for a solution to either the supply of or demand for a product or service. The second view is that opportunities are created by the action of the entrepreneur and his ability to act creatively. Finally is the view that opportunities are recognized by alert entrepreneurs since both the product/service (supply) and the market (demand) do exist.

In the absence of a generally accepted definition of what constitutes a small business, a variety of both quantitative and qualitative measures are used to distinguish small firms from other businesses. A business is considered to be small if it is independently owned and operated and typically has a small number of employees (as determined by the industry in the respective countries). Small business enterprises are found in all business sectors, mainly services, retailing, construction, wholesaling, finance, insurance, transportation, and manufacturing. The service sector remains by far the largest and fastest growing segment of small business.

Small businesses bring valuable rewards to their owners, including being one's own boss, the opportunity to fulfill a religious duty and serve the community, the opportunity to earn outstanding profits, the opportunity to make a difference, and the opportunity to contribute to society and be acknowledged.

Having a strong and profitable small business sector also benefits the broader economy and community. Small businesses are a source of innovation, job creation, training, contribution to big companies, and autonomy and economic independence.

The disadvantages associated with owning a small business include the uncertainty of income, multiple risks (financial security, careers, health, family, and social life), the risk of losing one's entire invested capital and more, the high level of stress, and the fact that one must assume total responsibility for the business.

The task of financing entrepreneurial activities continues to challenge the aspirations of many potential entrepreneurs. Islam prohibits all forms of interest-based financial transactions. Therefore, an alternative financial arrangement that is consistent with the religious convictions of Muslims and in harmony with their cultural values is sought to fulfill their business as well as personal financial needs.

The most common Islamic modes of business financing are *mudarabah* (silent partnership, passive partnership) and *musharakah* (partnership contract, active partnership). *Musharakah* and *mudarabah* are two PLS-based financial instruments that conform to Islamic financial principles. *Musharakah* is a contract between the entrepreneur and the financial institution that is identical to *mudarabah* except that the entrepreneur contributes starting capital and makes physical and mental contributions to the business venture.

The development of an effective entrepreneurship sector is influenced by a range of factors working together to ensure the success of the entrepreneurial venture and, consequently, the emergence of a thriving entrepreneurship sector.

Factors that enable or inhibit national entrepreneurship include the following:

(1) The entrepreneurs. It is entrepreneurs, with their high need for achievement, who create enterprises. Entrepreneurs identify business ideas, turn them into opportunities, and convert those opportunities into business enterprises through resource mobilization and risk taking.

(2) Sociocultural factors. Decisions of potential entrepreneurs to pursue or hold back on their entrepreneurial aspirations are affected by their society's values, beliefs, attitudes, norms, symbols, and customs. Moreover, religion, family, education, and the media are four influential sociocultural institutions that can sway tendencies and attitudes toward entrepreneurship.

(3) Environmental/institutional factors. Even an entrepreneurial culture needs a friendly business environment and enabling institutions in order for entrepreneurship to emerge and develop. Entrepreneurship success or failure depends largely on the prevailing legal, economic, political, and technological forces combined and supported by functional institutions.

(4) Other factors. External forces such as imposed ideological beliefs, colonization, globalization, the discovery of abundant natural resources, and being subjected to sudden waves of immigrants can influence the cultural and institutional setting of the entrepreneurial process in certain societies.

Key Terms

Accidental opportunity discovery	Institutional factors	Private ownership
Al-qard al-hasan	Islamic entrepreneurship	Property rights
Creativity	*Khalifah* vicegerent	Proprietorship
Economic environment	Legal environment	Public ownership
Enabling factors	Locus of control	*Rabb al-mal*
Entrepreneur	*Mudarib*	Reputation risk
Entrepreneurial activity	*Mudharabah* (silent partnership)	Resource mobilization
Entrepreneurial culture	*Musharakah* (partner- ship financing)	Restricted mudarabah
Entrepreneurial opportunity	Muslim entrepreneur	Risk
Entrepreneurial process	Opportunity creation	*Rizq*
Entrepreneurship	Opportunity discovery	Screening opportunities
Fard kefayah	Opportunity recognition	*Shariah*
Halal	Partnership	Small business
Ibadah	Political environment	Small business sectors
Inhibiting factors	Political stability	Sociocultural factors
Innovation		*Tawhid*
		Ummah
		Uncertainty

Discussion Questions

1. Discuss the three major phases of the entrepreneurial process and identify the basic conditions associated with the Islamic perspective of entrepreneurship.

2. Discuss the foundations of private ownership in Islam. Enforce your arguments with verses from the Holy Qur'an.

3. Identify six prohibited practices and transactions in Islamic entrepreneurship.

4. Describe the main differences between Islamic and Western entrepreneurship.

5. Identify key issues that must be addressed during the opportunity-screening process.

6. Briefly discuss five ways to generate good business ideas.

7. What is a small business? What contributions do small businesses make to communities and a nation's economy?

8. Identify key differences between small businesses and entrepreneurial ventures.

9. Describe the potential challenges most likely to confront a small business owner.

10. Describe major internal factors leading to the failure of small businesses.

11. Explain the differences between restricted and unrestricted mudarabah contracts in the context of their role in promoting Islamic entrepreneurship.

12. Identify key differences between mudarabah and musharakah as instruments for financing small business start-ups.

13. How can the economic environment be an enabling factor for the development of entrepreneurship?

14. Describe the role of Islamic culture in entrepreneurship development.

Comprehension Questions

1. How does an entrepreneur differ from a traditional manager? Compare and contrast the two with regard to the following characteristics: primary motives, focus of attention, attitude toward risk, skills, and decision-making style.

2. Some critics describe Islam as an anti-entrepreneurial religion, asserting that Islam's emphasis on the hereafter and disregard for material gain discourage would-be entrepreneurs from taking the entrepreneurial path.
How do you respond?

3. How do you link the importance of applying strict opportunity-screening procedures with the fact that over 80 percent of all new products fail?

4. Why is *musharakah* most likely to be the preferred option by banks for financing small business start-ups?

5. How does political stability contribute to entrepreneurship development?

Activities

1. Think of a local or national entrepreneur who you admire. Conduct preliminary research and prepare a two-page report on his/her entrepreneurial qualities, achievements, commitment to the rules of *Shariah* and Islamic business ethics while practicing entrepreneurship and his/her contribution to the community.
Share your report with your instructor and classmates.

2. Find a successful entrepreneur or a small business owner in your community, and conduct a semi-structured interview with him/her. You can start by asking:
What motivated you to start your own business?
How did you recognize the business opportunity?
How did you mobilize start-up finances? What kind of support, if any, did you receive from the government? From family and friends?
Based on the data you collect, would you define your interviewee as an entrepreneur or a small business owner? Why?
Discuss your findings with your instructor and classmates.

3. Based on the knowledge you have gained from this chapter regarding the definition and characteristics of the entrepreneur, do you consider yourself to be an entrepreneur? A potential entrepreneur? What entrepreneurial qualities do you possess?

4. Interview the customer service department of any Islamic bank or financial institution and identify the *Shariah* financial instruments it has adopted and employs (with practical examples). *Prepare the interview report for a 15-minute class presentation.*

5. Survey the attitude of at least 10 entrepreneurs/small business owners in your community toward their perspective of Islamic entrepreneurship. Prepare a 10- to 15-question survey to serve this purpose.

   Analyze the collected data and share your findings with your instructor and classmates.

References

Barringer, B.R. and Ireland, R.D. (2008). *Entrepreneurship: Successfully Launching New Ventures* (4th ed.). Upper Saddle River: Prentice Hall.

Bolton, J.E. (1971). *Small Firms: Report of the Committee of Inquiry on Small Firms.* London: Her Majesty's Stationary Office.

Bygrave, W.D. and Hofer, C.W. (1991). Theorizing About Entrepreneurship. *Entrepreneurship Theory and Practice*, 16(2), 13–22.

Campell, S. and Hartcher, J. (2007). Internal Control for Small Business. Retrieved March 2, 2017, from: https://www.whistleblowing.com.au/information/documents/InternalControls.pdf

Cusworth, J.W. and Frank, T.R. (1993). *Management Projects in Developing Countries.* Harlow: Longman, p. 11.

Day, G.S. (2007). Is It Real? Can We Win? Is It Worth It? Managing Risk and Reward in an Innovation Portfolio. *Harvard Business Review*, December, pp. 110–120.

Harper, M. (1984). *Small Business in the Third World: Guidelines for Practical Assistance.* Chichester: Intermediate Technology Publications.

Hassan, M.K. and Hippler, W.J. (2014, May). Entrepreneurship and Islam: An Overview. *Econ Journal Watch*, 11(2), 170–178.

Herbert, R.F. and Link, A.N. (1988). *The Entrepreneur: Main Stream Views and Radical Critique* (2nd ed.). New York: Praeger.

Hoover, K. (2014). Public Opinion of Big Business Improves, but Small Business Still Rules. https://www.bizjournals.com/bizjournals/.../public-opinion-of-big-business-improves

Hornady, J. (1982). Research About Living Entrepreneurs. In C.A. Kent, D.L. Sexton and K.H. Vesper (Eds.) *Encyclopedia of Entrepreneurship*. Englewood Cliffs: Prentice Hall.

Kao, J. (1991). *The Entrepreneur*. Englewood Cliffs: Prentice Hall.

Kayed, R. (2006). Islamic Entrepreneurship: A Case Study of the Kingdom of Saudi Arabia. Massey Research Online, Massey University, Palmerston North, New Zealand.

Lenko, M. (1995). Entrepreneurship: The New Tradition. *CMA Magazine*, 69(6), 18–20.

Public Affairs PULSE Survey (2015). Attitudes About Big Business and Small Business. Public Affairs PULSE Survey. https://pac.org/pulse/?p=478

Sadeq, A. (1993). Islamic Banking and Economic Development. Paper presented at International Conference on Islamic Banking, Sydney, Australia, November 1993.

Sahih Al-Bukhari, Vol. 2, Book 24, Number 549.

Sarasvathy, S., Dew, N., Velamuri, S. and Venkataraman, S. (2003). Three Views of Entrepreneurial Opportunity. In Z. Acs (Ed.) *Handbook of Entrepreneurship*. Boston: Kluwer Academic Press, pp. 141–160; Batten Institute Research Paper No. 2003 Vol 2.

Schaper, M., Volery, T., Weber, P. and Gibson, B.J. (2014). *Entrepreneurship and Small Business* (4th Asia-Pacific edition). Milton: John Wiley & Sons, pp. 32–33.

Schumpeter, J. (1934). *The Theory of Economic Development*. Cambridge: Harvard University Press.

Seth, S. (2014). *Entrepreneur vs. Small Business Owner, Defined*. New York: Investopedia, 25 September 2014.

Sheikh An-Nabhani, T. (2008). *The Economic System of Islam* (6th ed.). Charleston: Selfpublished via CreateSpace.

Timmons, J.A. (1994). New Venture Creation: Entrepreneurship for the 21st Century (4th ed.). Burr Ridge: Irwin Press.

Wall Street Journal (2010). Small Business. *Wall Street Journal*, December 16, p. B8.

Yildirmaz, A. (2015). 3 Trends Supporting Small Business Employment Growth. Retrieved March 12, 2017, from: https://www.forbes.com/.../3-trends-supporting-small-business-employment-growth/

Selected Bibliography

Adas, E.B. (2006). The Making of Entrepreneurial Islam and the Islamic Spirit of Capitalism. *Journal for Cultural Research*, 10(2), 113–137, doi:https://doi.org/10.1080/14797580600624745.

Alvarez, S.A. and Barney, J.B. (2007). Discovery and Creation: Alternative Theories of Entrepreneurship Action. *Strategic Entrepreneurship Journal*, 1(2), 11–26.

Anderson, A.R., Jack, S.L. and Dodd, S.D. (2005). The Role of Family Members in Entrepreneurial Networks: Beyond the Boundaries of the Family Firm. *Family Business Review*, 15(1), 45–58.

Baron, R.A. (2014). *Essentials of Entrepreneurship: Evidence and Practice*. Cheltenham: Edward Elgar Publishing Ltd.

Blackburn, R.A. and Schaper, M.T. (Eds.). (2012). *Government, SMEs and Entrepreneurship Development: Policy, Practice and Challenges*. London: Routledge.

Etemad, H., Madsen, T.K., Rasmussen, E.S. and Servais, P. (Eds.). (2013). *Current Issues in International Entrepreneurship*. Cheltenham: Edward Elgar.

Gillespie-Brown, J. (2009). *So You Want To Be an Entrepreneur?: How to Decide If Starting a Business Is for You*. Chichester: John Wiley & Sons.

Gumusay, A.A. (2015, August). Entrepreneurship from an Islamic Perspective. *Journal of Business Ethics* 130(1), 199–208.

Hassan, K., Kayed, R.N. and Oseni, U.A. (2013). *Introduction to Islamic Banking and Finance: Principles and Practice*. Harlow: Pearson Publications.

Kayed, R.N. and Hassan, M.K. (2011). *Islamic Entrepreneurship*. London: Routledge.

Kettell, B. (2011). *Case Studies in Islamic Banking and Finance*. Chichester: John Wiley & Sons.

Mariotti, S. and Glackin, C. (2016). *Entrepreneurship: Starting & Operating a Small Business* (4th ed.). Harlow: Pearson Publications.

Scarborough, N.M. (2014). *Essentials of Entrepreneurship and Small Business Management* (7th ed.). Harlow: Pearson Publications.

Wiedl, K.N. (2006). *The Islamic System-Not Conducive to Start-Up of Young, Innovative Business Firms*. Norderstedt: GRIN Publishing.

Notes

1. Private ownership is a shared natural propensity among humans. Islam recognizes such a tendency and protects the right to private ownership as long as it is understood that humans are God's servants who are entrusted with His wealth; wealth is lawfully (*halal*) gained with the intention to spend it in the way of the Almighty Allah; wealth is not hoarded and prevented from being invested, developed, and used freely for the good of humanity; wealth is not concentrated in the hands of the wealthy minority; and wealth is not used in promoting harmful activities or invested in *haram* (forbidden) business activities.

2. For a more comprehensive overview of the size and share of the global Small Business sector refer to the following reports:
   (a) Administration. US Small Business Administration. https://www.sba.gov/sites/default/files/advocacy/United_States.pdf;
   (b) 2018 Report - EU Start-up Monitor
       startupmonitor.eu/EU-Startup-Monitor-2018-Report-WEB.pdf
   (c) Small Business Counts - Australian Small Business and Family ...
       https://www.asbfeo.gov.au/sites/default/.../Small_Business_Statistical_Report-Final.pdf.au
   (d) An Overview of Small and Medium Enterprises in Malaysia and Pakistan
       https://pdfs.semanticscholar.org/f888/181d4bf5a5f3952ca08dea80dc3b933baa171.pdf

3. For more information about small business employment along with historical data, visit www.adpemploymentreport.com

4. A sole proprietorship in Islam, as is the case for other forms of business, must follow the rules of *Shariah* regarding: (1) products and services offered, (2) financial transactions, and (3) compliance with the principles and practices of the Islamic code of business ethics.

5. The loan must be an interest-free loan (*al-qard al-hassan*).

6. Pink-collar worker is one who is employed in a job that is typically considered to be women's work. However, the term is being used now to include all service jobs.

7. Blue-collar worker is a member of the working class, usually those who work in manual labor.

8. A white-collar worker is a professional or educated worker who works in either an administrative or managerial role.

BUSINESS ETHICS AND SOCIAL RESPONSIBILITY

4

Mohammad Adli Musa and Mohd Ariff Mohd Daud

International Islamic University, Malaysia
Institute for Research & Development of Policy, Malaysia

Learning Outcomes

LO1: Describe Islamic business ethics and identify factors that affect ethical behavior in organizations.

LO2: Describe corporate social responsibility and explain how Islam protects and improves both the welfare of society and the interests of an organization.

LO3: Explain useful strategies for implementing the social responsiveness of an organization.

LO4: Understand the social responsibility of organizations to their customers, employees, stockholders, and environment.

Contents

INSIGHT: UN Global Compact

Ethis Ventures aims to create markets that "feed the soul." Through eight crowd-funding platforms, it aspires to encourage collaboration to bring about good for humanity. It claims to "focus on values and outcomes" and "seek to create funding flows that have a social impact, along with sustainable growth." Umar Munshi, founder and CEO of Ethis Ventures, says that "Ethis Ventures believes in the ten universal principles of the UN Global Compact, which are in alignment with our own efforts to encourage ethical investment and sustainable charity. We pledge to strive to continuously improve and uphold these principles to circulate wealth for good."

Participants and signatories of the UN Global Compact, among which is Ethis Ventures, align their strategies and operations with universal principles of human rights, labor, the environment, and anticorruption and take actions that advance societal goals. The ten principles of the UN Global Compact are that businesses should: (1) support and respect the protection of internationally proclaimed human rights, (2) make sure they are not complicit in human rights abuses, (3) uphold the freedom of association and the effective recognition of the right to collective bargaining, (4) uphold the elimination of all forms of forced and compulsory labor, (5) uphold the effective abolition of child labor, (6) eliminate discrimination in respect of employment and occupation, (7) support a precautionary approach to environmental challenges, (8) undertake initiatives to promote greater environmental responsibility, (9) encourage the development and diffusion of environmentally friendly technologies, and (10) work against corruption in all its forms, including extortion and bribery.

All that has been mentioned is in line with the current notions of business ethics and social responsibility. Various verses of the Qur'an and many Prophetic traditions, from which business ethics and social responsibility principles can be derived, address how one should conduct business. Furthermore, the Prophet Muḥammad himself was a businessman and was born in an environment where trade was the main economic activity.

Further reading on Ethis Ventures: http://www.ethisventures.com/ and UN Global Compact: https://www.unglobalcompact.org/

4.1   Introduction

Business ethical norms are often universally appealing. For example, trustworthiness, honesty, and integrity are ethical values that everyone appreciates, while fraud and deception are unethical practices frowned upon by all. It is thus no surprise that the notions of mainstream business ethics resonate with Islamic business ethical norms. Nonetheless, the contemporary discourse on business ethics has somehow ignored religion in favor of ethical theories rooted in humanism. An understanding of religious traditions, in particular Islam, would hopefully place ethics with regard to business in a broader perspective. When comparing and contrasting between business ethics in Western and Islamic contexts, there seems to be no tension or dichotomy between the two. Both are alike but at the same time unique in their own right. Both serve a similar purpose – to promote ethical behavior in business – although their philosophical underpinnings and the ways in which they do so might be different.

It has been acknowledged that prior to the emergence of business ethics as an academic discipline, religious teachings were influential in promoting ethical behavior in all spheres of life, including business. Moreover, religious beliefs provide a binding framework of ethical norms for people involved in business. To a certain extent, legislation is an effective enforcement mechanism that ensures corporations behave responsibly. However, law is sometimes insufficient, the legislative process could take some time, and more often than not laws are enacted in response to the negative impacts of certain unethical practices of business organizations. For example, the Sarbanes-Oxley (SOX) Act of 2002 was enacted as a response to corporate accounting scandals that happened in the 2000–2002 period, in particular at the Enron Corporation.

The *Shariah*, which is often referred to as Islamic law *per se*, does offer guidance and prescribe instructions aimed at creating an ethical environment for business transactions to take place. The focus on the form of these instructions has somehow led to the spirit underlying such rules being lost. Thus, *Shariah* rules are insufficient to ensure that the ethical objectives of the *Shariah* are being translated into practice. A reemphasis on Islamic ethics could potentially bring about the desired outcome, where business transactions are underlined by ethical norms.

4.2   Business ethics

Business ethics refers basically to ethics as applied to business, which is studied to appreciate the nature of moral issues in business and how they might be resolved. Business ethics is "about acting responsibly" and "doing what is right" in connection with the values of an organization and considering the impact of actions upon others. Without ethics, neither businesses nor individuals can function since the absence of an ethical framework governing actions leads to the nonexistence of behavior standards of a civil society, which would result in chaos and disorder. Business ethics also deals with the "expectations and requirements" of society from businesses.

The rise of interest in business ethics was a response to the widespread and well-publicized problems in the economic sphere highlighting ethical lapses and raising moral questions. More fundamentally, the root of the economic crisis is in fact a moral crisis marked by a decline of personal and civic virtues. This is not new. In the 1930s Franklin Roosevelt also observed that America faced not just an economic crisis but a moral crisis during the Wall Street Crash of 1929. The fact that a broad cross section of society is affected by business scandals and economic crises in one way or another makes business ethics relevant. Business is in fact one of the most powerful and influential social institutions, affecting almost every aspect of contemporary life, and as a result any ethical shortcoming in business will have negative impacts on members of society.

Besides the pressure on businesses to perform ethically, the increased emphasis on ethics in business is attributed to the realization that "good ethics is good business." Business organizations are interested in business ethics not because of their overwhelming desire to do the right thing but because they consider it a means to prevent the consequences of illegal behavior and to avoid further government regulation of business. Apart from that, business ethics might also be construed as an advertising tool or window-dressing exercise to appease various stakeholders. Some people use business ethics as an expedient for the pursuit of narrowly defined economic self-interest when in fact it should be considered a matter of principle. Business organizations' interest in business ethics has often arisen reactively rather than being a result of proactive policy; businesses can act defensively in the face of public criticisms and realize the importance of projecting a good public image.

It is worth noting that business ethics is sometimes considered an oxymoron due to the perception that the aims of business and ethics are "fundamentally incompatible" based on the assumption that ethics is concerned with abstract principles while business is the practice of making money. In an article published in the *New York Times Magazine*, economist Milton Friedman accepts that individuals might have certain social responsibilities (Friedman, 1970) but rejects the idea that businesses too have social responsibilities. Instead, their sole responsibility is to make as much money as possible while abiding by the basic rules of the society embodied in both law and ethical customs. However, this proposition is rejected on the basis that businesses owe society for the basis of their very existence and thus are morally obliged to produce goods and services efficiently for society. Moreover, although business organizations are not literally individuals, they qualify as individuals on the basis that their decision-making structure permits the use of moral reason, and therefore, like individuals, they have obligations to behave in an ethical manner.

4.3   Islamic business ethics

The Qur'an, which Muslims believe to be the word of God that dates back more than 14 centuries, speaks about ethics in business. The Qur'an approves of business as long as it does not divert one from worshipping God.

Moreover, God instructs man to disperse after performing prayers to seek His bounty and remember Him while doing so.

The Qur'an only confines itself to disapproving fraudulent practices in business and requires abstention from certain forms of trade, which are deemed to be unethical and ultimately destructive to man. Allah SWT mentioned this in two different verses of the Qur'an.

The Prophet Muḥammad was born in Makkah, a major trading center of the time, and spent a considerable period of his life as a businessman before his Prophethood. The importance of business pursuits in Islam is thus reflected in the fact that the Prophet Muḥammad was a trader and that he was married to Khadījah, a very successful businesswoman. As early as age 12, Muḥammad was exposed to business by his uncle Abū Ṭālib, since it was the main activity of the people of Quraysh. He brought Muḥammad with him on a business journey to Syria, where they met a monk who informed Abū Ṭālib that Muḥammad had the signs of being appointed Prophet. At the age of 25, Muḥammad went to Syria as a merchant for Khadījah, who was a businesswoman of great honor and fortune and who later became his wife. He proved to be an excellent businessman, reaping more profits than usual while adhering strongly to good manners, honesty, deep thought, sincerity, and faith. More than successful, Muḥammad was a responsible businessman who cofounded a group called the League of Ethical Businessmen, intended to encourage the merchants of Makkah to be honest in their dealings and to share a part of their wealth with the poor. Suffice to say that the Prophet was an ethical leader during that period. After his marriage to Khadījah, Muḥammad contributed to the management of his wife's large business

---

Q 24:37
"[Are] men whom neither commerce nor sale distracts from the remembrance of Allāh and performance of prayer and giving of zakāh."

Q 62:10
"And when the prayer has concluded, disperse within the land and seek from the bounty of Allāh, and remember Allāh often that you may succeed."

Q 4:29
"...do not consume one another's wealth unjustly but only [in lawful] business by mutual consent."

Q 9:34
"...Indeed many of the scholars and the monks devour the wealth of people unjustly and avert [them] from the way of Allāh. And those who hoard gold and silver and spend it not in the way of Allāh – give them tidings of a painful punishment."

I swore allegiance to the Messenger of Allah, promising to hear and obey, and behave sincerely towards every Muslim. He [Abū Zurʻah] said: Whenever he sold and bought anything, he would say, "What we took from you is dearer to us than what we gave you. So choose [as you like]."

Narrated by Jarir ibn ʻAbdillāh. *Sunan Abī Dāwūd, ḥadīth* no. 4945

"The business transaction is only by mutual satisfaction [of the parties involved]."

Narrated by Abū Saʻīd al-Khuḍrī. *Sunan Ibn Mājah, ḥadīth* no. 2185 interests. It is thus no surprise that many Prophetic Traditions related to business ethics can be found in the books of *Ḥadīth*.

In another *hadith*, Al-Tirmidhī records a powerful statement praising the honest businessman. This statement can be conceived as the highest possible praise for honest and trustworthy business practitioners, acknowledging their considerable contribution to society's prosperity. The Prophet Muḥammad not only was God's Messenger but also enacted laws and had first-hand knowledge of trade and was concerned with contract law and economic affairs. Furthermore, when the Prophet Muḥammad migrated to Madīnah, people would refer disputes involving trade and commerce to him. The rulings he gave were recorded and formed the basis of Islamic commercial law.

> "The honest and trustworthy businessman [on the Day of Resurrection] will be amongst the Prophets, those who are truthful and the martyrs."
>
> Narrated by Abū Saʿīd al-Khuḍrī. *Sunan al-Tirmidhī*, *ḥadīth* no. 1212

4.4   Islamic business ethics framework

Many elements within Islam resonate with prevailing notions of business ethics. However, these elements remain dispersed, incoherent, and unsystematized. This section is aimed at developing a higher-order framework to organize and systematize these elements with a view to constructing a more coherent notion of business ethics in Islam.

The Qur'anic verse 16:90 encapsulates the three guiding principles that would serve as the basis for a framework of Islamic business ethics. The verse begins with God commanding, thus addressing those who have believed in Him and His Unity, followed by the command to be just and to act benevolently. *Tawḥīd*, *ʿadālah*, and *iḥsān* are the guiding principles that resonate with al-Ghazālī's in his acclaimed *Ihyā ʿUlūm al-Dīn* (*Revival of Religious Sciences*) in which he attempts to establish that justice and benevolence must be served by the legal forms of business transactions.

> **Q 16:90**
> "Indeed, Allah orders justice (*al-ʿadl*) and good conduct (*al-iḥsān*)..."

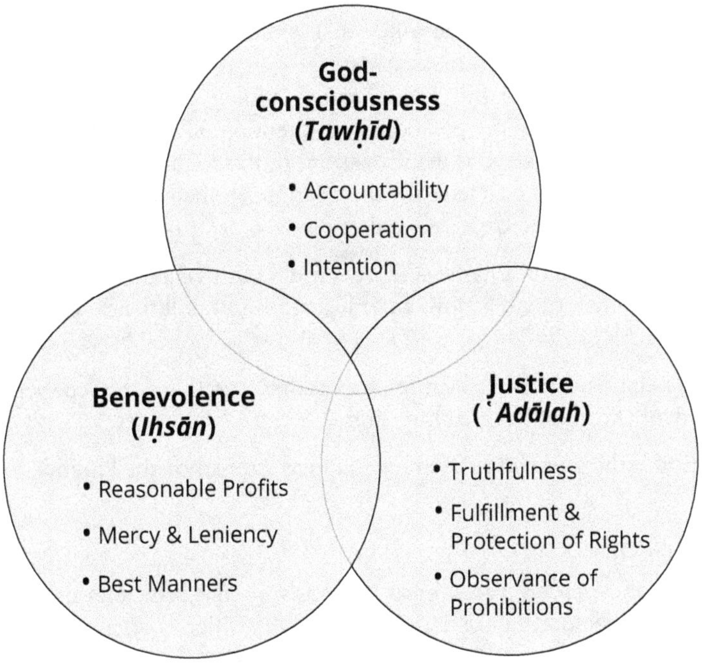

Figure 4.1   Conceptual framework of Islamic business ethics

This figure illustrates the interconnectedness of these principles and that these fundamental guiding principles are not mutually exclusive. There is in fact a degree of overlap between them and, consequently, a degree of commonality between the propositions of the fundamental principles and the resultant expectations. For example, the proposition of accountability under the principle of God-consciousness also embodies the principle of justice since it provides an impetus to be truthful. Being merciful and lenient, as proposed under the principle of benevolence, is related to God-consciousness in the sense that one hopes to be rewarded by God for an act of kindness. Justice and benevolence overlap when one seeks reasonable profits as opposed to profit maximization, which entails offering fair prices for products and services, thus minimizing exploitation. Those who observe the three fundamental guiding principles can be categorized as being in the ranks of the truthful (al-ṣiddīqīn) as in the *ḥadīth* of the Prophet, where he states: "The honest and trustworthy businessman (on the Day of Resurrection) will be amongst the Prophets, those who are truthful and the martyrs." Meanwhile, those who restrict themselves to justice join the ranks of the righteous (al-ṣāliḥīn), and those who add benevolence to justice join the ranks of those who are drawn close to God (al-muqarrabīn).

4.4.1   God-consciousness: *Tawḥīd*

Tawḥīd is the core of religious experience in Islam, and His presence fills the Muslim's consciousness at all places and times. Human beings are:

- God's *'abd* (servants), who strive to perfect their service and devotion to God; and

- God's *khalīfah* (vicegerents) on earth, who are answerable to God.

Tawḥīd, which characterizes a "person's relationship with God, His universe and His people," is considered to be a key to Islamic business philosophy and must broadly guide and inspire business activity.

How can we envisage this fundamental guiding principle in practice? The notions of accountability, cooperation, and intention, all of which are inherent in the *tawḥīdic* paradigm, serve as manifestations of this highly abstract principle. On a vertical plane, *tawḥīd* characterizes the relationship between human beings and God. Acknowledging the Unity of God implies:

- total submission to the Divine Will. As a result of this submission, human beings are accountable for their actions and must strive to fulfill their role as His vicegerents on earth;

- human beings are created equal to one another, and this means cooperation and equality of effort and opportunity; and

- intention is the foundation of every action as stressed by the Prophet.

4.4.2   Justice: *Adālah*

The Qur'an and *sunnah* placed great emphasis on the principles of uprightness, equity, and temperance. In classical Arabic, al-'adl, which is often translated as justice, means literally "a combination of moral and social values denoting fairness, balance, temperance, and straightforwardness." Al-'adl, the root from which the word 'adālah (justice) is derived, is the supreme attribute of God, and its denial implies a denial of God.

> **"Actions are but by intentions, and every person shall have that which he intended."**
>
> Narrated by 'Umar ibn al-Khaṭṭāb. Recorded in *Ṣaḥīḥ al-Bukhārī*, *ḥadīth* no. 17

> **Q57:25**
> "God sent Messengers with clear signs, the Scripture and the Balance, so that people could uphold justice."

The Qur'an contains over 200 admonitions against injustice and more than 100 expressions denoting the notion of justice, either directly or indirectly. The Prophet Muḥammad often warned his followers against oppression and exhorted them to be just in all their actions. Acts of injustice in the form of exploitation, oppression, and wrongdoing deprive others of their rights and also imply nonfulfillment of duties and obligations toward others.

The Qur'an's emphasis on justice in business transactions can be seen in God's command in 17:35. In addition to that, the first few verses of *sūrat al-Muṭaffifīn* (83:1–7) present another example in which God admonishes those who give short measure on one hand but demand full measure from others by warning them of the day they will be made accountable for their actions before Him. The importance given by the Qur'an toward full measure in the context of trade during the time of its revelation demonstrates the susceptibility of sellers to shortchanging their customers to increase profits. In our current context, where products and services might not be measured in weight, these Qur'anic injunctions demand fulfilling duties toward the counterparty in a transaction.

Many Prophetic traditions prohibit certain kinds of business transactions, which, when scrutinized, aim to uphold justice and protect the rights of parties engaged in business. These traditions are cited by Muslim jurists in discussions of the validity of contracts and business transactions, although it can be argued that in most instances references to ethics have been obscured by a focus on technicalities and the letter of the law. Therefore, it is not surprising that, although a contract or business transaction may be sound and fulfill the conditions stipulated by Muslim jurists, it may involve injustice. This can be attributed to the fact that not all prohibitions lead to the invalidation of contracts.

According to al-Ghazālī, a business transaction based upon injustice is that which causes harm to the public by means of unjust dealings, oppression, deceit, or fraud. He asserts that the Golden Rule: – that a person should love for others what he loves for himself – should typify the conduct between parties involved in a business transaction.

This fundamental guiding principle can be translated into practice by

- being truthful and trustworthy;

- fulfilling and protecting the rights of all stakeholders; and

- refraining from what has been prohibited in relation to business transactions and activities.

It is therefore expected that business entities should be transparent in their dealings and disclose material information, display a high level of integrity, fulfill their duties responsibly, and avoid any form of exploitation that would jeopardize justice.

4.4.3 Benevolence: *Iḥsān*

Al-Ghazālī argues that justice is a means to achieve success, while benevolence is a way of attaining success and felicity, and that God has commanded man to act in both a just and benevolent manner. Acting in a just manner is related to one's obligations and responsibilities, while benevolence means acting in a manner that benefits others even if one is not obliged to do so. Adam Smith makes a similar argument, suggesting that it is from human nature that people act benevolently. The absence of justice results in harm, but the absence of benevolence does not have the same effect, and the latter begins where the former ends.

"Injustice (ẓulm) is darkness on the Day of Resurrection."

Narrated by Jābir ibn 'Abdillāh. *Ṣaḥīḥ Muslim*, *ḥadīth* no. 2578.

Q 17:35
"Give full measure when you measure, and weigh with accurate scales: that is better and fairer in the end."

In a similar vein, *iḥsān* induces people to care about others and to treat them with consideration, which in turn encourages strong ties of love, brotherhood, solidarity, unshakable confidence, peace, and cooperation in all that is righteous. According to the Qur'an, justice is an essential legal requirement. But at the same time man is persuaded to behave benevolently in claiming his rights and discharging his duties. God also commands man to act in a benevolent manner toward parents, kinfolk, orphans, the poor and needy, neighbors near and far, travelers in need, and slaves.

Iḥsān is one of the foundations of Islamic ethics and implies goodness and generosity in interaction and conduct, which is then projected practically and spiritually by being merciful, just, forgiving, tolerant, and attentive. In business transactions, refraining from injustice is a lower grade of duty appropriate primarily to the lower class of virtuous people, while a higher duty is to conduct oneself in a way that others benefit. Besides benevolence, *iḥsān* also implies the quest for excellence and perfection. *Iḥsān* here means perfection or doing things in the best possible manner. Thus, besides being merciful and lenient, *iḥsān* requires that economic interactions be characterized by the best possible manners.

This fundamental guiding principle can be applied by

- pursuing reasonable profits;
- exhibiting mercy and leniency in dealings; and
- interacting with stakeholders with the best of manners.

Businesses are therefore expected to maximize the wellbeing of their stakeholders as opposed to maximizing profits, to be cognizant of those in need due to various circumstances, and to provide high-quality services in dealing with their clients, which would increase customer satisfaction and loyalty.

4.5   Responsibility to stakeholders

There are six primary stakeholders of business firms: customers, employees, stockholders, creditors, the environment, and communities. A business organization with ingrained ethical considerations should fulfill responsibilities toward its stakeholders to the fullest and not pursue profit maximization.

4.5.1   Responsibility to customers

Customers provide the reasons for the existence and success of a business. Customers have some expectations toward a business and its products, and these expectations must be managed accordingly. This responsibility is not limited to providing goods and services but should also incorporate the element of social responsibility. In this regard, the business entity should adhere to responsible production and marketing practices. Business firms should ensure their goods are produced in a responsible manner. For example, those involved in the food business should always maintain high hygiene standards and use the best and freshest produce, although the cost of doing so might be higher. Similarly, businesses should not oversell their products and services in the course of marketing, which might lead to deceiving existing and potential customers.

4.5.2   Responsibility to employees

Employees form the backbone of a business organization and contribute to the progress and success of the firm. Ethical business organizations are expected to treat their employees fairly and compensate them adequately, and in return employees must perform their duties responsibly and in the best way possible.

4.5.3   Responsibility to stockholders

The creation of a stock market represented a new era where firms are usually run by professional managers and owned by multiple individuals. The owners, who typically own equity in firms, have little information in the running of the business. It is then imperative for the managers to manage the firms accordingly, as well as provide sufficient information to the owners so they can make informed decisions. The concept is similar to the practice of *muḍārbah*. This practice even predates the Prophet Muḥammad, where the capital owner engages with a responsible merchant to do business for them, and the profit shall be shared accordingly.

4.5.4   Responsibility to creditors

The longest verse in the Qur'an concerns financial transactions. In 2:282, Allah SWT lays down certain rules and regulations that Muslims should adhere to when involving themselves in financial transactions, particularly when it comes to borrowing and lending. Allah specifically ordered for any transaction to be written down, with two witnesses overseeing the process. This is to ensure justice and protection for both borrowers and creditors.

4.5.5   Responsibility to the environment

Businesses should manage the production process to minimize harm to the environment. Companies should always find ways and innovate to mitigate the negative effects of pollution. Similarly, firms should avoid producing goods that are harmful to the environment. These elements of negative externalities should be compensated by the firm through the allocation of a certain portion of profit gained.

4.5.6   Responsibility to community

Businesses and the communities in which they operate cannot be separated. Businesses provide communities with goods and services. On the other hand, communities consume such goods and purchase services, in addition to providing labor. Besides providing quality goods and services for communities, businesses should also engage in community development projects, by providing funding and becoming directly involved. In a larger context, businesses should also try to optimize profits and not evade taxes, as businesses should also pay *zakāt* from their profits.

4.6   Law and ethics

Many prophetic traditions prohibit certain kinds of business transactions that, when scrutinized, aim to uphold justice and protect the rights of parties engaged in business. These traditions are cited by Muslim jurists in their discussions of the validity of contracts and business transactions, although it can be argued that in most instances reference to ethics is obscured by a focus on technicalities and the letter of

"Pay to the worker his wages before his sweat becomes dry."

Narrated by 'Abdullāh ibn 'Umar. *Sunan Ibn Mājah*, ḥadīth no. 2443

"The honest Muslim trustee who spends – sometimes he said who gives – what he is commanded to do and he gives that in full with his heart overflowing with cheerfulness and he gives it to one to whom he is ordered, he is one of the givers of charity."

Narrated by Abū Mūsā. *Ṣaḥīḥ al-Bukhārī*, ḥadīth no. 1438

Q 2:282
"O you who have believed, when you contract a debt for a specified term, write it down. And let a scribe write [it] between you in justice..."

Q 30:41
"Corruption has appeared throughout the land and sea by [reason of] what the hands of people have earned so He may let them taste part of [the consequence of] what they have done that perhaps they will return [to righteousness]."

the law. Therefore, it is not surprising that, although a contract or business transaction may be sound and fulfill the conditions stipulated by Muslim jurists, it may not be ethical. This can be attributed to the fact that not all prohibitions lead to the invalidation of contracts. Similarly, not all *Shariah*-compliant contracts are ethical.

For example, a couple of recent incidents have created a bad impression on the ethicality of Islamic finance, in which people might perceive it as similar to conventional finance because it is also susceptible to fraud. The case of DanaGas's *Ṣukūk* in UAE and 1MDB *Ṣukūk* in Malaysia proves this. DanaGas initially issued a *Shariah*-compliant *ṣukūk* and then claimed that it was not *Shariah*-compliant upon potential default and tried to pay creditors a lower amount. Similarly with 1MDB in Malaysia, where the company issued *ṣukūk*, yet the proceeds were allegedly fraudulently siphoned off. These cases highlight the possibility that *Shariah*-compliant instruments are being issued just to raise funds, whereas Islamic finance principles clearly stipulate that capital must be channeled toward *Shariah*-compliant activities. Islamic finance and any form of business underpinned by Islamic precepts should differentiate itself by imbuing its enterprise with ethics in accordance with the spirit and soul of Islam.

4.7   Conclusion

Both mainstream and Islamic business ethics provide guidelines to ethical business practices. There are similarities and differences in the way they do so. The discourse on mainstream business ethics appears to focus on the rules of conduct by which business decisions are made. These rules are determined by legislation, specific rules depending on the nature of business, specific organizational codes of conduct, and the personal morals of the individuals who are members of the business organization. Meanwhile, the discourse on Islamic business ethics seems to focus on *Shariah* principles as the basis from which legal and ethical instructions in relation to business are derived. In mainstream business ethics, that which is legally acceptable is not necessarily ethically acceptable. Likewise, in Islamic business ethics, that which is legally permissible or *ḥalāl* is not necessarily ethical.

The underlying difference between mainstream and Islamic business ethics is the reference to God in the latter. While references to God are almost absent from mainstream business ethics, notions related to *tawḥīd*, such as accountability to God, revelation as a source of ethical guidance, and emphasis on life in the hereafter, often appear in the discourse on Islamic business ethics. Moreover, Muslims believe that Islam is not merely a religion but a way of life, in which *Shariah* principles govern every aspect of one's conduct. The implication is that Muslims are supposed to be motivated to behave ethically as they are constantly being observed by God and will reap the reward for their ethical behavior in the hereafter.

The principle of God-consciousness implies the realization that human beings were created by God and that everything on earth and in the heavens belongs to God. Human beings are His *khalīfah* (vicegerents) on earth and are entrusted with managing the resources made available to them. Thus, human beings are accountable to God in the way they fulfill this trust and are responsible for their actions. This demands that human beings

- act in a socially responsible manner;

- take into consideration the impact of their actions on humanity as a whole; and

- be brothers in humanity and assist one another in goodness.

In Islam, the notion of justice is strongly emphasized and is manifested in many injunctions that involve human interactions. The Golden Rule is to treat fellow human beings in a way that one desires to be treated. Accordingly, it is expected that:

- all parties in financial transactions will be transparent and fully disclose pertinent information;

- businesses will fulfill their legal and ethical duties or obligations to their various stakeholders; and

- businesses will protect the rights of their stakeholders.

The legal and ethical prohibitions in relation to business transactions serve the purpose of curbing exploitation, which is the antithesis of justice. Any form of exploitation is unequivocally unacceptable as it inflicts harm upon the society in which businesses operate.

Benevolence is acting in a manner that benefits others, even if there is no legal compulsion to do so. Being benevolent is associated with being kind and charitable. Benevolence involves:

- seeking reasonable profits instead of profit maximization, where consideration is given to provide products and services at fair and reasonable prices;

- exhibiting mercy and leniency by being mindful of the constraints and circumstances of clients and employees; and

- providing a high level of quality of service to clients and other members of society who interact with a particular business.

In comparison to mainstream business ethics, Islamic business ethics has yet to undergo a development process that would transform it into a movement or distinct and independent discipline of its own. There seems to be no urgent need for Islamic business ethics to evolve in the way mainstream business ethics have evolved, because arguably personal ethics embraced by Muslims can be extended to all spheres of life and no special knowledge or skills are required to behave ethically when conducting business transactions. Furthermore, the *Shariah* rules governing these transactions are claimed to be ethically infused, and as such following those rules would ensure ethical behavior.

Chapter Highlights

There appears to be little difference between mainstream and Islamic business ethics. Both are aimed at providing guidelines for ethical business practices, though the ways in which they do so might differ. Mainstream business ethics relies on rules determined by legislation, nature-specific guidelines of a business, codes of conduct of individual business organizations, and personal morals of members of the organization in guiding businesses to make ethical decisions. Islamic business ethics, on the other hand, is mainly governed by *Shariah* principles that inform individuals and business organizations of their legal and ethical obligations. However, what is legal or permissible need not necessarily be ethical. What distinguishes Islamic business ethics from its mainstream counterpart is the *tawḥīdīc* paradigm. Accountability to God, revelation as a source of ethical guidance, and reference to life in the hereafter distinguish Islamic ethics in general from ethical theories and philosophical analysis underlying mainstream business ethics. Islamic business ethics has not undergone the developmental stages of mainstream business ethics and thus has yet to emerge as a distinctive academic field; it is part of the larger framework of Islamic ethics, economics, and finance all together. This is understandable as Muslims claim that ethical values are expected to permeate all aspects of life.

Tawḥīd is built upon the belief that human beings are created by God and that everything belongs to Him. Human beings are God's vicegerents on earth entrusted with managing its resources and thus accountable to Him in executing this trust responsibly. Before God, all human beings are equal and there are no preferences on the basis of natural traits such as gender or race. The implications of such a concept for business are that businesses must provide products and services that not only conform to *Shariah* principles but also have a positive impact on society, be aware that people are equal partners and that they should participate in the business and cooperate with one another in utilizing the resources made available to them, and give primacy to the centrality of intention in serving the needs of the community. The emphasis on truthfulness, transparency, and integrity and the reasons behind *Shariah* prohibitions are to ensure justice and fairness in business transactions. Businesses are expected to be truthful and trustworthy by practicing full disclosure of material information and not engaging in deceptive marketing. Companies and corporations must faithfully honor their contractual obligations with all stakeholders, and as such, the competency of their staff is of paramount importance. Companies are also expected to treat their employees fairly and compensate them adequately, and in return employees must perform their duties responsibly and in the best way possible. *Iḥsān*, on the other hand, encourages caring for others and treating them with consideration. *Iḥsān* also implies the pursuit of excellence and perfection. In relation to business entities, the expectations derived from *iḥsān* are that businesses should not reap outsize profits, be lenient and merciful in dealing with others, and provide the best possible services to clients.

Key Terms

ʿAbd	*Homo economicus*	Mercy
Accountability	*Homo Islamicus*	Profit maximization
ʿAdālah	*Iḥsān*	Prohibition
Cooperation	Intention	Qur'an
Deceit	*Khalīfah*	Reasonable profits
Exploitation	Law	Rights
Farḍ	Leniency	*Shariah*
Fiqh	Manners	*Tawḥīd*
Ḥadīth	*Maqāṣid al-Shariah*	Transparency
Ḥalāl	Marketing	Trustworthiness
Ḥarām	*Maṣlahah*	Truthfulness

Discussion Questions

1. What is Islam's attitude toward business?

2. What are the similarities and differences between mainstream and Islamic business ethics?

3. Are law and *Shariah* rules sufficient to regulate business?

4. How and why are ethics important and significant to business?

5. Why should businesses be expected to have social responsibilities?

6. Should God be considered as a stakeholder? If yes, how can this be manifested in practice?

7. Where and how do religion in general and Islam in particular guide business decisions?

8. Is being ethical good for businesses? Why and how?

9. What should be done if there is a conflict of interest between shareholders and society? Which should prevail?

10. Do authorities have to intervene to ensure that businesses not only abide by the law but also act in the best interest of society at large?

Selected Bibliography

Ahmad, M. (1995). *Business Ethics in Islam* [in English]. Islamabad: The International Institute of Islamic Thought.

Al-Ghazālī, A.H.M.I.M. (2013). *The Book of Proprieties of Earning and Living – Kitāb Ādāb Al-Kasb Wa Al-Ma'āsh*. Translated by A. Setia. Kuala Lumpur: IBFIM.

Ali, A.J. (2014). *Business Ethics in Islam*. Cheltenham: Edward Elgar Publishing.

Beekun, R.I. (1997). *Islamic Business Ethics* [in English]. Herndon: The International Institute of Islamic Thought.

Friedman, M. (1970). The Social Responsibility of Business is to Increase Its Profits. *New York Times*, September 13.

Hasanuzzaman, S.M. (2003). *Islam and Business Ethics*. London: Institute of Islamic Banking and Insurance.

Musa, M.A. (2007). Business Ethics in the Light of the Sunnah. MA Thesis, International Islamic University Malaysia.

Naqvi, S.N.H. (1981). *Ethics and Economics – An Islamic Synthesis*. Leicester: The Islamic Foundation.

Nik, Y. and Nik, M.A. (2002). *Islam & Business* [in English]. Edited by I. Noor. Selangor: Pelanduk Publications.

Rice, G. (1999). Islamic Ethics and the Implications for Business. *Journal of Business Ethics*, 18, 345–358.

Tripp, C. (2006). *Islam and the Moral Economy: The Challenge of Capitalism*. Cambridge: Cambridge University Press.

Wilson, R. (2001). "Business Ethics: Western and Islamic Perspectives." Chap. Part III – Ethics in Business. In K. Ahmad and A.M. Sadeq (Eds.) *Ethics in Business and Management: Islamic and Mainstream Approaches*. London: Asean Academic Press, pp. 135–168.

MANAGEMENT AND MARKETING

ISLAMIC COMMERCIAL JURISPRUDENCE

5

Abu Umar Faruq Ahmad

King Abdulaziz University, Saudi Arabia

Learning Outcomes

LO1: Define *Shariah, fiqh, fiqh al-mu'āmalāt,* and *maqāṣid al-Shariah* as the basis for commerce, finance, and economy.

LO2: Describe the sources of *Shariah* and *fiqh.*

LO3: Explain the *maqāṣid al-Shariah* to protect and promote the stakeholders' well-being of the contracting parties in Islamic business transactions.

LO4: Understand the underlying philosophy of business transactions in Islam.

LO5: Explain the meaning, types, key features, the main categories, and the key factors that make a contract invalid.

Contents

5.1   Introduction

This chapter briefly discusses *Shariah* and *fiqh* as the theoretical foundation for Islamic commercial jurisprudence, which includes commerce, finance, and the economy. It begins with the meaning and definition of *Shariah* and *fiqh*, followed by a discussion on the sources of *Shariah*, with *maqāṣid al-Shariah* being one of the cornerstones of contemporary Islamic commercial jurisprudence. It then elaborates on the underlying philosophy of business transactions in Islam. The chapter further elucidates the meaning and features of valid or invalid contracts, as well as the key categories of contracts, which include commutative, partnership, charitable, fee- and service-based, and supporting contracts. The chapter concludes with a discussion on the key prohibited contracts in business transactions that could render relevant transactions of the parties concerned null and void, followed by a short elaboration on the key reasons behind the invalidation of a contract and the way to rectify such a contract. The chapter concludes with a review of some discussion questions and answers to encourage learners to reflect on the topics and issues discussed.

5.2 *Shariah*: Theoretical foundations of commerce, finance, and economy

One cannot discuss commerce, finance, and the economy and the related disciplines from Islamic perspectives without first discussing *Shariah*. This is because *Shariah*, which has been translated *inter alia* as Islamic law, covers all aspects of human behavior, directs the life style of Muslims, and undeniably regulates commercial transactions. The *Shariah* has long been truly unpracticed and replaced by Western law. Nevertheless, as a result of Islamic reinforcement, the opportunity to adjust *Shariah* to the modern world has been considered in recent times. Although Islamic legal rulings are permanent in nature, the principles inherent in *Shariah* are adjustable and their application is adaptable to new circumstances, such as with respect to Islamic commercial jurisprudence, as they stand in modern usage.

The emergence of traditional Islamic commercial jurisprudence dates back to the revelation of the Glorious Qur'an to the final Messenger, the Prophet Muhammad (pbuh). Since then, the fundamental concepts of Islamic finance have been broadly applied, and these were continued until the fall of the Islamic Empire. However, with the increase of European influence during the colonial era, this system has been ignored and Muslim-majority countries have adopted an interest-based conventional financial system. This trend did not continue after the 1960s since, with the emergence of the Islamic Renaissance, Muslim countries have started to re-examine their economic systems and reintroduced the Islamic financial system that adheres to the requirements of the principles of *Shariah*. The revolutionary step of offering modern Islamic financial services started in the 1970s with the introduction of commercial Islamic banks and financial institutions in the Gulf and Middle Eastern countries.

The following subsections aim to briefly discuss the literal and technical meanings and definitions of key terms such as *Shariah*, *fiqh*, *fiqh al-muʿāmalāt*, and *maqāṣid al-Shariah* to integrate the relevant disciplines.

5.2.1   *Shariah*: Meaning and definition

The word *Shariah* (also spelled *Shariah*, Sharī'at, Shari'a, *Shariah*, *Syariah*, or *Shar'*) is derived from the three-letter root *sh-r-ʿa*, the verb of which is *sharaʿa*, meaning "to begin, start, introduce, prescribe or undertake (something)." It can also mean "to access, initiate an entry to a body or entity." Another meaning of the verb is "to make (something) apparent or manifest." The meaning of its verbal noun is "clear, well-trodden path to water, or a break in a riverbank allowing access to water that leads to a main stream, the road to a watering place, the clear path to be followed, the path which the faithful should step in." From this etymological meaning, *Shariah* has literally been used to refer to "a path or a passage that leads to an intended place, or to a certain goal" and is conceptually referred to as "a set of rules, regulations, teachings, and values that govern the lives of Muslims, manifested in the religion of Islam, the totality of Allah's commandments." Regarding this *Shariah* the Qur'an states, "For each We have appointed a divine law and a traced-out way" (Al-Qur'an, 5:48).

According to Muhammad Asad, the famous commentator of the Qur'an, "It is to be borne in mind that the literal meaning of the term *Shariah* is "the way to a watering-place," and since water is indispensable for all organic life, this term has in time come to denote a "system of laws," both moral and practical, which shows man the way to spiritual fulfillment and social welfare: hence, "religious law" in the widest sense of the term. Keeping in mind its literal meaning, *Shariah* has been defined by Muslim jurists as commands given by Allah to His servants, as brought by the prophets, whether they relate to the manner of action (known as subsidiary and applied law, to which the field of *fiqh* was developed) or manner of belief (known as the essentials and creeds for which the field of theology was developed).

5.2.2 Sources of *Shariah*

Various sources of *Shariah* are used by Islamic jurisprudence to elaborate the laws of Islamic financial and commercial transactions. These can be categorized as primary and secondary. The Qur'an and the *sunnah* are the primary sources unanimously agreed upon by Muslim jurists. The Qur'an is the first and foremost source of *Shariah* from which all other sources have been derived. It is the direct and unaltered words of Allah revealed to the Prophet Muhammad (pbhu), through the angel Jibril in Makkah and Madinah. It stipulates the moral, philosophical, social, political, and economic bases on which a society should be built. The Makkan verses of the Qur'an generally deal with theological and philosophical matters, while the Madinan verses consist of socioeconomic laws.

The second one is the *sunnah*, which consists of actions, utterances, and tacit approvals attributed to the Prophet Muhammad (pbhu), as related in his traditions (*ahādith*), handed down through a trustworthy chain of transmitters or narrators. The term *sunnah* is used sometimes in a wider sense to include the deeds and practices of his fellow Muslims or companions and successors. Justification for following the *sunnah* as a source of law has been repeatedly referred to in the Qur'an.

However, given the fact that the answers to all questions pertaining to Islamic legal matters that arose in Muslim communities were not addressed directly in the two primary sources of *Shariah*, Muslim jurists developed additional methods for deriving legal rulings. In the authoritative classification developed in the early ninth century by Imam al-Shafi'i there are two secondary sources of *Shariah*, the *ijmā'* and *qiyās*.

The *ijmā'* is the consensus of unanimous agreement of Muslim jurists on a particular legal issue at any given time. Muslim jurists cite many passages from the Qur'an that validate *ijmā'* as a source of *Shariah* and consider it as important as the Qur'an and *sunnah* as a source on matters related to legislation. The majority of Muslim jurists consider *qiyās* or analogical reason as the fourth source of *Shariah*. In support of *qiyās* as a source of Islamic law, they refer to some passages in the Qur'an that describe an application of a similar process by past Islamic communities. They also cite the Prophet's companions' practice of *qiyās* on some issues. They also argue that since the objective of all legal rulings is to safeguard human wellbeing, the *qiyās* can be similarly applied to cases that share similar causes.

5.2.3   *Fiqh* and *Fiqh al-Muʿāmalāt*

The terminology of *fiqh al-muʿāmalāt* is a combination of two words: *fiqh* and *muʿāmalāt*. We will first consider the meaning and definition of the word *fiqh,* and then explain the term *muʿāmalāt* with its meaning and technical definition.

5.2.3.1   *Fiqh: Meaning and definition*

The Arabic word *fiqh* is an infinitive noun that denotes sound knowledge, profound understanding, full comprehension, and aptitude. The word sometimes is merely used in its literal and essential meanings versus in a technical sense. Thus, the term *fiqh al-muʿāmalāt* is used to mean "understanding, investigation or establishing the meaning" of civil transactions or human interactions. In a broader sense, *fiqh al-muʿāmalāt* deals with issues related to all kinds of financial transactions in general and with endowments, laws of inheritance, marriage, divorce, child care, foods and drinks, penal punishments, warfare and peace, and judicial matters (including witnesses and forms of evidence), in particular.

As far as the proofs for using the word *fiqh* in the key sources of *Shariah,* namely the Qur'an and the *sunnah,* the term *fiqh* occurs in six different variations 20 times in many verses in the Qur'an in the sense of understanding. For example, at 9: 122 the word appears thus: "Why should not then a company from every party from among them go forth that they may apply themselves to obtain understanding in religion, and that they may warn their people when they come back to them that they may be cautious"[1] The word has also appeared in a *hadith* in which the Prophet (pbuh) is reported to have said: "Whom Allah wants to favor, He grants him comprehension of this religion" (Sahih Bukhari vol. 1 Hadith No. 71, Tirmidhi and Musnad Ahmad).

Technically, the term *fiqh* is confined to practical *legal* rules and rituals (devotional matters), so it has been defined by Amidi, al-Zarkashi, al-Baydawi, and Shawkani as "the knowledge of the rules of the Shariah that are derived from their elaborated evidences." (Kamali, 2003) This definition is similar to what was given earlier by the jurist Imam Shafiʿi as "the knowledge of the rules of the Shariah relating to the individual action or conduct derived from their elaborated evidences." Given the foregoing definition of *fiqh,* the rules that are known through any source other than *Shariah* are excluded from the realm of *fiqh.* Similarly, the rules of *Shariah* that relate to beliefs and the principles of *fiqh* are not included in *fiqh.* The term "derived" in this definition also implies that the subject matter of the science of *fiqh* includes the *Shariah* rules that are known by way of consideration, reflection, study, and search and as such the knowledge of Allah, the prophet, and angels is excluded from the domain of *fiqh* since it is received through revelation. Likewise, the expression of the words "elaborated evidences" excludes the knowledge of a follower of a particular school of jurisprudence about the precepts of the *Shariah* since it is not acquired through evidence.

5.2.3.2   *Muʿāmalāt: Meaning and definition*

Muʿāmalāt is the plural form of the term *muʿāmalah,* which literally means mutual transaction or dealing, social intercourse, behavior, transaction, and interaction. Broadly from Islamic jurisprudential perspectives, the sciences of *muʿāmalāt* are the branches of Islamic jurisprudence that deal with commercial and business activities in an economy. In other words, constitutes knowledge of the rules of conduct pertaining to commercial transactions that have been derived by Muslim jurists from specific passages in the Qur'an and *sunnah*. Thus, *muʿāmalāt māliyyah* are commercial transactions that are concluded through contracts permitted by *Shariah* as evidenced by the Qur'an, the *sunnah*, and other sources of *Shariah*.

There is no unified definition of *fiqh al-muʿāmalāt* on which the jurists have agreed upon. The most basic meaning of *fiqh al-muʿāmalāt* refers to the Islamic legal rulings related to the interpersonal relationship between a man and his fellow human beings. Thus, it covers matters pertaining to marriage, divorce, criminal procedures, dispute resolution, business and financial transactions, rights and responsibilities of rulers and their subjects, global transactions, and so on.

As per the definition given by al-Zuhayli, the term *fiqh al-muʿāmalāt* has been defined as "the knowledge of *Shariah* rulings that relates to the practical aspects of a *mukallaf* in the area of business and financial dealings and derived from its detailed evidences." From this definition it is observed that *Shariah* has a wider meaning than *fiqh*, and *fiqh* has a wider meaning than *muʿāmalāt*.

5.2.4 *Maqāṣid al-Shariah* and Islamic finance

The notion of *maqāṣid al-Shariah*, or objectives of *Shariah*, has gained momentum and attracted much attention from contemporary Muslim scholars due to its use and reference in resolving modern-day issues, particularly emerging issues confronting *muʿāmalāt* or human interactions.

The *maqāṣid al-Shariah* is a combination of two words: *maqāṣid* and *Shariah*. *Maqāṣid* is the plural form of the word *maqsad*, which literally means "will or determination of carrying out something to serve a purpose." Technically, the term *maqāṣid al-Shariah* refers to "a juristic-philosophical concept developed by the later generations of the classical jurists, who attempted to formulate the goals and purposes of the *Shariah* in a comprehensive manner to aid in the process of investigating new cases and organizing previous existing rulings." The aim of *Shariah* lies in the principle of eliminating agony, hardship, and difficulty from people and finding solutions to their problems. Emphasizing this principle, the Qur'an declares that Allah does not want to impose any hardship on His servants, although the context of the relevant text illustrates the rituals of ablution for prayer. The application of the contents of the text is eternal. The verse reads: "Allah does not want to impose any hardship on you, but wants to make you pure, and to bestow upon you the full measure of His blessings, so that you might have cause to be grateful" (5: 6).

The objectives of *Shariah* have either been directly referred to in the Qur'an and the prophetic traditions (*sunnah*) or have been stated by some of their predecessors among Muslim jurists. These objectives were recognized by almost all jurists as serving the common interests of all of humanity and protecting them from harm. For instance, the twelfth-century Muslim philosopher Al-Ghazali (d. 1058AH/1111CE) classified the *maqāṣid* into five key categories. He writes: "The very objective of the *Shariah* is to promote the wellbeing of the people, which lies in safeguarding (*hifz*) their faith (*din*), their self (*nafs*), their intellect (*ʿaql*), their posterity (*al-nasl*), and their wealth (*al-mal*). Whatever ensures the safeguarding of these five serves the public interest and is desirable."

Al-Shatibi (d. 790H/1388CE) endorses Al-Ghazali's five key categories of *maqāṣid al-Shariah* and points out that they are the most preferable in terms of their harmony with the fundamental nature of *Shariah*. However, mostly late and contemporary scholars have extended the scope of the *maqasid* to embrace other vital objectives of *Shariah*. The Maliki jurist Al-Qarafi (d. 684AH/1285CE) added the protection of *al-'ird* or integrity as the sixth objective of *Shariah*. Later, in the fourteenth-century, Ibn Taymiyyah (d. 728AH/1327CE) was perhaps the first scholar to depart from the perception of restricting the *maqāṣid* to a definite number. He provides a broader definition of *maqāṣid al-Shariah* by adding the preservation of the social order, promotion of the wellbeing and righteousness of the community, preservation of the family, and so forth to the previous list of his predecessors. He asserts: "Both its general rules and specific proofs indicate that the all-purpose principle of Islamic legislation is to preserve the social order of the community and insure its healthy progress by promoting the wellbeing and righteousness of that which prevails in it, namely, the human species. The wellbeing and virtue of human beings consist of the soundness of their intellect, the righteousness of their deeds as well as the goodness of the things of the world where they live that are put at their disposal."

The Muslim scholar Ibn al-Qayyim (d. 751AH/1350CE) considers the *maqāṣid* in a slightly different way. He observes: "Shariah is based on wisdom and achieving people's welfare in this life and the afterlife. Shariah is all about justice, mercy, wisdom, and the good. Thus, any ruling that replaces justice with injustice, mercy with its opposite, common good with mischief, or wisdom with nonsense is a ruling that does not belong to the Shariah, even if it is claimed to be so according to some interpretations." However, the contemporary scholar Shaikh Yusuf Al-Qaradawi further included in the list of the *maqāṣid* human dignity, liberty, social welfare, and human alliance, calling them the higher *maqāṣid* of the *Shariah*.

From the foregoing discussions it is evident that the objective of *Shariah* in general is to protect society and ensure the stability of its healthy growth and development. From these perspectives, *Shariah* encourages individuals and societies to be in complete harmony and well protected, with a sense of unity and trust where each member of the community renders help to others, honors what is good, and refrains from doing mischief.

Despite the history of *maqāṣid al-Shariah* one finds that as a discipline it was not in the realm of scholars' contributions until the early fourth century. According to Hashim Kamali (1998), "The recurrent references to it appeared in the works of Imam al-Haramayn al-Juwayni (d.478/1085), who was probably the first to classify the *maqāṣid al-Shariah* into the three categories of essential (*darûriyāt*), complementary (*hajiyāt*), and desirable (*tahsiniyāt*), which has gained general acceptance ever since." Therefore, there is a debate on the scope of *maqāṣid* in terms of what they may include. Some juristic schools, such as Zahiriyyah, view the *maqāṣid* as known only when they are identified and declared by clear text. According to other jurists, the majority of *Shariah* scholars did not confine the *maqāṣid* to clear text alone, as they believe that *Shariah* itself is rational and goal-oriented and its rules generally founded on identifiable causes. Beyond the debate of whether *maqāṣid* should be considered in connection with Islamic banking and finance practices, it can be concluded that if an Islamic bank or financial service provider does not comply with Islamic commercial jurisprudence but is in full compliance with *Shariah* rulings, which automatically include all *maqāṣid al-Shariah* in spirit and substance, though not in form, it is contributing to the shared responsibility of achieving the objectives of *Shariah*.

5.3 Underlying philosophy of business transactions in Islam

The Islamic financial system is an integral part of *Shariah* that can only be understood in the context of Islamic attitudes toward ethics, wealth distribution, social and economic justice, and the role of society or the state. Principles encouraging risk sharing, individual rights and duties, property rights, and the sanctity of contracts are all part of the Islamic code underlying the financial system. Muslims believe that human beings are Allah's representatives on earth who act as His trustees. The absolute ownership of man's property is not recognized in Islam. Therefore, transactions in an Islamic legal financial system should be carried out at both individual and corporate levels in accordance with *Shariah*. Individual interest is not the sine qua non in this system; rather, the interest of the public is based on bottom-line considerations (Vogel and Hayes, 1998).

Given the described attitude of Islam toward humanity, the core principles underlying an Islamic financial system revolve around the concept of equity and fairness. A business transaction in Islam is characterized by not simply obtaining benefits or maximizing profits but also seeking to promote social justice and a moral economy. The philosophy of transactions in Islamic law stems from a set of rules and laws referred to as the *Shariah*, which governs economic, social, political, and cultural aspects of Islamic societies. These rules and regulations dictate the rights and obligations of those involved in financial markets. They also may form the basis of regulation and legislation pertaining to financial markets (Ahmad and Hassan, 2007).

The philosophy and features of Islamic business transactions revolve around the nontransgression of any of the tenets of *Shariah*, such as avoiding transactions that involve *riba, gharar, maysir,* and *qimār*, as well as upholding the sanctity of contracts and preventing harm to contracting parties (Ahmad, 2010). These are discussed in the following subsection in more detail.

5.3.1 *Riba*-based transactions

Muslim jurists have defined *riba* as "all forms of gain or profit which were unearned in the sense that they resulted from speculative or risky transactions and could not be precisely calculated in advance by the contracting parties." In the legal terminology of the *Shariah*, *riba* has been defined as "an increment, which, in an exchange or sale of a commodity, accumulates to the owner or lender without giving in return an equivalent countervalue or recompense (*'iwad*) to the other party."[2]

Because *riba* is prohibited in Islam, all types of financial contracts and transactions must be free of it. Jurists base this prohibition on arguments of social justice, equality, and property rights. Social justice demands that borrowers and lenders share both rewards and losses in an equitable fashion and that the process of wealth accumulation and distribution in the economy be fair and representative of true productivity. The question of *riba* has been addressed in the literature on Islamic finance with much elaboration, and there is a near consensus about the meaning and implications of *riba*.[3]

5.3.2 Transactions based on *Gharar*

Literally, *gharar* means risk, uncertainty, and hazard. Technically, it is an element of deception either through ignorance and faulty description of the commodity or in its price, in which one or both parties stand to be deceived through ignorance of an essential element of exchange. Although the term *gharar* may equate to uncertainty and risk, these are things that occur in the normal course of doing business. But in *Shariah*, the prohibition of *gharar* is related to its insistence on fair and ethical dealings and based on its lack of tolerance for unjustified enrichment.

All forms of contracts and transactions must be free from *gharar* or excessive uncertainty.[4] This implies that contracting under conditions of excessive uncertainty is not permissible. Contracting under *gharar* is similar to gambling.[5] The prophetic *hadith*, in addition to prohibiting gambling or games of chance, also prohibits trading in *gharar*. Islamic scholars have identified the conditions and highlighted situations that involve excessive uncertainty and, consequently, invalidate a contract. Also, transactions should be devoid of any ignorance from both parties. Therefore, contracting parties should have perfect knowledge of the countervalues intended to be exchanged as a result of their transactions.

The Hanafi school of Islamic Jurisprudence defines *gharar* as "that whose consequences are hidden." However, the Shafi'i legal school defines *gharar* as "that which admits two possibilities, with the less desirable one being more likely." The Hanbali school defines it as "that whose consequences are unknown" or "that which is undeliverable, whether it exists or not." On the other hand, the Zahiri school says that "*gharar* is where the buyer does not know what he bought, or the seller does not know what he sold." The contemporary Islamic legal scholar Mustafa Al-Zarqa states that "*gharar* is the sale of probable items whose existence or characteristics are not certain, due to the risky nature that makes the trade similar to gambling."

Gharar is of three kinds: (a) excessive, which vitiates transactions; (b) minor, which is tolerated; and (c) moderate, which falls between the other two categories. Any transaction can be classified as forbidden activity due to excessive *gharar*. A number of *ahādith* forbid trading in *gharar* or transactions that are based on *gharar*.[6] Jurists have sought many complete definitions of the term. They have also come up with the concept of *gharar yasir*, or minor risk.[7] What *gharar* is, exactly, was never fully decided upon by Muslim jurists. This was mainly due to the complication of having to decide what is and is not a minor risk. Derivative instruments such as stock options have become common only relatively recently. Some Islamic banks provide brokerage services for stock trading and perhaps even for derivatives trading.

5.3.3   Transactions involving *Maysir* and *Qimar*

The literal meaning of the term *maysir* is "to achieve something without putting any effort into it," which explains the principle upon which gambling is prohibited in Islam. The Arabic noun *al-qimār* derives from *qamar*, or the moon, which waxes at certain times and wanes at others. It has been given this name due to the possibility that each gambler may lose his wealth to his counterpart and gain the wealth of another. Any monetary gain that can be earned so easily that no work is required to acquire it is unlawful. In Islam, gambling is considered a great evil of society and immensely harmful to the wellbeing of the human social order. As such, Islam categorically prohibits all forms of gambling, so human society is spared its ill-effects and harms. The Prophet emphasizes its prohibition to such an extent that even considering taking part in gambling is regarded as condemnable.

Jurists and scholars unanimously agree on the prohibition of gambling.

The Qur'an and the *sunnah* explicitly forbid gains made from *maysir* or gambling and games of chance. An uninformed speculation in its worst form is also akin to gambling. The term speculation always involves an attempt to predict the future outcome of an event. But the process may or may not be backed by the collection, analysis, and interpretation of relevant information. The relevant experts in financial institutions will assume risk after making a proper assessment of it using the required information. All business decisions involve speculation in this sense. It is only the gross absence of value-relevant information or conditions of excessive uncertainty that make speculation akin to a game of chance and, hence, forbidden.

5.3.4   Sacredness of contracts

Islam upholds contractual obligations and the disclosure of information as a sacred duty. This feature is intended to reduce the risk of asymmetric information and moral hazard. It also provides basic liberty to enter into transactions (Al-Qur'an, 2:275). The involvement of an element of compulsion for either party to a transaction invalidates the contract (Al-Qur'an, 4:29). However, this basic rule does not entail unhampered liberty to contract, and the liberty to do so may be relinquished with transactions involving other rules and regulations requiring unequivocal rulings.

5.3.5   Prevention of harm

This refers to the possibility of a third party being unfavorably affected by a contract between two parties. If a contract between two parties carried out with their mutual consent is detrimental to the interests of a third party, then that third party may have certain rights and obligations. The Prophet (pbuh) is reported to have said: "There should be no harming nor reciprocal harming" (narrated by Ibn Mājah, al-Dāraqutni and others on the authority of Abu Saʿid al-Khudri).

Now one may wonder in this regard how one prioritizes the various rules of Islamic financial transactions in the event of a conflict. An Islamic legal financial system has a clear scheme of priorities in legislation. Where there is a clear injunction in the Qur'an, for example, in the form of a prohibition of interest and games of chance, these must be observed at all costs. Next in importance are the rules that follow from the *sunnah* and *ʿijmāʿ* or consensus, in that order.

5.4   Valid and invalid contracts for business transactions in Islam

Islamic financial products are aimed at investors who want to comply with the tenets of *Shariah*. The most distinct component of Islamic finance, as illustrated in the *Shariah*, is the ban on *riba*. Other components include an emphasis on equitable contracts, the linking of finance to productivity, the desirability of profit sharing, and the prohibition of gambling.

5.4.1   Meaning and definition of contract

The corresponding Arabic term for "contract" is *ʿaqd*, and the literal meaning of its verbal form *ʿaqada* is "to tie, bond, join, lock, hold, fasten, link together." Technically, the *ʿaqd* is a connection of the words of one party, or offer (*ʿijāb*), to the words of another party, or acceptance (*qabul*), which carries legal implications on the subject matter. In a juristic sense, *ʿaqd* has been defined as "an agreement between two parties through offer and acceptance that constitutes an attempt to forge a binding agreement." Therefore, binding the contractual parties into a legal agreement will carry legal consequences. From the definition, the term *'aqd* more or less corresponds to the technical term "contract" in Western jurisprudence. The application of the notion of *'aqd* in an Islamic legal system has a wider application than the term *contract* in common law. Nevertheless, both are similar in their definitions in that a contract can be defined as a combination of an offer and acceptance or mutual agreement, which forms a contract.

The objectives of a contract are twofold: (a) to clarify, show, and manifest the real intention and willingness of the contracting parties; (b) to protect both contracting parties' interest and avoid misleading in the deal. The mutual consent of parties is the basis for the formation of a contract, which is clearly manifested in the Qur'an. It states: "*O you who believe! Eat not up your property among yourselves in vanity, but let there be among you trade by mutual consent*" [4:29]. It is also referred to in a *hadith*. The Prophet (pbuh) is reported to have said: "It is unlawful to take the property of a Muslim except by his consent." However, consent is an intangible mental fact, and as such this intention must be manifested in sufficient form of words or conduct that indicates a definite intention to contract. Expressing an offer (*'ijāb*) and acceptance (*qabul*) is a method to manifest the intention to contract. The contract is said to be concluded when the connection between the *'ijāb* and *qabul* takes place.

5.4.2   Valid and invalid contracts

With respect to validity, contracts are categorized mainly as valid and invalid. A contract is regarded as valid if all its elements are found to be in order and all its pillars or elements (*arkān*) and conditions (*shurut*) are satisfied and if the contract does not involve any *Shariah*-prohibited activities. However, a contract would be invalid if any of its key conditions is not met. A valid contract has legal effects whereby the contract is binding on the parties with immediate effect after the contract has been concluded. A straightforward contract basically requires the existence of two parties, found to be mature and sane in terms of being capable of entering into contracts; the existence of an offer and acceptance must be by free mutual consent; a subject matter that ought to be in principle legal, existing, valuable, usable, capable of ownership, in a deliverable state, specified and quantified, and the seller must have title and ownership; and lastly, the contract should not contradict any statutory or common law rules. The view of the majority of jurists is that if any of the aforementioned elements and conditions are not fulfilled, then the contract is invalid. However, Hanafi jurists hold that if certain conditions are not met, then the contract would be deemed *fāsid*, meaning that certain but not all legal consequences may still follow from the contract.

Furthermore, a contract whose basis is not legally recognized renders it invalid. When one of the necessary elements of a valid contract is missing, the contract will then be invalid. Hence, when one of the elements of a contract is not satisfied, the contract will have no legal effect and no title may be passed nor any payment made. The best example of this kind of contract is the sale of dead animals, blood, liquor, and pork.

5.5   Types and key features of valid contracts

Contracts in Islamic commercial transactions are of various types. Although this classification is commonly viewed with respect to their impact, effectiveness, and validity theoretically, contracts are divided into unilateral and bilateral in the sense that the former, which are also known as gratuitous or noncommutative contracts, favor recipients of such items as donations, gifts, rebates, wills, trusts, gratuitous loans, and so on; while the latter fulfills the requirements of parties to contracts. This latter type of contract covers all other permissible commercial transactions, namely exchange or commutative contracts that mainly deal with trading, buying, and selling activities; security contracts concerning guarantee, mortgage, and debt transfer; partnership contracts; contracts of safe custody; and service-oriented contracts such as agency and commission. The key difference between these two types of contracts is that what is normally tolerated in unilateral contracts would not necessarily be the same in bilateral contracts.

In this section, an in-depth discussion on the key features of different contracts is presented. These include (a) commutative contracts, (b) partnership-based contracts, (c) charitable contracts, (d) fee- or service-based contracts, and (e) supporting contracts. To this end, the definitions and key features of the aforementioned contracts are discussed in detail.

5.5.1   Commutative contracts

A commutative contract (also known as an exchange-based or debt-creating contract) is a type of contract whereby ownership is acquired through some kind of exchange between two parties. In a simplified way, it is a contract that involves the *exchange* of one countervalue for another. For example, exchanging a commodity for a consideration (price) is one type of *exchange-based contract*. In this contract, ownership is acquired through certain kinds of exchange between two parties. The object of exchange-based contracts must have value of some kind. The Shafi'is and Hanbalis view the usufruct of an asset (i.e., the benefit arising from the use of that asset) as property, and as such it falls under the category of exchange-based contracts. However, the Hanafis and Malikis depart from this view. Several types of exchange-based contracts include *bay' murābaḥah*, *bay' salam*, *bay' istisnā'a*, and *ijārah* modes of financial transactions.

5.5.1.1   *Concept and meaning of* Bay' Murâbaḥah

The term *bay' murābaḥah* is a combination of *bay'* and *murâbaḥah*. *Bay'* refers to any transaction in which ownership of an asset is exchanged between a seller and a buyer in return for money or by barter. The word *murâbaḥah* comes from a root (*r-b-ḥ*) meaning "profit," and thus it literally means "a sale on mutually agreed profit." However, technically it is a sales contract in which the seller declares his cost and the profit. As a financing technique used by Islamic banks, it involves a request by the client to the bank to purchase a certain item for him. The bank does that for a certain profit over the cost, which is stipulated in advance. For example, a coffee importer who wants to use Islamic financing would ask a bank to purchase on its behalf a shipment of coffee. The bank would make the purchase, take title to the coffee, and resell it to the importer. The importer would receive the goods immediately but would be allowed to defer payment to the bank. The bank would charge a fee to cover its work on the transaction and the cost of the deferred payment. In this arrangement, neither the agreement of the bank to buy nor the purchase itself obligates the customer to buy. On the other hand, the risk element is undoubtedly there until the customers fulfill their original promise, protecting the seller from any accusation of disguised *ribā*. Given this technical meaning of *murâbaḥah*, one can see that there are two essential ingredients for *murâbaḥah*. First, the seller must own the good before transferring title to the purchaser. Second, the seller discloses his cost for the product and then adds on a profit up front.

The difference between a conventional sale and a *murābaḥah* sale is that in the latter, the seller's cost price is made known to the buyer. Under a *murābaḥah* contract, the bank purchases goods on behalf of the buyer and then sells them to the buyer at an agreed upon mark-up. The *Shariah* allows in this case a justifiable profit in addition to the real cost incurred. To make it *Shariah*-compliant, some conditions are imposed on *murābaḥah* such as the prohibition of interest, a rebate on early payment, and penalty for default or late payment. Financing for unspecified purposes and overhead is not permissible under a *murābaḥah* contract.

5.5.1.2   Concept and meaning of Bay' Salam

The etymology of the word *salam* in *bay' salam* means "to hand over or deliver." It is a contract for deferred delivery that was originally sanctioned during the time of the Prophet (pbuh), to facilitate the trading activities of farmers who were awaiting crops. In more modern times, it has been applied to the production of raw materials and fungible goods (i.e., those that can readily be estimated and replaced according to weight, measure, and amount in general).

The scholars of the various schools of Islamic jurisprudence have each defined this term, and set its conditions, in accordance with their own view. The term *bay' salam* is best defined as "a contract in which a full payment of the price is made in advance at the time of contract for assets to be delivered later at a future date." It is necessary that the quality of the assets intended to be purchased be fully specified, leaving no ambiguity that could cause dispute. The objects of this sale are ordinary assets and cannot be gold, silver, or currencies because these are regarded as monetary values whose exchange is covered under rules of *bay' al-sarf*.[8] Barring this, *bay' salam* covers almost everything capable of being described as to quantity, quality, and workmanship. This sale contract is often applied in the agricultural sector, where a bank advances money for various inputs to receive a share in the crop, which it then sells.

5.5.1.3   Concept and meaning of Bay' 'Istisnā'a

Bay' 'istisnā'a is the second kind of sale where a commodity is transacted before it comes into existence. It means ordering a manufacturer to manufacture a specific commodity for the purchaser. If the manufacturer undertakes to manufacture the goods for him with material from the manufacturer, a transaction under a *bay' 'istisnā'a* contract comes into existence. However, it is necessary for the validity of a *bay' 'istisnā'a* contract that the price be fixed with the consent of the contracting parties and that the necessary specification of the commodity (intended to be manufactured) be fully settled between them.

Literally, the word *'istisnā'a* is derived from the root word *sanā'a*, or to manufacture or construct something. *'Istisnā'a* is an order or request to manufacture something, whereby the requestor invites, induces, or causes another to make or manufacture goods for him. Technically, it is a contract to purchase for a set price something that may be manufactured later on according to specifications agreed upon by the parties. In other words, it is a contract of sale of specified items to be manufactured or constructed with an obligation on the part of the manufacturer or contractor to deliver them to the customer upon completion. The contract of *'istisnā'a* creates a moral obligation for the manufacturer to manufacture goods, but before he starts working on the goods, either of the parties may cancel the contract after giving notice to the other. However, after the manufacturer has started the work, the contract cannot be cancelled unilaterally.

Bay' 'istisnā'a can be used to provide financing in certain transactions, especially in the housing sector. If the client has his own land and seeks financing for the construction of a house, the financer may undertake to construct the house on that open land, based on *bay' 'istisnā'a*, and if the client has no land but wants to purchase the land, the financer may undertake to provide him a constructed house on a specified plot of land. Since it is not necessary under *bay' 'istisnā'a* that the price be paid in advance or that it be paid at the time of delivery (it may be deferred at any time according to the agreement of the parties), the time of payment may be fixed in whatever manner the parties wish. Payment may also be made in installments.

5.5.1.4   Concept and meaning of 'Ijārah

'Ijārah literally means "to give something on rent." It refers to a contract of transfer of ownership of usufruct or service in exchange for a specified consideration for a fixed period. The primary objective of the *'ijārah* mode of transaction is to facilitate a lessee who does not intend to own certain assets but needs to use and benefit from the use of the assets against the payment of certain agreed-to rent to the lessor. In the context of Islamic finance, the Islamic financial service provider (IFSP), as the owner of the asset and usufruct, leases or transfers the usufruct of the asset for an agreed-upon rental amount and at a specified period to the lessee as its customer. Under the primary *'ijārah* structure, since the customer does not intend to own the asset but to benefit from it, at the end of the lease period, the asset remains with the IFSP as the lessor. The pillars of the *'ijārah* contract are: (a) expression, which includes both offer and acceptance; (b) the parties, both the lessor and the lessee or employer and employee; (c) wage/salary/rent; and (d) usufruct and service.

The *'ijārah* is of several types: (1) *'ijārah thumma al bay'* (hire purchase), under which the customer leases an object and agrees to purchase it, paying in installments so that by the end of the lease, he or she owns the object free and clear; (2) *'ijārah wa-iqtinā* (or *'ijārah muntahiah bi al-tamlik*), which may involve both a lease contract and a sale contract, but here the transfer of ownership occurs as soon as the lessee pays the purchase price of the asset—anytime during the leasing period; and (3) *'ijārah mawsufah bi al-dhimmah*, wherein the service or benefit being leased is well defined, but the particular unit providing that service or benefit is not identified. In contemporary Islamic finance, *'ijārah mawsufah bi al-dhimmah* contracts are combined with an *'istisnā'a* contract for the construction of whatever it is that will provide the service or benefit. The financer finances its production, while one party begins leasing the asset after "taking delivery" of it. While forward sales normally do not comply with the principles of *Shariah*, it is allowed using *'ijārah* provided rent/lease payments do not begin until after the customer takes delivery of the object. *Shariah* also requires that the asset is clearly specified and its rental rate is fixed.

5.5.2   Controversial debt-creating contracts

The Islamic banking and financial services industry has witnessed the introduction of some commercial contracts in recent times that are either not allowed by *Shariah* or at best controversial. These contracts have been the subject of intense debate. Some mechanisms permit *riba* through the back door. Others appear to be allowed in form only, not in substance. In the literature of Islamic commercial jurisprudence, these are documented as contracts of *hiyal* or legal tricks, but they have been permitted by mainstream scholars under certain conditions. The reason is that Islamic banks, like their conventional counterparts, face challenges in satisfying the needs of their customers, and they are under pressure to introduce and develop transactions that are *Shariah*-compliant. These include *bay' al-tawarruq*, *bay' al inah*, and *bay' al-dayn* contracts.

5.5.2.1   *Concept and legitimacy of* Bay' al-Tawarruq

The word *tawarruq* is derived from the word *al-wariq*, which means silver, because the one who buys the goods is only buying them for the sake of dirhams, and originally they were made from silver (silver coins). It also means money. Therefore, *tawarruq* has been defined as buying goods with a delayed payment and then selling it to someone else other than the seller [from whom one bought the goods] to obtain cash. In other words, it is a combination of two separate sales transactions whereby an individual in need of funds purchases a commodity from a seller on a deferred payment basis and then sells the same on a spot basis to yield cash to a party other than the original seller. In modern Islamic banking practice, the bank usually performs all the transactions needed as it first buys the commodity under its own name, then sells it to the customer on credit, and finally sells it on behalf of the customer to a third party for its cash value.

Scholars differ as to whether it is permissible. Some say that it is permissible and they argue that if a man buys an item because he wants the item itself or he wants its price (by selling it), both are valid aims. Scholars who have permitted *tawarruq* provided it fulfills a genuine demand for funds claim it does not violate the norms of *Shariah* including involving any *riba*. However, some scholars, like Imam Ahmad and Ibn Taimiyah, say that it is not permissible, because generally the aim of such transactions is to take dirhams for dirhams, and the item comes in between as a means of making the transaction permissible, and making a prohibited thing permissible by other means does not change anything. Therefore, *tawaruq* is considered a legal trick, since the individual concerned has no real intention of buying or selling the commodity (Moghul and Ahmed, 2003). He engages in these purchase and sales transactions to acquire cash. Scholars who do not permit *tawarruq* cite the famous *hadith* of Bukhari, "actions are but by intentions, and each man will have but that which he intended," as evidence to support their view.

5.5.2.2   *Concept and meaning of* Bay' al-'Inah

Bay' al-'inah is contracting a loan or purchasing on credit. It has been defined by some jurists as a sale of a commodity on credit and repurchasing it for a lesser amount in cash (Rosly and Sanusi, 1990). Therefore, the contract contains two sales transactions: one at a deferred price, and one at a lower cash price. These transactions can be described in the following manner:

1. The parties make an explicit statement of their intention to enter into a twin contract. Here, parties expressly declare through the contract that the vendor in the first contract that takes place on deferred payment will repurchase the asset at a cash price lower than the former deferred price.

   There is a consensus among all Muslim jurists and scholars that this is invalid and impermissible.

2. The parties enter into a twin sale where a commodity is sold to a second party on credit and the seller repurchases it at a cash price lower than the former credit price without any condition in the contracts that necessitate it.

5.5.2.3   *Concept and* Shariah *ruling on* Bay' al-Dayn

The word *bay' al-dayn* connotes the sale of debt or debt trading or the selling of debt. It can be defined as the sale of a payable right or receivable debt either to the debtor himself or to any third party. This type of sale is usually for immediate payment or deferred payment.

Shariah permits the selling of debt by its equivalent in quantity and time of maturity by way of *hawālah* or debt transfer. This form of debt trading is accepted by all schools of Islamic law provided it is paid in full and thus gives no benefit to the purchaser. The rationale for this ruling is that financial transactions involving debt should never allow deferred payment, as this would be regarded as *riba*.

According to most Hanafi, Hanbali, and Shafi'i jurists, it is not allowable to sell *dayn* to non-debtors or a third party. However, Malikis, and some Hanafi and Shafi'i jurists allowed selling of debt to third parties under the following conditions:

(a) The seller has the ability to deliver the debts;

(b) The debt must be confirmed and the contract signed on the spot;

(c) The debt cannot be created from the sale of currency (gold and silver) to be delivered in the future and the payment is not of the same type as the debt, and if it is, the rate should be the same to avoid *riba*;

(d) The debt should be goods that are saleable, even before they are received. This is to ensure that the debt is not of a food type, which cannot be traded to debtors.

5.5.3   Partnership-based contracts

In Islamic commercial jurisprudence, mainstream jurists differ in the way they define a partnership. While Hanafis define a partnership as a contract between partners on both capital and profit, the Shafi'is look at it as a contract giving the right to something to two or more people, making it common. Hanbalis define partnership as the coming together of two or more people in transactions. Partnership-based contracts, also known as equity-based contracts, are the financial contracts most frequently used by Islamic banks. These contracts mainly include the two-key mode of transactions: (a) *mushārakah* and (b) *mudārabah*. The concept, meanings, and rules of these contracts are discussed in the following subsection.

5.5.3.1   *Concept and meaning of* Mudārabah

Muslim scholars have used different terminology for this Arabic word when translating it into English such as "profit sharing," "trust financing," "trustee profit sharing," "equity sharing," "fund management," "sleeping partnership," and "commenda." The names for this kind of contract are themselves of some interest. The very word *mudārabah* seems to come from an idiomatic phrase that appears in the Qur'an, meaning to beat the earth or travel a great distance (4:101).

Mudārabah is defined as a contract between at least two parties whereby one party, the financer (known as *rabb al-māl* or *sahib al-māl*, i.e., owner of the property) entrusts funds to the other party, the entrepreneur (the *mudārib* or '*āmil*), to undertake a business activity. The entrepreneur returns the principal to the financer with a predetermined share of profit. In the case of loss, the financer loses some or all of his capital and the entrepreneurs receives no remuneration for her labor and effort. In Islamic banking, the *mudārabah* contract has been extended to include three parties: depositors as financers, the bank as intermediary, and entrepreneurs who require funds. The bank acts as an entrepreneur when it receives funds from depositors and as financer when it provides funds to entrepreneurs. For example, Islamic banks, after receiving funds from depositors, may enter into a contract with well-established commodity traders who have access to deals but lack capital to execute them. Profits from the deals will be split between the two parties, rewarding the banks for the provision of money and the traders for their expertise. This is called "two-tier *mudārabah*" as investors pool their funds with banks, which subsequently deal with entrepreneurs.

5.5.3.2   *Concept and meaning of* Mushārakah

The word *mushārakah* is normally translated into English as "partnership." In the context of Islamic banks, however, *mushārakah* means "participating financing" or "equity participation." It is a relatively new term in Islamic commercial law. Literally, it means a joint-venture agreement between two parties to engage in a specific business activity with the aim of making a profit. In other words, it is a participative arrangement in which all partners contribute capital. Unlike *mudārabah*, they are entitled to participate in management but not necessarily required to do so. Profit is to be distributed among the partners in a ratio agreed to by the partners in advance, while loss is borne by each partner strictly in proportion to the capital contribution.

The *mushārakah* corresponds in many ways to its conventional counterpart, but there are important differences. There are two kinds of *mushārakah*: *mufāwadah*, or a universal partnership in which complete equality of investment and profit and loss is obligatory, and *'inān*, or limited investment partnership under which all other types of partnership fall. Under an *'inān* arrangement, each partner is an agent but not the guarantor of the other, and the agency applies only to the field of business for which the partnership was established and to the extent of their joint capital. The *'inān* form of *mushārakah* is the form used by Islamic financial institutions today. The institutions usually translate *mushārakah* as participation rather than partnership, and it is in the sense of participating in the borrower's profits, in return for capital, that the *mushārakah* has come into its own, rather than as a working partnership in which both sides contribute the same kind of input (Al-Zuhayli, 2003).

5.5.4   Charitable contracts

Charitable contracts (*'uqud tabarru'āt*), also known as noncommutative or gratuitous contracts, are contracts based on voluntary charitable actions or donations. These are unilateral (one-sided or independent) contracts whose underlying purpose is to transfer to another party the ownership of an object or asset without the intention of receiving any gain or consideration from the recipient. Such contracts are made with the virtue of benevolence or an act of kindness (*al-ihsān*) and do not involve a commutative exchange or any countervalue. These contracts include *inter alia qard hasan* (benevolent loan), *hibah* (gift), *'i'ārah* (asset lending), and *'ibra'* (absolution).

5.5.4.1   *Concept and objectives of* Qard Hasan

The term *qard hasan* is a combination of two words: *qard* and *hasan*. The word *qard* is derived from the Arabic *qirād*, which means "to cut." It is called *qard* because it cuts certain parts of a lender's property by granting a loan to the borrower, while *hasan* is translated as beautiful, good, beneficial, gratuitous, benevolent, and handsome, for example. Chapra, a modern Muslim economist, defined *qard hasan* as a loan that is returned at the end of the agreed period without any interest or share in the profit or loss of the business.

Islam emphasizes brotherhood among Muslims, and since *qard hasan* is a gratuitous loan, it can help fellow Muslims who need money, and we can deduce the objectives of *qard hasan* as being:

- to help needy fellow Muslims;

- to establish better relationships among the poor and rich;

- to mobilize wealth among people in society;

- to perform a good deed that is encouraged and appreciated by Allah and the Prophet Muhammad (pbuh);

- to strengthen the national economy;

- to help the poor create new job markets and business ventures using their merits, skills, and expertise;

- to establish a caring society;

- to eradicate unemployment from society; and

- to remove social and economic discrimination in society.

5.5.4.2 *Concept and meaning of* Hibah

Hibah, literally meaning "gift" or "donation," is technically a method of ownership transfer whereby an asset or object is legally given away by one party to another without any consideration or countervalue (*'iwad*). In short, it is defined as a gift, meaning no compensation is given in return.

From the perspective of Islamic finance practices, the IFSP normally provides savings account holders this *hibah* as a token of appreciation for their deposits in the former, representative of a share of the profit made from the latter's deposits. The *Shariah* permits this practice as long as it is not considered as a cost. The *hibah* is also practiced in *takāful* products in such a way that, instead of transferring risks from *takāful* participants to the *takāful* operator in exchange for their contributions through a unilateral contract (popularly known as *tabarru'*), they help each other via this contribution to a participant in need.

A variant of *hibah* is *sadaqah,* which can be better translated as charity or alms, although there exists an insignificant difference between the two. While *hibah* is a gift given for no compensation for the sake of the recipient, and the giver usually knows who he is giving the gift to and there is direct contact between the two, *sadaqah* is given solely for the sake of Allah, and no commendation or reward is intended from the recipient. Also, in *sadaqah,* the donor usually prefers to hide his identity from the recipient, and hence there is usually no personal relationship between donor and donee.

5.5.4.3 *Concept and meaning of* 'I'ārah, Ju'ālah, *and* Ibrā'

(a) *'I'ārah:*
   Literally, the word *'i'arah* or *'ariyah* is used in connection with borrowing. In Islamic finance terminology, it is used to denote lending of a nonfungible item.

Technically, it permits the borrower to receive a benefit from the property of the lender without any compensation. For example, people may borrow small articles of household goods from neighbors and relatives. The borrowed item may remain with the borrower for a definite or indefinite period of time. The contract of '*i'ārah* is encouraged and recommended as a form of charitable deed. The property is held on trust by the borrower who is therefore not liable for its destruction, loss, or diminution of value, unless caused intentionally or by fault and negligence. The contract of '*i'ārah* has four pillars: (1) the lender (*al-mu'ir*), (2) the borrower *(al-musta'ir)*, (3) the borrowed item (*musta'ar*), and (4) the expression that includes offer and acceptance.

(b) *Ju'ālah:*

Ju'ālah literally means: (a) to determine, in the sense that the party wishing to offer *ju'ālah* or commission, will determine the rate of reward; (b) to make an obligation, on the premise that it is a binding promise to pay certain compensation to a person who performs some recognized tasks. In a broader sense, one of the contracting parties undertakes to pay a specified amount of money for rendering a particular service in line with the terms and conditions stipulated in the contract. Technically, *ju'alah* is a promise to grant a determined reward for either a determined or undetermined task that is considered burdensome to accomplish.

(c) *'Ibrā':*

'Ibrā' literally means release, removal, relief, abandoning, or absolution. Technically, it is a contract through which a person waives his or her right that is established as an obligation or liability on another. *'Ibrā'* has a dual function in that it implies both the waiving of the right and the transfer of the ownership of the debt are transferred to the debtor. The objects of '*ibrā*' are debts, rights, and claims over nonfungible property. Nonetheless, debts of fungible items can also be waived or withdrawn since they are considered debt that could be determined to be a liability. With regard to the relationship of '*ibrā*' to debts, '*ibra*' arises in situations in which a creditor waives the debt and releases the debtor from the obligation to repay it. It can also be practiced in relation to rights of one's fellow human beings in the sense that a borrower may release his guarantor in a *kafālah* contract, or he may release a transferee in a *hawālah* contract. Likewise, a contracting party may relinquish his right to use certain objects, his right to terminate the contract if the objects are found to be defective, or his right to claim compensation for the damage of his object(s).

5.5.5   Fee- and service-based contracts

In this section, the use of fee- and service-based contracts in Islamic commercial jurisprudence is examined. These contracts, though considered secondary to primary contracts such as commutative, partnership-based, and charitable contracts as discussed earlier, are a central part of the foundation of Islamic financial transactions.

5.5.5.1   *Fee-based contracts*

Modern commercial banking involves a wide array of services to customers, many of which are fee-based. These are distinct from products and services that are fund-based. Since these do not require the use of funds but still contribute significantly to the bottom line, their importance can hardly be overemphasized. Fee-based products also involve a lesser degree of divergence between Islamic and conventional practices. While Islamic banks currently offer a wide range of such services, we discuss a few of the more popular and commonplace ones.

5.5.5.2 *Service-based contracts*

Islamic banks, like their conventional counterparts, provide fee-based services, such as:

(i)   safekeeping of negotiable instruments, including shares and bonds and the collection of payments (based on an agreement of *wakālah* under which the Islamic bank acts as the *wakil* or agent of its client);

(ii) internal (domestic) and external transfer operations (based on an agreement of *wakālah* under which the Islamic bank acts as the *wakil* or agent of its client);

(iii) administration of property, estates, and wills; for example (based on an agreement of *wakālah* under which the Islamic bank acts as the *wakil* or agent of its client).

Lately Islamic banks have started offering various services related to real estate, property, and project management. These are fee (*'ujrah*)-based services offered to customers regardless of whether they avail themselves of financing or not. They are natural extensions of an Islamic bank's financing activities. Since financing activities are concentrated in property finance or project finance, banks benefit from the synergy that such fee-based activities provide.

5.5.6 Supporting contracts

Supporting contracts are often crucial because they act to complete many aspects of services, products, and banking. Many supporting contracts are created to cater mostly to specific situations, and most of this support requires proper *'aqd* as well. Such contracts are also considered a facility to provide specific outcomes for the customer. They also fall under bilateral arrangements.

Popular contracts include contracts of *kafālah*, which are guarantees aimed at securing obligations and protecting debts, either from being uncollected or from being in default. Other contracts include *hawālah*, which is used for transferring debt liability from the transferor to the payer, *rahn* or mortgage or pawn broking that has specific terms, *hāmish jiddiyyah* or security deposit, or even *wakālah*, which is defined by the Accounting and Auditing Organization for Islamic Financial Institutions (AAOIFI) in its *Shariah* Standard No. 23 as an act of one party directing another party to act on its behalf regarding what can be a subject matter of delegation (AAOIFI, 2010).

To sum up, a variety of services offered by conventional banks may be provided by Islamic banks without any need for modification in the nature of the product, as long as there is no debtor–creditor relationship involved in the process. Activities where such a relationship comes into existence at the beginning or at a later stage, however, need close scrutiny for the possible existence of *riba*. These often involve a mix-up of fees for services rendered and interest or *riba* for lending money. Where a loan is involved, it would be dangerous to allow the bank to receive revenues or fees based on a percentage of the loan value—to allay suspicions of *riba*. But where there is no loan involved, the fee would be based on the benefit to the customer, on the one hand, and efforts exerted by the bank or work done, on the other.

Where both these elements are present, the fee may be determined as an absolute amount taking into account the benefit conferred and costs incurred, and certainly not as a percentage of the value of the loan (El-Gamal, 2000).

5.6   Invalid contracts

A number of flaws may make a contract invalid for four key reasons: (a) internal or apparent mistakes arising from assumptions made by the contractors; (b) complete and incomplete coercion; (c) negligible and excessive unfairness; and (d) verbal and actual deception.

Examples of Invalid Contracts

Internal mistakes: A person purchases a cow thinking that it will produce a lot of milk, but there was no mention in the contract that it in fact produces milk. These kinds of mistakes do not affect the validity and execution of the contract, because the formulation of the contract matters but not the internal assumptions, which lack substantial proofs.

Apparent mistake: Selling semi-precious stones in a market for precious jewels may apparently be assumed to be the same category of value. If these sorts of mistakes concern the nature of the property, they render the contract invalid. However, if they concern the description of the property, then the contract is pending and can be revoked by the one who has been tempted to make the mistake.

Complete coercion: To force a person by threatening to kill him or cut off his limbs.

Incomplete coercion: To bully by whipping or imprisoning a person which effects the contract in a way that it would tantamount to be null and void.

According to the majority of scholars, the words and acts of the coerced do not affect the contract.

Negligible unfairness: This kind of unfairness happens in contracts, and within appraisers' assessments. Since this unfairness is negligible, it has no effect on the contract.

Excessive unfairness: An example is the purchase of a $10 book for $100. Here, if the contract is free from deceit, the unfairness is tantamount to negligence on the part of the one who was deceived, and as such he is responsible for any loss. However, if the unfairness is a result of deception, the one who is cheated will not be bound by the contract.

Verbal deception: This is a deception that occurs when one party lies to the other. If such verbal deception does not affect the authority of the contract, unless it causes injury to either party of the contract, the victim has the right to terminate the contract for being unfairly dealt with.

Actual deception: An example of an actual deception is letting milk accumulate in a cow's udder to make her appear as if she produces abundant milk. This kind of deception affects the contract, making it nonbinding, and the affected party has the right to void the contract.

Chapter Highlights

- *Shariah* constitutes the commands of Allah for His servants that were related by any of the prophets whether they relate to actions or beliefs.

- The objective of *Shariah* is to promote human wellbeing, which lies in the preservation of, for example, their faith, self, intellect, generations, wealth, social order, family, human dignity, liberty, social welfare, and human alliances.

- *Fiqh* is knowledge of the rules of *Shariah* relating to individual actions or conduct derived from their elaborated evidences from texts of the Qur'an and *Sunnah*, whereas the *usul al-fiqh* is the sound knowledge of the proofs or sources of *fiqh*, the method of application, and the condition of a person who applies them.

- The function of *fiqh* is to derive these rules from the sources of *Shariah* following the methods and underlying principles set forth by *usul al-fiqh*. The role of *usul al-fiqh* is to explicate and elucidate the methods of deducing the rules of *Shariah*.

- The philosophy of Islamic business transactions revolves around the non-transgression of the tenets of *Shariah*, which include avoiding transactions that involve *riba, gharar, maysir,* and *qimār*, as well as upholding the sanctity of contracts and preventing harm to contracting parties.

- Contracts in Islamic commercial jurisprudence are categorized mainly as valid and invalid. Valid contracts are contracts whose elements are found to be in order, and all its conditions set by *Shariah* are fulfilled. Otherwise, they are for all intents and purposes invalid.

- Commutative contracts are those involving the *exchange* of one countervalue for another, whereby ownership is attained through exchange between two parties.

- Partnership-based contracts can either be contracts between partners with respect to both capital and profit or giving the right in something to two or more people, making it common, or the coming together of two or more people in transactions, according to the majority of Muslim jurists.

- Charitable contracts are based on voluntary charitable actions or donations whose underlying purpose is to transfer to another party the ownership of an object or asset without the intention of receiving any gain or consideration from the recipient.

- Fee- and service-based contracts are not different from those used in conventional finance. However, they are a central part of the foundation of Islamic financial transactions.

- Supporting contracts act to complete many aspects of products and services. Many of these are created to cater mostly to specific situations. They are also considered a facility to provide specific outcomes for customers.

Key Terms

'Aqd	*Fiqh*	Service-based contract
Business transaction	Invalid contract	Supporting contract
Charitable contract	*Maqāṣid al-Shariah*	*Usul al-fiqh*
Commutative contract	Partnership-based	Valid contract
Debt-creating contract	contract	
Fee-based contract	*Shariah*	

Discussion Questions

1. Define the terms *Shariah, fiqh,* and *muʿāmalāt,* and describe the relationship between them.

2. Is the objective of *Shariah*—protecting and promoting the wellbeing of the people—limited to safeguarding the people's faith, self, intellect, posterity, and wealth, as the twelfth-century Muslim philosopher Al-Ghazali classified the *maqāṣid al-Shariah* into these five categories?

3. With respect to validity, contracts are categorized as valid and invalid. Briefly explain the situations where a contract would be rendered valid and when invalid.

4. Discuss the meaning and *Shariah* legitimacy of a *bayʿ al-dayn* contract as a controversial debt-creating contract used by some Islamic banks.

Selected Bibliography

AAOIFI (2010). *Shariah Standards for Islamic Financial Institutions 1432H – 2010, (2010).* Manama: Accounting and Auditing Organization for Islamic Financial Institutions.

Ahmad, A.U.F. (2010). *Theory and Practice of Modern Islamic Finance: The Case Analysis from Australia.* Irvine: Universal-Publishers.

Ahmad, A.U.F. and Hassan, M.K. (2007). Regulation and Performance of Islamic Banking in Bangladesh. *Thunderbird International Business Review,* 49(2), 251–277.

Al-Zuhayli, W. (2003). *Financial Transactions in Islamic Jurisprudence (Trans. of al-Fiqh al-Islami wa Adillatuhu),* 1. Beirut: Dar al-Fikr al-Muasir.

El-Gamal, M.A. (2000). *A Basic Guide to Contemporary Islamic Banking and Finance.* Houston: The Rice University.

Kamali, M.H. (1998). Maqāṣid al-Shariah: The Objectives of Islamic Law. *The Muslim Lawyer Journal,* 3(1).

Kamali, M.H. (2003). *Principles of Islamic Jurisprudence.* Cambridge: Islamic Texts Society.

Moghul, U.F. and Ahmed, A.A. (2003). Contractual Forms in Islamic Finance Law and Islamic Inv. Co. of the Gulf (Bahamas) Ltd. v. Symphony Gems NV & (and) Ors.: A First Impression of Islamic Finance. *Fordham International Law Journal,* 27, 150.

Rosly, S.A. and Sanusi, M.M. (1999). The Application of Bay Al Inah and Bay al-Dayn in Malaysian Islamic Bonds: An Islamic Analysis. *International Journal of Islamic Financial Services,* 1(2).

Saleh, N.A. (1992). *Unlawful Gain and Legitimate Profit in Islamic Law* (2nd ed.). London: Graham & Trotman.

Vogel, F.E. and Hayes, S.L. (1998). *Islamic Law and Finance: Religion, Risk and Return.* The Hague: Kluwer Law International.

Notes

1. The full text of the verse is: "And it does not beseem the believers that they should go forth all together; why should not then a company from every party from among them go forth that they may apply themselves to obtain understanding in religion, and that they may warn their people when they come back to them that they may be cautious?"
2. See Frank E. Vogel and Samuel L. Hayes, III. 1998. *Islamic Law and Finance: Religion, Risk and Return*, The Hague: Kluwer Law International, pp. 71–95. See also, Nabil A. Saleh. 1992. *Unlawful Gain and Legitimate Profit in Islamic Law*, 2nd ed., London: Graham & Trotman. pp. 11–43.
3. See Al-Sarakhsi. 438H. *Al-Mabsut*. Egypt: Matba'ah al-Sa'aadah.
4. The Qur'an clearly forbids all business transactions that cause injustice in any form to any of the parties. It may be in the form of hazard or peril leading to uncertainty in any business, or deceit or fraud or undue advantage.
5. The reason is that a gambler is ignorant of the result of his gambles.
6. This *ahādith* often gives specific examples of *gharar* transactions such as selling the birds in the sky or the fish in the water, the catch of the diver, an unborn calf in its mother's womb, the sperm and unfertilized eggs of camels etc.
7. Financial transactions with minor risk are deemed to be permissible while a transaction with a non-minor risk is deemed to be unlawful.
8. Mutual exchange from hand to hand without delay.

ORGANIZATIONAL CULTURE AND MANAGING CHANGE AND INNOVATION

6

Ahmad Rafiki and Sutan Emir Hidayat

University College of Bahrain, Manama,
Kingdom of Bahrain

Learning Outcomes

LO1: Understand the importance of organizational culture from an Islamic perspective.

LO2: Identify the impact of Islamic rules and culture on enhancing firm performance, knowledge creation, and organizational change.

LO3: Understand the role of ethics, leadership, and organizational commitment in creating improvements and promoting better performance.

LO4: Explain how Islam promotes creativity to support organizational success.

Contents

Organizational culture has been a hot topic in the management discipline for many years. Islam's being a comprehensive way of life creates cultures; it is not the product of a specific culture. Understanding organizational culture from an Islamic perspective leads to achieving the ultimate success (*falah*). Islam promotes continuous improvement, and in order to realize it, performance, knowledge creation, change management, ethics, leadership, and organizational commitment are essential. Therefore, it is important to discuss all topics related to organizational culture. This chapter presents the above six important topics in detail to offer readers an alternative perspective.

6.1   Introduction

The discussion of culture is widespread in many organizations among employees or other stakeholders. Culture is an abstraction created and derived by social and environmental situations, which must be understood comprehensively. The idea of a "culture" is actually a metaphor. It is an image or understanding that is symbolic of something that we can't actually access directly. In fact, the culture of an organization is the inferred and invisible agenda and customs of a given group of people.

Managers usually encounter resistance when attempting to change the behaviors of their subordinates, especially those behaviors that violate the rules of the organization. Most of the time, managers monitor the activities of their subordinates who continuously seem to be embroiled in conflicts more than ensuring that tasks are completed. Miscommunication or misinterpretation of information occurs that causes group members to act in ways they usually don't. Repeated reminders and explanations are given to avoid the reoccurrence of similar events; however, without positive awareness, the situation doesn't change. This is a common occurrence in many organizations.

In environments where tensions are ever present, leaders are aware of the importance of finding effective ways of running their organizations. In this situation, some individuals and groups will continue to do ineffective things and endanger the viability of the organization. Meanwhile, some groups cannot do their jobs without involving other groups. As a result, miscommunication occurs among groups, resulting in conflicts within the organization. These are among the situations often faced by leaders.

6.2   Application of Islamic organizational culture

6.2.1   The concept of Islamic organizational culture

Hofstede (1991) defined a culture as various kinds of interactions that can influence other people in their surroundings and involves the interactions of many complex assumptions, behaviors, and narratives. Organizational culture refers to a set of opinions or beliefs shared by members of an organization (Shahin and Wright, 2004). From an Islamic perspective, culture is any value, thought, or symbol that is based on Islamic norms that influence the behavior, attitude, faith, or habits of someone in a certain walk of life. The success of the Prophet Muhammad (PBUH) appears on how he had created the working atmosphere conductively through his attitude of feeling pity to other people as stated (QS. 3: 159). Islamic teachings consist of a combination of culture and profession. It explained in the Qur'an that professionalism is about having full of commitment in works and done it very well (QS. 17: 84).

Meanwhile, organizational culture from an Islamic point of view is a set of values based on the Qur'an, *sunnah*, *ijma*, and *qiyas* that helps the members of an organization in understanding the aims of their organization, the standards by which it is run, and what must be done to achieve ultimate success (*falah*). It is a process of disseminating a vision, mission, philosophy, beliefs, values, norms, knowledge, and skills among organizational members in light of the Qur'an and *sunnah* for attaining the objectives of the organization effectively and efficiently, thereby obtaining the pleasure (*rida*) of Allah (SWT). A culture plays an important role in forming the behavior of the organization's members, including that of managers.

6.2.2 Islamic culture: The prominent features

There are some unique features of Islamic culture, as elaborated in what follows:

(a) Putting trust in Allah

The term *tawakul* means that all Muslim employees or employers should submit themselves to Allah (God) in all their worldly affairs, including those related to the organization they work for. Allah will help His servants if they follow Islamic teachings. Trust allows work to be done optimally.

(b) Missionary spirit

The mission of Muslims differs from that of non-Muslims. The main mission of the Prophet Muhammad (PBUH) is to complete the *akhlaq* (ethics) of the people. Similarly, all Muslims have as their mission to invite and influence people through *da'wah* (sermons) to accept Islam as a belief and the ultimate true religion.

A missionary spirit is a good deed for every Muslim. This spirit causes Muslims to become sincere and enthusiastic in performing their duties within an organization. As a result, they are empowered to renounce their individual interests and help glorify the organization. Better performance causes the organization to surpass its competitors, which will indirectly confer more advantages to employees.

A missionary spirit encourages a person to work more closely with peers, subordinates, and top management. Driven by a mission, Muslims will be more confident, self-motivated, and precise in carrying out their duties, and they will never stop striving to make their organization achieve excellence.

(c) Honesty and truthfulness

A Muslim should be honest and truthful, both internally and externally, individually and collectively, privately and publicly (Ather, 2007). Honesty brings a sense of self-confidence to Muslim that is reflected in in their behavior, words, and deeds. This kind of confidence makes the believers feel self-satisfied and socially secure. Honesty leads individuals to trust in and be trusted by others. Honesty means unity of behavior, unity of standards, and integrity of personality. Honesty means striving to avoid internal opposition, social conflict, and self-contradiction. In a *hadith*, the Prophet (PBUH) said, "Truthfulness leads to righteousness and righteousness leads to Paradise ... A man continues to be truthful and encourages honesty until he is recorded with Allah as truthful ... Falsehood leads to wickedness, and wickedness leads to the Hellfire. A man continues to tell lies and encourages falsehood until he is recorded with Allah as a liar."

Islam encourages Muslims to be honest. Honesty needs to be applied in an organization. With honesty, an organization's environment is conducive to promoting happiness among employees and a trust culture.

(d) Accountability

Accountability is a significant feature of Islamic organizational culture. An organization cannot perform well in the absence of accountability, and its members need to promote an accountability culture (Altalib, 1991; Trad, 1998). Accountability refers to the duties or tasks of employees that must be reported to the organization. In other words, the organization has the right to ask managers or supervisors about what they are doing. This accountability relates to worldly affairs including businesses and the hereafter (Day of Judgment), where everyone is held responsible for everything they had done up to that point, good or bad deeds. Allah (SWT) will mete out punishment or reward accordingly. The Prophet Muhammad (PBUH) said, "Surely, all of you are responsible and will be questioned about your responsibilities."

(e) Consultative decision making

A consultation is needed to obtain advice from those who have knowledge and are experts on certain subjects. An example involves the Prophet Muhammad (PBUH), who frequently consulted his companions on all important matters. In other words, the Prophet (PBUH) made many decisions after listening to his companions' opinions and inputs and carefully considering them (Syed, 2002). This consultative decision making must be implemented in all organizations. The process enhances the quality of decisions and creates trust among employees. A good decision inspires employees. Islam clearly prohibits egoism, which is the opposite of a consultative culture (Ather, 2007).

(f) Doing good and prohibiting wrong practices

Muslims should always perform good deeds and avoid all types of harmful practices. Rewarding the best deeds and punishing the bad deeds are one of the most important social principles in Islam. An organization has the capacity to promote a healthy environment.

(g) Absolute sincerity

In many of today's organizations, people do not bring their souls to work but merely carry their limbs and brains (Mitroff, 2003). As a result, many organizations cannot find superior talent and creative employees. Thus, employees do not advance themselves as holistic human beings (Rego et al., 2007). However, workers and bosses in Islamic organizations should work with absolute sincerity for the blessings of Allah (SWT) and organizational growth. The Prophet Muhammad (PBUH) said, "All actions are only but driven by intentions, and verily, every man shall only but that which he intended. Thus, he whose migration (*Hijrah*) was for Allah and his Messenger, his migration was for Allah and His Messenger, and he whose migration (*Hijrah*) was to achieve some worldly benefit or to take some woman in marriage, his migration was for that for which he migrated."

The *hadith* elaborates that good intentions are crucial for actions to be accepted by Allah (SWT), i.e., truly for the sake of Allah (SWT). This is called *ikhlas* in Islamic teaching or an absolute sincerity, which means to ensure that every worship or affair is performed solely for the sake of Allah (SWT) and to gain His pleasure (*rida*). It is also known as a condition of acceptance on the performed deeds that give happiness to everyone who applies it.

Managers in Islamic organizations are required to understand the Qur'an and *sunnah* as references in life. It is important to note that they must understand both of them by having sufficient knowledge ('ilm). This includes knowing about Islamic principles and compliance with them. Every Muslim is encouraged to improve his/her skills and increase knowledge as urged repeatedly by the Prophet Muhammad (PBUH). The humbleness of man is created with excellence in his knowledge and will help him to acquire knowledge. With knowledge, employees can differentiate wrong from right.

(h) Good Behavior

Engaging in good behavior is a very meaningful cultural trait for a Muslim. With good behavior, enemies can be turned into new friends and others can show their respect; even the very learned will not be appreciated without good behavior. Good behavior brings positive effects and costs nothing. In an organization, the motivation for work and interpersonal relationships are promoted through the actions of managers. Thus, managers must behave with decorum around their subordinates. The Prophet Muhammad (PBUH) said, "All creations are the family of Allah and who behave well with the family of Allah is most likeable to Allah."

(i) Justice

Justice is synonymous with equality. Both are crucial in dealings with people who come from different backgrounds. Islamic organizational culture can be shaped through justice. The Qur'an reminds Muslims in many verses to be fair and just in all their affairs, even if decisions go against their parents or themselves.

The Prophet Muhammad (PBUH) carries out the instructions of Allah (SWT) with justice, even to his relatives, for instance, as he said, "If my daughter Fatimah had been guilty, she would not be spared" (Al-Bukhari, 1997, p. 409). Injustice creates conflict or disorder and brings negativity to all relationships, as the Prophet (PBUH) warned, "injustice is darkness in the hereafter" (An-Nawawi, 1993, p. 143), while justice results in happiness. Perhaps there is no reason for managers to ignore the adoption of justice, particularly in an Islamic organization.

(j) Cooperation

Islam encourages employees to cooperate with each other. Cooperation is associated with doing works on a team that lead to better results. It is an important part of a shared culture to be learned in an Islamic organization. Prophet Muhammad (PBUH) said, "The best people among you are those who benefit others." The Prophet (PBUH) also exhorted, "Allah shows no mercy to them who are not merciful to the people."

(k) Mutual Trust and Respect

Trust is related to respect, and both are imperative in an organization. Muslims must be trustworthy and not be suspicious of others without proof (Sharfuddin, 1987). Creating a culture of mutual respect can promote togetherness and solidarity among employees. The Prophet (PBUH) taught his companions: "Trust your brother and try to come up with reasons for him and justification for what he does even if he did it seventy times."

(l) Sacrifice

Employees in an Islamic organizations are expected to adopt a culture of sacrifice; in particular, managers should make personal sacrifices. Employees are expected to follow managers' lead by making even greater sacrifices. The Prophet (PBUH) never took anything for personal gain or for his family's. This is demonstrated in the attitudes of the second *khaliph*, Umar Ibn al-Khatab, and the third *khaliph*, Uthman Ibn 'Afaan. A culture of sacrifice can contribute to the development of harmony and unity of various groups working together in an organization. This will assist them in attaining the organization's goals.

(m) Physical Health

The physical fitness of employees is very crucial, and Muslims are reminded by the Prophet Muhammad (PBUH) that "a strong believer is better than the believer who is weak in physical strength." The physical health of employees is associated with their ability to perform their tasks. Sick employees cannot accomplish their assigned tasks. Islamic organizations have to ensure and accustom employees to engage in physical exercise frequently as well as to maintain their endurance for a certain period, which will benefit the organization.

(n)   Neatness and Cleanliness

Muslims' personal appearance should be neat and clean. Allah (SWT) loves Muslims who are physically presentable and very concerned with cleanliness. The Prophet Muhammad (PBUH) said, "Cleanliness is half of faith." The Prophet (PBUH) also said, "Allah is beautiful and He likes beauty." These also relate to dressing. Employees are encouraged to dress in an Islamic way, which can lessen problems in the workplace such as sexual harassment and create productive working surroundings.

(o)   Brotherly Relations

Islam introduces a typical and glorious cultural concept of employee management relations. All Muslims are brothers and should help each other. Islam teaches the maintenance of good relations, while many *hadiths* of the Prophet Muhammad (PBUH) instill the importance of brotherhood, including the following:

When you meet him, salute him, when he calls you, respond to him. When he seeks advice, give him advice. When he sneezes and praises Allah, respond to him. When he falls ill, visit him. When he dies, follow him (the funeral bier).

(p)   Performing Compulsory Prayer

In an Islamic organization, the rules for performing worship must be accommodated. For Muslims, performing compulsory prayers (five times daily) is an instruction from Allah (SWT). The Prophet Muhammad (PBUH) said that prayer (*salah*) is "the best deed." Prayer is so meaningful in Muslims' life. One day, the Prophet Muhammad (PBUH) asked his companions, "Do you think that dirt can remain on a person bathing five times a day in a brook running in front of his door?" "No," answered his companions, "No dirt can remain on his body." Then the Prophet (PBUH) said, "So, exactly similar is the effect of Salah offered five times a day. With the grace of Allah, it washes away all sins."

(q)   Forbidding libel and slander

Islam prohibits the libeling or slandering of anyone, Muslim or non-Muslim. These actions spread hostility and create conflict among people, including in an organization. Both can diminish good deeds and add bad ones that cause embarrassment. Islamic organizations have to ensure to avoid these disgraceful actions by their members.

Both libeling and slandering are strongly prohibited by Allah (SWT). One who does these things is like a person who eats the meat of his dead brother. The message

Table 6.1 Prominent Islamic teachings based on Qur'an verses

Prominent features of Islamic culture	Qur'an verses
Maintaining trust in Allah	Al Imran, 3:159
Missionary spirit	Ash Shura, 41:33; An Nahl, 16:125; Al Imran, 3:104; Luqman, 31:32; Yusuf, 12:108
Hard work	An Najm, 53:30; 40–41, Ar Rad, 13:11; Al Hajj, 22:41; Al Jumua, 62:10
Absolute sincerity	Al Bayyina, 98:5
Excellence	Al Baqara, 2:148
Accountability	Al Zalzala, 99:7–8
Consultative decision making	Ash Shura, 42:38
Cultivating good and forbidden practices	Al Imran, 3:104; Luqman, 31:32; Yusuf, 12:108
Morality	Al Qalam, 68:4; Al Ahzab, 33:21
Knowledge	Fatir, 35:28; Al Furqan, 25:67
Justice	An Nisa, 4:58;135
Mutual trust	Al Hujraat, 49:6;12
Good behavior	Al Hujraat, 49:13; Al Baqara, 2:83
Mutual respect	Al Hujraat, 49:13
Neatness and cleanliness	An Naba, 78:4–5; Al Araf, 7:31
Physical fitness	Al Qasas, 28:26, Al Baqara, 2:247
Brotherly treatment of employees	Al Anfal, 8:63; At Taubah, 9:71, Al Hujraat, 49:10; Al Imran, 3:103
Compulsory prayer	Al Hajj, 22:35; Al Ankaboot, 29:45
Dressing Islamically	An Noor, 24:30; 30
Prohibiting backbiting and slander	Al Hujraat, 49:12

Source: Authors

is clear that Muslims must hate slander. In an organization, libel will create anger, doubt, and jealousy among coworkers and ruin the working environment. Table 6.1 summarizes the prominent Islamic teachings based on Qur'an verses.

6.2.2.1   The Islamic organizational culture model

There are four phases of creating an inspired organizational culture from an Islamic perspective (Hoque et al., 2010). The descriptions of each phase are as follows:

• Initiatives of founders of organization

Islamic organizational culture is created through initiatives taken by the founders. The founders know what the organization should do based on an agreed vision (Robbins and Judge, 2009). A distinct organizational culture cannot be created if the founders deviate from their original vision or are unable to make the right decisions.

• Selecting managers and operatives

Founders should choose individuals with similar thoughts as them (Robbins and Judge, 2009). To form a strong culture, the founders need to follow the agreed vision and qualities at this stage. The founders may have their own preferences for finding and recruiting individuals with certain competencies, skills, and knowledge to carry out tasks effectively and who are able to realize the vision of the founders. At this stage, adequate information must be given to applicants concerning the mission and vision of the organization. Candidates can learn about the organization, but if they find that the organization's values conflict their own, they can retract their application. With this, the selection process preserves the organization's culture by choosing or rejecting individuals who might agree or disagree with the organization's values.

- Top managers' role

  A major effect of organizational culture derives from the decisions of senior-level managers (Hambrick and Mason, 1984). The top-level management disseminates instructions related to the organizational culture to all employees. The behaviors and actions of senior executives convey the organization's values to employees. Employees can learn how decisions are made; the degree of freedom managers allow their employees; suitable forms of dress; mutual collaboration among employees; effective ways to execute the works; policies on promotions, rewards, punishments, job descriptions, responsibilities, and other progress (Robbins and Judge, 2009).

- Socialization

  This process is meant for new employees in adapting to the organization's culture (Rollag, 2004). The success of this process depends on the process of recruiting and selecting employees conducted by the organization. New employees are not forced to implement the existing culture, but they need to learn and adapt to the culture gradually. The success of employees' acculturation also depends on the level of perceived values of new employees and the top management preferences regarding socialization method (Robbins and Judge, 2009).

- Feedback

  The intended organizational culture cannot be created by one action but needs feedback, which will be collected from time to time. The founders will monitor this process continuously. Feedback is crucial in forming an organizational culture from an Islamic perspective. It is acknowledged that the intended organizational culture is the result of integrated and continuous attempts initiated by the top management and founders. Thus, an effective monitoring system is required to establish the intended organizational culture from an Islamic perspective. After receiving feedback, the required actions should be done to eliminate obstacles that block the formation of the desired organizational culture.

6.2.3   Organizational culture and firm performance

The organizational culture that relates to firm performance are attitudes of hard work and excellence. These two things are crucial for organizational performance. Managers and employees must incorporate them into their daily operational activities. In Islam, work is considered an act of *ibadah* (worship). A work dedicated by a Muslim is meant to gain worldly materials for fulfilling the life needs. Those worldly materials also can be used as tools or facilities to worship Allah (SWT). Neglecting work is not a part of the Islamic teachings.

The Prophet Muhammad is an icon in Islam who has given good life examples to his adherents. He always prayed to Allah (SWT) to seek help to keep him from laziness. As an entrepreneur, he worked hard, which made his partner, Khadijah, appreciate him. All his merits and virtues are remembered by Khadijah, who later became his wife. The Prophet Muhammad (PBUH) showed all Muslims a harmony between work and worship that can boost the quality of life. Muslims must be consistent in their act of worship and they also have to put unlimited efforts in their lifework, as was mentioned in a popular statement of a Muslim scholar: "Work hard (for making a living and survival) as if you are going to die." The Prophet (PBUH) also advises Muslims on the importance of work and said, "Verily the best things which ye eat are those which ye earn yourselves or which your children earn." In fact, the Prophet (PBUH) always teaches Muslims how to be productive, work effectively, and contribute to society.

Imam Hasan Al-Basri (one of the scholars of Islam) was asked about the secret behind his asceticism. The Imam replied with four things: One, I believe that my sustenance will never be stolen by anybody (but I have to work to obtain it). Two, I realize that a work that is mine must be undertaken by me, so I do not reduce my attempts in doing it. Three, I believe that Allah (SWT) is the Omnipresent (Al-Basiir – The All Seeing), so I do not like him watching me committing sins. Four, I understand that death may come at any time for me, so I get ready for it (through good deeds).

The employees in an organizations should work hard. Effort made to produce an excellent outcome may boost an individual's talents, competencies, and authenticities. An individual who aims for superior performance intends to attain achievements for their advantages and the organization. The Prophet (PBUH) instructs his followers to look for perfection in all subjects. It is a basic principle in Islamic culture. The Prophet (PBUH) said, "Verily, Allah loves that when any one of you does a job to perfect it." The Prophet (PBUH) also said, "Verily Allah has enjoined goodness to everything." Attaining superiority requires exceptional effort, and must avoid taking advantage of other people in doing works. The Prophet's (PBUH) noble companions showed Muslims practices of perfection. The Prophet (PBUH) also said, "The most merciful in my Ummah is Abu Bakr, the most pious is Omar, the most genuinely honest is Uthman, the most fair is Ali bin Abi taleb, the one who knows best how to recite The Quran is Ubayy Ibn Ka'b, and the one who has most knowledge about what is lawful and what is prohibited is Mu'adh Ibn Jabal. All people have a trustworthy guardian, and the trustworthy guardian of this people is Abu Ubayd Ibn al-jarah."

Muslims achieve superiority by doing the best deeds, while they are struggling to attain good ethical values of *al-muhsineen* (those who do virtues). It also means that Muslims need to follow in the footsteps of other pious adherents of the Prophet (PBUH) who achieved excellence in worship and worldly works. The Prophet Muhammad (PBUH) said, "If you pray, pray well, and if you fast, fast well." Managing time properly is crucial for Muslims because it could give motivation to do great deeds that will be richly rewarded. Wasting time is not an action of Muslims. When Muslims abuse the time given to them, they are considered losers. Certainly, excellence is a basic aim of a Muslim life. Directors, managers, or supervisors who are Muslims must be sure to achieve excellent results in their daily works and for their organization.

Performance is the result of effort aimed at achieving a certain goal. Thus, performance is the ability to do a job based on certain knowledge. There are indicators for a good Muslim in implementing Islamic values. Among others, that a Muslim does not think only about happiness in the world but also happiness in the hereafter or looking after a balance in life, how to survive doing something in a better way by

Table 6.2 Dimensions of *Al-Falah*

Khalifa (2001):	Yousef (2001):
1. Dynamic (strive to thrive)	1. *Halal* – Livelihood in accordance with teachings of Allah SWT and *Shariah*
2. Universal (implying the endeavors of one's entire life)	2. *Qanaah* – Be pleased and thankful with one's earnings
3. Ethical (be righteous in intentions and deeds to be blessed)	3. *Taufiq* – Asking for the blessing of Allah in proportion to one's expectation
4. Continuity (enjoyed both in worldly life and in the hereafter)	4. *Sa'adah* – Spiritual happiness
	5. *Jannah* – Worldly success should act as the bridge to ultimate success in the life hereafter (paradise)

Source: Authors

working hard, and acquiring some wealth to give to orphanages or those in need. These are related to an intention, plan, or aim that could be created by an individual but all will be decided by Allah SWT.

The measures of performance are still debatable. Masuo et al. (2001) suggested that nonmonetary measures of satisfaction, personal development, achievement, and satisfaction are the most important (Haber and Reichel, 2005). However, many studies associated with performance measures exclude religiosity as a factor. The religiosity factor is discussed comprehensively in Islamic teachings as it is an integrated measure of financial or nonfinancial success that refers to everlasting welfare and blessing called *al-falah* (Ahmad, 2006). Meanwhile, Yousef (2001) explained *al-falah* as a way to attain greater reward by seeking the pleasures of Allah (SWT) and motivates all Muslims to make their best effort in their work. This is an outcome in the Islamic performance model. Siddiqi (1979) added that *al-falah* can be attained merely through an ethical approach to human matters. Below are the dimensions of *al-falah* proposed by both authors (Table 6.2).

Satisfaction in Islamic terms is *qonaah*. Muslims do not have this behavior except those who are given guidance and guarded by Allah from evil zeal, stinginess, and avarice (Khalifa, 2001). An instance of *qonaah* is shown in the salary received by a Muslim who works for an Islamic organization. He or she may get a smaller salary for his/her work but perceive higher satisfaction in his/her work because of the rights granted or allowed to perform Islamic obligations such as prayer (salah) during working hours (Sharfuddin, 1995). Thus, satisfaction in Islam refers to the act of meeting religious duties.

6.2.4   Organizational culture and knowledge creation capability

According to Barney (1986), organizational culture is one of the crucial driving factors behind any movement in an organization. It affects the dissemination of knowledge, interactions, and the perceived values of organization members. It also has an important impact on knowledge creation capability. To explore in detail the effect of organizational culture on knowledge creation capability, three components of organizational culture, individualism-collectivism, uncertainty avoidance, and power distance, must be in place and should be conceptualized as organizational values.

Hofstede (2001) posited that individualism-collectivism is a significant dimension of organizational culture. Individualism is defined as a condition in which personal interests are considered more important than the interests of the group, while collectivism means the converse (Wagner, 1995). Individualism focuses on independence, whereas collectivism stresses interdependence (Wuyts and Geyskens, 2005). In individualist organizations, employees are likely to be seen as individuals because they feel that their personal values are more important than the company's objectives, while in collectivist organizations employees maintain collaborations to uphold organizational values (Chen et al., 1998).

Wang et al. (2011) added that collectivism has a significant influence on knowledge creation capability for two reasons:

1. Collectivism emphasizes collaboration and teamwork (Chen et al., 1998). Nahapiet and Ghoshal (1998) posited that collaboration creates openness and motivates people to exchange knowledge. Moreover, teamwork is conducive to the dissemination of knowledge and is a way to encourages creativity (Wagner, 1995). Thus, collectivism has a significant effect on knowledge creation capability because it can be used in promoting knowledge exchange (Nahapiet and Ghoshal, 1998; Smith et al., 2005). Conversely, individualism focuses on the quest of personal goals but one must be always ready to communicate with any group members (Wagner, 1995). Thus, members in individualist organizations rarely exchange knowledge with others, which hinders knowledge creation (Bochner and Hesketh, 1994).

2. Members of collectivist organizations choose cooperation to promote organizational values and appreciate knowledge exchange (Bates et al., 1995). Conversely, members in individualist organizations consider personal values more significant than organizational objectives (Chen et al., 1998), so they recognize values only from knowledge exchange (Nahapiet and Ghoshal, 1998; Smith et al., 2005).

Uncertainty avoidance is associated with the degree to which an organization finds itself threatened by and attempts to avoid uncertainty (Hofstede, 2001). The impact of uncertainty avoidance on knowledge creation capability is negative. Organizations that are low in uncertainty avoidance perceive uncertainty, take risks, compromise on a diverse set of opinions and behaviors, and dare to oppose existing routines through forming new knowledge (Cakar and Erturk, 2010). Conversely, organizations that are high in uncertainty avoidance require consistency and conformity, and selections are likely to be rational (Erramilli, 1996), so they are more likely to defend the constancy of the current knowledge base rather than acquiring new knowledge (Bochner and Hesketh, 1994). Therefore, low uncertainty avoidance organizations have better motivation to form new knowledge and boost their knowledge creation capabilities.

Moreover, the eagerness of organizations to test new ideas and take risks has a positive impact on knowledge exchange (Cakar and Erturk, 2010). Organizations that are low in uncertainty avoidance drive employees to test and exchange ideas and knowledge. Conversely, organizations that dislike risk taking and testing new ideas will move against disseminating and combining ideas and knowledge (Smith et al., 2005). As a result, uncertainty avoidance drives such organizations away from promoting knowledge creation capability.

6.2.5   Organizational culture and organizational change

A change within an organization is associated with changes in tasks. A process of analyzing gaps between the past and present is needed for future outcomes. Organizational change indicates a diversity of human activities and interactions on technical aspects which are interrelated dimensions in the organization. Individual attitudes toward change may vary. It is hard to change attitudes because of resistance. Some are more resistant to change and others are more amenable to change. The resistance to organizational change may derive from one or more factors such as huge changes in task, reduced economic assurance, psychological threats, ruin in social compositions, and lowering of status.

There are three types of individual or group reactions to organizational change:

1. Affective. This reaction is related to the perceived satisfaction or anxiety about change.

2. Cognitive. This reaction is related to opinions associated with utility and necessity and about the knowledge required to deal with change.

3. Instrumental. This reaction is related to actions already undertaken or which will be undertaken to deal with change.

Meanwhile, there are three types of attitudes toward change:

1. The affective component includes how a person senses an object, which shows assessment and emotion, and is often expressed as like or dislike for the object.

2. The cognitive component of an attitude comprises the information possessed by a person about an individual or thing that is based on what he/she believes is true.

3. The behavioral trend emphasizes the manner of a person to act toward an object.

6.3   Work ethics, leadership, and organizational culture

6.3.1   Islamic work ethic and organizational culture

Ethics is one of the most commonly discussed topics in recent years, including the Islamic work ethic (IWE). The discussion on the IWE emerged with an emphasis on promoting better relationships among people. In Islamic teachings, all people have to build relationships with their God (*hablum mina Allah*) and among themselves (*hablum minannas*). The IWE is related to *akhlaqul karimah*, which the Prophet Muhammad (PBUH) asked the Muslims to adopt in their daily business activities.

Employees have a strong commitment to their organization not merely based on their benefits package or compensation but on the IWE as well. Muslims who wish to be granted the pleasure of Allah may achieve this by applying the core values of ethics (Ahmad, 2006).

The IWE is defined as the set of moral principles rooted in Qur'an and *sunnah*, which are closely related to *al-khuluq*, which concerns Islamic values, beliefs, and practices (Arslan, 2001). It inspires employees have trust in the workplace, which will strengthen social business accountabilities (Ali, 2005) through hard work, commitment, dedication, creativity, and cooperation (Yousef, 2001). The IWE is meant for life fulfillment and is related to business initiatives with the highest tribute (Ahmad, 1976), which also serves as criteria for evaluating performance in positive or negative terms (Al-Sa'adan, 2005). Believers in Islam who practice IWE seem to be more committed to their organizations (Yousef, 2001). As servants of God, Muslims must monitor and be involved in implementing IWE in business applications and actions within an organization (Beekun and Badawi, 2005). Nasr (1984) asserted that the IWE must be a serious consideration because it is the ideal which Muslims need to realize.

Yousef (2001) differentiated between Islamic and Protestant work ethics (IWE vs. PWE), though both emphasize dedication to work, commitment, hard work, creativity, avoidance of unethical means of wealth accumulation, collaboration, and competitiveness in the workplace. However, unlike the PWE, the IWE focuses more on intention than on outcomes, stresses duties to society, emphasizes goodness and justice, and sees involvement in economic activities as a duty. It is asserted by Esposito (2005) that Islam embraces both private and public life and affects not only religious aspects but also social behavior.

The most popular measurement scale of the IWE was developed by Ali (1988), which was then used by researchers in both organizational and management contexts (Yousef, 2001; Rahman et al. 2006; Ali and Al-Kazemi, 2007; Khalil and Abu-Saad, 2009; Kumar and Rose, 2010; Wahab and Rafiki, 2014). Table 6.3 shows the elements of the IWE as proposed by Ali (1988) with the reference from the Qur'an (Table 6.3).

Morality is associated with the culture of an organization. *Akhlaq*, or moral character, is important as an indication of the perfect Muslim. In fact, a knowledgeable person is useless without good character. The Prophet Muhammad (PBUH) said,

Table 6.3 Reference to the Islamic work ethic in the Qur'an

Subject	Al-Qur'an verses
Agreements and promises	Ar-Rad 13:25, Al-Qasas 28:28, Yunus 10:71
Consideration for others	An-Nisaa' 4:36, Al-Mumtahina 60:9
Consultation	Ash-Shura 42:38, Taha 20:103, Al-Kahf 18:22
Continuous improvement	Al-Araf 7:42
Cooperation	Al-Hujraat 49:9, Maryam 19:96
Equality and unity	Al-Isra' 17:35
Fairness in dealings	Al-Anaam 6:152, Al-Mumtahina 60:8, An-Najm 53:32, Al-Maida 5:8
Fairness in wages	Al-Imran 3:57, Saba' 34:37
Hard work	Al-Baqara 2:62; 82, Al-Anaam 6:135
Helping others	As-Saff 61:14, An-Nahl 16:97, Yunus 10:41
Honesty and justice	Al-Baqara 2:177, Az-Zumar 39:2; 3
Humble	Hud 11:23
Patience	Hud 11:11
Righteous intention	Al-Baqara 2:25; 225, Al-Baqara 2:62, At-Taubah 9:105, As-Saff 61:8, Al-Qasas 28:19
Social order	Al-Imran 3:110, Al-Baqara 2:273
Truth	Al-Anfal 8:27, Yunus 10:61, An-Nur 24:8

Source: Ali (1988) and Rafiki and Wahab (2014)

"Indeed I have been sent to complete the perfecting of good character." The Prophet (PBUH) also said, "The best among you are those whose character is good." Then the wise man said, "When money is lost, nothing is lost, when health is lost, something is lost, but when character is lost, everything is lost."

6.3.2   Leadership and organizational commitment

Leadership is defined as an ability to influence a group of people toward a vision or set of goals. Compatible leadership approaches are needed in an extremely competitive and unpredictable business environment. It also emphasizes the effectiveness of empowering people.

Leadership is a process of influencing people and society where one individual can garner the support of others in the completion of ordinary duties. A leader is able to organize, give guidance and examples, point out directions, define purpose, engage in a common mission, and urge others to achieve objectives. Hidayat et al. (2017) mentions three leadership styles: transactional, transformational, and laissez-faire, discussed in previous studies. Buon (2014) stated that transformational style is the most cited style which emphasized relations created between leaders and followers. Leaders motivate and inspire followers based on their vision, values, ethics, and norms. Buon (2014) added that an organization led by a transformational leader has superior performance. Such leaders also create hope and lend confidence to their subordinates to deal with uncertain obstacles.

Meanwhile, the Islamic leadership style has a unique approach where it is committed to principles related to spiritual aspects and practices. This made it superior than other modern styles of leadership (Aabed, 2005). Haddara and Enanny (2009) added that leaders in Islam lead people and manage organizations with *amanah* (trust) and responsibility. These two principles must be held to be important by the leaders of an organization. Trust comes from God and people, so leaders must feel accountable to God and people for their trust.

Beekun and Badawi (1999) posited that Islamic leadership reflects a psychological bond between a leader and his followers, where a leader is expected to give guidance and care to followers. There are two main roles of a leader, first to be a servant-leader, or *sayyid al qawn khadimuhum*, where the leader becomes the servant of his followers; and second to be a guardian-leader, where the leader promotes his followers' wellbeing and motivates them to do what is right. Moreover, leaders in Islam must be committed to promoting Islamic moral character traits of *iman, islam, taqwa*, and *ihsan*. Other Islamic values that must be adopted by Muslim leaders are justice (Qur'an, 5:8), trust (Qur'an, 8:27), righteousness (Qur'an, 2:177), struggle toward self-improvement (Qur'an, 22:77–78), and promise keeping (Qur'an, 5:1).

Meanwhile, Moten (2011) stated that there are misperceptions about the values of Islamic leadership compared to the leadership styles adopted by secular societies, for a few reasons. First, Islam makes no distinction between spiritual and worldly matters. It addresses the rules of human behavior covering all facets of human existence. Religion is not a unit, department, or organization concern but a comprehensive reference (Iqbal, 1962, 2006). Furthermore, Moten (2011) posited that Islam does not discourage involvement in politics, nor does it promote corruption in politics. Second, the main principle of Islam is the unity and sovereignty of Allah or *tawhid*; no one has the power of control and command except Allah. This denies anyone who claims absolute right and power over anything. Finally, Islam rejects all temporal primacy and warns believers against using spiritual and ethical values for personal benefit. Both Muslim leaders and followers desire a life in compliance with *Shariah*.

Muslim leaders learn about management based on the possession of revealed knowledge and other Islamic sources. They implement initiatives and actions that comply with Islamic beliefs and practices. This is related to the concept of *tawheed* as practiced by the Prophet (PBUH) (Khaliq, 2007a, b).

Khan (1998) mentions that human beings were created with great qualities that can contribute to exceptional achievements, which require the implementation of specific Islamic principles. Hossain (2007) urges Muslim leaders to acknowledge the importance of the revealed sources of knowledge (Qur'an and *sunnah*). Understanding Islamic values will promote the culture of God-consciousness and justice within organizations while guarding against oppression (Khaliq, 2009).

Muslim authors continuously summarize and list Islamic leadership principles to this day. One of the principles is team building. Leaders have to strengthen the mental and physical fitness of teams, and this can be done by attending Friday (Juma'at) sermons, congregational prayers, and zikr circles (Kassem and Al-Buraey, as cited in Ismail, 2007). Khan (1998) wrote that the Prophet Muhammad (PBUH) as a leader had positive thoughts and was a results-oriented person. He always strove to be productive (Table 6.4).

Definitions of the concept of organizational commitment include the description of an individual's psychological bond to the organization, including a sense of job involvement, loyalty to, and belief in the values of the organization. Organizational commitment is characterized by employee acceptance of organizational goals and a willingness to exert effort on behalf of the organization.

Organizational commitment has several dimensions that are related to values compatible with the organization, employee fidelity to the organization, readiness to put effort into representing the organization, and preserve relationships in the organization. It is used positively to measure the organization's objectives and as a common platform in connecting employees and employer.

The supervisor must motivate employees and not only direct them to complete tasks. Leaders must motivate workers and communicate effectively with them, while managers must persuade, help, and guide employees in the execution of their decisions.

Employees may show signs of commitment to their employer as an expression of satisfaction to get support from their employer. The support of a direct supervisor can have a positive impact on employees, motivating them to avoid wrongdoing. Leadership style represents an imperative role in promoting effectiveness and efficiency in the organization, which then influences employee commitment. Hence in many studies, leadership style has a prominent relationship with organizational commitment. Leaders have a crucial impact in an organization in terms of establishing employees' commitment in accomplishing their jobs. Leaders also need to understand employees' needs as they will influence organizational commitment significantly.

Organizational culture is used as a significant influencer that spurs commitment and improved performance. The commitment of employees is determined by the level of happiness at work. Employees' emotional commitment to their organization will wane if they are not given opportunities to excel as expected. This will influence an individual's organizational commitment. Meanwhile, organizational culture can

Table 6.4 Islamic leadership principles and qualities

Begin from the possible	Turn minus into plus	Gradualism instead of radicalism	Receiving the message; a principle equated to the act of seeking advice and knowledge to show the right ways to followers
See advantage in disadvantage	The power of peace is stronger than the power of coercion	To be pragmatic in controversial matters	Disseminating the message; referring to the act of assigning tasks and confirming that they are well completed
Change the place of action	Not to be a dichotomous thinker	Eloquence (*fasah*)	Morality and piety (honesty and trust)
Make a friend out of an enemy	To avoid the battle as one's own favourable field	Patience (*sabr*)	Superior communication
Faith and belief	Knowledge and wisdom	Enterprise (*iqdam*)	Justice and compassion
Courage and determination	Mutual consultation and unity (fraternity and brotherhood)	Leniency (*lin*)	Patience and endurance
Commitment and sacrifice	Lifelong endeavour	Gratitude and prayers	Conviction (*yaqin*)
Mutual consultation (*shura*)	Knowledge (*ma'refah*)	Justice (*'adl*)	Self-sacrifice (*tadhyah*)
Humility Enterprise (*iqdam*)	Eloquence (*fasah*) Sovereignty (*al-siyadah*)	Patience (*sabr*) Mutual consultation (*al-shura*)	Leniency (*lin*) Justice (*al-'adalah*)
Equality (*al-musawat*)	Freedom (*al-hurriyyah*)	Enjoining what is right and forbidding evil	

Source: Khan (1998, 2007), Khaliq (2007a, b), Ismail (2007), Adnan (2006) and Lukman (1995)

also be regarded as a mediator to assist in creating organizational commitment. If the organizational culture is accepted by employees, this will contribute to better performance. Normally, the bureaucratic culture in an organization affects employee commitment and can hamper employee work effectiveness.

When the culture is supportive, it will bring significant outcomes that lead to increased commitment and engagement of employees. These correlations were confirmed in a study by Odom et al. (1990). These researchers also stated that an organization should develop an achievement-based culture or a mission culture so employees can be more committed to company objectives. Employees' commitment must be consistent and it should support company goals. Bureaucratic issues result in less commitment by employees in their daily work.

Chapter Highlights

This chapter provides insights into Islamic organizational culture. It has highlighted the roles of revelation, namely the holy Qur'an and the sayings (*hadith*) of the Prophet (PBUH), in determining the salient features of Islamic organizational culture. Using revelation as the main source of knowledge for developing organizational culture is the main difference between conventional and Islamic organizational cultures.

Being a leader and entrepreneur, the Prophet Muhammad (PBUH) provided an example of how Islamic organizational culture applied in all types of organizations, including business organizations. Comparing Western and Islamic organizational cultures, it can be concluded that both organizational cultures have many similarities. In fact, Islamic organizational culture is more comprehensive than its Western counterpart. Therefore, Muslim leaders and entrepreneurs should learn and apply Islamic organizational culture in their respective organizations as demonstrated by the Prophet (PBUH) in his life.

The analysis presented in this chapter provides a solid understanding of:

- the meaning of Islamic organizational culture;
- the salient features of Islamic culture;
- the relationship between organizational culture and firm performance;
- the relationship between organizational culture and knowledge creation capability;
- the relationship between organizational culture and organizational change;
- the meaning of the Islamic work ethic;
- the relationship between the Islamic work ethic and organizational culture;
- the relationship between leadership and organizational commitment; and
- Islamic leadership principles and qualities.

Discussion Questions

1. Define Islamic organizational culture. Compare it with conventional organizational culture.

2. Discuss five salient features of Islamic culture.

3. Discuss the Islamic organizational culture model.

4. How does organizational culture affect firm performance?

5. Discuss the relationship between organizational culture and knowledge creation capability.

6. How does culture spur change in organizations?

7. What is meant by Islamic work ethic? Compare it with the Protestant work ethic.

8. Discuss the relationship between organizational culture and Islamic work ethic.

9. Discuss the relationship between leadership and organizational commitment.

10. As a leader in an organization, why do you need to apply Islamic leadership principles and qualities? Discuss.

11. As a manager, what are initiatives can you take to ensure that your organization's culture is successfully influencing the firm performance and knowledge creation capability in your respective country and organization? Provide logical suggestions to support your recommendations.

12. As a leader, what is your approach to implementing Islamic leadership principles and qualities in an organization with employees of multiple races and religions? Provide evidence to back up your answer.

13. The Islamic work ethic and Islamic organizational culture are applicable in all organizations. What are the key challenges confronting you as a general manager in implementing both Islamic kinds of ethics and culture? Provide evidence-based recommendations.

Abbreviations

SWT	*Subhanahu Wa Ta'ala* or Glory to Him, the Exalted
PBUH	Peace Be Upon Him
IWE	Islamic work ethic
PWE	Protestant work ethic

Key Terms

Akhlaqul Karimah	*Ihsan*	*Tawhid*
Al Falah	*Ijma*	*Taqwa*
Al-Khuluq	*Iman*	*Tawakkul*
Al-Muhsineen	*Qanaah*	*Ummah*
Amanah	*Qiyas*	*Zakat*
Haram	*Riba*	*Zikr*
Halal	*Sunnah*	

Online Resources

Useful Websites

Harvard Business Review: https://hbr.org/topic/organizational-culture

World Bank Blogs: http://blogs.worldbank.org/category/tags/organizational-culture

Ernst & Young Global Limited: https://consulting.ey.com/

Society for Human Resource Management: https://www.shrm.org/resourcesand-tools/tools-and-samples/toolkits/pages/understandinganddevelopingorganizationalculture.aspx

The Oxford Review: https://www.oxford-review.com/what-is-an-organisational-culture/

Selected Bibliography

Aabed, A. (2005). A Study of Islamic Leadership Theory and Practice in K-12 Islamic Schools in Michigan (Unpublished doctoral thesis), University of Brigham Young, United States. Available at: http://scholarsarchive.byu.edu/cgi/viewcontent.cgi?article=1407&context=etd (Accessed 8 November 2017).

Adnan, A. (2006). A Study of Islamic Leadership Theory and Practice in K-12 Islamic School in Michigan. Available at: http://contentdm.lib.byu.edu/ETD/image/etd1273.pdf (Accessed 30 January 2017).

Ahmad, K. (1976). *Islam: Its Meaning and Message*. London: Islamic Council of Europe.

Ahmad, K. (2006). *Management from the Islamic Perspective*. Kuala Lumpur: International Islamic University Malaysia.

Al Sa'adan, A.B.M. (2005). An Introduction to a Seminar "Work Ethics in Public and Private Sectors" Conducted in General Management College in Saudi Arabia – Riyadh on Thursday, 20/1/1426 Hijri – 1/3/2005 Gregorian titled "Work Ethics and Complain Department Experience in Controlling Them."

Al-Bukhari, M.I.I. (1997). *The Translation of the Meanings of Sahih Al-Bukkari*. Riyadh: DarusSalam (Translated by M.M. Khan).

Ali, A. (1988). Scaling an Islamic Work Ethic. *The Journal of Social Psychology*, 128(5), 575–583.

Ali, A.J. (2005). *Islamic Perspectives on Management and Organisation*. Northampton: Edward Elgar.

Ali, A. and Al-Kazemi, A. (2007). Islamic Work Ethic in Kuwait. *Journal of Management Development*, 14(2), 366–375.

Altalib, H. (1991). *Training Guide for Islamic Workers*. Herndon: IIIT & IIFSO.

An-Nawawi, I.A.Z. (1993). *Riyadh As-Salleheen (Gardens of the Rightous People)*. Cairo: International Islamic Publishing House (Translated by A. Nassar, Original Work Published in Thirteenth Century).

Arslan, M. (2001). The Work Ethic Values of Protestant British, Catholic Irish and Muslim Turkish Managers. *Journal of Business Ethics*, 31, 321–339.

Ather, S.M. (2007) *Islamic Management and Business* (1st ed.). Chittagong: Noksha Publications.

Barney, J.B. (1986). Organizational Culture: Can It Be a Source of Sustained Competitive Advantage? *Academy of Management Review*, 11(3), 656–665.

Bates, K.A., Amundson, S.D., Schroeder, R.G. and Morris, W.T. (1995). The Crucial Interrelationship Between Manufacturing Strategy and Organizational Culture. *Management Science*, 41(10), 1565–1580.

Beekun, R. and Badawi, J. (1999). The Leadership Process in Islam. *Proteus-Shippensburg*, 16, 33–38.

Beekun, R.I. and Badawi, J.A. (2005). Balancing Ethical Responsibility Among Multiple or Ganisational Stakeholders: The Islamic Perspective. *Journal of Business Ethics*, 60(2), 131–145.

Bochner, S. and Hesketh, B. (1994). Power Distance, Individualism/Collectivism, and Job-Related Attitudes in a Culturally Diverse Work Group. *Journal of Cross-Cultural Psychology*, 25(2), 233–257.

Buon, T. (2014). *The Leadership Coach*. London: Hodder & Stoughton.

Cakar, N.D. and Erturk, A. (2010). Comparing Innovation Capability of Small and Medium-Sized Enterprises: Examining the Effects of Organizational Culture and Empowerment. *Journal of Small Business Management*, 48(3), 325–359.

Chen, C.C., Chen, X.P. and Meindl, J.R. (1998). How Can Cooperation Be Fostered? The Cultural Effects of Individualism-Collectivism. *Academy of Management Review*, 23(2), 285–304.

Erramilli, M.K. (1996). Nationality and Subsidiary Ownership Patterns in Multinational Corporations. *Journal of International Business Studies*, 27(2), 225–248.

Esposito, J.L. (2005). *Islam: The Straight Path* (Revised 3rd ed.). Oxford: Oxford University Press.

Haber, S. and Reichel, A. (2005). Identifying Measures of Small Ventures – The Case of the Tourism Industry. *Journal of Small Business Management*, 43(3), 257–286.

Haddara, M. and Enanny, F. (2009). *Leadership: An Islamic Perspective*. Canada: Memorial University of Newfoundland. Available at http://manal.ca/sites/default/files/Leadership.pdf (Accessed 6 November 2017).

Hambrick, D.C. and Mason, P.A. (1984). Upper Echelons: The Organization as a Reflection of Its Top Managers. *The Academy of Management Review*, 9(2), 193–206.

Hidayat, S.E., Rafiki, A. and Aldoseri, M.M. (2017). Application of Leadership Style in Government Organizations: A Survey in the Kingdom of Bahrain. *International Journal of Islamic and Middle Eastern Finance and Management*, 10(4), 581–594.

Hofstede, G. (1991). *Cultures and Organizations: Software of the Mind*. London: McGraw-Hill.

Hofstede, G. (2001). *Culture's Consequences* (2nd ed.). Thousand Oaks: Sage.

Hoque, N., Mamun, A. and Kabir, M.J. (2010). Leadership Traits from Islamic Perspectives. *Bangladesh Journal of Islamic Thought*, 6(8), 87–108.

Hossain, M. (2007). Case Studies of Muslim Managed Organizations in Bangladesh. paper presented at International Conference, Management from Islamic Perspective at Hilton Kuala Lumpur, 15–16 May, Organized by KENMS.

Iqbal, M. (1962). *The Reconstruction of Religious Thought in Islam*. Lahore: Sheikh Muhammad Ashraf, p. 2.

Iqbal, M. (2006). *Bang-e-Dara*. Lahore: Allama Iqbal Urdu Cyber Library Network, Iqbal Academy.

Ismail, Y. (2007). A Proposed Approach to the Development of Islamic Management as a Discipline. paper presented at International Conference, Management from Islamic Perspective at Hilton Kuala Lumpur, 15–16 May, Organized by KENMS.

Khalifa, A.S. (2001). *Towards and Islamic Foundation of Strategic Business Management*. Kuala Lumpur: International Islamic University Malaysia.

Khalil, M. and Abu-Saad, I. (2009). Islamic Work Ethic Among Arab College Students in Israel. *Cross Cultural Management: An International Journal*, 16(4), 333–346.

Khaliq, A. (2007a). Leadership and Work Motivation from Islamic Perspective. paper presented at International Conference, Management from Islamic Perspective at Hilton Kuala Lumpur, 15–16 May, Organized by KENMS.

Khaliq, A. (2007b). *Management from Islamic Perspectives – Principles and Practices*. Kuala Lumpur: Research Centre, IIUM.

Khaliq, A. (2009). Leadership and Work Motivation from the Cross-Cultural Perspective. *International Journal of Commerce & Management*, 29(1), 72–84.

Khan, M.W. (1998). Prophetic Principles of Success. Minaret, September, pp. 8–9. Available at: http://makkah.wordpress.com/leadership-and-islam/ (Accessed 17 December 2017).

Khan, A. (2007). Islamic Leadership: A Success Model for Everyone and All Times. Available at: http://americanchronicle.com/articles/view/33073 (Accessed 5 January 2017).

Kumar, N. and Rose, R.C. (2010). Examining the Link Between Islamic Work Ethic and Innovation Capability. *Journal of Management Development*, 29(1), 79–93.

Lukman, T. (1995). *The Islamic Polity and Leadership*. Klang: Baron Production Sdn Bhd.

Masuo, D., Fong, G., Yanagida, J. and Cabal, C. (2001). Factors Associated with Business and Family Success: A Comparison of Single Manager and Dual Manager Family Business Households. *Journal of Family and Economic Issues*, 22(1), 55–73.

Mitroff, I.I. (2003). Do Not Promote Religion Under the Guise of Spirituality. *Organization*, 10(2), 375–382.

Moten, A.R. (2011). Leadership in the West and the Islamic World: A Comparative Analysis. *World Applied Sciences Journal*, 15(3), 339–349.

Nahapiet, J. and Ghoshal, S. (1998). Social Capital, Intellectual Capital, and the Organizational Advantage. *Academy of Management Review*, 23(2), 242–266.

Nasr, S. (1984). Islamic Work Ethics. *Hamdard Islamicus*, 7(4), 25–35.

Odom, R.Y., Boxx, W.R. and Dunn, M.G. (1990) Organizational Cultures, Commitment, Satisfaction and Cohesion. *Public Productivity and Management Review*, 14(2), 157–169.

Rafiki, A. and Wahab, K.A. (2014). Islamic Principles and Values in Organization. *Asian Social Science*, 10(9), 1–7.

Rahman, N.M., Muhamad, N. and Othman, A.S. (2006). The Relationship Between Islamic Work Ethics and Organizational Commitment: A Case Analysis. *Malaysian Management Review*, 41(1).

Rego, A., Cunha, M.P.E. and Souto, S. (2007). Workplace Spirituality, Commitment, and Self-Reported Individual Performance: An Empirical Study. *Management Research: The Journal of the Iberoamerican Academy of Management*, 5(3), 163–183.

Robbins, S.P. and Judge, T.A. (2009). *Organizational Behavior* (13th ed.). Upper Saddle River: Prentice-Hall.

Rollag, K. (2004). The Impact of Relative Tenure on Newcomer Socialization Dynamics. *Journal of Organizational Behavior*, 25, 853–872.

Shahin, A.I. and Wright, P.L. (2004). Leadership in the Context of Culture – An Egyptian Perspective. *The Leadership & Organization Development Journal*, 25(6), 499–511.

Sharfuddin, I.M. (1987). Toward an Islamic Administrative Theory. *The American Journal of Social Sciences*, 4(2), 229–244.

Sharfuddin, I.O. (1995). Motivation the Cornerstone of Human Performance: an Islamic and Comparative Perspective. In F.R. Faridi (Ed.) *Islamic Principles of Business Organisation and Management*. New Delhi: Qazi Publishers and Distributors.

Siddiqi, M.N. (1979). *The Economic Enterprise in Islam* (2nd ed.). Lahore: Islamic Publication.

Smith, K.G., Collins, C.J. and Clark, K.D. (2005). Existing Knowledge, Knowledge Creation Capability, and the Rate of New Product Introduction in High-Technology Firms. *Academy of Management Journal*, 48(2), 346–357.

Syed, I.B. (2002). Shoura, Islamic Research Foundation International. Available at: www.irfi.org (Accessed 19 September 2017).

Trad, K. (1998). Leadership. Available at: www.speednet.com.au/,keysar/leader,1.htm (Accessed 27 November 2017).

Wagner, J.A. III (1995). Studies of Individualism-Collectivism: Effects on Cooperation. *Academy of Management Journal*, 38(1), 152–172.

Wahab, K.A. and Rafiki, A. (2014). Measuring Small Firm Entrepreneur's Performance Based on Al-Falah. *World Applied Sciences Journal*, 29(12), 1532–1539.

Wang, D., Su, Z. and Yang, D. (2011). Organizational Culture and Knowledge Creation Capability. *Journal of Knowledge Management*, 15(3), 363–373.

Wuyts, S. and Geyskens, I. (2005). The Formation of Buyer-Supplier Relationships: Detailed Contract Drafting and Close Partner Selection. *Journal of Marketing*, 69(4), 103–117.

Yousef, D.A. (2001). Islamic Work Ethic: A Moderator Between Organizational Commitment and Job Satisfaction in a Cross-Cultural Context. *Personnel Review*, 30(2), 152–169.

ISLAMIC MARKETING

7

Hurrem Yilmaz, Osama Sam Al-Kwifi and Zafar U. Ahmed

American University of Ras Al Khaimah, UAE

Qatar University, Qatar

Learning Outcomes

LO1: Understand the development of marketing concepts and how Islam supports effective marketing strategies.

LO2: Describe marketing strategies and understand challenges of targeting Muslim markets.

LO3: Explain the main concepts related to creating, pricing, branding, packaging, and labeling products to satisfy Muslim consumers.

Contents

Islamic marketing has made great strides since its formal conception and has managed to establish itself as a distinct discipline. This chapter provides a comprehensive review of Islamic marketing and its recent evolution as an important field that complements current marketing practices. To establish a foundation for an ethical framework, the chapter starts by introducing the relationship between Islam and business activities, which is built upon creating a value-maximizing approach based on the interests of all stakeholders. Resources and reports that describe Islamic markets across the world are reviewed to define ways to segment the large Muslim population. Then the principles of Islamic marketing are presented as a guide for businesses aiming to penetrate Muslim markets through an appropriate mixed marketing strategy. Examples of successful companies and social media platforms are presented as case studies. The chapter ends with a review of state-of-the-art research on consumer neuroscience.

Egeturk

In the 1960s certain European countries that were steadily reaching the heights of economic development compensated for their own shrinking workforces by importing workers from underdeveloped or developing nations. Worker migrations flowed not only from regions like Spain, Portugal, Greece, Italy, and the Balkans but from Muslim-majority countries like Turkey as well. Along with a variety of other issues arising from cultural differences, Muslim immigrants also encountered obstacles concerning food and drink.

These dietary difficulties advanced along two major lines:

1. The prevalence of pork or pork-related products and inevitably running into them.

2. The absence of tastes and flavors that were familiar to Muslims. Turkish immigrants, for example, longed for items like spicy sausage (*sujuk*), seasoned dried cured beef (*pastirma*), olives (*zeytin*), salty white cheese similar to feta (*beyaz peynir*), pickles, and certain types of vegetables that were rare or not found in Europe at that time.

While such small details may seem insignificant, they were in fact crucial to our lives, and the solutions to these sorts of dietary differences were not easily found and actually took many years to figure out. Some individuals with enterprising spirits turned these cultural differences into opportunities and eventually went from running small-scale shops to heads of giant corporations. Consider Burhan Ongoren, for example, also known as the founder and owner of Egeturk, which is the leader in Germany in Turkish sausage products. He started out making sausages at home for his family, but after offering some to friends as well, he found there was great demand for them and started producing more. Eventually, his small-time home-based operation turned into the major meat and sausage empire it is known as today.

7.1   Introduction

Between 2010 and 2050, the world's population is expected to rise to 9.3 billion, an increase of 35 percent. During the same period, the Muslim population—a relatively young population with high fertility rates—will grow by 73 percent (Pew Report, 2009). With an approximate 1.8 billion Muslims in the world today (23 percent of the world's population), it is unquestionable that the Muslim consumer segment represents a remarkable opportunity for businesses and marketers across the world. In fact, Western companies are becoming increasingly interested in Muslim markets, and some companies that have already started to build their brands across the Islamic world are working hard to reach inclusive global domination by expanding within the largest segment of the world's population.

While Muslim consumers are distributed across more than 65 countries, they all have their local preferences. For instance, India (a Hindu-majority country) has more Muslims than any other country in the world (even more than Indonesia, the largest Muslim nation in the world). Although there are commonalities in Muslim consumers' behaviors, such as dietary, lifestyle, and financial rules related to the Islamic faith, they are not entirely homogeneous. Other than following the same faith, the Muslims of Indonesia, Bosnia, and Nigeria have little in common. They have even less in common with the predominantly Turkish Muslims in Germany, and very little in common with the Algerian and Moroccan Muslims of France or the South Asian Muslims of Britain. Such variations in Muslim consumer tastes stem from variables related to the social and cultural manifestations of each country and to the percentage of the Muslim population in that country, whether it is a majority or minority. Because Islam has no geographic boundaries, we can find large Muslim-minority communities across countries including China, Britain, the United States, Russia, Canada, Australia, Germany, and France. In addition, the wealth of Muslim countries has a huge impact on Muslim consumer behavior, such as the Arabian Gulf Cooperation Council (GCC), a regional intergovernmental political and economic organization, which has major purchasing power compared to other countries.

Since Islam came into existence, Muslims have been conducting their business activities based on Islamic laws (*Shariah*), where business practices and regulations are known and well documented. While no specific books talk explicitly about the current link between Islam and modern business activities, recent interest in exploring the influence of Islam on various business activities and marketing practices has grown (Saeed et al., 2001; Rice, 1999; Wilson, 2006; Alserhan, 2015).

Thus, it is imperative for companies to understand the dynamics of Muslim consumers when marketing to countries that contain a Muslim population. In the past, Western companies used their product and brand names to enter global markets; however, with the rapid development of Islamic countries and the ambition of Muslims in a branded world, these companies need to have a better understanding of the Islamic perspective of Muslim consumers. This issue is relevant for all companies from Muslim and non-Muslim countries because it enables these companies to act on the basis of factors that shape the behavior of Muslim consumers (Saeed et al., 2001). For this reason, there is a need to understand the concept of Islamic branding and marketing and to know how it fits within modern marketing practices.

7.2 Islam and business

The relationship between Islam and business has deep roots, going back to the Prophet Muhammad's (pbuh) era of Islam 14 centuries ago. However, interest in understanding the relationship between Islam and consumer behavior and marketing activities has grown rapidly in recent years. This can be seen by tracking: (1) the interest in creating specialist journals and the mounting number of research publications; (2) the increased number of organizations worldwide that authorize *halal* (permissible) products; (3) the increased activities of multinational companies to expand globally in Muslim countries, which represent an important market segment; (4) the growing movement toward establishing a Muslim trading bloc, which will take some time to bring to fruition; and (5) the financial crisis of 2008, which devastated world markets and revealed the need for more socially responsible business practices.

Islam is a way of life that touches all aspects of daily human actions, including commercial, social, and spiritual activities. Islamic teachings cover all aspects of economic activities, including marketing, financing, contracting, selling, and promotion. In Islam, all business activities are governed by two doctrines: (1) obedience to the moral order of God and (2) empathy and mercy to other humans, which involves avoiding doing harm to others and preventing unethical practices (Niazi, 1996).

Islamic teachings and laws are based upon primary and secondary sources. The primary sources are: (1) the Qur'an (Islamic holy book), which includes many commandments, rules, and principles on the behavior and actions of Muslims; the commands of the Qur'an are fixed and represent the main foundation of Muslim daily practices; and (2) the *sunnah*, which represents the behaviors and known practices of the Prophet Muhammad, most of which have been documented in the *hadith* literature. The *sunnah* contains many things that the Prophet Muhammad said, did, or agreed to, which showed his life as a true reflection of the Qur'an. The Prophet Muhammad was also a very successful businessman before receiving the prophecy. Thus, he was familiar with the business domain and best practices that were shaped by the commands of the Qur'an. The Prophet Muhammad also taught people how to carry out fair business activities, such as avoid increasing prices in competition and cheating in the selling process. The *sunnah* provides details of what is stated generally in the Qur'an.

The secondary sources are (1) *ijma* (consensus), where Islamic scholars can agree on matters within the limits of the Qur'an and the *sunnah* after extensive evaluation; (2) *qiyas* (analogy), which generalizes the general principles from the Qur'an and the *sunnah* to similar settings; and (3) *urf* (tradition), where a common practice among Muslims is adopted based on their common habits, providing it does not contradict the primary sources. This wide spectrum of resources provides Muslims with rich references to use when addressing any issues that could arise in their daily lives and offers them remarkable flexibility for finding solutions to challenges as they arise in the business domain. Some solutions might be customized to fit the needs of Muslims in a specific culture or region based on its unique characteristics and conditions, which could thus lead to slight variations in Muslim consumer practices across the world.

7.3   Islamic values for an ethical framework

The Islamic perspective on business practices has been largely ignored by Western researchers, which could be due to the weak economic activities and contributions of Muslim countries (Prahalad, 2004). However, recent years have witnessed a rising interest in exploring the influence of Islamic laws on business activities and understanding how Islamic institutions and principles can provide essential guidance for today's business practices (Rice, 1999; Siddiqi, 1992; Khan, 1995). Many researchers have devoted efforts to studying the linkages between religious practices and business ethics since this has become a critical subject for investigation (Saeed et al., 2001; Dubinsky et al., 1991; Green, 1993; Vasquez-Parraga and Kara, 1995).

Based on the aforementioned sources of Islamic laws, it is possible to build an entire socioeconomic system that guides the ethical behavior of Muslims and provides practical solutions that cover the relationship between consumers and sellers and employers and employees (Rice, 1999). Islam provides a set of key values that guide the behavior of all involved parties to establish an ethical system aimed at creating fair business practices and ensuring each individual behaves responsibility and honestly (Alserhan, 2015; Siddiqi, 1981). The following values reflect the most important key business ethical values: (1) prohibition of bribery: as a form of corruption, bribery is strongly condemned, and any business activities based on this action are considered unethical; (2) prohibition of deception and cheating: because honesty and clear communication are the foundation of business, sellers should not exaggerate or lie about their products and services, and it is prohibited to acquire assets or capital by deception or fraud; (3) greater social responsibility: though individuals have the freedom to conduct their business and make decisions, they are expected to contribute to the community's welfare and social responsibility; and (4) justice: all business parties under various conditions are required to ensure justice is a central business matter; for example, abusing monopoly power to overcharge consumers is condemned (Wilson, 2006).

While Islam cannot force businesses to sell their goods at a certain price or increase market domination, it sets certain guidelines to conduct business in a way that guarantees a fair outcome for all involved parties and emphasizes social responsibility (Chapra, 1992). The concept of social responsibility is at the heart of ethical values in Islam, which is much needed in the current business environment to sustain the interests of stakeholders, the natural environment, and the community (Beekun, 1996).

Saeed et al. (2001) argued that current international marketing ethics should be developed in the direction of a global moral order to reflect the natural universal desire for a stricter ethical system. They proposed a value-maximization approach based on equity and justice (Miskawayh Ibn, 1968), which constitutes "just dealing" and "fair trading" based on Islamic marketing practices. Such an approach can achieve a broader welfare for society in a number of ways: (1) it is grounded in principles based on the Qur'an, which are absolute in their terms and not subject to vague interpretation by individual quirks and needs; and (2) it is focused on value maximization for all parties involved in business activities rather than an egocentric search for profit maximization.

This demonstrates that Islamic values and principles have a strong foundation on which to influence human conscience toward establishing a reliable ethical system, and it emphasizes value maximization for society at large based on the concept of justice. In practice, this involves fair trading practices that consider the interests of consumers and sellers and avoid causing harm (or loss) to others to increase self-interest.

7.4   Islamic consumer behavior

The interest in understanding Islamic consumer behavior and its roots in religiosity has increased significantly in the last few decades and is under constant development (Mustafar and Borhan, 2013; Wilson and Grant, 2013; Alserhan, 2010; Alam et al., 2011). The literature contains a significant number of studies that explore Islamic consumer behavior from different perspectives, including, for example, Islamic banking (Zebal and Saber, 2014), Islamic mortgages (Amin et al., 2014), Muslim shopping behavior (Al-Kwifi et al., 2019), Islamic food selection (Awan et al., 2015), *halal* cosmetic products (Abd Rahman et al., 2015), and Muslim clothing choices (Bachleda et al., 2014).

Culture is the main external factor that shapes consumption behavior (Shaw and Clarke, 1998; Schouten and McAlexander, 1995), where it symbolizes lifestyles and beliefs that are manipulated by our environment and transferred to future generations. In other words, it incorporates patterns of behavior, acquired reactions, fundamental beliefs, customs, and conventional ways of thinking. Thus, the effect of culture on individuals' lives is so intense that it can even alter consumer intentions and choices (Chang, 2005). Although culture is the most central determining factor of human desires and behavior, religion is a key determinant influencing consumption behavior. Based on recognition, many scholars have suggested that religion is part of a culture that can influence consumer behavior (Kotler, 2000; Al-Kwifi et al., 2019), which emphasizes that consumers who follow a religion hold certain values that can influence their shopping patterns and decisions. Although religion was found to be an important cultural factor that impacts consumer behavior, Islam is not a culture that evolves over time but rather is a unique lifestyle that can create a set of behaviors called "Islamic consumer behavior." Such behavior is reflected in every aspect of one's daily activities, causing individuals to follow specific consumption patterns that are slightly different from those of the mainstream market.

As Islamic markets continue their steady growth, trends in Islamic consumer behavior will continue to attract the attention of scholars, leading to increasing interest in exploring this behavior and understanding its theoretical foundation. As a result, many theories have been applied to investigate this behavior, such as the theory of consumer behavior, the theory of reasoned behavior, and the theory of planned behavior. However, these theories fail to capture Islamic perspectives of consumerism because traditional theories consider materialism and pleasure seeking to be an individual's purpose in life (Lada et al., 2009). In response to this, Khan (1995) proposed a framework of Islamic consumer behavior theory, in which he explained consumption behavior after applying Islamic parameters. He highlights that consumption in the West, in which the consumer acts rationally, tends to maximize utility and minimize costs, whereas from an Islamic perspective, the consumer is expected to engage in moderation when acquiring and using resources, considering the welfare of and justice for others. Hence, the choice of a Muslim consumer is based on two aspects: its immediate effect in this life and its later effect in the lives of others (Khan, 1984).

Hamdani and Ahmad (2002) proposed a divine economics or faith model to investigate Islamic consumer behavior based on afterlife values. Wilson and Liu (2010) later introduced the theory of a *halal* decision-making paradigm for Muslim consumption behavior by considering the *Shariah* parameter. They found this behavior to be guided by cognitive and affective factors, resulting in conative factors. In brief, this demonstrates that Islamic consumer behavior is an important issue that requires more attention from academics and practitioners. In practice, businesses need to accurately define the underlying reasons for Islamic consumer behavior in various markets worldwide in order to determine the appropriate marketing and advertising strategies that will appeal to these unique market segments. Failing to implement this task could lead to missing significant opportunities to take advantage of local Muslim markets or to expand globally into Muslim markets distributed across various countries. Interestingly, many international companies, such as Nestle and some fast-food chains, were eager to explore Muslim consumption behavior across various countries and adapt their products to reflect these consumption patterns.

7.5   Islamic markets

Reliable information about the structure of Islamic markets has started to appear recently because Muslim consumers are spreading globally and little information is available about some Islamic countries and communities. One of the most trust-worthy reports is the Pew Report (2009), which presents data about the behavior of Muslim consumers worldwide. Though it is not a comprehensive report on all aspects and possible influences of consumer behavior, it provides reliable insights into Muslim consumer variations among diff countries and confirms that Muslim market segments are not fully homogeneous (Kearney, 2007). Based on the country of residence, Muslim consumers communicate in different languages, wear various styles of clothing, and eat different foods. Over time, these variations in lifestyle could shape consumers' behavior. Despite such deviations in behavior, Minkus-McKenna (2007) showed that 70 percent of all Muslims worldwide prefer products and services based on Islamic principles and teaching.

In general, Muslims look for *halal* (*Shariah*-compliant) products and services, which are made based on Islamic laws. These laws require all inputs, processes, and outcomes to be *Shariah*-compliant. If products and services are not *Shariah*-compliant, they are considered un-*halal* or *haram*, and Muslims are not allowed to buy them. *Halal* (allowed) and *haram* (forbidden) apply to all aspects of a Muslim's life, including food and nonfood items, lifestyle goods, and services. Companies that produce *haram* products find it difficult to market to Muslim consumers because their purchasing behavior is determined by the mutual understanding of what is permissible and what is forbidden under Islamic law. Thus, being *Shariah*-compliant is the fastest way to ensure acceptance of a company and its products among Muslim consumers.

Alserhan (2010) pointed out that the global Islamic market is projected to grow 15 percent annually, making it the fastest expanding market segment worldwide. This rapidly growing segment is a result of the high birth rate of Muslims compared to that of Western countries, which is well below the natural replacement rate. Based on these birth rates, the United Nations Population Fund forecasts that Muslims will account for 30 percent of the world population by 2050, and two-thirds of this global population under the age of 18 will be Muslims. In addition, official predictions state that the Muslim population in developed countries will increase sharply in coming decades, especially in Europe, due to the massive immi-gration and high birth rates; these changes will likely shift the market structure of certain developed countries.

Research by J. Walter Thompson (JWT, 2009) examined three major reports about the Muslim population in selected countries around the world. These reports provide important demographic information that companies can use to analyze Muslim markets for branding and marketing activities. In 2009, the Gallup Coexist Foundation presented a global study of interfaith relationships (Gallup, 2009) that studies attitudes and perceptions among Muslims and the general public in diverse Muslim and non-Muslim countries. This study provides good information about the economic and social standing of Muslims, showing that Muslims, regardless of their country of residence, have similar positive attitudes toward interfaith living.

Subsequently, Ogilvy and Mather (2010) initiated a special project called the Ogilvy Noor Brand Index, which focuses on understanding Muslim consumers' attitudes toward global brands. They asked Muslim consumers in the Kingdom of Saudi Arabia (KSA), Egypt, Pakistan, and Malaysia to rate brands on a 100-point index that was built according to this testimony: "This brand is completely

Shariah-compliant" (Ogilvy and Mather, 2010). The index ranks 35 global brands from within five groups: beverages, food and dairy, personal care, financial services, and aviation industries. Notably, Lipton, Nestle, and Nescafe scored above 120, and Lipton received the highest brand score of 131. Other global brands such as Kraft, Pringles, and 7-Up were also ranked in the top ten. The majority of the financial services and airline brands that were studied, including Citibank, Singapore Airlines, Emirates, and HSBC, received some of the lowest scores on the index. An important implication of this index is that, in the eyes of Muslim consumers, an Islamic brand does not have to be produced in a Muslim country. Much more important to Muslim consumers is a genuine consideration of their needs, demonstrated through different aspects of the brand's behavior in line with Islamic law (*Shariah*-compliant).

ASDA'A Burson-Marsteller, a public relations agency that specializes in studying consumer behavior in the Middle East, issued an annual survey on global brands that appeal to young people. The findings suggest that young Muslims across the Middle East perceive brands from various countries differently. For example, US brands appeal more to Muslim youth in GCC countries and North Africa compared to Levant youth, whereas young Muslims in the Middle East all perceive French brands equally. Figure 7.1 shows which brand's country of origin appeals most to Muslim youth, thereby indicating that Muslim markets are not homogeneous.

Worthy of note is that Muslim consumers are not looking for specific products and services; they are receptive to many kinds of products and services provided they are *Shariah*-compliant. For example, travel and tourism, which is known to Muslims as *halal* tourism, is a rapidly growing industry in the Islamic world. *Halal* tourism has an estimated market value of $220 billion (JWT, 2016), which is expected to grow at a rate of 20 percent annually. Additionally, in the promotions industry, an increasing number of TV advertisements, promotion banners, and product packaging in the Muslim world involve using women wearing head scarves because it is an effective and appealing way to approach the majority of consumers.

Previous global studies and reports have found similarities and differences across global Islamic markets. The similarities include (1) mutual faith and values, (2) comparable dietary needs, and (3) comparable lifestyle requirements (e.g., finance,

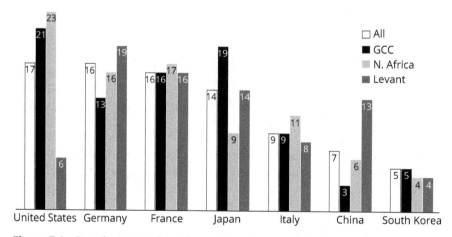

Figure 7.1   Brand country of origin appealing to young Muslims

tourism, leisure), while the differences relate to (1) their global distribution, (2) language, (3) cultural background, (4) level of education, and (5) Islamic adherence.

7.6   Segmenting Islamic markets

While traditional segmentation is executed based on characteristics such as demographics, geography, and psychographics, features that include cultural background and tradition are often used to serve as a foundation for segmentation (Athanassopoulos, 2000; Sohail et al., 2017). Consequently, if the Muslim community is to be segmented, sets of common actions, preferences, or habits must be identified. Studying the behaviors, motivations, and customs of Islamic communities can be used to segment within the broader Islamic population. The following categories can be used to classify Muslim consumers' behavior and attitudes:

1. *Halal* (Permissible)

   This category encompasses actions that are permissible according to Islamic principles. Therefore, Muslims can freely practice these actions without worry of committing a sin. This category consists of three subcategories:

   (a) *Wajib*: This refers to compulsory actions. According to this tenet, failure to perform such activities amounts to a sin. For a business, a *wajib* activity is to work toward the improvement of society and create value in the community within which it operates. Thus, it would be a sin (*haram*) for a business to only look for profits and not give back to society.

   (b) *Mandoob*: This comprises activities that are preferable but not obligatory. Thus, failing to perform these actions is not a sin. Helping a community member would be an example of a *mandoob* activity.

   (c) *Makrooh*: This subcategory includes deeds that are frowned upon and are not considered to be the norm. While these activities are not considered a sin, they can lead to sin. Therefore, in contrast to *mandoob*, *makrooh* activities ought to be avoided whenever possible. Divorce is an important example of *makrooh*.

2. *Mustabeh*

   Mustabeh is the category of deeds that are doubted in nature. For example, a *Mustabeh* activity might either be *haram* (nonpermissible) or lead to a *haram* activity. As a result, Muslims refrain from acts that constitute a *mustabeh* activity.

3. *Haram*

   These activities amount to committing a sin and are denounced in accordance with the sacred teachings of the religion. Consuming drugs and alcoholic beverages and gambling belong to this group.

The following five segments represent prominent Muslim segments based on the values and attitudes of Muslim consumers (Vohra et al., 2009):

1. Conservatives

   This segment captures those consumers who devoutly practice Islam in all of their activities throughout their lives and consider Islam the supreme law governing their existence. They tend to be older and are socially very conservative. For example, male conservatives maintain beards and pray five times a day. They detest gender interactions and Western habits and apparel. They adhere strictly to the religious societal norms enumerated in the religious texts of Islam (or Muslim scholars) and even believe religious dogma supersedes their personal preferences.

2. New age Muslims

Progressive Muslims who accept recent developments in technology and consent to the mingling of different communities. These Muslims accept Islam as their religion but understand that society is not one-sided. Thus, they are tolerant of other religions, interested in new networks of information, and fascinated by new trends in the market. For example, these Muslims believe in female empowerment, use the Internet to their advantage, and might seek an education abroad. Mostly, middle- and upper-class Muslims living in big cities such as Riyadh, Cairo, Ankara, Tehran, Kuala Lumpur, and Jakarta form this group.

3. Societal traditionalists

This group involves consumers who are not religious, yet they believe that one should live according to Islamic societal norms. They prefer decisions of others (clerics, elder relatives) in their communities to personal choice and preferences. To outsiders, they seem to lack characteristics of self-confidence because they depend on the decisions of others. Muslims of the lower working class are part of this segment.

4. Practical strivers

Practical strivers include consumers who are unorthodox and open-minded. They belong to the affluent class of Muslims and accept other cultures freely. For example, they might want to own a sports club or a German luxury car such as a Porsche. They are also risk takers and want to be financially successful in life. They practice religion only for social conformance.

5. Liberals

Liberals stand at the opposite end of religious conservatives. Some of them are highly educated and deem their religious identity to be less relevant and important than their national pride and individuality. These Muslims are interested in international news, the latest gadgets, travel, music, and adventure. Young and assertive, these Muslims might not be religious at all and like to enjoy their life without following Islamic principles.

7.7   Principles of Islamic marketing

Since Islam appeared 14 centuries ago, Muslims have been conducting business on a global scale and engaging in trade activities with various countries. Back then, the ethical practices of Muslims were known and highly admired by non-Muslim traders. However, the term *Islamic marketing* only appeared recently (probably around the 1980s), when Western companies started to explore Muslim countries as a highly attractive market segment. These Western companies found that, to be accepted by Muslim consumers, products and services need to meet certain criteria related to Islamic laws. Later, companies discovered that Muslim consumer demands differ from one Muslim country to another depending on cultural and economic factors. Thus, to gain wider access to these promising markets, there is a need to explore the key principles that influence Muslim consumers' behavior.

The term Islamic marketing, which started to appear frequently in various venues and discussions, was defined by Jafari (2012) as "the study of marketing phenomena in relation to Islamic principles and practices or within the context of Muslim societies" and by Alserhan (2010) as "Religion-based marketing, in which your marketing activities are guided within the framework of Islamic Shariah." Other researchers also defined Islamic marketing by linking it directly to Islamic principles. Since 2000, a significant number of research papers have investigated this new field of Islamic marketing from various perspectives and examined how it contributes to the existing body of knowledge (Saeed et al., 2001; Rice, 1999; Wilson, 2006). A better understanding of Islamic marketing concepts will facilitate its application to contemporary Western ideas on marketing.

Companies aiming to appeal to Muslim consumers need to understand how the concept of Islamic marketing, as a philosophical concept, can be turned into a modern marketing concept. Thus, there is a need to present the steps to follow in connection with Islamic teachings in a marketing mix. Sula and Kartajaya (2006) presented 17 principles of Islamic marketing that companies should apply to ensure *Shariah* compliance. These principles are divided into four groups. The first group refers to the landscape of Islamic marketing, which contains all components of a business: competitor, change, customers, and company. The second group belongs to the elements of strategic marketing. In this group, all elements are defined within the scope of "justice" for all involved parties. For example, in differentiation, the moral obligation of the seller is to tell consumers the weak and strong points of a product (Al-Fatih, 2009). The seller should never hide anything from his customers, including any defects his products might contain. The third group refers to the *Shariah* scorecard, which is utilized to balance company values with the interests of all stakeholders. Finally, the fourth group is linked to "Sharia enterprise," where company values and goals have a strong link with "inspiration," culture," and "institution." For the purpose of this chapter, the following section extends the discussion on the marketing mix from an Islamic perspective involving the second group.

7.8 Islamic marketing mix

One of the major concepts in the modern marketing mix is to set up an effective marketing program that blends all of the marketing elements into one strategy designed to deliver value to customers (Kotler and Armstrong, 2006). For Muslims, the perception of a marketing mix is shaped by its *Shariah* compliance, which could vary across Muslim countries. The following sections present some basic conditions involved in implementing marketing mix elements from an Islamic perspective.

7.8.1 Product

This element includes the production process and all inputs that lead to the final product. The main goal of the production process is to provide and satisfy basic consumer demands. Miller and Deiss (1996) proposed that the main reason behind unethical decisions to reduce the quality of a product is the company's cost-leadership strategies. However, the Islamic perspective inspires a social and welfare approach rather than only profit maximization because the decision-making process is controlled by the principles of lawfulness, existence, deliverability, precise determination, and purity (Al-Misri, 1991). These principles dictate that the following conditions be mandatory in the process of introducing a product: (1) the product must be lawful and not cause dullness of mind or lead to public immorality; (2) the product must be in the actual possession of the seller; (3) the product must be deliverable at the time of sale; (4) agreement on the sale must identify precisely the quantity and quality; and (5) the product must be clean (not contaminated), which could reduce its usefulness. These principles indicate that Islamic laws place a strong emphasis on product quality and purity from beginning to end based on a moral approach that ensures consumers are free from harm and negative consequences (Al-Faruki, 1992). These principles are essential to conducting business, but many conditions still have to be considered during the process of selling products. For example, low-quality and high-quality products cannot be sold in the same place because it is considered a form of cheating, which confuses consumers (Al-Fatih, 2009). To ensure transparency, items of differing quality should be clearly separated and identified so that customers can easily distinguish between high- and low-quality products.

To show that a product or process conforms to Islamic principles, companies must obtain a *halal* certificate to confirm that they comply with the aforementioned principles. The *halal* certificate is issued by a specialized government agency (or authorized agency) in each country. Non-Muslim companies, such as Nestle, Subway, Carrefour, and McDonald's, have entered Muslim countries by obtaining this certification and presenting it with their products. Kasriel (2008) claimed that a *halal* certificate (or its symbol) attracts not only Muslim consumers but also non-Muslims, because they associate *halal* products with safety and purity. The real Muslim market could thus be larger than originally expected, because of the emerging groups containing non-Muslim consumers.

Noteworthy is that some products deemed acceptable in Malaysia, such as a Barbie doll without a headscarf, are banned in countries such as KSA. Therefore, understanding what constitutes *halal* could vary among countries. For example, some Muslims consider meat products *halal* if they are not pork or mixed with pork, while other Muslims only eat meat that is certified *halal* to ensure that the animal was not stunned and that it was treated humanely and fed natural ingredients while alive.

A Product: Scent the Middle Eastern Way

The Arab world is full of rich and diverse communities, groups, and cultures. Differences exist not only among countries, but within countries as well. Fragrances have always been an integral part of Middle Eastern traditions and heritage, and this continues today with consumers being very knowledgeable and selective about the kinds of fragrances they will buy. Fragrances that are custom made in the store by adjusting the concentration of various notes to suit individual tastes to create a highly personalized fragrance are the new norm, as is layering, where consumers mix two or more perfumes themselves to create their own signature scent.

According to Euromonitor International (EMI), the retail value of the Middle East and African fragrance market is expected to reach US$8.5 billion by 2021, up from the US$6.1 billion level of 2017, with the United Arab Emirates (UAE) establishing itself as an international destination and a strategic business hub for the perfume industry.

In the GCC, the retail value of fragrances is estimated to reach US$3.6 billion in 2021, of which US$2.1 billion will be attributed to the KSA and US$807 million to the UAE, the two big spenders. Some regional perfume brands have enjoyed tremendous success, such as Kayali (Huda Beauty), Anfas (Emirati perfumer Asim Al-Qassim), Arcadia (Emirati perfumer Amna Al-Habtoor), Odict (Kuwaiti-Saudi brand), Fragrance Kitchen (Kuwait), and Lootah (UAE). We will introduce the reader to one of these brands that have gained popularity especially within the GCC countries, namely Rasasi Perfumes.

Rasasi Perfumes: A Brand of UAE

Rasasi Perfumes LLC was founded in 1979 by Abdul Razzak Kalsekar and is strategically located in Dubai in the UAE. The company has built a solid company on the basis of pioneering entrepreneurial vigor over the course of some four decades, making a number of highly desirable and exclusive fragrances to establish a worldwide name connoting quality, luxury, and magnificence. Founder Abdul Razzak Kalsekar's vision is currently being carried forward by his six sons. The Rasasi brand, with its Oriental and Occidental perfume lines, is widely recognized and sought across the world.

The company pioneered the concept of a mono-brand fragrance store, which became a trend in the regional perfume retail industry.

Rasasi's geographical footprint includes 165 stores in leading malls and prime market locations across the GCC (UAE, KSA, Oman, Kuwait, Bahrain, and Qatar). Rasasi products are exported to more than 60 countries across the globe through a strong distribution network, supported by a state-of-the-art manufacturing facility in Jebel Ali Free Zone, Dubai.

7.8.2   Price

A product is worth what consumers are willing to pay for it; however, pricing policies are formulated to manipulate and influence human psychology, leading to setting a price that is often considerably higher than what sellers truly charge. This pricing approach is used to give consumers the false perception that they are getting a bargain (Shaw, 1996). This kind of pricing is unethical and banned under Islamic law because it is forbidden to gain something too easily without working for it (Shaw, 1996). In reality, such actions will increase the profit of sellers in the short term but reduce the purchasing power of consumers in the long term because they will run out of cash as a result of these pricing practices, leading to a slowdown in economic activity.

Islam does not force sellers to set specific prices or ban price controls and adjustments to reflect the supply and demand of the market by, for example, setting higher prices resulting from a normal shortage of a given product or setting price ceilings to control opportunistic movements among sellers. In Islam, self-operating mechanisms of price manipulation and healthy competition are encouraged in practice because they increase market dynamics and encourage business owners to offer the best products. However, the important conditions for the successful application of a pricing mechanism require that there should be no cornering of a market, no hoarding, no (unjustified) price adjustment, no movement toward a monopoly, and no restrictions on trade (Niazi, 1996).

When business owners set unfair prices, it is important in Islam that the government take action for the sake of consumers and prevent a monopoly, especially for products that the average consumer has a high need for (Al-Ukhuwa, 1938). Once,

Umar Al-Khattab (one of the early Islamic rulers) was passing by a business owner and saw that he was trading raisins at a much lower price than his competitors, trying to undercut his competitors to force them to sell their product at a loss. Umar Al-Khattab told him: "Either raise your price or get out of our market" (Malik, 1989). Hoarding of any product is prohibited in Islam because it leads to a dramatic increase in prices, especially for commodities in great demand. In certain cases, government officials and market leaders will look at certain products to arrive at a consensus on a fair price that safeguards the public interest and ensures an acceptable profit for sellers.

The role of government officials is to ensure that prices remain fair and to act on any ethical gaps within the price setting. Price fluctuations without valid reasons can shake consumer confidence and cause them to delay product purchases in the hope that prices will be lower in the near future. Changes in prices should be consistent with changes in the quantity or quality of a product. It is acceptable in Islam for prices to increase as a result of the natural scarcity of a product because this is consistent with Islam's normative position about price determination by market forces to enhance the goal of healthy and fair competition.

7.8.3 Promotion

Promotion is a way to publicize a product and explain its features; thus, business owners should make sure to advertise the true value of their products without making false claims because all such actions are prohibited by Islam (Trim, 2008). In terms of Islamic ethics, it is unethical for business owners to overhype their products and advertise them as having features they do not actually have (Al-Ukhuwa, 1938). Such actions represent cheating and fraud, which are banned under Islamic laws. For example, the Prophet Mohammad used to advertise his products by telling the truth and describing their good and bad features. This sincerity and honesty caused him to be held in high esteem among other business owners and consumers because he not only promoted the product he sold but also promoted himself as an honest trader. This led consumers to trust him and his word when it came to his products, and his example represents the optimal approach to effective advertisement.

Islam also forbids salesmen from making false pronouncements in their sales pitches or unethical claims to push their products in a way that deceives customers. Therefore, all means that lead to fraud and deception are prohibited in the promotion process within an Islamic ethical framework. Based on Islamic promotion principles, marketers should promote their products according to the following rules:

1. Avoid false and misleading advertisement.

2. Reject high-pressure manipulation or misleading sales tactics.

3. Avoid sales promotions that use deception or false testimonies.

4. Use promotional techniques that are not based on sex, emotion, or fear.

5. Ensure promotions do not contribute to dullness of the mind (promotions that could lead to long-term mental or physical deterioration).

6. Avoid the use of suggestive language and behavior and the depiction of unreal, fantasy-like scenes in advertising.

7. Avoid stereotyping women in advertising as objects to lure and attract consumers.

Based on these rules, marketers are required (in their advertisements) to tell the truth about their products and disclose all faults in their goods, whether obvious or hidden. This disclosure can be done in a professional way to present the real capabilities of products while keeping in mind that the goal is to promote the product and not to demonstrate that the product is useless and thus dissuade the consumer from buying it. The ultimate objective is to tell consumers the truth and let them decide whether the product meets their needs.

Since global Muslim consumers are not a homogeneous market segment, different levels of perception exist with respect to Islamic promotional activities. For example, Muslim communities (where they represent a majority) are highly restrictive about the collective rules outlined earlier; however, in countries where Muslims are minorities, less emphasis is placed on some of the rules because of the pressure of the wider sociocultural environment. For example, pictures that were used in promotional activities targeted at Muslim consumers in conservative communities use the Islamic dress code and avoid any appeals to emotions or sexuality, a widely used technique when marketing to non-Muslim consumers.

7.8.4   Place

Products reach consumers through distribution channels. In this process, companies might use certain distribution approaches that add significant costs to the total price for a shorter delivery time, delay the delivery to create a shortage in products and increased prices, or dominate the distribution channel with the intention of raising the price level. While these actions are used in the profit-maximization approach to increase the monopoly power of companies, they are forbidden in Islam because they place an additional financial burden on consumers. Other cases of unethical practices that can occur in product distribution include using packaging designs without sufficient product safety and protection, aggressive driving on public roads, improper wrapping, and transporting hazardous or toxic products on public highways without taking suitable precautions.

Enabling goods delivery and product acquisition by agencies is not prohibited in Islam, as long as these are done for the appropriate delivery of products and not to increase prices. The main objective of distribution in Islam is to create value for all stakeholders and to provide satisfactory products and services (Saeed et al., 2001). From an Islamic perspective, failing to meet these conditions during the buying and selling process will result in unethical practices.

7.8.5   People

The public face of a company is its contact personnel; thus, employee satisfaction can lead to customer satisfaction. In other words, to satisfy your customers, you must satisfy your employees. As an important part of a company's delivery of its products and services, employees must exercise a deep understanding of customers' needs by being patient, honest, fair, and accountable.

Islam emphasizes the employee's rational judgment in serving customers' needs and ethically achieving the company's objectives. Employees should not use any form of coercion to convince someone to perform an action without his free will. Employees must, under all conditions, respect the consciousness of customers to ensure that their hard-earned money is not wasted (Hassan et al., 2008). From an Islamic perspective, employees are expected to receive comprehensive training before performing their work, where they learn to implement the value-maximization approach to protect the interest of all parties. Based on consumers' awareness level, employees should be able to think rationally and show interest in customers' feelings and attitudes. They must provide accurate and reliable information for customers and avoid disclosing any private information without formal consent.

Some businesses use their employees, or other companies' employees, to promote their products through sexual and emotional appeals. According to Islamic principles, these unethical practices are forbidden because they mistreat humans by using them as a marketing tool for seducing consumers. Overall, employees should have a pleasant appearance and follow an acceptable dress code. These rules are particularly applicable to women, who need to wear a headscarf and should refrain from wearing excessive makeup or tight clothing, which could be considered seductive; female staff must dress in attire that complies with the Muslim code. Islam respects individual rights, which are an essential prerequisite for traditional Islamic law. Individuals should not be used or forced to conduct themselves in a way that suppresses their "independent judgment." Islam emphasizes the importance of consumers' "decision-making freedom."

7.9   A short story

Malaysia: Building a Global *Halal* Hub

Malaysia is set on becoming a global *halal* hub. A set of standards developed by Malaysia are widely recognized by Muslim countries around the world. The country's Department of Islamic Development Malaysia (JAKIM) has overall responsibility for implementing the *halal* certification system and for monitoring and enforcing *halal* guidelines across the country. Malaysia recognizes 56 *halal* certification bodies across 33 countries that are able to certify imported products. Here are a few examples of the basic requirements for securing *halal* certification in Malaysia:

- The company must produce or supply *halal*-only products and services. In other words, the business must be dedicated to the production or provision of solely *halal* products or services.

- A company listed in the multinational and small and medium-sized enterprise (SME) category is required to establish a Halal Assurance System (HAS) to oversee and ensure compliance with the *halal* certification procedures.

- An applicant must have at least two permanent Muslim Malaysian members on its staff working in the kitchen/handling/food processing section.

- The transportation used must be specifically for *halal* product delivery only.

7.10   Successful companies

Companies that have taken significant steps toward complying with Islamic principles in conducting their business activities have attracted Muslim consumers and built a successful business model. In reality, there are a large number of such companies from both Muslim and non-Muslim countries. Here we list a few of these companies and discuss the approach they took to reach Muslim consumers.

7.10.1   Tekbir clothing (Turkey)

This company started as a small shop in the well-known conservative district of Fatih in the Turkish city of Istanbul. In 1982, the shop started catering to conservative Muslim women seeking new lifestyles. These women sought to go out in public, attend college to advance their careers, and contribute to family income. The shop offered them various coats and scarfs with a certain aesthetic unlike anything they would normally wear at home or buy at the local market. These items were more modern and easier to wear and included certain attractive "styles" while still being conservative and nonrevealing. Such clothing geared toward women who covered their heads and respected the Islamic principles of hijab had not existed until that time. Women had to seek skilled friends, neighborhood tailors, or large stores that accommodated secular styles to obtain such clothing.

The founders of Tekbir (Mustafa Karaduman and his two brothers) explained their motives as being beyond just a desire to make money. More importantly, they wanted to provide stylish and easy-to-wear clothing for women observing Islamic dress codes. A venture that began as a single store has now multiplied into 45 shops located across the city of Istanbul (Tekbir, 2017). A seven-floor factory building built on a spacious site in the industrial zone of Istanbul now produces fabric that passes through different stages to become dresses, coats, headscarves, and other clothing in large quantities. Even though Tekbir clothing started out alone, and even though it now faces competition from a variety of stores, big and small, it continues along its bright, self-determined path with confidence.

7.10.2   Wardah *halal* cosmetic (Indonesia)

Long ignored or misunderstood by the mainstream, Muslim women's beauty needs are being championed by a new wave of niche brands—and enjoying outstanding commercial success. The *halal* label gained popularity in cosmetics when the Malaysian government introduced a *halal* cosmetics standard in June 2010. Table 7.1 shows the response to the growing line of *halal* beauty products among Muslim consumers, where the annual growth rate of this market is around 10 percent, indicating that it represents a promising market for potential investors.

Many Muslim women fear that mainstream cosmetic products might contain alcohol, pork, dead animals, or other animal byproducts forbidden by Islam. This condition laid the groundwork for the establishment of Wardah, a specialized

Table 7.1 Growth in *halal* beauty market in different Muslim communities

Halal beauty market (US$ millions)			
Market	2013	2014	2015
Australia and New Zealand	1.34	1.36	1.37
China	17.30	19.98	18.74
Thailand	20.40	21.61	23.01
India	77.89	84.62	92.23
Pakistan	119.70	130.52	142.85
Indonesia	255.00	283.00	315.74
Malaysia	306.68	340.41	379.56
Total	798.31	881.50	973.50

company in *halal* cosmetic products, which has become widely popular across Indonesia for its product line made from all-natural and *halal* ingredients and designed specifically for Asian Muslim women's skins. Recently, Wardah has expanded to serve the broader public because an increasing number of non-Muslim women have started to choose this brand for its purely natural ingredients. Research has shown that marketing by Western brands fails to appeal to Muslim women because it shows "a flamboyant type of beauty" that fails to speak to Muslim women.

7.11   Digital platforms and Islamic marketing

Digital strategies to target Muslim consumers are vital given the Muslim consumer segment's geographic dispersion. Such strategies are powerful tools for reaching Muslim consumers worldwide and addressing their needs, leading to a better approach to serving them. The influence of these digital strategies is considered significant for the future of Islamic branding and marketing. The following are some examples of successful online platforms targeting Muslim consumers.

7.11.1   Alchemiya.com

Alchemiya.com is an on-demand video platform that "presents the world's best content about Muslim life." Alchemiya was the first Muslim media company to debut a public equity crowdfunding campaign. The company secured £117,320 from 153 investors through Crowdcube (a leading investment crowdfunding platform).

7.11.2   Zilzar.com

Zilzar.com, founded by Muslim entrepreneur Rushdi Siddiqui, is an online retailer aiming to be the Muslim world's Amazon. The e-commerce platform has a presence in 57 Muslim countries. The business-to-business and business-to-consumer platform offers several categories of products and services. Its core product groups are electronics; food and beverages; health and beauty; machinery, industrial parts, and tools; fashion, textiles, and accessories; and gifts, sports, and toys.

7.11.3   Halaltrip.com

Halaltrip.com is another successful website for the Muslim target market. The Muslim tourism concept began over a decade ago with the flow of visitors to Malaysia and Turkey. However, the spread of digital technologies has enabled millions of Muslim families to change the way they book their holiday vacations. One example is the distribution of travel services through Halaltrip.com. This website specifically targets Muslims for travel. Hotels are rated not only on their quality and service but also on other features such as whether they are located near mosques or *halal* restaurants.

7.12   Consumer neuroscience and *halal* products

Consumer neuroscience is an emerging field that uses functional magnetic resonance imaging (fMRI) technology to track brain activation while making a decision to select a product or a certain brand. Since product images influence consumer behavior, many researchers have started to use fMRI technology to explore consumer behavior by tracking brain activity. From a marketing perspective, this issue is important for understanding the stimulation that causes more brain activation during the decision-making process for selecting a product. Al-Kwifi (2015) explored the impact of destination images on tourists' decision making using fMRI technology and found that the level of brain activation at the ventromedial prefrontal cortex (vmPFC) increased when participants were asked to assess attractive destination images compared with the level of activation for unattractive ones. The positive attitude toward an attractive destination led to a higher intention to visit that destination. In 2016, he conducted another study to investigate the role of fMRI in detecting attitudes toward brand switching for smartphone products and found increased brain activation at the vmPFC when participants were asked to judge images that reflected a brand's perceived usefulness compared with judging images that reflected pleasure derived from a given brand (Al-Kwifi, 2016). These studies, among others, present solid evidence that product images have a significant impact on consumer psychology when selecting a particular product or brand.

Recently, the authors examined Muslim consumers' behavior in connection with *halal* products using fMRI technology. In this study, participants were put in a MRI scanner for approximately 60 minutes and shown different images of *halal* and non-*halal* products. The participants were asked to think about their intention to buy the shown products. A complete description of a similar experiment can be found in Al-Kwifi (2015). The authors concluded that our internal consciousness responds differently to brands based on our inner beliefs. Their study was the first to investigate Muslim consumers' behavior toward *halal* products using fMRI technology, and it opened the door to more research exploring Muslim consumers and their psychology.

The fMRI studies on Muslim consumers represent a new body of evidence showing that Muslim consumers constitute a unique market segment that follows special rules regarding consumption based on Islamic beliefs. Unlike previous studies that used conventional approaches to studying consumer behavior, using fMRI technology to investigate the internal response of Muslim consumers to *halal* products represents a significant advancement in exploring consumer behavior. There is no doubt that the findings from this new technique significantly contribute to the existing consumer behavior literature by monitoring and studying brain activities while making decisions about selecting products and defining the settings that cause more activation in favor of a specific product. This is important in terms of expanding our knowledge of the underlying mechanisms and associated conditions when consumers are subjected to different promotional strategies. Advanced neuroscience studies can be used to determine the brain region that impacts a Muslim consumer's decision to select a *halal* product and then try to find better advertising strategies that increase the probability of this choice.

Islamic markets are relatively large and continue to grow worldwide, so marketing managers of food and cosmetics companies must have a better understanding of this market segment's consumers. Such understanding would enhance their advertise in strategies and make them more effective in influencing the purchasing decisions of Muslim consumers. Since Muslim consumers are widely dispersed around the globe, it is impotent that promotional strategies take into account the distinctiveness of the local environments that Muslims live in because consumers in each region are defined by certain cultural and social aspects. Although different promotion strategies would accommodate local flavors, presenting a *halal* product in a way that reflects Islamic values is the key to success in any promotional activities.

Chapter Highlights

Muslim markets are expanding rapidly and are unquestionably the next important (and largely untapped) global opportunity. The *halal* market alone is worth US$2.1 trillion a year and is increasing at a rate of US$500 billion annually thanks to the growth of the global Muslim population. The global Muslim consumer market is therefore expected to reach US$30 trillion by 2050 (Alserhan, 2010), which represents a tremendous business opportunity for Muslim and non-Muslim companies to create new products and services that fit the needs and requirements of niche Muslim markets. It is therefore essential that non-Muslim companies interested in serving Muslim consumers understand Islamic marketing principles before commencing business activities in the relevant markets.

The globalization of the world economy requires global businesses to familiarize themselves with the Islamic perspective on business and understand the factors shaping the behaviors of Muslim consumers. Additionally, the current emphasis on learning and utilizing business ethics, at the local and international levels, emphasizes the laws of Islam as the ultimate source of value maximization, which is essential in reshaping business practices to serve all stakeholders.

Key Terms

Halal	Islamic marketing mix	Segmentation of Islamic
Halal cosmetics	Muslim consumer	markets
Islamic marketing		

Discussion Questions

1. Discuss from an Islamic perspective the broad guidelines that must be followed and adhered to in advertising.

2. Discuss pricing policies in Islam.

3. How can business executives discover business opportunities in Muslim markets?

4. Define Islamic marketing.

5. What are the four Ps of marketing? Give examples from Islamic marketing.

6. What is the difference between Islamic marketing and Islamic branding?

7. The sales orientation to marketing assumes that aggressive selling is what is needed to increase demand. Does Islamic marketing support this notion?

8. Name an online platform targeting Muslim consumers and discuss its strategy.

9. Discuss the importance of consumer neuroscience in Islamic marketing.

Case Studies

Ajmal Perfumes: An Islamic Brand from UAE

Ajmal Perfumes was established in 1951 by the late Haji Ajmal Ali. The company has grown rapidly from a modest trading outfit into a national corporation. The family-owned business, operating in Dubai, UAE, is driven by the passion of the second and third generations of Ajmal's family, each playing a major part in building the business brand. Since its beginnings, Ajmal has been an innovator in making perfumes for various occasions; notably, it introduced different types of perfumes appropriate for Islamic celebrations and events. According to its founder, Mr. Haji, "A fragrance is all it takes to travel through time, such is the bond between memory and fragrance." Ajmal uses this concept as the basis of its business: to unlock old memories using smell, be it the memory of lost love or of a dear friend. This approach was very unique and creative in helping Ajmal to focus its marketing strategy on recreating those memories through specific kinds of perfumes.

Over time, Ajmal was able to introduce many distinctive products to the market, enabling its recognition as a luxury brand, as shown below. It was able to build a strong corporate entity with an outstanding portfolio of over 300 of the finest and most fascinating scents. The company has over 150 exclusive retail outlets across the GCC and a presence on the international market: it exports to 30 countries. A brand with a rich heritage and rooted in Islamic culture, Ajmal Perfumes has carved out a niche for itself in the perfume industry.

Modanisa: A Turkish Brand of Islamic Fashion

Modanisa was launched on Mother's Day in 2011 as a dream and vision to meet modest women's desire to wear clothes that fit their lives and reflected Islamic values. Modanisa is the first Turkish fashion platform to make online clothes shopping accessible to customers worldwide. It was able to introduce a wide range of products to fit the needs of women on various occasions; its range includes hijabs, outerwear, stylish wear, sportswear, swimwear, shoes, and accessories. Modanisa uses a professional team of designers to create a wide range of clothes that reflect modern consumer needs, with a strong consideration of Islamic principles, as shown below.

The clothes offered by Modanisa have enjoyed an increased market base that includes customers in 130 countries. To enhance communication activities with customers worldwide, the company posts content on its website in five languages, Turkish, Arabic, English, French, and German, and has employees to communicate with customers using these languages. This move significantly enhanced the company's global presence and increased its market base. Each month, 16 million people around the world visit its website via the Internet or its app. Surprisingly, it sells over 650 brands and 70,000 products, which can be shipped to 5 continents. The passion and dedication to introducing fashionable products have instilled in its customers a love for and trust in the brand. In 2016, Reuters selected Modanisa as the world's most popular Islamic apparel website, and in November 2017, it won the prestigious Islamic Economy Award in the Islamic Arts category.

References

Abd Rahman, A., Asrarhaghighi, E. and Ab Rahman, S. (2015). Consumers and Halal Cosmetic Products: Knowledge, Religiosity, Attitude and Intention. *Journal of Islamic Marketing*, 6(1), 148–163.

Al-Faruki, I.R. (1992). *AL TAWHID: Its Implication for Thought and Life* (IIIrd ed.). Kuala Lumpur.

Al-Fatih, E. (2009). *Pesan Nabi Tentang Dagang (Prophet Muhammad's Messages on Doing Business).* Bandung: Garis.

Al-Kwifi, S.O. (2015). The Impact of Destination Images on Tourists' Decision Making. A Technological Exploratory Study Using fMRI. *Journal of Hospitality and Tourism Technology*, 6(2), 174–194.

Al-Kwifi, S.O. (2016). The Role of fMRI in Detecting Attitude Toward Brand Switching: An Exploratory Study Using High Technology Products. *Journal of Product & Brand Management*, 25(2), 208–218.

Al-Kwifi, S.O., Abu Farha, A.K. and Ahmed, Z.U. (2019). Dynamics of Muslim Consumers' Behavior Toward Halal Products: Exploration Study Using fMRI Technology. *International Journal of Emerging Markets*, 14(4), 689–704.

Al-Misri, A.I.N. (1991). *The Reminiscences of the Traveler: A Classical Manual of Islamic Sacred Law*. Translated by N.H.M. Keller. Abu Dhabi: Modern Printing Press.

Al-Ukhuwa, D.-D.M.I. (1938). *The ma'alim al-Qurab fi Ahkam al-Hisbah* (Edited by R. Levy). London: Luzak.

Alam, S.S., Mohd, R. and Hisham, B. (2011). Is Religiosity an Important Determinant on Muslim Consumer Behavior in Malaysia? *Journal of Islamic Marketing*, 2(1), 83–96.

Alserhan, B.A. (2015). *The Principles of Islamic Marketing*. Gower: London.

Amin, H., Abdul-Rahman, A. and Abdul Razak, D. (2014). Theory of Islamic Consumer Behavior: An Empirical Study of Consumer Behavior of Islamic Mortgage in Malaysia. *Journal of Islamic Marketing*, 5(2), 273–301.

Athanassopoulos, A.D. (2000). Customer Satisfaction Cues to Support Market Segmentation and Explain Switching Behavior. *Journal of Business Research*, 47(3), 191–207.

Awan, H.M., Siddiquei, A.N. and Haider, Z. (2015). Factors Affecting Halal Purchase Intention – Evidence from Pakistan's Halal Food Sector. *Management Research Review*, 38(6), 640–660.

Bachleda, C., Hamelin, N. and Benachour, O. (2014). Does Religiosity Impact Moroccan Muslim Women's Clothing Choice? *Journal of Islamic Marketing*, 5(2), 210–226.

Beekun, R.I. (1996). *Islam and Business Ethics*. Herndon: International Institute of Islamic Thought.

Chang, L.-C. (2005). The Study of Subculture and Consumer Behavior: An Example of Taiwanese University Students' Consumption Culture. *Journal of American Academy of Business*, 7(2), 258–265.

Chapra, M.U. (1992). *Islam and the Economic Challenge*. Herndon: International Institute of Islamic Thought.

Dubinsky, A.J., Jolson, M.A., Kotabe, M. and Chae, U.L. (1991). A Cross-National Investigation of Industrial Salespeople's Ethical Perceptions. *Journal of International Studies*, 22(Winter), 651–670.

Gallup (2009). Gallup Coexist Index: A Global Study of Interfaith Relations. http://www.olir.it/areetematiche/pagine/documents/News_2150_Gallup2009.pdf

Green, R.M. (1993). Centesimus Annus: A Critical Jewish Perspective. *Journal of Business Ethics*, 12(12), 945–954.

Hamdani, S.N.H. and Ahmad, E. (2002). Toward Divine Economics: Some Testable Propositions. *The Pakistan Development Review*, 41(4), 609–626.

Hassan, A., Chachi, A. and Abdul Latiff, S. (2008). Islamic Marketing Ethics and Its Impact on Customer Satisfaction. *Journal of King Abdulaziz University: Islamic Economy*, 21(1), 27–46.

Jafari, A. (2012). Islamic Marketing: Insights from a Critical Perspective. *Journal of Islamic Marketing*, 3(1), 22–34.

JWT (2009). Understanding the Islamic Consumer. www.wpp.com/NR/rdonlyres/0EE122EE-C956-431A-BFC9-78BED42011D1/0/marketing_to_muslims.pdf

JWT (2016). Travel and Hospitality: Halal Tourism. https://www.jwtintelligence.com

Kasriel, D. (2008). Spotlighting Europe's Muslim Consumers. *Euromonitor International*, September 10. Available at https://blog.euromonitor.com/spotlighting-europes-muslim-consumers/

Kearney, A.T. (2007). Addressing the Muslim Market. Available at: www.atkearney.com/images/global/pdf/AddressingMuslimMarket_S.pdf

Khan, M.F. (1984). Macro Consumption Function in an Islamic Framework. *Journal of Research in Islamic Economics*, 1(2), 3–15.

Khan, M.F. (1995). *Essays in Islamic Economics*. Leicester: Islamic Foundation.

Kotler, P. (2000). Consumer Market and Consumer Behavior. In *Principles of Marketing* (8th ed.). Upper Saddle River: Prentice-Hall.

Kotler, P. and Armstrong, G. (2006). *Principles of Marketing* (11th ed.). New Delhi: Prentice-Hall.

Lada, S., Tanakinjal, G.H. and Amin, H. (2009). Predicting Intention to Choose Halal Products Using Theory of Reasoned Action. *International Journal of Islamic and Middle Eastern Finance and Management*, 2(1), 66–76.

Malik, I.A. (1989). *Al-Muttawa of Imama Malik bin Anas – The First Formulation of Islamic Law*. Translated by B. Aisha. London: Kegan Paul International.

Miller, A. and Deiss, G.G. (1996). *Strategic Management*. New York: McGraw Hill.

Minkus-McKenna, D. (2007). The Pursuit of Halal. *Progressive Grocer*, 86(17), 42.

Miskawayh Ibn, A.I.M. (1968). *The Refinement of Character*. Translated by C.K. Zurayk. Beirut: The American University of Beirut.

Mustafar, M.Z. and Borhan, J.T. (2013). Muslim Consumer Behavior: Emphasis on Ethics from Islamic Perspective. *Middle East Journal of Scientific Research*, 18(9), 1301–1307.

Niazi, L.A.K. (1996). *Islamic Law of Contract*. Lahore: Research Cell, Dyal Sing Trust Library.

Ogilvy & Mather (2010). Brands, Islam and the New Muslim Consumer. Available at: www.ogilvy.com/News/Press-Releases/May-2010-The-Global-Rise-of-the-New-Muslim-Consumer.aspx

Pew Report (2009). *The Pew Forum on Religion and Public Life. Mapping the global Muslim population*. Washington, DC: The Pew Research Center.

Prahalad, C.K. (2004). *The Fortune at the Bottom-of-the-Pyramid*. Upper Saddle River: Wharton School Publishing.

Rice, G. (1999). Islamic Ethics and the Implications for Business. *Journal of Business Ethics*, 18, 345–358.

Saeed, M., Ahmed, Z.U. and Mukhtar, S.M. (2001). International Marketing Ethics from an Islamic Perspective: A Value Maximization Approach. *Journal of Business Ethics*, 32(2), 127–142.

Schouten, J.W. and McAlexander, J.H. (1995). Subcultures of Consumption: An Ethnography of the New Bikers. *Journal of Consumer Research*, 22(1), 43–61.

Shaw, S.A. (1996). *Business Ethics*. Belmont: Wadsworth Publishing Company.

Shaw, D.S. and Clarke, I. (1998). Culture, Consumption and Choice: Towards a Conceptual Relationship. *Journal of Consumer Studies and Home Economics*, 22(3), 163–168.

Siddiqi, M.N. (1981). Muslim Economic Thinking: A Survey of Contemporary Literature. In K. Ahmad (Ed.) *Studies in Islamic Economics*. Leicester: The Islamic Foundation.

Siddiqi, M.N. (1992). Islamic Consumer Behavior. In S. Tahir et al. (Eds), *Readings in Microeconomics in Islamic Perspective*. Kuala Lumpur: Longman, pp. 49–60.

Sohail, M.S., Al-Jabri, I.M. and Wahid, K.M. (2017). Relationship Between Marketing Program and Brand Loyalty: Is There an Influence of Gender? *Journal for Global Business Advancement*, 10(2), 109–124.

Sula, M.S. and Kartajaya, H. (2006). *Shariah Marketing*. Bandung: Mizan.

Tekbir (2017). Tekbir Clothing. https://www.tekbir.com.tr

Trim, B. (2008). *Business Wisdom of Muhammad SAW: 40 Kedahsyatan Bisnis Ala Nabi SAW* (Business Wisdom of Muhammad SAW: 40 Business Breakthrough of Prophet SAW). Bandung: Madania Prima.

Vasquez-Parraga A.Z. and Kara, A. (1995). Ethical Decision Making in Turkish Sales Management. In N. Delener (Ed.) *Ethical Issues on International Marketing*. Binghamton: International Business Press.

Vohra, M., Bhalla, G. and Chowdhury, A. (2009). Understanding the Islamic Consumer. *Research and Society: Research World*, February, pp. 40–43.

Wilson, R. (2006). Islam and Business. *Thunderbird International Business Review*, 48(1), 109–123.

Wilson, J.A.J. and Liu, J. (2010). Shaping the Halal into a Brand? *Journal of Islamic Marketing*, 1(2), 107–123.

Zebal, M.A. and Saber, H.M. (2014). Market Orientation in Islamic Banks – A Qualitative Approach. *Marketing Intelligence and Planning*, 32(4), 495–527.

Selected Bibliography

Alserhan, B.A. (2010). Islamic Branding: A Conceptualization of Related Terms. *Journal of Brand Management,* 18, 34–49.

Muhamad, N., Leong, V.S. and Mizerski, D. (2016). Consumer Knowledge and Religious Rulings on Products Young Muslim Consumer's Perspective. *Journal of Islamic Marketing,* 7(1), 74–94.

Wilson, J. and Grant, J. (2013). Islamic Marketing – A Challenger to the Classical Marketing Canon? *Journal of Islamic Marketing,* 4(1), 7–21.

HUMAN RESOURCE MANAGEMENT AND DECISION MAKING

HUMAN RESOURCE MANAGEMENT AND LABOR RELATIONS

8

Pawan Budhwar and Vijay Pereira

Aston Business School, Birmingham, UK

Faculty of Humanities and Social Sciences,
Khalifa University, Abu Dhabi, United Arab Emirates

Learning Outcomes

LO1: Develop an understanding of the nature of human resource (HR) management functions and practices in the Middle East.

LO2: Explain the determinants of human resource management (HRM) in the Middle East.

LO3: Describe how organizations manage the employment relationship and help to share responsibility between management, human resource specialists, and employees from an Islamic perspective.

LO4: Explain future directions for the HR function to tackle key HR challenges in the region.

Contents

As highlighted in the initial chapters, the Middle East is a vast and diverse region on which there remains a serious dearth of reliable information (except for a few countries such as the United Arab Emirates [UAE]) regarding the nature and pattern of management systems in general and human resource management (HRM) functions and practices in particular (see Budhwar, Pereira, Mellahi and Singh [2019] for a comprehensive review of HRM in the Middle East). This chapter aims to provide an overview of the latter. To put matters in context, it first provides a brief presentation on what HRM is in general and then presents developments in HRM in the Middle East in particular. This is followed by a discussion on the main factors that influence HRM functions and practices in the region. The chapter concludes by highlighting the main challenges facing human resource managers in the Middle East and by pointing to a way forward.

8.1   What is Human Resource Management (HRM)?

8.1.1   HRM in general

To gain a broader perspective on the topic of HRM, an overview of the various developments that have taken place in the field is essential. Learning about such developments can be inspirational for both students and HR practitioners because they demonstrate what has happened and indicate the expected direction of future developments. The field of HRM in the West (mainly Anglo-Saxon nations like the USA, the UK, Canada, Australia, and New Zealand) is now well developed. Its roots can be traced back to the scientific management movement in the late nineteenth and early twentieth centuries (e.g., the link between work design and rewards); the social reform movement launched in the early twentieth century by Robert Owen and George Cadbury in the United Kingdom (e.g., emphasizing worker welfare); to the creation of professional bodies like the Society for HRM in the United States and the Chartered Institute of Personnel and Development (founded in 1913 as the Institute of Industrial Welfare Workers); and the emergence of human relations, organizational development, and behavioral science (from the 1930s to the 1960s). Thus, debates in the field have evolved from being related to the nature of HRM (e.g., soft versus hard variant of HRM or personnel management versus HRM), the strategic nature of HRM, HRM as a source of competitive advantage, and the extent to which HRM helps to improve organizational performance. For details see Crawshaw et al. (2017).

The literature (e.g., Ulrich and Brockbank, 2005) also highlights a variety of roles performed by HR managers. These can be categorized as operational/tactical (e.g., administrator, regulator), strategic (e.g., change agent, advisor), and HR leadership. Similarly, the HR function in the West is now organized in a variety of ways, such as HR business partner, HR centers of excellence, HR shared services, her, and self-HR, and via HR outsourcing (Crawshaw et al., 2017). Accordingly, over the years a number of definitions have been proposed to explain what can be incorporated within the broad topic of HRM. For example, Storey (1995, p. 5) defines HRM as *"a distinctive approach to employment management which seeks to achieve competitive advantage through the strategic deployment of a highly committed and capable workforce using an array of cultural, structural and personnel techniques."*

However, the aforementioned developments have not taken place in a similar manner in other parts of the world, though there is evidence that they are now, but they simply have yet to happen on such a large scale. In the case of the Middle East, it is believed that the developments in HRM in most countries in the region are in their infancy (Budhwar and Mellahi, 2016). Hence, while analyzing the nature of HRM in such a context, it is important to define HRM in the broadest sense. This makes sense because several HRM approaches can exist within firms in different countries, each of which depends on a number of distinct internal labor markets (Budhwar and Sparrow, 2002). Within each labor market, HRM incorporates a range of subfunctions and practices, which include systems for workforce governance, work organization, staffing and development, and reward systems. For this chapter, we define HRM *"… concerned with the management of all employment relationships in the firm, incorporating the management of managers as well as non-management labor."*

8.1.2   HRM in the Middle East: An overview

In this overview of HRM for the Middle East, it is important to remember that there are few similarities (e.g., religion based) and many differences (e.g., economic development, availability of skills) between countries within the region, which have direct implications for the nature of the HRM function. To conduct a meaningful analysis, it would be sensible to focus on countries where sufficient cultural homogeneity exists and exclude countries that have significantly different HRM models. This will allow for a comprehensive discussion of countries operating within distinct contexts in terms of HRM practice. In this regard, the focus is on countries where Islam is the dominant religion. It is believed that Islam can be the major differentiator in the practice of HRM for the region because of its influence on the way people are managed in organizations (e.g. Mellahi and Budhwar, 2010; Budhwar et al., 2019). Although the Middle East is the birthplace of Islam, Judaism, and Christianity, Islam is the main religion of the Middle East, with approximately 95 percent of the total population following it.

Existing information on the region clearly indicates that most countries in the Middle East are now emphasizing the development of their human resources. In particular, the oil-rich countries want to reduce their dependence on oil and develop other sectors, which requires skilled human resources. Similarly, the non-oil-producing countries in the Middle East tend to rely on an efficient reserve of human resources for sustained economic growth. However, most countries in the region tend to overly rely on a foreign workforce, and given the rapidly increasing indigenous population and unemployment in the region, there is an increased emphasis on the development of so-called locals and a reduction in the number of foreigners in the workforce, for example by Saudi Arabia, UAE, and Oman. Such developments have resulted in the initiation of major nationalization programs (i.e., creating recruitment for locals). This has clear links to the creation of the right kind of marketable skills in the region and to changing the mindset of locals to work in the private sector and lower-level positions, which is proving to be a major challenge. These developments have serious implications for HRM in the region (Budhwar and Mellahi, 2012).

The existing literature highlights attempts to provide a country-specific HRM overview. In this regard, see, for example, the works of Al-Jahwari and Budhwar (2016) on Oman, Waxin and Bateman (2016) on UAE, Ali and Al-Kazemi (2006) on Kuwait, Tlaiss and Elamin (2016) on Saudi Arabia, Abdalla (2006) on Qatar, Ramdani et al. (2016) on Algeria, Zeynep (2006) on Turkey, El-kot (2016) on Egypt, Hatem (2006) on Sudan, Yahiaoui and Zoubir (2006) on Tunisia, and Hassi (2016) on Morocco (cited in Budhwar and Mellahi [2006, 2016]). These scholars discuss the nature and emerging patterns of HRM systems along with their key determinants in their respective countries. Additionally, two volumes by Budhwar and Mellahi (2006, 2016) and a few special issues of journals (Budhwar and Mellahi, 2007, 2010; Alfiouni et al., 2014) have helped to put together an overview of the HRM scenario in the region.

An analysis of the existing literature highlights the emergence of a number of key HRM-related themes. Perhaps the dominant one highlights the influence of Arab cultures and values on management systems and the immense impact of Islamic values, Islamic work ethics, and Islamic principles on HRM. Also, in addition to the influence of Arab values, the colonial legacy has continued to shape HRM practices in the region. Expectedly, owing to sociocultural similarities, a number of countries, such as Egypt, Morocco, Turkey, Kuwait, and Qatar, tend to be similar with respect to various aspects of cultural value orientations. For example, they tend to be high on group orientation, strong on hierarchical structures, high on masculinity, strong on following Arab traditions, and low on future orientation.

Mellahi and Budhwar (2006) report a strong impact of high power distance on managers' perceptions of the delegation of authority to lower-level employees and interactions with them in countries like Kuwait, Saudi Arabia, Morocco, and Egypt. As a result, managers in such countries practice centralized decision-making processes, are less willing to delegate responsibility, and discourage active employee participation. In such circumstances, and stemming from sociocultural and traditional expectations, loyalty to one's family and friends is expected to override loyalty to organizational procedures, and this often results in the use of inequitable criteria in recruitment, promotion, and compensation. Mellahi (2006) further highlights the influence of Islamic values and the principle of *shura* i.e., consultation, social harmony, and respect that are manifested in consensus decision-making styles, respect for authority and age, and concern for the wellbeing of employees and society at large in countries like Kuwait and Saudi Arabia. Further, several ideal Islamic values such as equity and fairness are often not adhered to in practice. This explains the widespread adoption of some HRM practices in the Middle East that are not compatible with Islamic values, such as nepotism in recruitment and compensation, known as *wasta* in Gulf Cooperation Council (GCC) countries, and *piston, m'aarifa,* and *k'tef* in North African countries.

Linked to the aforementioned nationalization programs is the theme of human resource development for enhancing the skills of locals. This has implications for the kind and nature of management education, its impact on managerial effectiveness, and the need for and mechanisms of management development in the Arab world. Given the presence of a large number of foreign nationals in the region, there is also a strong need for foreign firms and employees to be strongly responsive/adaptive to local requirements in order to be successful in the Middle East. This is more important given the significant cultural diversity of the foreign workforce in the Middle East, where it is crucial for managers to recognize, understand, and acknowledge the cultural differences of subordinates and, accordingly, adopt a relevant leadership style. Because of the high power distance in most Middle Eastern nations, an employee-oriented approach tends to be more successful than others.

8.2   Factors influencing HRM

8.2.1   Framework of factors influencing HRM in a cross-national context

Budhwar and Sparrow (2002) developed a framework of three levels of factors and variables that are known to determine the nature of HRM policies and practices in different national settings. These include national factors (e.g., national culture, national and international institutions, such as labor laws and educational and vocational frameworks, resulting in the creation of skills and dynamic business environment), organizational-level variables (such as age, size, nature, life cycle stage of the organization), and organizational strategic emphasis (e.g., cost reduction or an emphasis on rapid growth). It is beyond the scope of this chapter to provide an analysis of the impact of all factors and variables on HRM in the Middle East. Given that HRM is in its infancy in most Middle Eastern countries and the notion that HRM in a cross-national context can be best analyzed by examining the influence of national factors, the focus here is on national–international factors and their influence on HRM in the region.

8.2.2   Factors influencing HRM in the Middle East

Over the past couple of decades or so, countries like Jordan, Turkey, Egypt, Algeria, and Tunisia have been actively pursuing the process of privatization via liberalization of their economic systems, as a result of which central government control over HRM practices has been greatly reduced, which has serious implications for the HRM systems of those countries. Some of the obvious impacts are reflected in job security in the public sector (which is now eroding quickly) and the downsizing and closure of poorly performing firms. The growing high level of unemployment has had a significant impact on employment relations in Tunisia, Egypt, Algeria, and Morocco in the form of declines in union membership and decreases in their bargaining power.

As mentioned earlier, the national governments of many countries emphasize the development of local human resources and accordingly give organizations freedom in HRM matters, though within a legal framework. As a result, the names and nature of traditional personnel departments are changing to emphasize developing effective HRM systems to help firms compete at home and abroad. However, in the absence of skilled HRM professionals in most Middle Eastern countries, HR managers have been muddling through, often relying on "trial and error" to cope with the impact of market liberalization and severe international competition. To compensate for such skills gaps, many countries like Algeria, UAE, Oman, Jordan, Kuwait, and Saudi Arabia are heavily investing in the development of their human resources. A number of systems issues in these countries, such as the lack of a vocation-based educational system, supply and demand imbalance, negative perception of locals with respect to working in the private sector or in lower-level positions, and the lack of participation of women in the main workforce, are proving to be the main bottlenecks (Budhwar and Mellahi 2012; Ali et al., 2017). Further, the strong emphasis on localization (i.e., giving priority to local nationals when it comes to job offers and promotions) is not helping either private-sector or multinational firms with the rationalization of their HRM systems.

Also, new laws have been put in place that give public-sector organizations greater autonomy when it comes to HRM issues; nevertheless, it is still rather challenging to fire employees in the public sector. For example, in public-sector organizations in Saudi Arabia, HR needs to overcome numerous legal challenges before they get rid of an employee. However, in the private sector, there has been a strong move away from the traditional lifetime employment and seniority-based reward systems to flexible employment arrangements that include performance-related and merit-based (evidenced through required levels of formal education and relevant work experience) pay. Thus, such individualized HRM practices have evolved, where relevant person-based performance and profile are becoming the key factors of an individual's remuneration, promotion, and so forth and this is evident in countries such as Turkey, Egypt, Algeria, and Morocco.

Other important determinants, such as economic and institutional aspects that impact and define HRM in diverse Middle Eastern countries, also vary, and this leads to divergent HRM models in each Middle Eastern country. For instance, given their geographical positions, countries such as Turkey, the North African countries Morocco, Algeria, and Tunisia, and Egypt have been significantly influenced by European culture more than GCC countries because of the obvious historical colonial presence. Thus, for example, the issue of gender inequality, though still present, is relatively and comparatively less in Morocco, Algeria, Tunisia, Egypt, Israel, and Turkey than in other GCC countries.

Additional evidence from countries like Algeria illustrate that contemporary HRM models echo the diverse historical contexts within which they evolved. There is evidence in the three North African countries (Morocco, Algeria, and Tunisia) suggesting that a comparable influence of French colonialism on HRM procedures, such as the use of the French language as a criterion for professional status, is often used as a criterion for recruitment, selection, and other areas of career advancement.

In addition to the foregoing factors, national wealth, composition of the workforce, trade unions, and employment legislation combine to create a unique country- or region-specific HRM model. For instance, the Middle East has some of the richest countries in the world, such as the UAE and Qatar, and some of the poorest, for example, Yemen and Sudan. This radical disparity in national wealth, understandably, results in different approaches to HRM. For example, in poor countries it is rare for small and medium-size organizations to invest in formal training. While this is partly due to the fact that managers are not convinced of or perhaps do not value the possible impact of HRM on improving organizational performance, the cost of conducting such training is prohibitive, especially for small organizations. This is not the case in GCC countries, where training and development of locals are extensive.

This drastic disproportion in national wealth plausibly result in diverse slants HRM approaches. For example, in poor countries it is rare for small and medium size organizations to invest in formal training of their employees. Whilst this could be partly credited to the that managers are not persuaded and influenced or possibly do not value the conceivable influence of HRM on cultivating organizational performance. Further, the cost of conducting such training is unaffordable and may be unreasonable, especially for small organizations. However, this is not the case in many GCCs countries, where training and development of locals is a priority and extensively used.

Apart from the fact that wealth inequality significantly influences human resource development, the configuration and composition of the labor market have caused differentiated HRM systems. Another are where this is evident is in the indigenous population, which the GCC countries must rely and, hence, require a wide-ranging use of foreign labor (expatriates) to develop their evolving infrastructure and to have successful economies, especially following the discovery of oil. However, these countries, from a more recent point of view, have started to rely on changing economic landscapes through investments in differentiated areas. An example of this is the UAE's strategy of investing in and utilizing artificial intelligence and innovation to pursue its strategy of global competitiveness. As a result, the composition of the labor market in these few GCC countries is more diverse than other Middle Eastern countries. While unemployment is greater in both GCC countries and the wider Middle Eastern countries, the reasons behind such unemployment are diverse in GCC countries compared to factors driving unemployment in other Middle Eastern countries. For example, in Algeria, Egypt, Morocco, and Tunisia, unemployment is largely said to be driven by the very absence and lack of jobs in the labor market, which has an adverse effect on the countries' ability to absorb the large number of young people entering the job market. Further, in some GCC countries, many locals will not accept socially undesirable jobs, and this is a cause of unemployment. Another very important and interesting factor is that while many Middle Eastern countries offer workers the right to form and join trade unions, a few GCC countries ban trade unions. That said, newer arrangements of work associations started to emerge in the 2000s, though the role of such associations is restricted to dealing with areas of abuse of foreign expatriate workers, which includes cases of delay in payments of salaries and arbitrary deportation. Additionally, the right to strike is acceptable in Algeria, Morocco, Tunisia, Egypt, Israel, and Turkey, but in GCC countries, strikes are illegal.

8.3 Challenges for HRM in the Middle East

The field of HRM seems to be evolving rapidly in terms of the function and role of HR managers in the Middle East (Budhwar et al., 2019). As discussed previously, there is a growing trend toward individualization in HRM policies, which includes areas such as rewards and promotion in Algeria, Morocco, Turkey, and Egypt. Also evident more recently in most Middle Eastern countries is a movement away from relationship-based practices toward greater performance-based measures when it comes to areas such as recruitment, selection, rewards, and promotion within HRM. Such an evolution of changes in HRM policies and practices has been encouraged, driven, and influenced by the volatility and ever-shifting transformations within the macro business environment. These include, among other key drivers, the escalation of global competition and its impact on Middle Eastern countries, the intense surge in information technologies—especially in the GCC countries—and the impact of Western approaches to work organization and management, predominantly in countries such as Morocco, Algeria, Tunisia, Egypt, and Turkey.

Unfortunately, though, the transformation needed to take on the aforementioned challenges is not keeping pace, and changes are happening too slowly. The explanations for such sluggishness are manifold and diverse. Thus, organizational inhibitors leading to greater organizational change in the Middle East could consist of quality of leadership leading to indecision, incompetence in managing change, and organizational inertia and politics in embedded routines and traditional non-productive ways (Budhwar and Mellahi, 2016; Budhwar et al., 2019). Further, the immature status of HRM in most Middle Eastern countries could be seen as another inhibitor of quicker and more reliable change in HRM policies and practices. Thus, HRM in many Middle Eastern countries has a low standing and often consigned to a "common sense" role—and the role and positioning of top management are such that HR management does not require professional skills. Because of this low standing of HRM, HR managers lack professional training, which would allow them to obtain requisite and relevant skills that would in turn develop and advance the competences needed to effect change and tackle existing and future challenges. Additionally, given the absence of skills and capabilities to deal with existing and future challenges, HR departments are prone to making rash decisions largely grounded on incomplete and disjointed measures to deal with the challenges posed by the constraints of a free market economy faced by additional and ever growing global competition. The failure to "upgrade" HRM as a discipline and develop "new" HRM skills and competences will have very important and productive implications for HRM in the Middle East. Developing a large pool of competent HRM managers takes time, effort, and dedication in training and development. However, there is a current dearth of HRM courses, and given the low standing in the region of HRM as a discipline (which is currently evolving at a fast pace), the absence of skilled HRM staff exacerbates the status quo.

The next most pressing area of action is the crucial necessity to change the mindset about unbalanced relationship-based HRM policies linked to cultural concepts that include *wasta* and *piston*—toward more competence or merit-based attitudes. This challenge is more important in the current context because of the obvious effects the countries in the Middle East are facing owing to the dynamic pace of global economic integration, and this may have a sizeable effect on the survivability and sustainability of ailing organizations in the region. This challenging shift will spur local management to be more committed by being transparent and fair when it comes to equal opportunities in recruiting, training, and rewarding employees. Therefore, the survival and sustainability of a large number of Middle Eastern organizations going forward will depend on fundamentally unlearning old, ineffective, or obsolete HRM practices and learning new, successful, globally accepted ones.

Another challenge, the high unemployment levels in the Middle East, is of concern. High past and present birth rates have compounded and added to the pressure on labor markets in most Middle Eastern countries. While one could argue that the risky and possibly precarious levels of unemployment can be immensely subversive in the Middle East, the key point of enquiry is who is responsible for enduring the price of falling unemployment, and this needs some thought. Here, the state along with the evolving private sector will need to develop a system whereby, on the one hand, the state subsidizes the cost of training locals and, on the other hand, this encourages private-sector firms to recruit more local workers.

In the context of existing and predictable economic and political challenges in the Middle East, where HRM is concerned the future will require serious trade-offs. One significant trade-off will involve, on the one hand, the necessity for augmented global competitiveness and economic competence and, on the other hand, adherence to resilient traditions and tensions for needs of social security and welfare. Thus, owing to the ever-increasing global business environment along with global competitiveness, we believe social security and welfare needs would decline in favor of more liberal and market-oriented socioeconomic development. Hence, within GCC countries, governments largely subsidize public-sector (and, to a certain extent, a few private-sector) firms that create employment largely for locals. However, this scenario is now quickly moving toward a more economically efficient and rationalized model, which predicts that unskilled workers, people possessing irrelevant skills, and those who had previously been employed in the public sector would be the most affected. This is because existing and future social and economic reforms will affect the existing scenario. Thus, the discussed trade-offs are currently evident and more trade-offs are expected in all Middle Eastern countries in the near future. As implications and regulation complications will differ and diverge within each country because of institutional and economic differences, studying HRM in the Middle East region becomes interesting and topical. For example, while richer countries such as Qatar and UAE will continue to be able to provide a relatively generous social safety net, less-rich countries, such as Egypt, Sudan, and Morocco, will struggle to keep pace.

8.3.1   The way forward

Moving forward, future emphasis should be on the connection between macro (i.e., organizational-level) and individual (i.e. employee-level) aspects and HRM procedures and practices to deliver insights into the important factors of HRM in the Middle East. In particular, there is a need to recognize and organize the distinctive region-specific features of national culture and other determinants, political institutions, and other probable external factors that affect HRM in the Middle East (see the comprehensive review in Budhwar et al. [2019]). Others area worth investigating are the association between organizational strategy and control and HRM consequences and the relationship between microlevel individual values and characteristics and macrolevel HRM practices in organizations.

Further, there is a need to understand how HRM policies and practices influence organizational performance and recognize which HRM influences and policies are associated with greater performance in the Middle Eastern region. In this regard, case-study research of high-performing firms in the Middle East can help recognize those influences and practices that correlate with high performance. It would also be worth including both indigenous HRM practices based on Islamic principles and practices that were developed elsewhere for such investigations. For instance, there is evidence in high-performance work systems (HPWSs) in other parts of the world, but literally nothing on HPWSs in the Middle East.

8.4 Summary

Based on the foregoing analysis, it can be concluded that there is a dearth of studies on different aspects of HRM systems in the Middle East, as a result of which it is difficult to form a conclusive and comprehensive picture of the situation. Also, it is difficult to confidently say whether there is such a thing such as a Middle Eastern HRM model, i.e., a single HRM model with distinct Middle Eastern characteristics. Perhaps for a number of reasons related to diversity within the region (e.g., historical contexts; institutional, geographical, cultural, political, legal, social, and developmental stages of nations; the support of relevant agencies; national wealth, poverty, and priorities; and issues related to terrorism, the role of unions, reliance on foreign labor), organizations in the Middle East seem to use a whole range of different HRM policies and practices, and the professionalization of HRM functions is at different stages in different countries.

Chapter Highlights

The analysis presented in this chapter will provide a good understanding of the following issues:

- The meaning of HRM
- Developments in the field of HRM in general
- Developments in HRM in the Middle East in particular
- Factors influencing HRM in the Middle East
- Key challenges faced by the HRM function in the region
- The way forward for the HRM function

Key Terms

Human resource management (HRM)
Islamic values
National factors
Piston
Shura
Wasta

Discussion Questions

1. Define HRM. Provide a rationale for incorporating various aspects of employment relations in the definition.

2. Discuss the key developments in the field of HRM in the West.

3. Summarize the emerging nature of HRM in the Middle East.

4. Identify and discuss the key determinants of HRM in the Middle East.

5. What are the key challenges confronting the HRM function in the Middle East? As an HR manager, how would you deal with them? Discuss.

6. As an HR manager, how would you ensure that your nationalization program is successfully implemented in your country and organizations? Provide logical suggestions to support your recommendations.

7. Considering the key challenges faced by the HR function highlighted in the chapter, how would you approach dealing with them? Provide evidence-based recommendations.

Online Resources

Useful Websites

Fact Sheet: http://www.doingbusiness.org/~/media/GIAWB/Doing%20Business/Documents/Fact-Sheets/DB15/DB15MENAFactSheetEnglish.pdf

World Bank: http://www.worldbank.org/en/region/mena

GCC: http://www.worldbank.org/en/country/gcc

Arab League: http://www.arableagueonline.org

Middle East Media Research Institute: http://www.memri.org

Middle East Institute: http://www.mei.edu

ILO in the Arab States: http://www.ilo.org/beirut/lang%2D%2Den/index.htm

The Society for Human Resource Management MEA: http://www.shrm.org/pages/mena.aspx

https://www.hbmsu.ac.ae/research/research-portfolio/middle-east-case-studies-centre

Selected Bibliography

Alfiouni, F., Ruel, H. and Schuler, R. (2014). HRM in the Middle East: Toward a Greater Understanding. *International Journal of Human Resource Management*, 25(2), 133–143.

Ali, F., Malik, A., Pereira, V. and Al Ariss, A. (2017). A Relational Understanding of Work-Life Balance of Muslim Migrant Women in the West: Future Research Agenda. *The International Journal of Human Resource Management*, 28(8), 1163–1181.

Budhwar, P. and Mellahi, K. (Eds.) (2006) *Managing Human Resources in the Middle East*. Routledge: London.

Budhwar, P. and Mellahi, K. (2007). Introduction: Human Resource Management in the Middle East. *The International Journal of Human Resource Management*, 18(1), 2–10.

Budhwar, P. and Mellahi, K. (2012) Human Resource Management in the Middle East. In C. Brewster and W. Mafrhofer (Eds.) *Handbook of Research on Comparative Human Resource Management*. Cheltenham: Edward Elgar, pp. 512–527.

Budhwar, P. and Mellahi, K. (Eds.). (2016). *Handbook of Human Resource Management in the Middle East*. Cheltenham: Edward Elgar.

Budhwar, P. and Sparrow, P. (2002) An Integrative Framework for Determining Cross-National Human Resource Management Practices. *Human Resource Management Review*, 12(3), 377–403.

Budhwar, P., Pereira, V., Mellahi, K. and Singh, S.K. (2019). Emerging Patterns of HRM in the Middle East: Challenges and Future Research Agenda. *Asia Pacific Journal of Management*, 36(4), 905–933. doi:https://doi.org/10.1007/s10490-018-9587-7.

Crawshaw, J., Budhwar, P. and Davis, A. (Eds.) (2017) *Human Resource Management: Strategic and International Perspectives*. London: Sage.

Mellahi, K. (2006). Human Resource Management in Saudi Arabia. In *Managing Human Resources in the Middle-East*. London: Routledge, pp. 115–138.

Mellahi, K. and Budhwar, P.S. (2006). Human Resource Management in the Middle East: Emerging HRM Models and Future Challenges for Research and Policy. In *Managing Human Resources in the Middle-East*. London: Routledge, pp. 309–319.

Mellahi, K. and Budhwar, P.S. (2010). Introduction: Islam and Human Resource Management. *Personnel Review*, 39(6), 685–691.

Storey, J. (1995). Human Resource Management: Still Marching On, or Marching Out? In J. Storey (Ed.) *Human Resource Management: A Critical Text*. London: Routledge.

Ulrich, D. and Brockbank, W. (2005). *The HR Value Proposition*. Boston: Harvard University Press.

EMPLOYEE BEHAVIOR AND MOTIVATION IN THE LIGHT OF ISLAM

9

Soleman Mozammel

Business Studies Program, Arab Open University,
A'ali, Kingdom of Bahrain

Learning Outcomes

LO1: Analyze the impact of Islamic values on individual, team, and organizational behavior and performance.

LO2: Understand employee motivation (intrinsic and extrinsic) in an organization.

LO3: Identify the nature and importance of job design.

LO4: Identify the factors affecting individual motivation, behavior, and performance in Islam.

LO5: Explain the tools used by Islamic and modern businesses to measure employee performance.

Contents

INSIGHT: Muslim Always on Duty: A Story of Motivation: We're Always 100 Percent on Duty

When a new European airline was launched, an educated Muslim gentleman was flying first class. A flight attendant approached him with a complimentary drink, but it was an alcoholic drink, so the man politely refused.

The flight attendant returned after a few minutes, but this time with the drink on a platter so as to appeal to and impress the man. However, the Muslim man again politely refused, explaining that he doesn't drink alcohol. The flight attendant was concerned and informed the cabin manager. The manager, thinking that the passenger might be dissatisfied with the service, which is why he turned down the drink, brought the man a second platter, now with flowers, and asked, "Sir, is there something wrong with our service? Please enjoy the drink; it's complimentary."

The man replied, "Thanks, but I am a Muslim and I do not drink alcohol." The manager still insisted that the man accept the drink.

Then the Muslim man suggested that the manager give the drink to the pilot first. The manager said, "How can the pilot drink alcohol, he's on duty?" and added, "And if he drinks, the plane could crash."

The passenger replied, "Sir, I am a Muslim and I'm always on duty protecting my *iman*, and if I drink, I will crash my whole life here and in the hereafter."

9.1   Introduction

Religious beliefs impact the background of an individual or a team in an organization. Therefore, they may play an important role in employee behavior, affecting employee motivation and, hence, organizational performance. The degree of influence of religious beliefs may not be limited to any particular territory, but it has expanded throughout the world due to rapid diversification in the workforce.

Business is an important element in the Muslim world, as in any part of the world. Therefore, rapid business growth has given rise to the rapid growth of organizations. In a competitive and dynamic business setting, identifying one's competitive edge is a key success indicator (KSI) for all organizations. Numerous organizations give a lot of thought to the KSI as a main objective. To meet that objective, there is a need of an effective work force management approach to motivate employees Therefore, a human resource management system should be in place that provides guidelines on recruiting and retaining motivated employees through effective job design.

The purpose of this chapter is to explain employee behavior and motivation in connection with Islamic values as they relate to individuals and teams and their consequent effect on organizational behavior and performance. At the same time, the chapter will discuss the importance of job design, which can enhance employee motivation and behavior. Finally, the chapter discusses the tools used by Islamic and modern businesses to measure employee performance.

9.2   Impact of Islamic values on individual, team, and organizational behavior and performance

Employee performance plays a crucial role in an organization's ability to achieve and sustain success (Bonache and Noethen, 2014). Important factors leading to superior organizational performance include work ethic, work attitude, employee engagement, employee motivation, and job satisfaction. But in Islamic management, these attributes of organizational performance are not sufficient. In an Islamic organizational setting, instilling in employees an Islamic mindset that leads to individual awareness about one's intent at work is essential. In the following section, some attributes of Islamic values are discussed in relation to performance.

9.2.1 Islamic values: Ethics

Muslim employees must not forget that their only intention to work is to worship Allah in order attain blessing from Allah (Abeng, 1997; Sharabi, 2012). The impact of such a value is so strong that through this awareness, employees are able to demonstrate great enthusiasm in performing their responsibilities, regardless of any obstacles. The main idea behind this value is that no one besides Almighty Allah has the power to help, guide, and give blessings to his servants who are patiently waiting. At the same time, Islamic values teach Muslims not to surrender to any form of laziness but to believe that Allah is watching his servants. Therefore, this awareness and value lead the individual or team to behave ethically.

Islamic values play an imperative role, impacting individuals, families, and the professional life of Muslims. In light of Islamic values, dedicated Muslims never complain about their duties but just become resolved to carry out their responsibilities, like everything they do with the utmost sincerity so as to receive Allah's blessing. Devout Muslims are keen to attain not only worldly rewards but also rewards in the hereafter. Muslims report high job satisfaction when they exert considerable effort to demonstrate their sincerity in carrying out work assignments, as well as *tawakal* on rewards.

9.3 Islamic values: Employee behavior and organizational performance

Employment is one of the main necessities of life. But it takes both great achievement and execution to lead a productive life for an individual or a team (Pfeffer and Veiga, 1999). However, a Muslim is required to have a different approach, such as that dictated by Islamic values, than the theoretical approach of Western philosophy, to accomplish and sustain high job performance. Islamic values mean that the work of a Muslim is an act of worshipping Allah (Basharat, 2009). It is stated in the Holy Qur'an (Surah Adh-Dhāriyāt verse 56): "And I did not create the jinn and mankind except to worship Me." This verse clearly indicates that one of the main devotions behind the creation of humans is to make them realize that the significance of intention before beginning and completing a task is that taking on a given task must relate to worshipping Allah and seeking Allah's blessings (Sulaiman et al., 2014). This cognizance inspires Muslim employees to carry out their work successfully.

At the same time, through nurturing Islamic values and awareness, Muslim employees are expected to demonstrate behavior both in their daily life and working life that totally prevents them from engaging in any unethical behavior. Again, this is due to their love for, fear of, and belief, in light of Islamic values, that Allah is always watching them wherever they are and whatever they are doing.

Organizations conduct appraisals or audits in order to measure and enhance the quality of their employees' performance. To measure the ethical standard and performance of Muslim employees, it is essential to understand whether or not Muslim employees are following Islamic values to a significant degree. Theoretically, a Muslim society that is under the guidance of the Holy Qur'an and *hadith* must possess high ethics and refrain themselves from behaving unethically. Islam and Islamic values guide all aspects of Muslims' lifestyle, leading to both individual and organizational success if they all learn and implement Islamic values and guidance in their daily life (Beekun and Badawi, 2005).

There is a significant relationship between Islamic values, ethics, and job performance, and many scholars have asserted that employees with higher Islamic values have been found to be inclined to higher job productivity, leading to overall higher organizational performance. This chapter implies an organization is determined to recruit and retain employees with higher Islamic values that can lead to a stronger work ethic. At the same time, the chapter also stressed the importance of an awareness and understanding of Islamic values in an employee's daily activities, which brings greater prosperity and satisfaction to the individual or the organization.

9.4   Identify the nature and importance of job design

Organizational leadership is responsible for creating and maintaining a proper atmosphere to assist employees develop their full potential. Failure to do so could cause frustration, resulting in reduced motivation and engagement with work and lower job satisfaction. As a result, poor performance and productivity, increased withdrawal from work, and reduced retention are inevitable. The major challenge that organizations face is motivating their diverse workforce. Management must recognize the various needs of their employees along with the factors that affect their motivation impacting the achievement of organizational goals and their own performance and career prospects (Ali, 2009).

If employees are not motivated appropriately, no system can ensure efficiency in the utilization of resources or fairness in their distribution. To motivate employees to do their best and use limited resources with maximum efficiency, it is necessary to address their personal needs and interests. Socialism is very simplistic and unrealistic because it expects individuals to work efficiently, even if they are deprived of the opportunity to pursue personal interests. Capitalism is considered to be unrealistic when it assumes that personal and social interests are always balanced. Secular and capitalist perspectives do not create a mechanism for motivating individuals to serve in line with societal interests when those oppose employees' personal interests. Motivating employees to work efficiency and fairly simultaneously is impossible, unless a spiritual dimension is injected into their personal interests so that societal interests are not threatened, even when they oppose personal ones (Chapra, 1995). Islamization implies the serious implementation of an Islamic strategy to improve the spiritual goodness as much as the material prosperity of employees and establish social–economic justice, which is the central purpose of job design.

9.4.1   Job design: Importance

Job design or job analysis aims at outlining and organizing tasks, duties, and responsibilities into a single unit of work for the achievement of certain objectives. It also outlines the methods and relationships that are essential for the success of a certain job. Job design essentially involves integrating job responsibilities or content and certain qualifications that are required to perform them. It outlines the job responsibilities very clearly and also helps in attracting the right candidates to the right job. Further it also makes jobs look interesting and specialized.

9.4.1.1   Benefits

The following are the benefits of a good job design:

1. **Employee input:** A good job design enables helpful job feedback. Employees have the option to vary tasks according to their personal and social needs, habits, and circumstances in the workplace. This also increases motivation and engagement by employees when they are aware of their duties and responsibilities.

2. **Employee training:** Training is an integral part of job design. Contrary to the philosophy of "leave them alone," job design lays due emphasis on training people so that they are well aware of what their job demands and how it is to be done. It is essential for employees to be trained in order to be technologically competent and use updated tools.

3. **Work/rest schedules:** Job design offers a work and rest schedule by clearly defining the number of hours workers must spend on their job.

4. **Adjustments:** A good job design allows for adjustments for physically demanding jobs by minimizing the energy spent doing the job and by aligning manpower requirements for such jobs.

Job design is a continuous and ever-evolving process aimed at helping employees make adjustments to changes in the workplace. The end goal is reducing dissatisfaction and enhancing motivation and employee engagement in the workplace.

9.4.1.2   Job description

Job description includes basic job-related data that are useful for advertising a specific job and attracting a pool of talent. It includes information such as job title, job location, supervisors and coworkers, job summary, the nature and objectives of the job, tasks and duties to be performed, working conditions, machines, tools, and equipment to be used, and related hazards.

9.4.1.3   Purpose of job description

- The main purpose of a job description is to collect job-related data in order to advertise for a particular job. It helps in attracting, targeting, recruiting, and selecting the right candidate for a given job.

- A job description is given to establish the deliverables of a particular job. It clarifies what employees will be expected to do if selected for a particular job opening.

- It gives recruiting staff a clear understanding of what kind of candidate is required by a particular department or division to perform a specific task or job.

- It also clarifies who will report to whom.

9.4.1.4   Job specification

Also known as employee specifications, a job specification is a written statement of educational qualifications, specific qualities, level of experience, and physical, emotional, technical, and communication skills required to perform a job, as well as the responsibilities involved in that job and other unusual sensory demands. It also includes, for example, general physical health, mental health, intelligence, aptitude, memory, judgment, leadership skills, emotional ability, adaptability, flexibility, values and ethics, manners, and creativity.

9.4.1.5   Purpose of job specification

- Presented on the basis of a job description, job specifications help candidates analyze whether they are qualified for a particular job or not.

- It helps the recruiting team of an organization understand what level of qualifications, qualities, and set of characteristics should be present in a candidate to make him or her eligible for the job opening.

- A job specification gives detailed information about a job, including job responsibilities, desired technical and physical skills, social skills, and much more.

- It helps in selecting the most appropriate candidate for a particular job.

A job description and job specification are two integral parts of job analysis. They define a job fully and guide both employer and employee on how to go about the whole process of recruitment and selection. Both data sets are extremely relevant for creating a right fit between job and talent, evaluating performance, analyzing training needs, and measuring the value of a particular job.

9.5   Identify the factors affecting individual motivation, behavior, and performance in Islam

9.5.1   Motivation

The word motivation originates from *movere*, a Latin word related to "moving." Therefore, motivation means moving an individual from tediousness to attentiveness. It resembles steering the wheel of a car that directs our actions. Motivation may be defined as a psychological process that instigates arousal, direction, and persistence of goal-oriented activities (Mitchell, 1982). Motivation may also be defined as an energized behavior providing direction and underlying the tendency to persist (Bartol and Martin, 1998). This definition clearly recognizes that individuals must have goal-oriented energy to focus on accomplishing what needs to be achieved. At the same time, individuals must persevere for a long enough time to realize their goals. Motivation is an important aspect or leading function of management that impacts individuals' motivation to achieve organizational goals.

There are two main types of motivation:

- **Extrinsic motivation**

  Extrinsic motivation is connected with the external characteristics of a job and usually relates to material means. Mainly, the importance of extrinsic motivation lies in its importance based on certain material benefits and rewards that exist at the bottom level of human needs (Ghauri, 2009).

- **Intrinsic motivation**

  Intrinsic motivation, in contrast to extrinsic motivation for external rewards, such as money and rank, is established in the heart of an individual. This motivation derives from the pleasure of work. Therefore, intrinsic motivation is defined as the desire of an individual to work willingly in order to obtain the internal satisfaction (Zaman et al., 2013). Employees with increased intrinsic motivation perform a job with passion because the job is interesting and enjoyable. Therefore, there is a significant relationship between intrinsic motivation and job satisfaction that impacts positive organizational commitment and job performance.

  Iintrinsic motivation reflects the internal aspect of individuals, rooted in their heart in the following two ways:

- **Religious/spiritual motivation**

  Individuals under this type of motivation are more guided by their spiritual characteristics, where these characteristics may lead to more energy and motivational force toward achieving their goals Religious motivation has an everlasting influence and it is the passion inside that aids individuals to consider themselves in a higher position compared to all individuals.

- **Rational motivation**

  Rational motivation is driven from specific purpose igniting a positive energy to accomplish a certain task. This motivation type satisfies talented individuals with a curious mind who enjoy the internal satisfaction of facing challenging work that has a long-term effect as opposed to material gain.

- **Spiritual/religious motivation in light of Islam**

  Spiritual or religious motivation is considered to be at the top of the list as it is recognized as an internal force (Ghauri, 2009). Only spiritual motivation can be a real force. Motivation theory in Islam contemplates two types of human behavior. First, it contemplates the inner world of individuals relating to Islamic faith. Second, it connects the outer world of individuals to physiological needs, that is, material needs. The prophet of Islam stated, "Remember that there is a piece of meat in your body. If it is good, the whole body becomes good and if it is bad, the whole body becomes bad. This piece of meat is your heart." This relates to the intrinsic personality, reflected in the will power of success or failure. Muslims believe that the motivational spirit of Islam is the main factor behind success (Ahmad et al., 2013).

9.5.2 Motivation: Other schools of thought

Other motivation theories have been classified into three major categories:

(a) Needs theory

(b) Cognitive theory

(c) Reinforcement theory.

9.5.2.1 Needs theory

Needs theory was developed by Abraham Maslow, and therefore, it is known as Maslow's motivation theory of hierarchical needs. There are five basic levels of needs that must be satisfied sequentially. They are:

- Existence: The type of needs that include physiological factors, namely, food, shelter, clothes, good pay, fringe benefits, safety at workplace.

- Relatedness: Relationship with others like family, friends, peers.

- Growth: Professional growth, self-esteem, and self-actualization.

9.5.2.2 Hygiene factors

Hygiene factors were developed by Herzberg, Mausner and Snyderman. According to Herzberg, et al. (2011), there are two factors, motivators and hygiene, in employee motivation. The theory argued that eliminating the cause of dissatisfaction (through hygiene factors) does not necessarily result in a state of satisfaction. Satisfaction (or motivation) transpires only as a consequence of using motivators.

9.5.2.3   Cognitive theory

Cognitive theory explains three types of needs: achievement, affiliation, and power. But it is argued that the strength of a propensity to act with determination is dependent on the strength of the anticipation that the action will be followed by a given positive outcome and on the attractiveness of that outcome to the individual.

9.5.2.4   Equity theory

Equity theory concedes that employees are concerned not only with the outright amount of remuneration they receive for their work, but also with the relationship of this amount to what their peers receive. Based on one's contributions, such as energy, knowledge, education, and capability, an employee can compare outcomes like remuneration, gratitude, and other considerations. Tension arises when people observe an imbalance in their outcome–input ratio relative to their peers. Equity theory is based on three main assumptions. First, the theory embraces employees developing beliefs about constituting a fair and equitable return for their contributions in the job. Second, the theory assumes that employees always compare what they perceive as the conversation their peers have with their employers.

9.5.2.5   Goal-setting theory

In goal-setting theory, it has been proven that if people are provided with a goal followed by a reward, then they become motivated. But the goals must be specific and measurable, challenging but attainable, relevant to the organization, and must be accomplished within a specific period of time. It is usually considered a powerful motivational tool by many leaders and employees.

9.5.2.6   Reinforcement theories

Reinforcement theories may be considered the antithesis of cognitive theories as the theories do not seem to relate to human thought processes. According to reinforcement theory, employee behavior can be rationalized by the effects of environment, and therefore, it is not necessary to look for cognitive explanations. The theory is mainly dependent on the law of effect, which says that behaviors ending with positive consequences are likely to be repeated and behaviors ending with unpleasant or negative consequences are less likely to be repeated (Bartol and Martin, 1998).

The previously mentioned Western theories provide the foundation for a significant amount of organization and managerial development practices. These theories mainly concentrate on explaining both employees' motivation and the effective influence of various motivating factors on employees' career achievement and on overall organizational performance. But at the same time, because they have their roots mainly in the Western social perspective of needs, these theories are mainly based on their orthodox value system. Therefore, the religious perspective of needs, especially the Islamic perspective, is not very evident in these theories.

9.6   Islamic perspective

Unlike the Western perspective, the Islamic perspective of human behavior and needs differs by concentrating more on the view that life is a test for Muslims to achieve success based on the blessings of Allah in the hereafter. It is only possible to achieve those blessings by worshipping Allah and through following *Shariah*, the code of laws in Islam. From this point of view, this chapter aims to explore and understand motivation and employee performance from an Islamic perspective in relation to Islamic management. The study has three main objectives: (1) understand Muslim managers' perspective of employee motivation and the factors that influence it, (2) understand the factors that influence the motivation of Muslim employees, and (3) understand the effect of the idea of a second life (i.e., the hereafter) on Muslim employees while looking at career success.

Traditional motivational theories do not provide the whole picture of human motivation as per the literature on motivation based on an Islamic perspective. Some Islamic scholars argue that fulfillment of spiritual needs should be recognized and considered as essential for Muslims (Rahman and Al-Buraey, 1992). But Western theories do not consider spiritual needs and mainly concentrate on worldly rewards. Therefore, the spiritual aspect of motivation is missing in Western theories.

It has been argued by Islamic scholars that material motivations and spiritual motivations complement each other, so they are interdependent and interrelated to each other. The following factors are considered in an Islamic perspective:

- Knowledge

- Free will

- *Taqwa* (piety)

- *Iman* (faith)

- *Ihsan* (perfection)

- *Amanah* (trusteeship)

- *Falah* and *Amal Saleh* (virtuous deeds)

- *Tahrid* (arousal)

- *Tawbah* (repentance)

- Reward and punishment

- Justice

- *Shura* (mutual consultation)

- Discipline and commitment to work.

The above attributes are to be fulfilled with respect to others and to Allah, the almighty God. Therefore, Islamic motivation comprises four main components: drive, instincts and innate biological determinants of behavior, commitment, and incentives.

The characteristics that are covered in Islamic motivation are as follows: (1) agreement with the hierarchical nature or the vertical interdependency of motives of Maslow's theory regarding the human hierarchy of needs; (2) the clear objectives and aims of Muslims in regard to achieving the acceptance and forgiveness of Almighty Allah; (3) the objectives and aims stating that both the goals and objectives of this life and hereafter are very important to achieve; (4) human needs, behavior, and nature must be related realistically to motivation; and (5) irrespective of small or unimportant matters in life, Muslims must be aware that Islamic motivation is derived from the comprehensive Holy Qur'an and Islamic teachings of the Prophet Muhammed, Peace be Upon Him (Alawneh, 1998).

The Islamic perspective illustrates the different factors impacting human motivation. Ihsan (perfection), the first factor, implies purification or perfection of human behavior and action. The expression of this divine factor is witnessed in the following *hadith* as per the Islamic conception by the authority of Omar bin Al-Khattab, stating, "The Prophet was asked, what is *ihsan* (perfection and goodness)?"

He replied, "It is to worship Allah as though you are seeing Him, and while you see Him not yet truly He sees you" (Sahîh al Bukhârî and Sahîh Muslim). Therefore, it is evident that the divine factor expresses the special relationship between God and the individual: "As for those who pursue most earnestly the quest in Us (Allah), we surely guide them in our paths. And certainly Allah is with those who practice Ihsan" (Qur'an 29:69).

Ihsan is also exemplified well by Saheeh Muslim in the following *hadith*: On the authority of Abu Ya'laa Shaddaad bin Aws (ra), the Prophet says, "Verily Allah has prescribed *ihsan* (proficiency, perfection) in all things. So if you kill then kill well; and if you slaughter, then slaughter well. Let each one of you sharpen his blade and let him spare suffering to the animal he slaughters" (Muslim).

This *hadith* emphasizes the importance of applying perfection or *ihsan* in every action and deed of a Muslim. The *hadith* also emphasizes *ihsan* in other actions. For example, when slaughtering animals, Muslims should apply goodness and perfection or *ihsan* in their daily life and work in order to receive rewards and acceptance of prayers directly from Almighty Allah.

The idea of commitment to practice both *ihsan* (perfection) and *ikhlas* (sincerity) in every action of a Muslim is considered to be an *ibadah* (worship) to Allah and, therefore, is recognized as a religious duty.

Good work is considered to be both *ibadah* (worshipping Allah) and *amanah* (trust), and both factors highly impact employee motivation as both are also in line with *Shariah*. Trust is considered to be a psychological contract between two or more individuals that carries both responsibility and accountability. Therefore, it needs to be built consistently as an important element of the life of Muslims in order to receive the *falah* (forgiveness) of Almighty Allah, leading to pure success in worldly life and in the hereafter.

Based on the foregoing discussion, a conclusion may be drawn on the subject of motivation as leading to a successful career from an Islamic perspective, suggesting that it differs from the Western perspective. Since Islamic factors give more attention to psychological rewards, it is evident that the Islamic perspective puts more emphasis on intrinsic motivation factors and variables related to performance. But at the same time, the Islamic perspective does not ignore the existence of extrinsic motivation factors. The Islamic perspective clearly emphasizes the impact of both religion (Islam) and the might of Allah on employees' perspective on life and its purpose. Purpose provides Muslims with the motivation to perform better in completing tasks in the world as well as receive the acceptance of Almighty Allah to achieve success in the hereafter.

9.7   Tools used by Islamic and modern businesses to measure employee performance

9.7.1   Employee engagement

The quality of service, irrespective of whether it is production or customer service, can only be determined by how much motivation employees have derived from their current profession (Sarker, 2009). According to Little and Little (2006), the US gross national product suffered a loss of nearly $300 billion resulting from inefficient employee output. Scholars have researched employee engagement in recent years addressing the connection between employee engagement and organizational success. As economic realities have forced organizations to reduce workforce levels, there has been a corresponding increase in the expected productivity of each worker (Catteeuw et al., 2007).

Organizational leaders must find new ways to improve employee engagement because it increases productivity, customer satisfaction, and organizational profitability (Bakker et al., 2010). Similarly, leaders must improve employee engagement in order to address the concerns of organizations.

Employee engagement is one of the most significant elements of organizational productivity and is directly related to the intrinsic motivation of employees. It pertains to the degree of effort exerted by an employee in pursuit of the organizational goals and refers to an employee's commitment to professional development in the organizational office. Employees with high engagement take pride not simply in earning the formal indicators of success but in understanding the new knowledge and incorporating or internalizing it in their lives (Mozammel, 2015). Engaged employees demonstrate higher value, morale, and self-respect at work for the accomplishment of work tasks.

9.8   Transformational leadership: A tool

Transformational leadership theory is based on leaders' ability to provide and develop an environment in which employees are engaged and motivated. Transformational leaders influence followers' behavior and attitudes toward their work. In a workplace where transformational leadership theory is practiced, there are high levels of trust among the leaders and the followers, and the leadership style plays an important role in employee engagement. Previous studies have determined the influence of transformational leadership on an organization's employees, specifically their engagement. Employee engagement refers to the degree of effort exerted by employees toward achieving the goals of their organization. Furthermore, engaged employees are proud to be part of the organization. Leaders' use of a transformational leadership style and employee engagement are some of the factors that lead to organizational success.

Transformational leaders must require managers to evaluate work processes in order to provide support for the engagement of employees. Transformational leaders are proactive and find ways to optimize organizational commitment and involvement among employees (Avolio and Bass, 2004). Finally, transformational leaders encourage stakeholders to aim for higher levels of ethical and moral standards. Thus, employees are more engaged by increasing productivity in their work.

In today's workplace, the employer requires employees to punch in their cards to make sure they are coming to work and on time. Some employers place cameras in the workplace to monitor the workforce. Some ask for daily reports, send patrolling supervisors, or use other means of monitoring performance. In management books, students learn of the Hawthorne effect—the idea that employees who are closely monitored perform better than those who are not.

An Islamic perspective on monitoring adds two types of such activities: self-monitoring and God's monitoring. Self-monitoring is the believer's effort to restrict himself from being immoral or from shirking on his duties.

An important description of piety in Islam is called *al ihsan*. *Al ihsan* has several meanings in Arabic, one being charity or giving alms to those who need it. Another meaning, more germane to our subject, translates into "Observing Allah." Its definition is to worship God as if you are seeing, (watching) Him, and is explained as follows: "*Ihsan is worshipping God as if you can see Him, for if you do not see Him, He sees you.*" (Imam Nawawi Forty Hadiths, Hadith 2). A Muslim who believes in this concept and embraces its meaning is more strongly deterred from committing unethical acts or shirking than an employee who is only concerned with traditional means of monitoring. This notion of being watched by Allah is a recurrent theme in the Qur'an. The Qur'an emphasizes this notion by declaring that even one's thoughts are known to Allah, as in (2:29): "*Say if you conceal that which in your souls or reveal it, Allah knows it.*"

A story from the time of the Caliph Omar bin al Khattab illustrates the point. Omar had prohibited the sale of diluted milk. He was walking in the city one evening when he heard a woman suggesting to her daughter to add water to the milk they were selling. The daughter replied, "How can I mix when Omar has prohibited it?" The mother retorted by saying that others were doing it and profiting from doing so and that Omar will never know. The daughter answered famously, "If Omar does not know, certainly the Lord of Omar would know and I would not do such a thing."

When Muslims believe they are being monitored by the Lord of the Worlds, the One, the Omnipotent Creator who asked them to act righteously and with integrity, they will be careful about how they act within their organizations. They will be efficient work, minimize waste, and refrain from deceiving and cheating. These benefits combine increase profits for the organization while reducing the cost of creating layers of supervisors and monitoring systems.

9.8.1   Leadership in Islam

According to Islam, the two major roles of a leader are those of servant-leader and guardian-leader. A leader is the servant of his followers (Saiyyad Al-Qawn Khadimuhum). He is to seek their welfare and guide them toward good. On the other hand, as guardian-leader, a Muslim leader should protect his community against tyranny and oppression, encourage God-consciousness, and promote justice.

Leadership in Islam is rooted in a belief in and willing submission to the Creator, Allah. It aims at serving Allah. To serve God, a Muslim leader is to act in accordance with the order of God and His Prophet (s.a.w.) and must develop a strong Islamic character. The four moral bases of Islamic leadership are *Islam, iman* (faith in God), *taqwa* (inner consciousness), and *ihsan* (love of God) (Kazmi and Ahmad, 2006). *Islam* means achievement of peace, with oneself and with the creation of God, through willing submission to Him. *Iman* implies Oneness of God and the prophethood of Muhammad (s.a.w.). A leader with strong *iman* will consider himself and all his possessions as belonging to God. He will bend his ego, his ideas, his passions, and his thinking to God. A leader with firm *iman* will not dodge responsibility for his actions and will continuously emphasize good deeds. *Taqwa* is the all-encompassing inner consciousness of duty toward God and awareness of one's accountability to Him. *Taqwa* restrains a Muslim leader or follower from behaving unjustly, whether to community members, customers, suppliers, or anybody else. *Ihsan* is the love of God that motivates the individual Muslim to work toward attaining God's pleasure. The Prophet (s.a.w.) describes *ihsan* as follows: "To worship God as if you see him, and if you cannot achieve this state of devotion, then you must consider that He is looking at you."

Key Terms

Employee engagement
Islamic value: ethics
Job description

Job design
Job specification
Leadership in Islam

Motivation theories

Discussion Questions

1. What are the two main Islamic values an employee should possess? How do they relate to employee engagement?

2. In the light of "Islamization," discuss the importance and benefits of job design.

3. Discuss the differences between job description and job specification in terms of their purpose.

4. What factors affect individual motivation, behavior, and performance in Islam?

5. Elaborate on the various types of motivation.

6. How does intrinsic motivation reflect the internal aspects of individuals in relation to Islam?

7. Critically appraise how the consideration of ethical values is pivotal in the application of motivation theories.

8. While bringing motivation in practice, explain the importance of a leader's personality, its role, and its impact on motivation.

Selected Bibliography

Abeng, T. (1997). Business Ethics in Islamic Context: Perspective of a Muslim Business Leader. *Business Ethics Quarterly*, 7(3), 47–54.

Ahmad, S., Rofie, M.K. and Owoyemi, M.Y. (2013). Islamic Work Ethics: An Appraisal of the Qur'anic View on Work Ethics. *The Social Sciences*, 8(5), 437–444.

Al-Jayyousi, O.R. (2012). *Islam and Sustainable Development: New Worldview*. London: Routledge.

Alawneh, S.F. (1998). Human Motivation: An Islamic Perspective. *American Journal of Islamic Social Sciences*, 15(4), 19–39.

Ali, A.J. (2009). Levels of Existence and Motivation in Islam. *Journal of Management History*, 15(1), 50–65.

Avolio, B. and Bass, B. (2004). *Multifactor Leadership Questionnaire* (3rd ed.). Menlo Park: Mind Garden.

Bakker, A.B., Albrecht, S.L. and Leiter, M.P. (2010). Key Questions Regarding Work Engagement. *European Journal of Work and Organizational Psychology*, 20(1), 4–28. doi:https://doi.org/10.1080/1359432X.2010.485352

Bartol, K.M. and Martin, D.C. (1998). *Management* (3rd ed.). New York: McGraw-Hill.

Basharat, T. (2009). The Characteristic Features of Worship as Propounded by Islam. *Al-Adwa*, 24, 27–41.

Beekun, R.I. and Badawi, J.A. (2005). Balancing Ethical Responsibility Among Multiple Organizational Stakeholders: The Islamic Perspective. *Journal of Business Ethics*, 60(2), 131–145.

Bonache, J. and Noethen, D. (2014). The Impact of Individual Performance on Organizational Success and Its Implications for the Management of Expatriates. *International Journal of Human Resource Management*, 25(14), 1960–1977.

Catteeuw, F., Flynn, E. and Vonderhorst, J. (2007). Employee Engagement: Boosting Productivity in Turbulent Times. *Organizational Development Journal*, 25(2), 151–158.

Chapra, M.U. (1995). *Islam and the Economic Challenge* (Islamic Economics Series 17). Markfield: Islamic Foundation: International Institute of Islamic Thought.

Farooq, M.O.(2011). *Toward Our Reformation: From Legalism to Value-Oriented Islamic Law and Jurisprudence*. Herndon: IIIT.

Ghauri, M.T. (2009). Religious Motivation: A Multiplying Force. *The Dialogue*, 6(2), 103–123.

Herzberg, F., Mausner, B. and Snyderman, B. (2011). *Motivation to Work*. London: Transaction Publishers.

Kazmi, A. and Ahmad, K. (2006). Management from Islamic Perspective. In *Instructors' Resource Manual*. Kuala Lumpur: International Islamic University.

Little, B. and Little, P. (2006). Employee Engagement: Conceptual Issues. *Journal of Organizational Culture Communications and Conflict*, 10(1), 111–120.

Mitchell, T.R. (1982). Motivation: New Direction for Theory, Research, and Practices. *Academy of Management Review*, 7, 80–88.

Mozammel, S. (2015). A quantitative Examination of the Relationship Between Transformational Leadership and Employee Engagement in the Branch Banking Sector of Bangladesh. Ph.D. Thesis Published in ProQuest (UMI).

Mozammel, S. (2016). *Relationship Between Transformational Leadership & Employee Engagement*. Saarbrücken: Scholars' Press. ISBN: 978-3-639-86242-3.

Pfeffer, J. and Veiga, J.F. (1999). Putting People First for Organizational Success. *The Academy of Management Executive*, 13(2), 37–48.

Rahman, M. and Al-Buraey, M. (1992). An Islamic Perspective of Organizational Controls and Performance Evaluation. *American Journal of Islamic Social Sciences*, 9(4), 499–514.

Robbins, S. (1993). *Organizational Behavior* (6th ed.). Englewood Cliffs: Prentice Hall.

Sarker, S. (2009). Employee Empowerment in the Banking Sector. *IUP Journal of Management Research*, 8(9), 48–66. Retrieved from: http://ssrn.com/abstract=1484372

Sharabi, M. (2012). The Work and Its Meaning Among Jews and Muslims According to Religiosity Degree. *International Journal of Social Economics*, 39 (11), 824–843.

Sulaiman, M., Ahmad, K., Sbaih, B. and Kamil, N.M. (2014). The Perspective of Muslim Employees Towards Motivation and Career Success. *e-BANGI: Jurnal Sains Sosial dan Kemanusiaan*, 9(1), 45–62.

Zaman, H.M.F., Nas, Z., Ahmed, M., Raja, Y.M. and Marri, M.Y.K. (2013). The Mediating Role of Intrinsic Motivation Between Islamic Work Ethics and Employee Job Satisfaction. *Journal of Business Studies Quarterly*, 5(1), 93–102.

Zamani, A. and Talatapeh, M. (2014). Discussion of the Motivation in the Islamic and Non-Islamic Worlds. *Journal of Applied Environmental and Biological Sciences*, 4(4)68–73. ISSN: 2090-4274.

DECISION MAKING

10

Mohammad Selim

College of Business Administration,
University of Bahrain, Zallaq, Kingdom of Bahrain

Learning Outcomes

LO1: Understand the scope of the decision-making process in organizations.

LO2: Explain the importance of decision making in business.

LO3: Evaluate key types of business decisions.

LO4: Establish a link between *Shariah* rules and decision making.

Contents

10.1 Introduction

Effective and right decision making is the fundamental aspect and cornerstone for success for any venture. Decision making refers to making a choice on a certain course of action from among all the available alternatives to achieve certain objectives or goals. According to Herbert Simon, "To make a decision means to make a judgment regarding what one ought to do in a certain situation after having deliberated on some alternative course of action."

In an economy, there are agents or actors, and they have certain objectives or goals. The agents or actors can choose different alternative courses of action for achieving those objectives or goals. When an agent chooses a course of action among all the alternatives to achieve his or her objectives or goals, it is called decision making. In other words, decision making is an action on the part of an agent or actor to choose a certain course of action because that agent considers that course of action to be the right action among all the alternative courses of actions available at that moment and the purpose of the agent or actor is to fulfill or achieve certain objectives or goals at that point of time.

Effective and right decision making brings success in the form of profits, gains, social wellbeing, prosperity, or happiness. Faulty decision making may bring losses or ruin while no decision making, often called inaction, is technically a decision because the agent decides not to do anything at that point of time because he or she thinks that inaction is the right action under uncertainty. However, if inaction becomes the cultural norm and the agent makes no decision over a long period of time until the critical moment arrives when it might be too late to make a decision, such procrastination and reluctance in decision making can bring disaster, ruin, and destruction. Therefore, effective and right decision making spurs growth, development, and progress, while procrastination in decision making or faulty decision making can very well ruin chances for potential success. Right and effective decision making is crucial for success for any agent, government, firm, community, family, or even individual. Right and effective decision making is so important that we must all know how to make right and effective decisions for success, prosperity, and sustainable development. The consequences of not making decisions until the last critical moment when it is too late are disastrous and bring ruin, destruction, or even loss of life, and such an eventual sad ending is evident in the writings of Anthony Robbins in the Niagara Syndrome in the following box:

INSIGHT: Not Making a Decision on Time

If decisions are not made on time, this can bring ruin and disaster. Robbins (2007) writes in his famous book where he mentions the Niagara Syndrome as follows:

> "Life is like a river for many people, they just jump in the river of life without ever deciding where they want to end up, so they quickly get caught up in the current, current events, current challenges, current fears. And then they come to the forks in the rivers, they don't consciously decide which way to go, they just go with the flow of the river...continue to drift down stream until one day the sound of the raging water wakes them up and they realize they are 5 feet from the falls and they are in a boat with no oars and then they say, "Oh shoot," but it's too late. They are going to take a fall, it may be a financial setback or the breakup of a relationship or maybe even a health problem, in almost all of the cases the fall could have been prevented by making better decisions upstream."

If the Admiral of a ship fails to decide to stop and seek shelter during an oncoming cyclone -just thinking that the ship will reach the destination before the cyclone starts, such an underestimation in decision making will not only cost the utter ruin of the ship in the powerful cyclone but will also cost the lives of thousands of passengers. How many ships were sunk in cyclones and in stormy seas and how many millions of people were drowned in cyclones, floods, and storms because of the failure of correct decision making on time—either because of underestimation or not taking proper or alternative action plans?

If a swimmer plans to cross a swift current river or channel and makes an emotional decision without investigating the temperature of the water or the speed of the current or the distance, and above all his ability and strength to withstand such odd challenges, it may cost him his life and the person may be swallowed up and swept away by the speedy current. How many swimmers have drowned and been swept away by a swift current because they failed to make the right decision at the right time after considering circumstances and the surrounding environment?

If the driver of a vehicle fails to decide to change lanes or take an exit at the right time without observing the oncoming vehicles behind him and makes a quick decision as many young drivers do, it will not only cost him his life and property but the lives and properties of other drivers and passengers in multivehicle accidents.

If a pilot fails to decide how much fuel the plane may need to reach its destination and thinks the plane has enough fuel, and suppose bad weather delays the journey about two to three hours to reach the destination, the Plane may just crash because of the lack of fuel. How many Planes were crashed because the pilot failed to decide to take more than enough fuel as precautionary measures?

If an individual or car fails to decide to stop and wait at Railway crossing and underestimates the speed of the oncoming train and starts to cross the track and the train just smashes and pulls the entire car or individual under the crashing steel wheels. How many individuals and vehicles meet such fate every year because of the failure of making correct decision to wait?

If there are minor problems in the Airplane engine and the Pilot ignores it as a minor problem or because of the pressure of the Airline or time constraints, and all such pressures led to the Pilot to make a quick decision without considering the consequences and the opportunity cost, the Pilot plans to cross the Atlantic Ocean which may take 6–7 h and often there are hardly any spot for emergency landing because there is water everywhere. If such minor engine problem persists and requires emergency landing and there are no Airports within 3–4 h flying time, it may cause disasters and the Plane may crash. How many Planes were crashed because of wrong and quick decision making? Alternatively, the Pilot could simply and strongly insist in his decision not to fly before the problem was fixed.

If an entrepreneur develops a new car for the market but fails to decide the testing of the product prior to mass production and marketing, it may just happen that the engine catches fire during ignition in extreme heat conditions. If all the engines are defective and prior to testing this dangerous fire hazard, if the company produces millions of cars and market them in the winter and in early summer, thousands of such cars catch fire and hundreds of drivers are dead and cause heavy damages to lives and properties, it will not only ruin the reputation but will incur enormous costs which may result heavy losses and bankruptcy for the entire business.

If the ski player fails to decide alternative plans for possible Avalanches, the sudden Avalanches can cost his life. How many ski-adventurers are buried alive in Avalanches because they did not take into considerations all the factors prior to make decision?

If a mountain climber fails to decide to test the rocks of the mountain and how solid those rocks are and whether those rocks are strong enough to carry the loads of his body weight when he will fasten his hooks on those rocks-his life will be in extreme risks and the eventual outcome may be either death or handicap for life.

If a person fails to decide the right course of his actions of good deeds in this life before his death, he may face ruins and may fail to enter into Paradise. Right and timely decision is crucial for the success in all spheres of life. A successful decision maker always considers the uncontrollable factors, circumstances and surrounding environment prior to making any decision.

10.2   Steps in decision making

Are we really decisive in our life? When we wake up early in the morning, many of us wake up late because we are not decisive. If we are really decisive, we will sleep early as planned, get enough sleep, and wake up early. As American Founding Father Benjamin Franklin rightly put it, "Early to bed and early to rise makes a man healthy, wealthy, and wise." Sakhr al-Ghamidi (may Allah be pleased with him) stated that the Prophet Muhammad (may the peace and blessings of Allah be upon him) said, "O Allah, bless my *ummah* (people) in their early mornings" (Sunan Abu Dawud, Hadith Number 2606).

10.2.1   Decisive and indecisive groups of people

There are two groups of people in this world: One group, composed of people who are decisive, makes plans and decisions at every stage of their life, while the other group hardly makes any decisions. As soon as the decisive group wakes up early in the morning, they immediately decide and plan for the entire day. Those who are not decisive often put things off and procrastinate, and days can pass without much of anything getting done. Every day, we get caught up in so many things, and if we do not make decisions, time will pass by without any future direction being set, the speed of our progress will be slowed down, and we may fall behind those who make decisions and pave their way forward. They are the successful high achievers. They continuously make decisions and take off to higher and higher levels, and indeed, the world belongs to them. These are the people who are most productive in society.

10.2.2   How to make decisions

So how does one make decisions? What are the steps and how do we really follow and make decisions? "Decision making," according to Herbert A. Simon, "comprises three principal phases: finding occasions for making decisions, finding a possible course of action, and choosing among courses of action."

10.2.3   What are the steps?

First we have to explore how to identify occasions for making decisions. Indecisive individuals do not know what to do, what to decide, how to make progress in life. This group of people have to "brainstorm," think and reflect, and even then they may need help for deciding on the right course of action.

This indecisive group needs to set priorities in life, what they want to be in the future, what direction they want their life to take, identify the areas in which they excel or have a comparative advantage. Therefore, they should set the direction of their life in which they have expertise and skills, things they love to do and can do well and areas in which they can achieve significant success without much hardship.

There is one other group of people who may be decisive enough and ready to make decisions, but they may face hundreds of issues in a single day; they have to make decisions on each of the issues and act on them as soon as possible. Such people need to set priorities and determine the logical sequence for completing tasks. To make the right decisions, they need to collect information and gather data. Once they have all the necessary information and know all the available and possible courses of action or alternatives, they need to consult with experts and stakeholders for further in-depth evaluation and determine the feasibility of each alternative.

Then they have to seek divine guidance about which course of action will be best for them, and then they will come up with a decision. Once they make their decision, that is not the end of it; rather, that is a new beginning, and at this stage they have to put all their trust in Allah, the most merciful who is the final accomplisher of all things and they themselves must make sustained and continuous efforts to reach their destination and finally accomplish the tasks they decided upon at the beginning.

10.2.4   Six steps in decision making

Successful decision making involves the following six steps:

1. Setting priorities

2. Collecting information and gathering data

3. Consulting with experts and stakeholders

4. Seeking divine guidance

5. Making a decision

6. Putting one's trust in God and engaging in continuous efforts.

These steps are explained below.

10.2.4.1   *Setting priorities and the logical sequence for completing tasks*

Those who know how to set priorities must decide and accomplish their tasks within a certain period of time are the most successful. In setting priorities, they have to follow a logical sequence as well.

Suppose there are three tasks:

a. Build a road or highway

b. On the same road or highway, lay underground cable

c. Install a natural gas pipeline.

Now priorities must be set and a logical sequence followed so the road doesn't have to be dug two or three times or the road paved more than once, and so on. Not setting priorities or following a logical sequence of task completion may cause problems. For example, suppose the road is paved, and now the cable company comes in and starts digging the road. Now the road and highway company comes and starts filling in the trenches and paves the road again. Of course this will incur additional costs. Now the natural gas company comes in and starts digging again, and guess what? The natural gas company may damage some of the cables and the cable company will have to redo some of its work and of course the roads and highway company must finish paving again after all the digging by both the cable and natural gas companies. By this time winter sets in and snow covers everything, and nothing is completed. Instead, the companies could set priorities and the sequence of work, and both the natural gas and cable companies could work together and even share the costs of digging, and there will be no damage to cables or natural gas pipes on either side. Once they are done, the road and highway company could decide the work to be done once and for all. Therefore, setting priorities and the logical sequence for completing the work will save money and make the decision making effective and efficient. Thus, one needs to set priorities about what should be done first and follow a logical sequence and coordinate tasks for success and efficiency.

10.2.4.2   Collecting information and gathering data

When we decide to do any tasks, we must have all the information, we need to gather all the data about the task itself, how many alternative ways it can be done, its impact, short-run and long-run consequences. In addition, we need to analyze and evaluate all possible benefits and costs, both direct and indirect, and environmental and sustainability issues.

Suppose a student decides to earn an undergraduate degree in business and plans to apply for admission. If he or she obtains information from only one university and applies to that university only and, for some reason, he or she is not accepted, his or her decision on higher education will fail but if he or she applies to many universities, say 25, and gets offers from 5 universities for admission, he or she has now 5 alternatives to choose from. Now with all the information he or she has it will be easier to choose one of the best possible alternatives and the success in decision making for higher education is now much brighter compared to the other scenario. Now just by collecting more information and deciding to send applications to 25 universities, the student improves her chances of success. This is a true story for a student, exactly like you. However, you will find similar examples in business. A young entrepreneur plans to market her new product. She negotiates with a big shopping mall to rent a small space to display her product. The store manager tells her to wait three months until they complete several consumer surveys for her product and decide whether to display it in the store or not. If she just waits for this decision, after three months either her request will be accepted or rejected. Even if it is accepted, maybe the rent will be too high to afford. Instead, if she negotiates with 40 other stores on renting space for her new product, there will be a higher probability that some stores will offer her similar or better service at a very reasonable rent and she will be able to choose from more options, so her decision making will be more effective and her new product will have a better chance at being seen by potential consumers, and in the future sales for her new product could increase.

The more information we have, the easier it is to determine the right course of action. Such decision making will not only save money, but it will also increase the probability of success. In addition, such informed decision making will minimize navigation in unknown territory and, thus, will help to avoid risk taking, pointless effort, and ultimate failure.

This is perhaps one of the main reasons why around 50 percent of corporate decision making eventually fails (Paul C. Nutt, 2002).

10.2.4.3   Consultations with experts and stakeholders

Of course, those who are specialized in certain areas know more than the average person. Experts know the inside story, the advantages and disadvantages of a particular situation or decision, consequences, in both the short run and long run, and can provide an overview and prognosis about certain issues and alternative courses of action. Allah the Exalted has said, "So ask those who possess knowledge if you do not know (Q 16:43). Therefore, it is important to make *istishara* (seek and consult) with others who have knowledge about the matter and issues. The whole process of consultations or *shura* is immensely important in decision making, and there will be further discussions, procedures for mutual consultations, and its analysis in the next section. The Prophet Muhammad, may the peace and blessings of Allah be upon him, said, "He who consults others in matters will not regret it" (Al-Tirmidhi, Vol. 1, p. 241, Beirut, Lebanon).

Consultations with all stakeholders are also important. It is crucial to get all on board as much as possible for successful and smooth decision making because the stakeholders will have to deal with the consequences, positive and negative, of every decision. They should be aware of decisions and they should know the possible direct and indirect benefits and costs of those decisions, as well as their impact on them (the stakeholders), their health, the environment, and sustainability. For example, uranium mining in Sahara Desert in North Africa created irreparable damage to water wells, and as a result, uranium-polluted water caused organ damage in many children and adults, and they became incapacitated and eventually stricken with cancer and many deadly diseases. Consultations with the stakeholders and disclosures of the long-term consequences will help to avert many such disasters and harm to humans, animals, the environment, and the food chain.

10.2.4.4 Seeking divine guidance

This is a key step for a successful decision-making process. Once we finish consultations with other people, who of course have limited and partial knowledge, we must seek the guidance of Allah, the most exalted and most high, the One with complete and perfect knowledge who has the power to make things happen. If He says, "Be," it becomes. Prophet Muhammad, may the peace and blessings of Allah be upon him, has taught us to seek guidance by *istikhara* prayer.

Jabir Ibn 'Abdullah, may Allah be pleased with him, said: "The Prophet Muhammad, may the peace and blessings of Allah be upon him, would instruct us to pray for guidance in all of our concerns, just as he would teach us a chapter from the Qur'an. He would say 'if any of you intends to undertake a matter then let him pray two supererogatory units (two *rak'ah naafilah*) of prayer and after which he should supplicate: 'O Allah, I seek Your counsel by Your knowledge and by Your power I seek strength and I ask You from Your immense favour, for verily You are able while I am not and verily You know while I do not and You are the Knower of the unseen. O Allah, if You know this affair—and here he mentions his need—to be good for me in relation to my religion, my life, and end, then decree and facilitate it for me, and bless me with it, and if You know this affair to be ill for me towards my religion, my life, and end, then remove it from me and remove me from it, and decree for me what is good wherever it be and make me satisfied with such" (Bukhari, Hadith Number 1162, 6382, 7390; Abu Dawud, Hadith Number 1538; Al-Tirmidhi, Hadith Number 480; An-Nasa'i, Hadith Number 3253; Ibn Majah, Hadith Number 1383).

The benefits of *istikhara* prayer are so profound and great that if a person is sincerely seeking direction from Allah, the Exalted, with firm faith in Allah, glory be to Him, surely Allah, the Mighty, the Exalted, will show him the way to success. Such a process of seeking guidance and direction about unknown matters and relying on Allah and seeking the right direction from Allah, the person will be brought closer to the Exalted One. Allah, the Exalted, has said, "And those who strive for Us—We will surely guide them to Our ways. And indeed, Allah is with the doers of good" (Q 29:69).

10.2.4.5   *Decision making in action*

After duly following the above four steps, one may proceed to make a decision and not procrastinate. One must remember that there are competitors, so procrastinating may lead to lost opportunities. If you do not make a decision, your competitors may decide sooner than you think and steal your opportunity—and it may be gone for-ever. Sure, you have to be careful, but following all the steps for making a decision will breed success after success, but inaction can lead to missing out on opportunities.

10.2.4.6   *Put your trust in Allah, the exalted, and engage in continuous efforts*

Once a decision has been reached based on due diligence, one must put trust in Allah, Glory be to Him, the Exalted, the Highest, who has the power and ability to realize the dream. Allah the Exalted has said, "Then, when thou hast taken a decision put your trust in Allah. For Allah loves those who put their trust (in Him)" (Q 3:159).

You have to supplicate and seek the help of Allah, the Exalted, for the success of your decision and continuously apply yourself for a successful outcome. It is like steering and driving your car to a destination of success. You cannot just put it on auto pilot and fall asleep at the wheel; the path is not always straight and you are not the only one on the highway; your competitors are there too, so you have to be vigi-lant and steer with speed but also with caution so that eventually you arrive at your destination of success without mishaps and accidents. These are the six steps for successful decision making; anyone who follows them passionately and puts all his or her efforts into them with complete trust in Allah, the Exalted, will not regret his or her decision. These are the ways Muslims during the golden era of Islam made decisions, and they succeeded time after time. Even occasional failures brought them to the core faith and strengthened and rejuvenated and prepared them for continuous success. If we follow in their footsteps, the world is ours, and the future will be better than the past.

10.3   *Shura* and consultative decision making

> **Q 17:7**
> "If you do good, you do good for yourselves; and if you do evil, [you do it] to yourselves."

Shura, or a consultative decision-making process, not only yields better decisions but also promotes peace, goodwill, trust, cooperation, coexistence, cohesion, com-mitment, motivation, and progress for the group or organization or for the nation at large. *Shura*-style decision making is much like shared values where all members together contribute to make the best possible decisions, not only for the organiza-tion to which they belong but also for all humankind.

Human beings are asked to do good, and if anyone does good, that goodness will positively enrich him or her in the days to come.

10.3.1   *Shura* strengthens the bonds of unity and cohesion

Often one group makes decision or imposes decision on another group but *Shura* facilitates the unity for those who will make decision and for whom the decision will be made. If both groups are same and together, with mutual consultations, their decision making will be more successful and universally accepted and everyone will mutually seek what is best for all stakeholders and thus will promote unity, cohesion and strong bond of mutual respect and honor.

10.3.2 The scope of *Shura*

However, *shura*, or consultation process, is not applicable for matters that are clearly and precisely defined in the Qur'an and in the traditions of the Prophet Muhammad, peace and blessings of Allah be upon him, because problems or issues with clear and optimum solutions have already been given. Similarly, if an issue is discussed and the final results do not contradict the standard rules and injunctions as set out in divine revelations in the Qur'an and wise and exemplary traditions of the Prophet Muhammad, may the peace and blessings of Allah be upon him, because if it does contradict these sources, the decision reached by the participants are not optimum, and as such, an optimum decision must be sought through mutual consultations in light of the Qur'an and *sunnah* as well as *ijtihad* (in-depth research), *ijma* (consensus), *qias* (analogical reason) conducted by the Scholars in Islam since the golden era of Islam throughout Islamic history. Such a journey will not only enrich the final outcome of the decision but will also enlighten the participants and bring further cohesion, unity, dedication, and strength in implementing the decision and the group will eventually be better off than earlier, at the initial stage. All such research and scholarship in the field will further shine new rays of light and hope for better decision making in the days to come.

10.3.3 *Shura* is participatory decision making

In *shura*, people's participation is not only required but obligatory. A leader is accountable to Allah, the most High, and Allah, the Exalted, has asked the Prophet Muhammad, peace and blessing be upon him, to consult with believers in the decision-making process in all pertinent matters.

Thus, *shura* style decision making covers all aspects of decision making, whether for public affairs at the government level or the firm level or even at the community or family level. Participation in *shura* by all stakeholders ensures cohesion, transparency, a clear vision, accountability, integrity, collective responsibility, cooperation, mutual respect, tolerance, and unity in hope and purpose and action. Therefore, *shura* recognizes the will of the people and their views as well as the views of all stakeholders.

The interests and views of all stakeholders should be accommodated, and often the leader will serve as facilitator to ensure that the opinions and wishes of all participants are evaluated and taken into consideration fully prior to making the final decision.

Such *shura* style decision making creates an environment of harmony, cooperation, and motivation, which often serve as the foundation and strength for the success of new decisions. *Shura* style decision making leads to the right direction. Ibn'Umar (may Allah be pleased with him) told of how the Messenger of Allah (peace and blessings of Allah be upon him) said, "Allah, may He be Exalted, will not cause my *ummah* to agree on falsehood, the hand of Allah, may He be Exalted, is with the *jamaa'ah* (the main body of Muslims) and whoever deviates, he deviates to the fire." This *hadith* is classed as *hasan* by al-Albaani (Al-Tirmidhi, Book Number 31, Hadith Number 2167).

Q 3:159
"It is part of the Mercy of Allah that thou dost deal gently with them. Wert thou severe or harsh-hearted, they would have broken away from about thee: so, pass over (Their faults), and ask for (Allah's) forgiveness for them; and consult them in affairs (of the moment)."

Q 42:38
"And those who have responded to their Lord and establish regular prayer, who (conduct) their affairs by mutual consultation, who spend out of what we bestow on them for sustenance."

10.3.4   Qualities and acumen of *Shura* members

According to Mawardi (1982), the members of the *shura* who also work as expert consultants in decision making should have certain qualities and acumen, so that they can give sound counsel on matters related to any issues facing the *ummah*:

1. Sound *iman* or faith

2. Ability to conduct *ijtihad* or research

3. Sound and in-depth knowledge of Qur'an, *sunnah*, and current affairs

4. Trustworthiness

5. Justice

6. Adult as per Islamic law

7. Reliability.

The success of decision making depends largely on the accuracy and quality of advice of the members of the *shura*.

10.3.5   *Shura* is an obligation and requirement for effective decision making

Leaders have the obligation to consult their followers in matters of decision making where there is no clear-cut, precise injunction in the Qur'an or in the tradition of Prophet Muhammad, peace and blessings of Allah be upon him, and it is expected that such mutual consultations in decision making will continue after the Prophet Muhammad, peace and blessings of Allah be upon him, for future generations to come. Indeed, such a tradition continued during the rightly guided *Khulafa-e-Rashedeen* and afterwards to some extent. Therefore, to reap the full benefits of successful decision making, there are no alternatives to mutual consultations as emphasized in the Qur'an. An entire *sura* or chapter, titled *Shuara* (Mutual Consultation), was revealed, and it signifies the importance of mutual consultation in decision making and maintaining social harmony, peace, and cooperation. Ali, may Allah be pleased with him, asked, "O Prophet! (may peace and blessings of Allah be upon him), if we have a matter in which we do not find a command or prohibition, then what is your advice? He (may peace and blessings of Allah be upon him) said, "Consult the righteous wise people and do not depend upon individual opinion" (Tabrani).

10.4   Types of decisions

Basically, there are two types of decisions: programmed decisions and nonprogrammed decisions. Nonprogrammed decisions include

*   Rational decision making;

*   Bounded rationality decision making;

*   Intuitive decision making; and

*   Creative decision making.

10.4.1   Programmed decision

Suppose certain events take place on a regular basis. For example, customers will always return some items. To deal with such reoccurring events, there are certain programmed decisions or decision rules, also known as a return policy in this case. The company sets its policy and applies it as part of its programmed decisions for future events.

10.4.2   Nonprogrammed decisions

Nonprogrammed decisions require the application of all the preceding six steps for decision making, and as such these decisions require much more attention and careful consideration, as elaborated in Section 10.2.4. Nonprogrammed decisions are more challenging and time consuming.

10.4.2.1   Rational decision making

In rational decision making, a series of steps are followed as outlined earlier in Section 10.2.4 to maximize the quality of decision making and not make poor decisions. In addition to the foregoing steps, in rational decision making, costs and benefits are also evaluated, and final decisions are made.

10.4.2.2   Bounded rationality model of decision making

In this model, the decision maker knowingly limits her options and makes a decision as soon as her minimum criteria are met. The decision maker does not consider all options, only the limited options, and as soon as she determines which option meets the minimum criteria, she decides and goes for it. For example, say someone wants to buy a house. Instead of checking all the houses on the market, the buyer makes a decision as soon she finds a house that meets her minimum criteria regarding price, size, and location.

10.4.2.3   Intuitive decision-making model

In this model, the decision maker makes a decision without conscious reasoning; this could be risky, but still around 89 percent of managers make intuitive decisions like this at least once in their life. If it is risky, why make decisions in this way? Because they are working under time constraints and immense pressure. They do not choose the best alternative; they only consider only one option at a time. Mainly emergency workers such as firefighters, police, and doctors take an intuitive decision-making approach, and they often consider their successes to be the result of good luck and failures the result of bad luck. Through their experience with emergencies, they discover a kind of pattern and simply makes decisions based on their intuition.

10.4.2.4   Creative decision-making model

In this model, decision makers come up with new and imaginative ideas that allow them to cut costs and make their company more profitable. They also focus on new ways of doing business. In this model the six steps outlined in Section 10.2.4 are followed for effective and creative decisions.

10.5   Faulty decision making

Faulty decisions are incorrect decisions that could lead to losses or even ruin, and decision makers must be aware of the pitfalls under this kind of decision making and avoid them. Decision makers must take precautionary measures so that their decisions do not turn into faulty decisions. Faulty decisions result from overconfidence bias, hindsight bias, anchoring bias, framing bias, and escalation of commitment, and these are explained below.

10.5.1   Overconfidence bias

Decisions made on the basis of overconfidence can lead be faulty. For example, a swimmer might be overconfident about swimming across the English Channel, but when he is only halfway across, he loses all his strength and can't continue. Not only is his decision a faulty one because of his overconfidence, but now his life is even in danger.

10.5.2   Hindsight bias

Hindsight bias the opposite of overconfidence bias, and decisions made on the basis of hindsight information may be faulty.

10.5.3   Anchoring bias

Decision making may be faulty when the entire decision is made on the basis of a single source of information. If there are additional sources of information and those data are not considered, then obviously the decision will be one sided and biased, and it may turn out to be the wrong decision. Suppose a manager decides to buy raw materials, checks the price of raw materials from only one source, and then makes a purchase, but it turns out that other sources show that the same raw materials can be purchased from other suppliers for 50 percent cheaper. Thus, the decision on the basis of only one source of information will be faulty.

10.5.4   Framing bias

Framing bias can often lead to faulty decisions. Framing bias refers to the way information is presented. For example, fish is a healthy food compared to meat. But fish may contain mercury, say 1 percent. Now if it is framed that there is 1 percent mercury in a certain fish, customers may walk away and not buy it, but if it is advertised as 99 percent pure fish, customers may like it. Therefore, inappropriate framing may lead to faulty decisions.

10.5.5   Escalation of commitment

Suppose a contractor plans to build a dam, and every time he is close to building the dam, a strong current sweeps away all the materials, and the dam is gone. Since he invested a lot of money in building this dam, but his expenses just keep rising with no return on his investment, if he continues in building the dam, he will incur more costs with no success. Therefore, the right decision would be to put a stop to the project and walk away or pass it on to someone with the right equipment and resources to complete the job. Failing to do so, he will face financial ruin.

Key Terms

Anchoring bias
Bounded rationality
  model
Cohesion
Collective responsibility
Commitment
Conscious reasoning
Cooperation
Creative decision
  making
Current challenge
Decision making
Decisive group
Escalation of
  commitment
Faulty decision making
Framing bias
Goodwill

Hindsight bias
Ijma
Indecisive group
Integrity
Inside story
Isthikhara prayers
Istishara
Ijtihad
Intuitive decision making
Logical sequence
Minimum criteria
Motivation
Mutual respect
Nonprogrammed
  decision
Overconfidence bias
Participatory decision
  making

Prognosis
Programmed decision
Procrastinating
Qias (consensus)
Rational decision
  making
Return policy
Shura style decision
  making
Seeking divine
  guidance
Setting priority
Sound opinion
Stakeholder
Tolerance
Trust
Unity in hope

Discussion Questions

1. Why is decision making important? What are the consequences of poor decisions made in an untimely manner? Explain with examples.

2. What are the six steps in decision making? Explain each step with an example.

3. Explain the role of seeking divine guidance in decision making. Why is decision making expected to be better in this process of seeking divine guidance?

4. Explain the role of *shura* in decision making. How and why does the *shura* style of decision making strengthen bonds of unity and cohesion?

5. What kind of qualities and insight should *shura* members have? Explain.

6. What are the different types of decisions? Explain with examples.

7. What is overconfidence bias in decision making? How does one overcome this bias in this kind of faulty decision making?

8. What is anchoring bias in decision making? Why does it lead to faulty decisions?

9. How can a business owner protect her business from faulty decision making? Give examples.

Selected Bibliography

Al Mawardi (1982). *Ahkamus Sunnah Wal Walaita Dinia*. Beirut: Darul Kutub Almiah.
Finkelstein, S. and Sanford, S.H. (2000). Learning from Corporate Mistakes: The Rise and Fall of Iridium. *Organizational Dynamics*, 29(2), 138–148.
Herbert, A. (2000). *Decision Making System*. London: Dekart Publication.
Ireland, R.D. and Miller, C.C. (2004). Decision Making and Firm Success. *Academy of Management Executive*, 18, 8–12.

Li, S., Sun, Y. and Wang, Y. (2007). 50% Off or Buy One Get One Free? Frame Preference as a Function of Consumable Nature in Dairy Products. *Journal of Social Psychology*, 147, 413–421.

Mohiuddin, M.G. and Islam, M.M. (2016). Decision Making Style in Islam: A Study of Superiority of Shura (Participative Management) and Examples from Early Era of Islam. *European Journal of Business and Management*, 8(4), 79–88. www.iiste.org. ISSN 2222-1905.

Nutt, P.C. (1999). Surprising But True: Half the Decisions in Organizations Fail. *Academy of Management Executive*, 13, 75–90.

Nutt, P.C. (2002). *Why Decisions Fail*. San Francisco: Berrett-Koehler.

Postmes, T., Spears, R. and Cihangir, S. (2001). Quality of Decision Making and Group Norms. *Journal of Personality and Social Psychology*, 80(6), 918–930. doi:https://doi.org/10.1037/0022-3514.80.6.918.

Robbins, T. (2007). *Awaken the Giant Within: How to Take Immediate Control of Your Mental, Emotional, Physical and Financial Destiny*. New York: Simon and Schuster.

Wong, K.F.E. and Kwong, J.Y.Y. (2007). The Role of Anticipated Regret in Escalation of Commitment. *Journal of Applied Psychology*, 92, 545–554.

Zell, D.M., Glassman, A.M. and Duron, S.A. (2007). Strategic Management in Turbulent Times: The Short and Glorious History of Accelerated Decision Making at Hewlett-Packard. *Organizational Dynamics*, 36, 93–104.

PART
4

FINANCE AND ACCOUNTING

FINANCIAL MARKETS AND INSTITUTIONS

11

Bora Aktan and Saban Celik

College of Business, University of Bahrain,
Manama, Bahrain

Department of Business Administration, Izmir Katip
Celebi University, Izmir, Turkey

Learning Outcomes

LO1: Explain various types of financial markets and their roles in serving business and the economy.

LO2: Describe the ways in which financial markets and institutions support and facilitate business enterprises.

LO3: Understand the fucntions of financial markets and institutions.

LO4: Explain the phenomenon of financialization and its impact on the real economy.

Contents

The Vestel Group of Companies (hereafter Vestel) is active in producing consumer electronics, white goods (in general durable goods), and information technologies. Vestel is the leading "*flagship*" company of the Zorlu Group, which comprises 30 companies, 16 of which are located abroad. There are two production plants of Vestel: one is located in Manisa, Turkey (indoor production area of 600,000 m^2), the other in Alexandrov, Russia. The firm carries out its sales and marketing operations through its eight subsidiaries which are mainly located in Europe. Deloitte (2010) reported that Vestel ranks 195th on the list of the world's largest 250 consumer products companies based on the figures reported in 2008 financial statements. Moreover, the firm is among the four fastest growing companies in terms of revenues according to the listing made for the Europe, Middle East, and Africa (EMEA) region. The Istanbul Chamber of Commerce publishes the 500 largest industrial corporations every year. In 2009, Vestel was ranked ninth, up six places compared to the previous year. Vestel reported considerable losses for 2008, whereas it generated profits of TRL 94 million for 2009 during the global financial crises. One of the top executives of the firm pointed out that *"the main reason was to have a short position in foreign currency in 2008. We did not evaluate this position before 2009. Our risk management policy has been reshaped using strategies to prevent us reporting such losses again. We are in a much better position after initiating this strategy. We are trying to strengthen our working capital and decrease the net debts"* (Topay, 2011). How should one manage a business in the context of a complex global and national financial market? Which financial markets and instruments are suitable for this practice?

This chapter explains financial markets and instruments within the scope of conventional financial systems in line with examples from Islamic finance in brief. We categorized our purposes within four categories. First, we explain various types of financial markets and their roles in serving business and the economy. Second, we describe the ways financial markets and institutions support and facilitate business enterprises. Third, we elaborate the mechanism and channels through which financial markets and institutions take place as a financial intermediation. Lastly, we emphasize the phenomenon of financialization and its impact on the real economy.

11.1   Financial markets

In the conventional financial system, financial markets are the one that bring suppliers and demanders of funds together and where financial assets are traded. Actors in the financial system make their transactions in the financial markets. These actors are consumers (households), businesses, the government, foreign actors and financial institutions. Financial markets can be classified using various criteria. These markets are divided into debt markets vs. stock markets depending on the nature of the financial instrument used in funding; money markets vs. capital markets, depending on the maturity of the financial instrument; primary markets vs. secondary markets, depending on whether the securities traded in the market were issued for the first time or not; and spot markets vs. futures markets, depending on when the exchange takes place. The financial market is important not only for conventional financial system but also for the significant role in plays in Islamic finance. Islamic financial institutions often try to benefit from financial markets.

The fundamental characteristics of Islamic finance come from the Quran and *sunnah*. The most characteristic difference between a conventional and an Islamic financial system is the prohibition of interest (*riba*). Charging interest of any kind is forbidden. No institution or economic entity may charge interest for contractual transactions. Although there is an interest-free lending mechanism known as *qard-hassan*, it offers no pecuniary reward for lenders. This is treated as social-economic solidarity. Consequently, there is no place for interest-based credit in Islamic finance, in contrast to conventional finance. This feature of Islamic finance implies that (1) there is no need for credit expansion or contraction, (2) interest if fixed by that state authority, and (3) this is a solution to conflicts of interest between lenders and borrowers. An Islamic financial system can best be described by the following two principles (Krichene, 2013:15):

- a 100 percent reserve depository and safekeeping banking system for domestic and international payments;
- a profit-loss-sharing type of investment banking that places real savings directly in private or public projects or indirectly via the stock market. Investors are shareholders.

The first principle implies that the system keeps the money (e.g., cash, gold, silver) and settles payments via clearing, withdrawals, and other forms of payment. The second implies that the system takes savings and puts them in profitable investment through mutual funds or stock shares. In return, investors receive transferable or liquid assets for their investment. In principle, the Islamic financial system prevents the emergence of the concept of interest, allowing lenders and borrowers to share the profit and loss of an investment. The main types of Islamic financial institutions include investment banks, mutual funds, and risk-sharing institutions.

11.1.1   Debt markets and stock markets

There are two ways of acquiring funds from financial markets: by borrowing and by issuing share certificates. Borrowing takes place in return for a debt security, and the borrower repays the lender the principal plus interest on the principal. When issuing share certificates, on the other hand, funds are acquired in return for the stock of the company, and the fund provider becomes a shareholder of the company by the amount of funds they provide.

Financial markets are divided into debt markets and stock markets on the basis of the financial assets traded. Markets where debt securities are exchanged are called debt markets, and markets where stock certificates are traded are called stock markets. In this sense, stock and bond markets account for a considerable amount of trading. From an Islamic finance perspective, *sukuk* (which is similar to a bond) is a dominant financial instrument.

Islamic indices consist of shares that qualify as *halal* (*Shariah*-compliant). *Shariah*-compliant is a legal guideline for monitoring shares. A share is considered *halal* if the firm does not operate in any prohibited sectors such as interest (*riba*), gambling, intoxicants, and pork.

11.1.2   Money markets and capital markets

Markets where securities with maturities of up to a year are traded and where loans with maturities of up to a year are given are called money markets, whereas markets where securities with longer maturities are traded and where loans with longer maturities are given are called capital markets. Money market securities are traded more frequently than capital market securities, which have longer maturities. Therefore, they are more liquid. Those with a surplus of short-term funds invest them in money markets, and those with sufficient long-term funds meet their needs in the capital markets. Capital market securities, such as share certificates and long-term bonds, are usually bought by financial intermediaries that are able to provide long-term funds, such as insurance firms and pension funds.

The longer the maturity, the higher the risk of facing unforeseen events. Therefore, risk in capital markets is higher than risk in money markets. There is a relationship between the interest rates of two bonds that are the same in all respects except their maturities, one with a longer and the other with a shorter maturity. The yearly interest rate of the longer-term bond depends on the yearly interest rates of the short-term bonds until its maturity. When the maturity is long, short-term interest rates may change because of unexpected events in a given period. This is reflected in the interest rate of the long-term bond covering the same period and affects its price. The interest rate and the price of a long-term bond can fluctuate significantly before its maturity. Therefore, the longer maturities in capital markets mean higher risks due to uncertainty. To the extent that they avoid risks, investors prefer financial assets in money markets, hence the higher liquidity in the money markets.

11.1.2.1   Money market instruments

A money market by definition is a market where short-term securities are traded. The term defined here is a period of less than a year. In a money market, those with excess funds benefit from the excess position by lending through the financial system to those that have short-term position. In a conventional financial system, the main principle is to charge the time value of money and real profit over lending. Therefore, as a result of borrowing in the market, there is a cost associated with the transaction. This cost is commonly defined as interest, which is the cost of using the borrowed funds. The following short-term money market instruments are commonly traded in conventional financial systems. In contrast, there are two fundamental reasons why it is difficult for Islamic banking to trade in money markets. The first has to do with a lack of collateral backing money market instruments. It is forbidden to trade in Islamic finance to issue a financial product without collateral. The second reason is known as the prohibition of cash borrowing without collateral. As a result of these constraints, Islamic financial institutions have developed specific money market instruments. Some of these are commodity *murabaha*, SWAP transactions (which is specific to Islamic finance), and short-term *sukuk*.

Treasury Bills: These are short-term debt instruments. The treasury meets its short-term funding needs by issuing treasury bonds. Treasury bonds do not have an interest coupon. However, because they are issued at a discount, in practice, interest is paid.

Negotiable Certificates of Deposit: These are bearer certificates that are given to depositors in return for their time deposits in the bank, specifying the amount and maturity of the deposits. These certificates are transferable and can be returned to the bank. Depositors can return the certificate back to the bank and withdraw the deposits. Thus, the investor would both benefit from the interest paid by time deposits and be able to transfer funds easily as if it were a checking account.

Commercial Papers: These are short-term debt instruments that public joint stock companies can issue at a discount, in proportion to their equity.

Repo and Reverse Repo: Repo (repurchase agreement) is the sale of securities with the stipulation that they will be repurchased at a future date. Because the repurchase price is higher than the original sale price, an interest payment takes place. Using this method, the seller of the security acquires funds, whereas the buyer earns interest. The security sold can be delivered to the buyer. In practice, however, the security is kept by the financial institution on behalf of the customer, and the customer is given a certificate stating that the securities will be repurchased on the specified date. In its essence, a repurchase agreement is borrowing in return for a short-term security; thus, it can be viewed as a sort of debt instrument.

Reverse repo, on the other hand, is the purchase of securities to be resold later. The same transaction is a repo agreement from the perspective of one of the parties and a reverse repo agreement from the perspective of the other party. Banks can invest the funds they acquire via repo in reverse repo transactions at higher interest rates.

Banker's Acceptances: Banker's acceptances, in particular, support the funding of exports and allow banks to provide funds on favorable terms. A banker's acceptance is a sort of time draft issued by a firm, payable at a future time. The bank, by accepting the draft, guarantees payment and puts its own reputation on the line. The bank can trade this draft in the money market or sell it at a discount.

Bank Bills: Bank bills are bills of exchange that are issued by a bank as a debtor. They are sold at a discount, with an interest rate at maturity. They have maturities of 1 year or less.

> ## Problem Question
>
> A T-bill with face value $1000 and 150 days to maturity is selling at a bank discount ask yield of 2.5 percent annually. What is the price of the bill?
>
> Bank Discount of 150 days: 0.025 × (150/360)=0.0104

11.1.2.2   *Capital market instruments*

A capital market is by definition a market where long-term securities are traded. Common stocks (which do not have a maturity) and bonds (which do have a maturity longer than 1 year) are two prevalent financial instruments. While common stocks represent ownership in a firm, bonds represent a contingent claim on firm assets. Capital markets are the primary source of long-term investment for firms. There are various types of bonds in a conventional financial system. In Islamic finance, *sukuk* is the dominant financial instrument in capital markets. At least 14 different types of *sukuk* are traded in capital markets. Examples include *sukuk al ijara, sukuk al istisna, sukuk al mudaraba, sukuk al murabaha, sukuk al musharaka,* and *sukuk al salam.* The role of *sukuk* is vital in the development of Islamic finance. The main reason it is so important is that Islamic financial institutions can launch new types of Islamic funds based on the *sukuk* market. Trading on common stock is allowed in Islamic finance under a set of rules.[1] Some of these rules include (1) prohibition on trading in alcohol, drugs, weapon products, (2) prohibition on non-interest-free transactions; (3) prohibition on having a higher ratio of debt to market value of 30 percent. Common stocks that conform to the set of rules are considered Islamic common stock and can be freely traded.

Sukuk as an Islamic capital market instrument can be categorized into two groups: sale-based *sukuk* and participatory *sukuk.* The fundamental difference between these two groups is the purpose of issuance. In the case of sale-based *sukuk,* the purpose is to finance a trade. On the other hand, there is an investment purpose behind issuing participatory *sukuk.* In addition to this fundamental difference, the profit-and-loss sharing principle is applicable in participatory *sukuk,* whereas there is a fixed payment in the case of sale-based *sukuk.* In this sense, participatory *sukuk* resembles ordinary shares owing to the profit-and-loss sharing principle. *Sukuk murabaha, salam, istisna,* and *ijarah* are well-known and widely traded *sukuk* in the sale-based sukuk category.

Sukuk Murabahah: This reflects a sale in which a commodity (asset) is sold with a profit margin (known as mark-up). The buyer knows the cost price and mark-up of the underlying asset in advance. The price of the asset can be paid at predetermined dates. When this happens, the buyer of the asset issues *sukuk murabahah* to show the seller evidence of the asset.

Sukuk Salam: In this type of *sukuk,* the transaction includes a future delivery of the underlying asset at a prepaid price.

Sukuk istisna: This is a contract that gives an obligation to the financial institution to buy the commodity (not yet completed) from producer at a prepaid price.

Sukuk ijarah: This is a *sukuk* certificate that makes it possible to sell an asset and then lease it back over a period of time.

Government Bonds: Bonds issued by governments in return for long-term borrowing from individuals and companies are called government bonds. Government debt securities are bearer securities, are sold by auction, and have an interest coupon. Bearers of these bonds receive periodic interest payments.

Corporate Bonds: Bonds issued by joint stock companies are equivalents of commercial bonds, only with longer maturities. These securities have standard maturities and interest rates and are usually issued by large, prestigious firms. The sales of these bonds issued by companies are undertaken by an underwriter.

Bank-Guaranteed Bills: These are bills of exchange drawn as loan collateral by corporations that receive loans from a bank, in their capacity as debtors, and given to the creditor bank. Guaranteed by the creditor bank, these bills can be publicly traded.

Certificates of Participation: Certificates of participation in security investment funds represent the ownership of a portfolio of funds. In this sense, they are similar to share certificates. However, because they are targeted at small investors, their values are relatively small.

Financial Leasing Agreements: Financial leasing agreements allow for leasing equipment to a firm for a specified amount of time in return for a specified rent. These agreements have two benefits for the lessor. First, the lessor retains ownership of the equipment provided, and risk is eliminated. Second, the lessor enjoys the same tax benefits. The lessee, on the other hand, pays to rent the equipment they use over a period of time and claim the rent payments as expenses. Financial leasing arrangements are commonly used as long-term debt instruments for the purchase of vehicles, computers, and the like.

Revenue Sharing Certificates: These are certificates that are issued so that real and legal persons can share in the revenue of state-owned bridges, dams, power plants, highways, railways, telecommunication systems, ports, airports, and the like. These certificates are unrelated to the ownership or management of the facilities in question; they are variable-interest bonds.

Share (Stock) Certificates: These are certificates that are issued by corporations with capital that is divided into stocks and that can issue share certificates in return for these stocks; they represent ownership of a specific number of stocks in the corporation and confer upon their holders the right to participate in the management of the corporation in proportion to their shares. Stock certificates are instruments that allow the issuing corporation to raise equity capital. They confer upon their holders the right to dividends, participation in management, voting, first refusal, and knowledge of company activities. When stock certificates change hands, these rights are transferred to the new owner.

Stock certificates are funding instruments that eliminate intermediaries. In other types of funding instruments, the company borrows from fund providers and pays interest in return for using the funds for a specified period of time. Stock certificates, on the other hand, do not create new debt. Funds acquired in return for stock certificates are added to the equity of the company. Buyers of stock certificates are motivated by the expectation of dividends and future increases in the value of the stock.

Problem Question

A 6-year government bond has a yield to maturity (YTM) of 4 percent and a coupon rate of 5 percent. The face value of the bond is $1000. What is the market price of this bond?

$$\text{Market price of bond} = \text{Present value of coupon} + \text{Present face value}$$

$$= (0.05 \times 1000)\left[\frac{1}{0.04} - \frac{1}{0.04\left((1.04)^6\right)}\right] + \frac{1000}{1.04^6}$$

$$= 1050$$

11.1.3   Primary and secondary markets

Primary markets are markets where debt securities or share certificates are sold to the first buyers. Secondary markets, on the other hand, are the markets where securities previously sold in the primary market are traded second-hand. In primary markets, securities are sold for the first time by intermediary institutions and investment banks. When a bank or an intermediary institution undertakes the sale of securities issued by a company, this is called underwriting. This transaction also serves as a sort of insurance as the intermediary institution guarantees the sale of all securities.

Securities exchanges and currency markets are examples of secondary markets. There is no direct relationship between transactions in secondary markets and the institutions that issue the securities traded in these markets. The institution that issues a debt security or share certificate acquires funds only from their sale in the primary market. The institution that issues a security does not get a direct benefit from the exchange of the said security in the secondary market. Such institutions receive funds only when they issue securities or certificates in the primary market. In the case of secondary market transactions, funds move between sellers and buyers in this market. For example, the treasury receives money when it sells the treasury bonds it has issued in the primary market. The treasury does not get any benefits when the same bonds change hands between individuals in the secondary market.

However, secondary markets have two important functions: providing liquidity and setting prices of financial assets. Secondary markets increase liquidity by facilitating sales of financial assets. In addition, the price set in the secondary market serves as an input when pricing the securities sold in the primary market. The higher the price of a security in the secondary market, the higher its price in the primary market. Therefore, the existence of secondary markets is important for the functioning of primary markets.

For most investors, secondary markets are the ones where most transactions take place. In terms of organization, secondary markets are divided into organized markets and over-the-counter markets. Markets where the transactions involving securities take place in an organized manner in a given space are called organized markets, whereas markets in which buyers and sellers do not meet in a space and the trading takes place online are called over-the-counter markets.

11.1.4   Spot markets and futures markets

Financial markets are divided into spot markets and futures markets depending on when the exchange takes place. Spot markets are markets where the financial instrument that is the subject of exchange is delivered and paid for immediately. However, depending on the market, "immediately" may also mean within a day or two.

Futures markets are markets where commodities, precious metals, capital market instruments, or currencies of a specified amount and quality are traded at a specified price with delivery set at a specified time in the future. There can be different reasons for trading in the futures market. For example, the futures market can be preferred to fix the future price of a security today, against potential changes in its price, in order to limit risk. In addition, speculators may choose to trade in the futures market to benefit from price movements in the future or to take advantage of price differences between the spot market and the futures market.

Derivative instruments whose prices are determined by the prices of the underlying assets play a significant role in financial markets. They are called derivatives due to the fact that their values are derived from or dependent on the underlying asset. In this sense, forward, futures, options, and swap contracts are well-known examples of derivatives. There are variant versions of the derivatives in financial markets, whereas we give a rather short description of the main types here for the sake of simplicity.

11.1.4.1   Forward and futures contracts

Forward and future contracts are the most important financial products for hedging the foreign exchange risk associated with firm operations. Forward and futures contracts give an obligation to issuers of an arrangement calling for future delivery of an asset at a predetermined price, quantity, and time. Despite the similarities between forward and futures contracts, there are fundamental differences in terms of market dynamics. On the one hand, forward contracts are customized and unregulated, carry high counterparty risk, and require no initial payment; on the other hand, futures contracts are standardized and regulated, carry low counterparty risk, and require initial margin payment. These contracts are used by hedgers, speculators, and arbitrageurs for different purposes. Contracts can be written on commodities, currencies, metals, and oil, among others. The fundamental purpose is to reduce uncertainty surrounding future prices. Since having a futures contract ensures that the asset will be bought or sold at a predetermined price, quantity, and time, a certain outcome can be expected as a result of the contract.

In Islamic banking, forward contracts are commonly used for hedging foreign exchange risk, with two fundamental differences. The first difference is that one of the parties involved in the transaction should have a right to terminate the contract. Since there are two parties, this right is given to the dominant side. For example, if a forward contract is set between a firm and an Islamic bank, the dominant side is the bank. On the other hand, if a forward contract is set between a bank and governmental institution, then the dominant side is the governmental institution. The second difference is that Islamic banks do not set a forward contract with those who want to speculate in the market. Therefore, these types of contracts are usually made between Islamic banks and corporate firms. Futures contracts are not considered by Islamic banks due to their features.

11.1.4.2   Option contracts

Option contracts are the most attractive derivative instruments.[2] These contracts are standardized and traded on stock exchanges, as is the case for futures contracts. By definition, these are contracts that give holders a right but not obligation to buy or sell the underlying assets at a predetermined price, quantity, and time. There are two classic types of option contracts, calls and puts. A call (put) option is a right to buy (sell) the underlying asset at a predetermined price, quantity, and time. Since it is a right to do so, the premium of the contract is relatively low compared with the underlying asset. This means that holders have a leveraged advantage to make a transaction. If prices go against them, holders may not exercise the option, so the maximum loss will be the premium only. In the case of American style options, holders can exercise the contract at any time before maturity, whereas European style options can be exercised only at maturity.

Option contracts (or, similarly, warrants) are not considered an appropriate financial product in Islamic finance. The main reason for this is that a right to buy or sell is not defined in Islamic finance.[3] In the case of an option contract, a right to buy or sell is bought, not the entire product, at the beginning of the transaction.

11.1.4.3 Swap contracts

Swap contracts (or in short swaps) are a multiperiod version of forward contracts. Instead of delivering Bahrain dinars for US dollars at a predetermined forward exchange rate and date, a foreign exchange swap would be arranged for more than one period. As an example, we may exchange 1 million Bahrain dinars for 0.4 million US dollars for the next 3 years. In a similar vein, interest rate swaps are an arrangement for exchanging a series of cash flows proportional to a given interest rate for corresponding series of cash flows proportional to a floating interest rate. In this example, one may wonder why someone would want to have fixed or floating interest rates. This has to do with a firm's creditworthiness, which could force the firm to borrow money at a floating interest rate. Swap contracts are commonly used financial instruments in Islamic banks.

11.1.5   The role of financial markets

So far, we have introduced the type of financial markets and the main version of financial instruments traded within these markets. Each of these financial instruments was created upon a need expressed by market participants. Broadly speaking, financial markets are places where firms can raise capital, seize opportunities, and manage uncertainty (Figure 11.1).

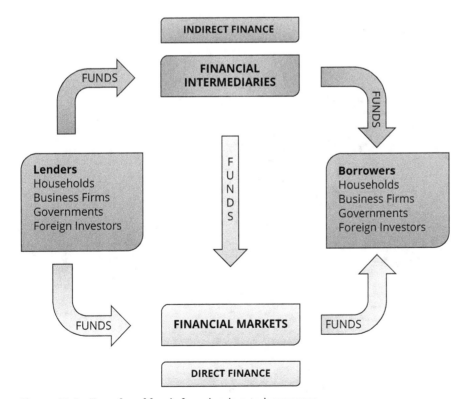

Figure 11.1   Transfer of funds from lenders to borrowers

From a firm's point of view, a financial market is a platform where firms meet their external financing needs. External financing can be either in the form of debt financing (issuing bonds or taking out loans) or equity financing (issuing equities) through initial public offerings (IPOs). From investors' point of view, a financial market is an efficient market that allocates funds to their most productive uses. The term **efficient market**[4] implies that asset prices reflect all available information so that asset prices approach their true (fair) value in the market. Asset prices are determined by the demand and supply of market participants. If the market is efficient, asset prices will represent an unbiased estimate of the assets' true value. This view is considered one of the main themes of neoclassical finance. At the other end of the spectrum, certain pitfalls, so-called anomalies, can be seen as a pattern in asset prices. This view falls under the purview of the field of behavioral finance. Proponents of this school argue that asset prices can deviate from their fair values even if asset prices fully reflect the available information since the term *market efficiency* is defined as prices fully reflecting relevant information, it is not clear that how correctly prices reflect the information. This definition implies that prices do not ignore information, but there is a problem related to how accurately information can be reflected in prices. The main source of confusion[5] is that proponents of market efficiency and behavioral finance have focused on and described the various definitions of efficiency. Supporters of the efficient market theory have tended to focus on definitions based on the absence of arbitrage, whereas supporters of behavioral finance have tended to define market efficiency in terms of objectively correct prices, rather than the absence of arbitrage profits.

Figure 11.2 shows a general circle of cash flows taking place between firms and financial markets. CF_1 represents the external capital needed for the firm to maintain its operations in which it invests in real assets. This takes the form of issuing equity shares or bonds. CF_2 represents cash outflows that take the form of interest and principal payments. CF_3 represents internal financing (retained earnings) that

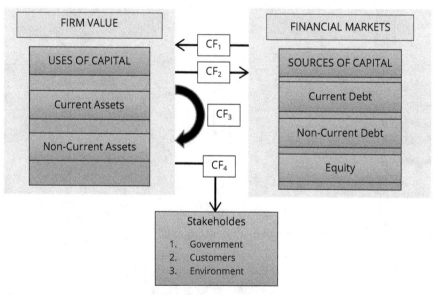

Figure 11.2 Cash flows between firms and financial markets

are not distributed to shareholders. CF_4 represents cash outflows in the form of taxes and other expenses.

11.2   Financial institutions

Financial institutions are the institutions that serve as intermediaries in the exchange of funds in the financial system. Due to this role, they are also called financial intermediaries. Most funds in the financial system are transferred using an indirect finance channel, that is to say, via financial institutions. Therefore, financial institutions play a crucial role in the transfer of funds in the system. Financial institutions will be examined in four groups: depository institutions, insurance and pension funds, exchange intermediaries, and other investment intermediaries. In Islamic finance, Islamic banks play a major role in serving as a financial intermediary. They innovate Islamic financial products and uphold Islamic rules governed by the legal authority.

11.2.1   Depository institutions

Depository institutions are the basic form of financial intermediaries whose main role is to transfer excess funds from depositors to borrowers of capital. On the side of depositors, these institutions create a platform where liquid, safe, and appropriate investments can be made. Depositors can withdraw their deposits any time they need in an efficient way. On the side of borrowers, these institutions provide alternative sourcing platforms that can be costly under certain conditions. If borrowers are big enough, depository institutions may provide them greater funds and for a longer term. However, if borrowers are small or even nonexistent (start-ups), then the importance of depository institutions becomes more apparent. Depository institutions can collect detailed information from borrowers, monitor them, and arrange for customized debt contracts that best fit their needs. These factors may justify a depository institution's lending in circumstances in which security issuance would either be infeasible or entail a higher cost of capital. Banks collect deposits from those with surplus funds and provide loans to those with insufficient funds. Banks are the most important intermediaries in the financial system. In addition to banks being the most important institutions in the system, depository banks occupy a special place in the system because they are part of the process of money creation (Figure 11.3).

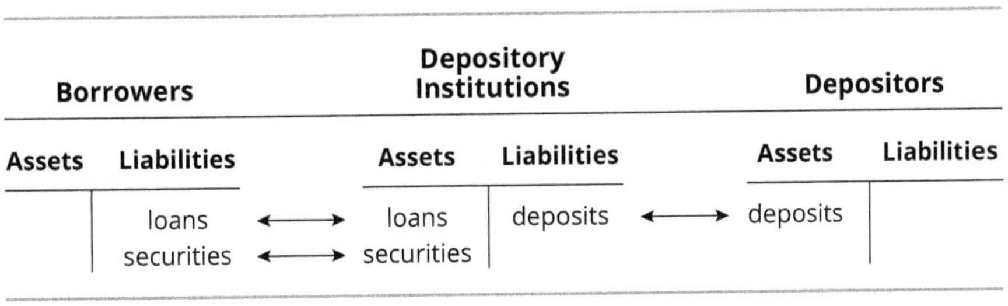

Borrowers		Depository Institutions		Depositors	
Assets	Liabilities	Assets	Liabilities	Assets	Liabilities
	loans	loans	deposits	deposits	
	securities	securities			

Figure 11.3   Balance sheet structure of depository institution

11.2.2   Insurance and pension funds

Insurance and pension funds are the institutions that collect funds at fixed intervals specified in agreements. Because they know about the amount of payments they will make in the future, according to a plan, unlike banks, they do not face the problem of sudden withdrawals. Therefore, they can invest their funds in long-term financial assets.

Insurance firms underwrite the risks of their customers via insurance agreements. Insurance policies are a type of financial asset. Insurance is an agreement between the policyholder and the insurance firm, allowing the policyholder, in return for a specified premium, to receive money from the insurance firm in the event of an unforeseen loss. For example, in the case of vehicle insurance, if the vehicle is damaged as a result of an accident, the insurance firm will pay for the damage in return for the premiums paid. These agreements transfer the risk from the policyholder to the insurance firm.

Private and public pension funds also fall in this category. Individuals who join this system build up savings via the premiums they pay as they work, so as to have a source of income when they retire.

In Islamic finance, an insurance agreement is commonly arranged and known as *takaful*. The fundamental difference between an insurance contract in a conventional financial system and *takaful* in Islamic finance is that the collected premiums are invested in Islamic financial instruments and distributed to the insured at maturity after covering damages. There are three types of *takaful* agreement: general *takaful*, family *takaful*, and *retakaful*.

11.2.3   Exchange brokers

Brokerage firms operating in securities markets are another type of financial intermediary. To serve in this capacity, they need to be licensed by the relevant regulatory body, such as the US Securities and Exchange Commission (SEC). Firms that have this license and operate in securities exchanges are also called intermediary institutions. These firms act as intermediaries in the IPO of securities in primary markets and their trading in secondary markets. In addition, they provide investment consultancy and portfolio management services.

11.2.4   Other investment intermediaries

Intermediaries in this group will be examined under four groups: financial leasing companies, factoring companies, consumer finance companies, and asset management companies.

11.2.4.1   Financial leasing companies

Leasing companies allow investors to lease financial assets. Financial leasing is based on a trilateral financial relationship between lessor, lessee, and seller. A financial lease agreement is a contract by which the ownership of an investment good that the investor would like to acquire is retained by the lessor, whereas the lessee retains usage rights of the good, in return for a rent. Once the contract expires, ownership is transferred to the lessee. For example, if a farmer chooses financial leasing to buy a tractor, he will acquire the right to use the tractor in return for some rent as specified in a contract, and once the contract expires, the farmer will acquire ownership of the tractor he had been using for the duration of the contract.

11.2.4.2 Factoring companies

Factoring companies use factoring agreements to facilitate the collection of creditor companies' accounts receivable. With this agreement, the factoring company buys from its customer the accounts receivable arising from the sale of all sorts of goods and services, and the customer is paid before the maturity of the receivables. Another aspect of this agreement is that the management of receivables is transferred to the factoring company. Factoring companies provide liquidity to creditor companies in return for their accounts receivable. These agreements facilitate the collection of receivables and improve the cash flow of companies.

11.2.4.3 Consumer finance companies

Consumer finance companies use consumer financing agreements to finance the planned purchase of goods and services using resources other than equity. These agreements of course create costs for the debtor, which vary depending on the type of finance. Consumer finance can take the form of vehicle loans, personal loans, home equity loans, mortgages, and so forth.

11.2.4.4 Asset management firms

Asset management firms are companies that offer financial products to allow financial-sector organizations to liquidate their nonperforming loans, nonperforming receivables, and other assets. These firms buy nonperforming loans from banks in return for a certain amount of money. The firms are then expected to collect debts in these portfolios by making restructuring deals with the debtors.

11.2.5   The role of financial intermediaries

In the current economic environment, there is obviously a positive correlation between economic prosperity and financial development. The most developed financial markets are located in advanced economies. Why is this so? To understand the dynamics behind this positive correlation, we need to understand the role of financial intermediaries. In this respect, we may identify the main functions of financial intermediaries and their additional services.

The functions of intermediaries can be classified into five functions that improve economic efficiency: (1) facilitating transactions, (2) facilitating portfolio creation, (3) easing household liquidity constraints, (4) spreading risks over time, and (5) reducing the problem of asymmetric information. In addition to these functions, financial intermediaries also act as a brokerage that brings buyers and sellers together to execute financial transactions. For example, stockbrokers specialize in brokerage, while others engage in brokerage in addition to serving as intermediaries. It is worth noting that there is an increasing trend of providing more than one type of financial service. This complicates the categorization and identification of financial intermediaries.

There is another concept usually mentioned in association with financial intermediaries: externalities. The term refers to spillover effects, positive and negative, generated by the actions of financial institutions in particular and the financial system in general. The risk from such circumstances is called systemic risk.[6] The systemic risk of financial intermediaries such as banks, investment companies, insurance companies, or credit unions can be enormous when interactivity is high. The logic is simple: if one fails, then everyone will lose. This is the reason behind why there must be strict regulations in financial systems.

Financial intermediaries sell their own liabilities to raise funds that are used to purchase liabilities of other corporations. Despite the numerous tasks financial intermediaries do, we explain their three principal functions here: fund aggregation, trading and investment, and risk management.

11.2.5.1   Fund aggregation

Fund aggregation can be identified as one of the primary tasks of financial intermediaries, which implies collecting relatively small deposits from market participants. Commercial banks are a concrete example of this function, whereas insurance companies, pension funds, and even hedge funds do fund aggregation as well. As they raise capital, they may decrease transaction costs substantially by utilizing economies of scale. Possible sources of economies of scale are transaction costs that fall in percentage terms with trade size, the sizable up-front costs of performing financial research, the expanded investment opportunities available to larger investors, and the greater ability of larger investors to diversify investments.

11.2.5.2   Trading and investment

Financial institutions do not just raise capital but also often trade or invest in financial assets on their own accounts. They believe that they can use information asymmetry in pricing financial assets better than anyone else in the market. For example, derivatives dealers hold trading portfolios of derivatives. Hedge funds very actively try to outperform the market using financial expertise.[7]

11.2.5.3   Risk management

The role of risk management in financial intermediaries is that they adjust the risk exposure of their customers downward. They have two options for reducing risk. They may either absorb risk themselves, spreading it among their portfolios, or transfer it through derivative contracts. The classic examples of risk management are insurers, whereas commercial and investment banks offer derivative-type products to reduce risk exposure.

11.3   How the financial system functions

The most important function of the financial system is to facilitate fund flows between lenders and borrowers. A well-functioning financial system improves overall efficiency in the economy by directing funds to efficient investments. However, if the financial system is unable to distinguish investors who target efficient investments from investors who tend to take high risks, the overall risk in the system will increase. Making that distinction is not always easy because one of the features of the financial system is that those with surplus funds and those with insufficient funds do not have the same amount of information. In financial systems, lenders always have less information than borrowers.

This means that financial markets contain more uncertainty and risk compared to other markets. Although it may look like there is abundant information, ordinary investors are more likely than not to be in doubt as to what to do with their money. It is not easy to decide on the most efficient way to invest one's savings. When risks and uncertainty increase, the functioning of the financial system may suffer. In an environment of scant information concerning which investments are riskier and which are less risky, the financial system will experience problems if funds are directed to investors who take a lot of risks.

When the risks in a financial system increase, exposing the system to potential crises, it creates problems not only for local units but also for other economies connected to that system, because of the global nature of such connections. Problems in financial systems may bankrupt banks or financial companies. When developments lead to a crisis, the effects of the crisis may rapidly contaminate other economies, and even create a global crisis. Therefore, understanding the dynamics behind the functioning of the financial system and how and through which channels this system affects the general functioning of the economy is crucial for understanding not just how national economies work, but also the dynamics behind the global economy. To this end, we will first examine information-related problems in financial systems.

11.3.1 Basic functions of the financial system

The financial system, in addition to facilitating fund transfers, performs other basic functions as well. These functions are the distribution of risk, providing liquidity, and transmitting information.

11.3.1.1 Distribution of risk

Investors invest their savings to earn additional revenue. Their goal is to maximize their earnings. However, the market is full of risks and uncertainties. Every individual investor has only limited information about the market. There is a risk that the attempt to earn higher revenues might result in the loss of savings. Therefore, investors take certain measures to limit risk in the face of future uncertainty. These measures are based on the basic principle of not putting all your eggs in one basket. Distribution of eggs to multiple baskets lowers the risk of all eggs breaking at once. By diversifying their investments, investors divide their investments among alternative financial assets. The word *portfolio* refers to all the financial assets that an investor owns. In a portfolio that consists of assets that can move in different directions, the return on one asset may increase as the return on another asset decreases. Thus, the total return on the portfolio may be stabilized, even though asset prices change.

To be able to create a portfolio that contains different financial assets and distributes the risk, the financial system should offer alternative financial assets. The more successful a financial system is in spreading out risk, the more fund transfers will take place in that system. In addition, the amount of funds accumulated in the financial system will increase and the risk distributed among alternative financial assets.

11.3.1.2 Liquidity

The second function of a financial system is to offer more liquid investment opportunities via alternative financial assets in the system. It is important for investors to own financial assets that they can turn into cash when they want, so that they can invest or buy goods and services. If you pay no transaction costs when turning assets into cash and can make that conversion at will, then you have invested in highly liquid assets.

Owning liquid assets is important for investors so that they do not miss important and profitable investment opportunities that require fast action. Financial assets such as stock certificates, bills, checks, and bonds are more liquid compared to nonfinancial assets such as cars, construction equipment, and immovable property. The financial system allows investors to invest in these liquid options.

11.3.1.3 *Information transmission*

The third function of the financial system is to collect and transmit information. Investors looking to invest their surplus funds in the financial system need information to gauge the future value of financial assets. The financial system plays an important role in the collection and transmission of this information.

For example, consider one of the most important financial institutions: banks. Banks are financial institutions that transfer the funds they collect from units with surplus funds to units with insufficient funds. Let us assume that the party with insufficient funds is a company. When banks provide funds to this company, in the form of a loan, they will examine the company in detail. They have experience that arises from being in this business for a long time. In the absence of banks, small investors would have difficulty locating companies that need funds. Assuming they found the company, they would have difficulty assessing the creditworthiness of the company. The financial system does not completely eliminate this problem, but it limits the lack of information of this type. The financial system and intermediary institutions in the system provide information to willing investors, in return for a price, about alternative financial assets.

11.3.2   Asymmetry in financial markets

Information plays a very important role in the functioning of the financial system. The functioning of financial markets requires distributed information; this is a prerequisite of healthy functioning markets. Collecting information, however, is costly. When this cost increases, the functioning of the market suffers. Due to the costs associated with acquiring information, financial markets are the most problematic of all markets. The most important problem in financial markets is that lenders have less information than borrowers. Lenders usually do not have complete information about the nature of investments to be made by borrowers or about the risks involved and potential return. Borrowers in financial agreements, however, can be assumed to have complete information, that is to say, they know where they will use the money and what the risks and potential returns are. However, lenders only have as much information as is provided by borrowers, that is to say, less than borrowers. Imbalance of information between parties to a debt agreement is called information asymmetry or lack of information. Lack of information in financial systems can lead to two problems: adverse selection and moral hazard.

11.3.2.1 *Adverse selection*

If the lender does not have sufficient information when deciding whom to lend to, this might result in adverse selection.[8] Adverse selection takes place before the debt agreement is signed. Adverse selection is ultimately caused by the fact that investors who tend to take more risks are more willing to borrow. To see why this is the case, assume you have two friends, Jane and Joe. Jane tends to borrow only when she is confident that she can pay the loan back because she does not like to take risks. Joe, on the other hand, likes to take risks. If you know both of your friends well and have information about their behavioral patterns, you prefer to lend to Jane rather than

Joe when both say they need money. However, if you do not know them very well, you cannot predict how they will behave when they borrow money, and you would face the problem of incomplete information in your lending. Of the two candidates who would like to borrow, Joe, the one that likes to take risks, would probably be more insistent on borrowing, whereas Jane would be more reluctant. In this case, it is highly probable that investors like Joe would receive more funds than investors like Jane, who do not like to take risks and are more conservative. When lenders do not have reliable information about the risks associated with potential borrowers and most potential borrowers are investors who like to take risks, this will result in adverse selection: high-risk actors would receive more funds.

Similarly, buyers of debt securities (e.g., bonds, bills) and share certificates have difficulty in deciding which firms are riskier and which are low-risk firms with higher profit potential. In this case, sellers of securities (i.e., borrowers) know about the financial situation of their firms, but buyers of bonds or share certificates (i.e., lenders) do not have this information. In terms of the value of financial assets, the real value of the bonds sold by a low-risk firm is higher than the real value of the bonds sold by a high-risk firm, other things being equal. However, because buyers in the market have incomplete information, they would not be able to distinguish between the bonds of good and bad firms, and most bonds would command an average price. In this case, good (low-risk) bonds would be underpriced and bad (high-risk) bonds would be overpriced. As a result, low-risk firms would not prefer to acquire funds by selling bonds in the market, whereas high-risk firms with financial problems would be more willing to sell bonds. In short, the problem of incomplete information would result in more bad bonds being sold in the market than good bonds, and a problem of adverse selection would emerge for buyers. In the event that risks are too high and the problem of incomplete information too severe, buying bonds will stop being a preferred investment option for buyers, and the market will stop functioning. This is frequently observed in times of financial crisis.

The simplest way to solve the problem of adverse selection is to remove lack of information. When there is complete information, buyers can distinguish between high-risk and low-risk securities, meaning that complete information would solve the problem of adverse selection. However, there are costs associated with access to information. Lowering these costs would improve access to information and lower the probability of adverse selection. To minimize the problem of adverse selection and to ensure healthy functioning of markets, the following solutions can be used.

Public Agencies Dealing with the Problem of Lack of Information: One way to achieve this goal would be to require market actors to share more information about their financial situation with the public.

Private Companies Collecting and Selling Information: Even when information about actors in financial markets is public, making sense of this information and predicting the current and future course of risks in different markets is not an easy undertaking. Therefore, examining financial statements disclosed by companies and reading reports about the financial sector prepared by public agencies may not be enough to assess the risks in the markets and predict future developments. This is why, in addition to publicly disclosed information, private companies also collect and sell information, accompanied by experts' assessments.

Collateral: Another way to solve the problem of adverse selection, besides removing lack of information, might be the inclusion of collateral terms in debt agreements. When collateral is pledged in debt agreements in return for the loan, the lender would be protected against loss that might result from the borrower's default. In this case, lenders would be more inclined to lend.

Company Equity: The equity of the borrowing company can also serve as a sort of collateral. The equity of a company refers to assets that remain after liabilities are deducted. Companies with strong equity, even when they have trouble repaying their debt, have at least assets that can be turned into cash, serving as a sort of assurance for lenders. Therefore, equity contributes to the functioning of debt markets by making it easier to lend.

11.3.2.2   Moral hazard

Another problem created by lack of information, one that emerges after the agreement is signed, is moral hazard. Moral hazard[9] refers to the risk that the borrower may use the money in inappropriate investments. To eliminate or at least minimize this risk, information is needed about whether the company is in a position to be able to meet its obligations. As mentioned earlier, the moral hazard in debt financing can be minimized by requiring collateral for the loan. In addition, the equity that companies have can also act as a sort of collateral. When lending to a company with strong equity, in the case of default, debt can still be collected by liquidating the company's assets.

Moral hazard also exists for financial institutions. Problems in the financial system can be very costly for the overall economy. In times of financial crisis, economic activity slows down, and unemployment and risks in the financial sector increase. If a large bank or financial institution were to go bankrupt, this might endanger the whole sector. Therefore, authorities try to ensure that the financial system functions without serious problems; they try to prevent big financial institutions, especially big banks, from going bankrupt. This policy is known as too big to fail. The policy of too big to fail might result in big financial institutions assuming larger risks compared to small institutions. This, in turn, makes it difficult for the latter to compete with big institutions. In addition, the policy of too big to fail increases the risk of moral hazard in financial markets. As a principle, financial institutions, banks in particular, are expected to try to minimize their risks. However, managers that count on the policy of too big to fail may engage in riskier activities. A financial system composed of such institutions would inevitably be unstable. The status of being too big to fail and the belief that this is a generally accepted government policy have the potential to destabilize the financial system and increase the risk of moral hazard.

11.3.3   Crises in financial markets

Economies have been facing financial crises with increasing frequency. The first financial crisis of the twenty-first century emerged in late 2008 in the US and became a huge global financial crisis. As a result of this latest financial crisis, economic activity has dropped to a level not seen since the Second World War. Global production has decreased and global trade has contracted.

There can be two types of crisis: a currency crisis and a banking crisis. Large, sudden movements in the exchange rate as a result of speculative attacks targeting the foreign exchange market, triggered by balance-of-payments issues, can lead to a currency crisis. Banking crises can be defined in two ways. First, a bank's customers may lose their confidence in the bank, resulting in rapid withdrawal of deposits (bank run) and the bank facing troubles. Second, banks may face crises for reasons other than bank runs. In either case, the confidence in the sector is shaken, and the crisis rapidly spreads to the entire sector as the balance sheets of institutions other than the problematic ones also start to deteriorate.

Channels Through Which Financial Crises Affect Economic Activity: Financial crises lower production and trade volume and increase unemployment. The main channels through which financial crises affect the real economy are as follows: increasing cost of borrowing, credit crunch, risk avoidance, company and household equity, exchange rate, and confidence.

Increasing Cost of Borrowing: In times of crisis, the cost of borrowing increases because the prices of securities decrease overall, and interest rates rise.

Credit Crunch: During financial crises, the problem of a lack of information is aggravated and profit expectations fall, making banks less willing to loan money, resulting in a credit crunch. Higher funding costs and a credit crunch make it more difficult to finance investments and consumption. As a result, investments decrease, and consumption spending, particularly spending on durable consumer products, falls. This, in turn, leads to a slowdown in economic activity.

Risk Avoidance: Another important indicator of financial crises is that investors tend to avoid taking risks. The tendency to avoid risks decreases demand for assets in general and lowers asset prices. Prices of stocks and real property decrease, along with those of other assets. The fall in asset prices negatively affects the balance sheets of companies and households.

Company and Household Equity: During crises, the fall in asset prices lowers equity, which is the difference between assets and liabilities on the balance sheets of companies. Because equity also serves as a sort of collateral, a decline in equity makes it more difficult for companies to borrow. Similarly, the fall in asset prices also lowers the equity of households, that is to say, the value of their net assets. As is the case with companies, this lowers the value of collateral that households can pledge when borrowing, making borrowing more difficult. As a result, funding their investments becomes more difficult for companies, households lower their spending, and economic activity slows down.

Exchange Rate: Risk avoidance during financial crises leads capital to shift to safer currencies, depreciating the currency of the country experiencing a crisis. A change in the exchange rate affects not only trade flows but also balance sheets. Depreciation of the local currency can have a positive effect on the trade balance by facilitating exports and making imports more difficult. This can spur economic activity. However, it takes time for changes in the exchange rate to be reflected in trade flows. In the short term, on the other hand, if households and companies have more liabilities than assets in foreign currency, depreciation of the currency would deteriorate their balance sheets, and the balance sheet impact mentioned earlier would increase.

Confidence: During crises, economic actors have negative expectations. Consumers, companies, and investors have lower confidence in the economy. The lack of confidence slows consumption, investment, and, ultimately, production activity.

As these considerations show, financial crises create similar problems regardless of their cause. The aforementioned factors interact with one another to depress economic activity. Therefore, financial crises, whether currency crises, banking crises, or both, decrease production, lower income, and increase unemployment.

11.3.4   Contagion of financial crises

We have seen how a crisis in the financial sector can spread to the entire economy of a country. However, a more dramatic impact of financial crises is that a crisis that starts in one country can spread to other countries, affecting a much larger area. When a financial crisis that starts in one country spreads by triggering financial crises in other countries or creating similar economic effects; this is called a contagion of financial crises. The most striking aspect of the contagion effect is that the crisis spreads from country to country very rapidly, and sometimes its effects are felt even more strongly in some countries than in the country of origin. The spread of the crisis that started in the US in late 2008 to first European countries and then to the entire world was an example of rapid contagion. Financial crises spread via three channels: herd behavior, commercial ties, and financial ties.

11.3.4.1   Herd behavior

The problem of a lack of information in financial markets is an important factor that triggers herd behavior. People who do not have sufficient information to guide their behavior act in concert with others. Therefore, when some investors in financial markets act in a certain way, other investors emulate their behavior and act similarly. Thus, when international investors in country A start fleeing the country, thinking that risks are too high there, investors in country B, where the market is similar to country A's, do the same. Herd behavior in international capital movements leads to sudden changes in the direction of capital flows.

11.3.4.2   Commercial ties

Commercial ties between countries, as well as competition in the same international markets, can facilitate the spread of contagion effects. Assume country A and country B have large-scale trade relations. In this case, a financial crisis that starts in country A would not only lower the demand for the products of country B but also interrupt the supply of production inputs that country B receives from country A. For this reason, country B will also be affected by the crisis. However, such trade channel effects are expected to make themselves felt in the medium term.

Therefore, a large volume of trade between two countries may not be very important in terms of contagion effects in the early stages of a crisis. Nevertheless, there is the possibility that the trade channel will have greater significance. When two countries are competitors in international markets, this can serve as another trade channel triggering the contagion of a crisis. For example, if the currency of country A depreciates as a result of a financial crisis, this may lower the competitiveness of country B. If country B in turn devalues its own currency to protect its competitiveness, this might result in a currency war between countries. Currency wars will increase the devastating effects of the crisis.

11.3.4.3   Financial ties

There can be two types of financial ties. First, financial ties may exist because the capital that flows to the countries may spring from the same source. Assume that countries A and B receive capital from the same international funds. In this case, the decrease in the risk appetite of international investors who pull their capital from country A because of a financial crisis might result in their pulling out of capital B, too. The second type of financial tie exists when the financial assets of countries with highly liquid financial assets are included in a large number of international portfolios. For example, assume a country B, whose bonds and stock certificates are much in demand in international markets. Even if the crisis is in country A, when international investors take new positions with less risky instruments, the demand for the bonds and stock certificates of country B will fall. In short, because of changes in international portfolios, the crisis would jump from country A to country B. Such rearrangements in international portfolios might result in the contagion of financial crises, in particular to countries with highly liquid financial assets.

11.4 Financial market and economy

The financial system contributes to economic growth. This section discusses the channels through which the financial sector supports economic growth. The emergence of financial institutions is based on market conflicts that result from the cost of acquiring information and cost of transactions. Because of information and transaction costs, lenders in the economy do not know about the risks associated with different investments, and borrowers do not know which funds are available at what cost. The high cost of acquiring information and conducting transactions led to the emergence of financial markets and institutions. In an environment of uncertainty, the financial system allocates resources through time and space.

11.4.1   The financial system and economic activity

The financial system transfers savings to the economy, provides information about investments, contributes to the efficient allocation of resources, and facilitates risk management and trade. Through these functions, the financial system also contributes to economic growth. Because the general functions of the financial system were explained in the previous sections, the present section will not examine them in detail; instead, the focus will be on the functions of facilitating change and contributing to growth.

The financial system facilitates the trade of goods and services by transferring savings to the economy. For example, consider an individual who does not have sufficient funds to buy a home or a firm that does not have the resources to finance the expansion of its business. The financial system makes it easier for this individual and this firm to borrow, thereby facilitating the sale of goods and services.

Economic growth refers to the increase in total production, that is to say national income, in a country. Economic growth is the only way to improve welfare in a country, and therefore, it is the primary objective of economic policy.

Economic growth has two sources: increase in production capacity via capital accumulation and increase in efficiency via technological innovation. An efficient financial system contributes to growth through both of these channels. Facilitating the transfer of savings to the economy, minimizing risks, enhancing the efficiency of resource allocation, and expediting the trade of goods and services raise the rate of capital accumulation in the economy. An efficient financial system also makes it easier for entrepreneurs and companies with the potential for technological innovation to access funds. This, in turn, facilitates the funding of technological innovation.

The relationship between the financial system and economic growth is, in fact, two-way. In a growing economy, the demand for financial services increases. Thus, the growth of the economy and increasing prosperity spur the development of the financial system. On the other hand, technological advances make the financial system work more efficiently and develop faster. Recent developments in information and communication sectors have caused rapid changes in the structure of the financial system and increased the diversity of financial services. A well-functioning financial system contributes to economic growth, whereas problems in the financial sector depress economic activity. When the system is in crisis, interruption of resource allocation results in a sharp decline in the economic activity of businesses, consumers, and actors in the public sector who need those resources.

11.4.2   Globalization of financial markets

The globalization of financial markets is a development that kicked in especially after the 1990s as a result of the advances in information and communication technologies and the implementation of financial liberalization policies. Today, when companies need resources, they can easily look for them overseas or foreign companies can invest in domestic markets. Thanks to computers and the Internet, investments can be made in many countries around the world at any given moment.

International financial markets can be divided into two categories: euro-currency markets and eurobond markets

11.4.2.1   Eurocurrency markets

Eurocurrency means money held in overseas banks. The most important eurocurrency is the eurodollar, which refers to deposits of US dollars held in banks outside the US. Even though this term was initially used to refer to US dollars in Europe, later, other currencies that were kept outside their domestic markets came to be called eurocurrencies as well. The eurocurrency market is an example of over-the-counter markets where trades are made over the phone, via fax or online. The most important eurocurrency markets are in London and New York. The interest rate that applies in the interbank eurocurrency market in London is called LIBOR.

How did the eurodollar emerge? The eurodollar market started to develop after World War II as the US dollar started to play an important role in the international economy. The eurodollar market emerged because many countries in Europe started to expand their dollar reserves, large amounts of US dollars entered Europe as a result of US economic aid after World War II, multinational American companies increased their investments outside the US, and investors wanted to invest in non-US markets because interest rates were capped in the US. Due to certain advantages that the eurodollar markets offered, the volume of US dollars traded outside the US reached massive levels. Among these advantages are the lower interest rate of eurodollars, fewer regulations on the eurodollar markets, and exemption from the withholding tax on profits earned in these markets. Multinational companies prefer trading in eurodollar markets because of these advantages.

11.4.2.2   International bond markets and eurobonds

Eurobond markets are markets where bonds issued outside their domestic market are traded. Eurobonds are sold in countries where the currencies in which they are denominated are not used. For example, a bond denominated in US dollars and sold in London is a eurobond. Eurobonds should not be confused with foreign bonds. Foreign bonds are issued in the country where the currency in which the bonds are denominated is used. For example, if the German automaker Porsche issues a dollar-denominated bond in the US, this is a foreign bond.

Eurobond markets are important because they make it easier for companies and governments to acquire resources from overseas. Eurobond markets confer certain advantages to those who trade in these markets. These include the flexibility and freedom of action that eurobond markets provide because they are not subject to strict regulations, implementation of the principle of confidentiality to avoid national controls, and exemption from the withholding tax on interest revenues earned from these bonds.

11.4.3   Regulation and supervision of financial markets

Because the healthy functioning of the financial system is very important, the system is regulated and supervised by public authorities all over the world. Yet, even though regulation and supervision make the financial system safer, market regulation may also impose costs because they limit economic activity. Excessive restrictions could hinder the development of markets and economic growth. Two extremes are possible: first, a lack of regulation may result in the uncontrolled growth of the financial system, increasing risks and aggravating the problem of incomplete information, and second, overregulation of the financial system may slow down economic growth. In short, if crises are the price to be paid for market freedom, low growth might be the price to be paid for regulation. A balance needs to be struck between these two extremes such that regulation and supervision allow for the healthy functioning of the financial system.

One component of regulation is to make information public to solve the problem of incomplete information in the financial system. To this end, various public agencies and bodies collect and share information with the public. However, it is also very important to improve confidence in financial institutions.

During financial crises, a lack of confidence in the system hinders economic activity. To protect the economy from such risks, authorities regulate financial institutions. These regulations include limiting entry, transparency, supervision of banks' balance sheets, and deposit insurance:

- **Limiting Entry:** Operating in the banking sector as well as in other fields of the financial sector requires a license. Only financial institutions that meet certain criteria are allowed to operate in the sector, and the types of activities they can engage in are also regulated.

- **Transparency:** Financial companies are required to submit statements about their financial situation to authorities on a regular basis. They need to keep their accounts following certain accounting principles, and they must undergo regular auditing.

- **Supervision of Banks' Balance Sheets:** Regulation of the types of assets that can be held on the balance sheets of banks is important to control banks' risks. Various regulations require banks to have portfolios that consist of low-risk and high-yield assets. In addition, to ensure a sufficient level of equity, banks are required to maintain a minimum capital adequacy ratio.

- **Deposit Insurance:** Deposit insurance is a common practice found in many parts of the world. Government insurance of the deposits held in banks ensures that customers will not face losses even when a bank fails, which serves to increase confidence in the banking system.

Chapter Highlights

Financial markets are markets that bring suppliers and demanders of money together and where financial assets are traded. Actors of the financial system make their transactions in financial markets. These actors are consumers (households), businesses, governments, foreign actors, and financial institutions. Financial markets can be classified using various criteria. These markets are divided into two groups, debt markets vs. stock markets depending on the nature of the financial instrument used in funding; money markets vs. capital markets depending on the maturity of the financial instrument; primary markets vs. secondary markets, depending on whether the securities traded in the market were issued for the first time or not; and spot markets vs. futures markets, depending on when the exchange takes place.

Financial institutions are institutions that serve as intermediaries in the exchange of funds in the financial system. Due to this role, they are also called financial intermediaries. Most funds in the financial system are transferred using indirect finance channels, that is to say, via financial institutions. Therefore, financial institutions play a crucial role in the transfer of funds in the system. Financial institutions are examined in four groups: depository institutions, insurance and pension funds, exchange intermediaries, and other investment intermediaries.

The most important function of the financial system is to facilitate fund flows between lenders and borrowers. A well-functioning financial system improves overall efficiency in the economy by directing funds to efficient investments. However, if the financial system is unable to distinguish investors who target efficient investments from investors who tend to take high risks, the overall risk in the system would increase. Making that distinction is not always easy because one of the features of the financial system is that those with surplus funds and those with insufficient funds do not have the same amount of information. In financial systems, lenders always have less information than borrowers.

The financial system contributes to economic growth. This section discussed the channels through which the financial sector supports economic growth. The emergence of financial institutions is based on market conflicts that result from the cost of acquiring information and the cost of transactions. Because of information and transaction costs, lenders in the economy do not know about the risks associated with different investments, and borrowers do not know which funds are available at what cost. The high cost of acquiring information and conducting transactions led to the emergence of financial markets and institutions. In an environment of uncertainty, the financial system allocates resources over time and space.

Key Terms

Adverse selection	Commercial paper	Eurocurrency market
Banker's acceptance	Common stock	Finance company
Capital market	Contagion of financial	FOREX market
Casualty insurance	crises	Information
company	Corporate bond	transmission
Certificate of deposit	Derivative market	
Commercial bank	Distribution of risk	

International bond market and eurobond
Life insurance company
Liquidity
Money market mutual fund

Money markets
Moral hazard
Mortgage
Mutual fund
Over-the-counter market
Pension fund

Primary market
Regulation
Repurchase agreement
Secondary market
Thrift institution
Treasury bill
Treasury bond

Discussion Questions

1. Why would a firm want or not want to be listed on a stock exchange?

2. What are the benefits of having access to capital markets?

3. Why does market efficiency become a critical problem in financial markets?

4. How do financial intermediaries reduce transaction costs and risk?

5. Is there any relationship between a financial system and economic growth?

6. What does the financial system do? What are its basic functions?

7. What is the most important feature of financial assets?

8. Compare debt securities and share certificates from the perspective of an investor.

9. How are factoring companies and asset management companies different?

10. Explain the importance of secondary markets for primary markets and for the issuers of securities.

11. Compare money markets and capital markets.

12. How does the financial system affect technological innovation in an economy?

13. Explain the problems of adverse selection and moral hazard, problems that result from lack of information. How are the two different?

14. Explain the solutions to the adverse selection problem.

15. What is a financial crisis? What are the different types of financial crises?

16. Explain the channels through which financial crises affect economic activity.

17. How do financial crises spread?

18. Explain special regulations for financial institutions.

Case Study

Read Edwards (1999), and then answer the following questions:

1. What is a hedge fund?

2. How was LTCM created?

3. How did it become successful?

4. What are the factors behind its collapse?

Online Resources

Visit https://www.msci.com/ to explore global equity exchanges.
Visit https://finance.yahoo.com/ to explore common stocks.
Search key terms in http://www.investopedia.com/.
Search bond market indicators at https://asianbondsonline.adb.org/regional/data.php.

Selected Bibliography

Akerlof, G. (1970). The Market for "Lemons": Quality Uncertainty and the Market Mechanism. *Quarterly Journal of Economics*, 84, 488–500.

Black, F. and Scholes, M. (1973). The Pricing of Options and Corporate Liabilities. *Journal of Political Economy*, 81(May–June), 637–654.

Choudhry, M. (2004). *Fixed Income Markets: Instruments, Applications, Mathematics*. Singapore: Wiley.

De Bandt, O. and Hartmann, P. (2000). Systemic Risk: A Survey. ECB Working Paper No. 35.

Dede, K. (2017). *Katilim Bankalarinda Hazine Ürünleri Ve Sermaye Piyasasi Uygulamalari* (Treasure Products and Capital Market Practices in Participation Banks). Istanbul: TKKB Publications.

Edwards, F.R. (1999). Hedge Funds and the Collapse of Long-Term Capital Management. *Journal of Economic Perspectives*, 12(2), 189–210.

Fama, E.F. (1970). Efficient Capital Markets: A Review of Theory and Empirical Work. *The Journal of Finance*, 25, 383–417.

ISRA (2017). *Sukuk: Principles & Practices*. Kuala Lumpur: International Shariah Research Academy for Islamic Finance and Securities Commission Malaysia.

Krichene, N. (2013). *Islamic Capital Markets Theory and Practice*. Singapore: John Wiley & Sons Singapore Pte. Ltd.

Merton, R.C. (1973). An Intertemporal Capital Assets Pricing Model. *Econometrica*, 41(5), 867–87.

Rowell, D. and Connelly, L.B. (2012). The History of Moral Hazard. *Journal of Risk and Insurance*, 79(4), 1051–1075.

Shefrin, H. (2005). *A Behavioral Approach to Asset Pricing*. Burlington: Elsevier Academic Press.

Topay, F. (2011). *Vestel*, MSc in Strategic Planning and Investment, Newcastle University.

Notes

1. These rules are set by the Accounting and Auditing Organization for Islamic Financial Institutions.

2. The literature on options holds a special place in finance. Fischer Black and Myron Scholes (1973) and Robert Merton (1973) contributed option pricing theory. In 1997, Merton and Scholes were (in collaboration with the late Black) awarded the Nobel Prize for their contribution to option pricing theory.

3. See Prophet Muhammed Hadith in Suyuti, El-Camius-Sağır, 6/330.

4. Efficient market hypothesis is one of the key differences between neoclassical finance and behavioral finance. Fama (1970, p. 383) was literally the first to define market efficiency in general as follows: "A market in which prices 'fully reflect' available information is called 'efficient'." Fama was awarded a Nobel Prize for his contribution in 2014.

5. Shefrin (2005) clarifies this point by the following example: An example of the confusion can be found in a side-by-side debate conducted on the pages of The Wall Street Journal on 28 December 2000. The paper published two opinion pieces: "Are Markets Efficient?: Yes, Even if They Make Errors" by Burton G. Malkiel, and "No, Arbitrage Is Inherently Risky" by Andrei Shleifer. A key difficulty with that debate was that the two authors did not subscribe to a shared definition of market efficiency. Shleifer focused on the mispricing of particular securities, whereas Malkiel focused on the absence of abnormal profits being earned by those he took to be informed investors.

6. Systemic risk in a very general sense is in no way a phenomenon limited to economics or the financial system. A full systemic crisis in the financial system may have strong adverse consequences for the real economy and general economic welfare (see a detailed taxonomy of systemic risk in De Bantd and Hartmann, 2000).

7. Can a hedge fund beat the market using financial expertise? LTCM was a dramatic case in financial history that is worth mentioning (Edwards, 1999).

8. The term was first used and popularized by Akerlof (1970).

9. The term moral hazard has a long history, originating not only from the insurance literature but also from the probability and economics literature (see more details in Rowell and Connelly, 2012).

ISLAMIC BANKING AND FINANCE

12

Abdus Samad

Department of Finance & Economic,
Utah Valley University, Orem, UT, USA

Learning Outcomes

LO1: Explain the role of banking and finance in the economy and its historical development.

LO2: Describe the principles and the conceptual foundation of Islamic banking and finance.

LO3: Understand the basics of the operation of the Islamic banking and finance industry.

LO4: Describe the contemporary experience of the industry as an alternative to the conventional financial system and its merits, limitations, and constraints.

Contents

Evolution of Modern Islamic Banking and Finance

In the 1960s Islamic banking and finance was in its theoretical stage. Today Islamic banking and finance is a reality. According to a Bloomberg report from January 5, 2017, *Shariah*-compliant financial assets of Islamic banking are forecasted to be $3 trillion in the next decade from an estimated $2.1 trillion at the end of 2016. Sales of *sukuk*, Islamic bonds, increased 24 percent to $44.1 billion last year. The UK is set to become a global center of Islamic finance and the first non-Muslim country to raise funds by selling *sukuk*. Its successful operations in the Middle East and Malaysia have encouraged other Muslim countries to follow suit. Today Islamic banking and finance operates in more than 53 countries. Pakistan has established 100 percent *Shariah*-based Islamic banking and finance. The Middle East and North Africa (MENA) as well as South and Southeast Asia have also witnessed the establishment and operation of Islamic banking and finance. The growth and popularity of Islamic banking and finance in Muslim countries has inspired non-Muslim countries to introduce it along with conventional (interest-based) banking. As a result, Western countries like the USA, Canada, the UK, and Switzerland, in particular, have witnessed the establishment of Islamic banking and finance.

12.1   Role of banking and finance

12.1.1   Introduction

A financial system consists of financial institutions such as commercial banks, credit unions, savings institutions, life insurance companies, property/casualty firms, and the regulatory authorities that regulate the system. Among financial institutions, commercial banks are the most important player in any economy. The distribution of the US financial institutions' assets in 2009 demonstrates the relative importance of the various sectors of financial institutions in the US economy.

Unlike conventional banking and financial institutions, Islamic banking and financial institutions consist of Islamic banks, Islamic finance companies, and Islamic Insurance companies. Islamic insurance is called *takaful*, which consists of life insurance and property and casualty insurance. Among Islamic financial institutions, the Islamic banking sector is the dominant sector in terms of assets and numbers. According to a global report, the Islamic banking sector is the dominant component and accounts for more than three-quarters of the industry's assets.

12.1.2   Role of banking and financial institutions

Banking and financial institutions play a vital role in a country's economic development. Economists such as Bagehot (1873), Schumpeter (1935), Goldsmith (1969), and McKinnon (1973) were explicit about the positive role of financial institutions in the economic growth of developed countries.

Bagehot (1873) and Hicks (1969) held that financial institutions played a critical role in the industrialization of the UK. Banks and financial institutions facilitated the process of industrialization of the UK by providing the essential capital needed for industrial development. Capital was the key factor in the Industrial Revolution, and banks and financial institutions supplied that essential capital through their mobilization of savings.

Schumpeter (1935) argued that financial institutions, by providing services such as mobilizing savings, evaluating projects, monitoring project management, managing risks, and channeling funds, facilitated technological innovation and economic growth. Thus, banks promoted economic growth by providing financial services and resources to those entrepreneurs who had the potential to innovate with respect to technology and production processes. The key element of economic growth, according to Schumpeter, is the entrepreneur, who takes risks in product and technological innovations. Banks lend support to successful entrepreneurs by channeling funds to their innovations.

In the US, during its early period, banks were engaged in merchant lending because of the mercantile philosophy of the early banks—lending for the very short term (Redlich, 1968). However, during the antebellum period from 1840 to the Civil War, the US demand for banking growth was unprecedented. The historic economic growth was accompanied by the establishment of a free banking system.

The free banking system was a natural choice when President Andrew Jackson vetoed the rechartering of the Second Bank of the United States in 1836. The establishment of a bank, under the free banking law, was almost automatic with minimum capital of $50,000. Consequently, a large number of banks were established and catered to the growing need. Banking and financial institutions play a vital role in a country's economic development.

Current empirical studies support the idea that financial development and intermediation played an important role in the economic growth of less developed countries (LDCs). Based on Odedokun (1998), financial institutions contributed about 85 percent of economic growth of LDCs. The growth-promoting impact of financial development was much more prominent on low-income LDCs than on high-income LDCs. According to him, financial intermediation had a significant positive impact, about 38 percent, on the GDP of the 21 sub-Saharan African countries.

12.2 Historical development of Islamic banking and finance

12.2.1 Historical background/underpinning of origins of Islamic banks

The emergence of Islamic banking and finance was inspired by three important sources (Samad, 2006). **First,** the principle of Islamic banking can be traced back to its origins in the Prophet Mohammed (SAS) 1500 years ago. He set the example of accepting deposits (deposits of gold, ornaments, and valuable assets) from tribal peoples free of charge and engaged in trade based on profit and loss sharing when he was entered into a business contract with a woman, Khadija, whom he married later. **Second** was the emergence of an Islamic renaissance. From the mid-nineteenth century, Muslim populations, intellectuals, and governments of almost all Muslim countries were under direct pressure to integrate *Shariah*-based business reforms in their laws and legal systems. Among the pioneers of the twentieth century who inspired the revival of Islam as a way of life different from the secular way of life were Abdul Aala Maudidi (1903–1979), Sayyid Qutb (1906–1966), Hassan Al-Banna (1906–1949), Mohammad Hamidullah (1908–2002), and Naiem Siddiqui (1948). The writings of these scholars not only inspired Muslims but also laid the foundation of critical thinking in the emergence of Islamic banking. **Third** are the writings on a theoretical model of Islamic banks. The theoretical foundations on the functioning of Islamic banks and the superiority of Islamic banks vis-à-vis conventional banks in providing stability during the business cycle were developed in the writings of many scholars. Among scholars whose critical thinking carried weight and inspired were Siddiqi (1983), Khan and Mirahkor (1986), Chapra (1985) and Mannan (1998). They deliberated on various issues, including principles and the institutional issues of Islamic banking operations and governance.

12.2.2 First attempts and the operation of Islamic banks

There are two opinions as to the creation and operation of the first Islamic bank. According to Wilson (1983), the first attempt to establish an interest-free Islamic bank was made by Muslim landlords in rural Punjab in Pakistan. In some accounts, the bank was established in 1953, while in other accounts, the bank was established in 1957. The most important element of the bank was the interest-free loans. Inspired by a religious spirit, some landlords in Punjab initiated interest-free loans and banking. The motivation of the landlords was to provide interest-free loans to help improve the economic condition of the poor farmers. The landlords made large deposits without interest and the bank distributed these funds to the needy and to poor agricultural farmers. The borrowers of loans paid no interest except for minimum costs to cover the bank's administrative expenses. The bank charged no interest. Basically, loans were interest free. They were made primarily for the purpose of house construction, buying seeds, and machinery (handlooms and agricultural tools). Although the establishment of the bank was a modest attempt to ameliorate the economic conditions of poor and needy farmers, the bank faced numerous problems. First, there was a shortage of funds. Because bank loans carried no interest, there was greater demand for them. However, supply could not accommodate the demand, i.e., the bank was unable to mobilize enough deposits. Second, the bank was unable to recruit enough bankers who were knowledgeable about banking and interested in working in rural areas. Bankers did not like working in rural areas at a small salary because they could live in cities with a higher salary, along with other amenities and features of urban life. Because of these problems, the infant Islamic bank did not survive for long.

According to others, including Alharbi (2015), Samad (2006), and Chachi (2005), the first attempt to establish an Islamic bank was made in Egypt. The first Islamic bank was Mit Ghamr Savings Bank in the rural area of the Nile Delta. The experiment of establishing an interest-free Islamic bank combining the idea of a savings bank with the principles of rural banking was based on Islamic *Shariah* (Ahmed, 1993). Mit Ghamr was established in 1963 by el-Naggar. The purpose of the bank was to mobilize the savings of rural Muslims and provide loans free of interest based on *Shariah* principles. The bank was managed by a group of enthusiastic Muslims who had some level of banking skills. The bank soon became a source of capital formation. The bank became an institution for mobilizing the idle savings of the community and provided loans for investment. The bank extended loans for a variety of purposes, such as buying machinery, tools, seeds, sewing machines, and other items. The bank was very successful and met its objectives. However, according to Wilson (1983), the bank merged with a government bank in 1967.

12.2.3   Development of Islamic banking in Muslim countries

Egypt

With the closing of the Mit Ghamr bank of Egypt in 1967, the Nasser Social Bank of Egypt was established in 1971 by presidential decree. The Nasser Social Bank of Egypt was the first Islamic bank under Act 13. The bank established under this act clearly specified that the bank was not permitted to charge interest; it was a not-for-profit institution established to cater to the needs of low-income Muslims. However, it was not mentioned that the bank was to adhere to Islamic *Shariah*. Faisal Islamic Bank of Egypt, the first commercial Islamic bank, was established in 1977 with capital of $50 million. The bank was completely based on the principle of *Shariah*; the bank's charter clearly stated that the bank must comply with Islamic *Shariah* rules in its operations.

United Arab Emirates

The first Islamic bank of Dubai was the Dubai Islamic Bank, established in 1975 under the Amiri Decree with capital of AED 50 million.

Sudan

Faisal Islamic Bank of Sudan was established in 1976 by Prince Mohammad Al-Faisal in collaboration with some Sudanese businessmen with the approval of former Sudanese presidents. It was the first Islamic bank in Sudan to cater the needs of Muslims.

Saudi Arabia

The Islamic Development Bank (IDB) was established in Jeddah in 1974 for the purpose of promoting economic growth in Muslim countries. Al-Rajhi bank, the first Islamic commercial bank of Saudi Arabia, was established in 1984 with capital of $5 billion.

IDB is a great source of development. By late 2000, IDB had financed trade of over $8 billion, mostly using the principle of mark-up pricing. It also provides loans with service charges based on actual administrative expenses.

Bahrain

The first Islamic bank of Bahrain was Bahrain Islamic Bank. The bank was established in 1979 with bank assets of BD 267 million. Faisal Islamic Bank was the second bank of Bahrain. The bank received its charter in 1993 and has been in operation since then. Bahrain is currently an import hub of Islamic financing. There are 11 Islamic banks operating side by side with conventional banks, with average total deposits of $2,738,298 (million) in 2014.

Malaysia

The first Islamic bank of Malaysia was Bank Islam Malaysia Berhad, established in 1983. The bank originated with the development of a financial institution called Tabung Hajji, which was established in response to Sharia needing money to perform the Hajj. Money deposited in Tabung Hajji to perform the Hajj (pilgrimage to Mecca) must be clean and untainted from *riba* (interest) (Samad, 2006). Tabung Hajji was established in 1963 and offered interest-free deposits to Muslims who intended to perform the Hajj. Later on, with the recommendation of the National Steering Committee, Bank Islamic Malaysia was set up in 1981 and began operations in 1983.

Bank Islam Malaysia is the third largest Islamic bank in Malaysia with total assets of RM32 million.

There are now **17** Islamic banks operating side by side with Islamic finance companies and Islamic insurance companies. Among Muslim countries, Malaysia has the highest number of Islamic banks and financial institutions. Malaysia is also the largest Islamic financial hub in Southeast Asia.

Indonesia

Indonesia is the largest Muslim country in Southeast Asia, with a population of more than 210 million. Though almost 90 percent of the population adheres to Islamic *Shariah*, the growth of Islamic banking and finance was limited. One reason for the lack of banking growth, including the growth of Islamic banking, was the lack of banking knowledge and banking habits. Based on a World Bank report, only 31.6 percent of Indonesia's adult population has a bank account.

However, recently the Islamic banking assets of Indonesia have shown remarkable growth, from US $8 billion to $22 billion, i.e., an annual growth rate of 29.2 percent.

The introduction of Islamic banks and financial institutions was a late phenomenon, and there are currently 11 Islamic banks in Indonesia operating side by side with conventional banks. Indonesia's first Islamic bank, Bank Muamalat, was established in 1994 under state patronage and has about 400 branches around the country.

Bangladesh

Bangladesh is a Muslim country with a Muslim population of about 150 million. To meet the requirements of Islamic *Shariah*-based banking, the first Islamic bank of Bangladesh was established in March 1983 under the auspices of Islamic Development Bank, Jeddah, with capital of TK 500 million. The name of the bank is the Islami Bank Bangladesh Ltd. It is the largest Islamic bank in Bangladesh. Today there are seven Islamic banks in Bangladesh operating side by side with conventional banks.

12.2.4 Development of Islamic financial institutions in the Western world

The growth of Islamic financial institutions is not confined to the Muslim world. The news of successful Islamic financial institutions in Muslim countries and the growing Muslim population in Western countries who want to follow interest (*riba*)-free banking inspired the growth of Islamic financial institutions and services in the West. Consequently we have observed the development of Islamic banking and finance in following Western countries.

United Kingdom (UK)

There is a large Muslim population in the UK. In response to Muslims' demand for Islamic financial products, the first financial institution, Islamic Finance House, was established in London in June 1983. In 2004, the Islamic Bank of Britain became the first fully fledged Islamic bank in UK. At present, 13 banks in the UK also provide Islamic financial services (Samad, 2006).

United States of America (USA)

Approximately seven million Muslims live in the USA. The growth of Islamic finance occurred largely in response to the growing demand of the increasing Muslim population. In 2006, there were about 20 Islamic financial services institutions and a conventional bank with a window of Islamic finances (Samad, 2006). Devon Bank of Chicago was the first bank to open a window for Islamic finance. Among the 20 financial services institutions, the prominent ones were Al Baraka Bancorp Inc., Chicago; Al Median Realty Inc., New Jersey; Ameen Housing Cooperative, San Francisco; Amana Mutual Fund Trust, Bellingham, Washington; Dow Jones Islamic Index Fund; Islamic Credit Union of Minnesota; Fuloos Inc. Toledo, Ohio.

Canada

In response to the needs of the growing Muslim population in Canada, the first *Shariah*-based institution was the Islamic Co-operative Housing Corporation. The Islamic Co-operative Housing Corporation was established in Toronto with paid-up capital of $30 million. The bank was involved in real estate business transactions as well as other businesses.

Switzerland

Switzerland was the first county in Europe to introduce Islamic financing. The first Islamic financial institution, Dar Al Maal Al Islami Trust (DMT), was established in 1981. It is a large multinational company. The objective of DMT was to foster *Shariah*-based financing. It concentrated on three kinds of activities: Islamic investment, Islamic insurance, and Islamic banking operations.

In addition to Dar Al Maal Al Islami Trust, there are few financial services companies that offer Islamic financial services. Among them, Faisal Finance, Geneva; Pan Islamic Consultancy Services, Geneva; and Cupola Asset Management, Geneva are well known.

Denmark

The first Islamic financial institution in Denmark, Islamic Bank International of Denmark, was established in 1982. Faisal Finance is another financial company in Denmark that offers a variety of Islamic financial services.

12.3 Principles and conceptual foundation of Islamic banking and finance

12.3.1 Principles of Islamic banking and finance

Islamic banking and finance is a special breed of entity that provides a variety of services and products that are consistent with Islamic principles and guided by Sariah law. It is a special breed because, unlike conventional banking and finance, which is based on exploitative profits and one-sided risk sharing, Islamic banking and finance is based on fairness and equitable risk sharing and is guided by the Qur'an and *Sunnah*. Because of this, Islamic banking and finance must adhere to the following fundamental principles.

First Principle The first principle to which Islamic banking and finance must adhere is the absence of *riba*, i.e., usury. The Qur'an clearly, without explanation and elaboration, prohibits *riba* (usury).[1] At 2:275 the Qur'an states: "whereas Allâh has permitted trading and forbidden Ribâ (usury)" and at 3:130 it states: "O you who believe! Eat not Ribâ (usury)." However, neither the Qur'an nor the Prophet of Islam defined what *riba* actually is. The absence of clarification of riba led to controversy among scholars.[2] At present, *riba* is interpreted as interest. Modern scholars of *Shariah* agree that a predetermined fixed rate of return, called interest, is not permitted in Islamic banking and finance. The declaration that usury (interest) is forbidden provides the most important foundation of the principle in Islamic banking/financial institutions that all business and financial transactions must be free from usury. Islamic banking and finance is an embodiment of usury-free transactions. Islamic banks do not charge any interest when financing loans and mobilizing deposits. All transactions at Islamic banks are free of interest. On the other hand, conventional banking and finance is deeply involved in interest. Interest is the life blood of conventional banks.

Second Principle The second principle of Islamic banking and finance is the development of a profit-and-loss-sharing (PLS) contract. Interest (usury) is considered to be highly exploitative and socially unjust because just one party, the borrower, not the bank, bears the credit risk. By fixing a predetermined rate of return (interest), lenders in conventional banking and finance receive assured income irrespective of business outcome. Because borrowers have to pay a fixed interest irrespective of the outcome of their business, financiers do not bear the risk of financing, except default risk. Fairness and social justice demand that the risk of financing be equitable, i.e., the risk of investment must be borne by both financiers and borrowers. Islamic banking and finance is a solution to this unfair and unjust practice. In Islamic banking and finance, the bank (the supplier of funds) is not a lender but an investor working side by side with borrowers. Supplying funds, Islamic banks bear the risk of the business venture with the borrower. Because the outcome of venture, failure or success, is not in one party's control, Islamic banking is more fair and equitable since risk of business is shared with borrowers.

This feature of sharing risk in business ventures gives rise to the PLS contract. The PLS contract is a unique feature of Islamic banking and finance. The fixed return from the **venture**, i.e., interest, is replaced by the PLS under which both parties, the supplier of funds, i.e., banks, and entrepreneurs share profits or losses based on a prearranged contract. PLS in a business venture is permitted in Islam and is, thus, an important cornerstone of Islamic banking and finance.

Third Principle The third principle of Islamic banking and finance is the prohibition against unpredictable speculation such as gambling (*maysir*) and *ghurar* (extreme uncertainty). Gambling is a business whose probability of outcome (success or failure) is unpredictable. Thus, the risk in gambling is unlimited. Since the probability of success is unpredictable, financing gambling or any element of gambling is prohibited in Islamic finance. Similarly, *gharar* arises when the probability of the outcome (success or failure) is unpredictable. *Gharar* is a situation of extreme uncertainty or extreme risk whose probability of outcome cannot be predicted. A well-defined contract is not possible. For example, the sale of a five-prong, 300-pound deer that has not yet been hunted in the forest is forbidden.

The difference between *gharar* (uncertainty) and risk in business is that the probability of risk in business is predictable, whereas the probability in *gharar* is unpredictable because in *gharar* the events are unknown and do not even exist. Thus, financing a business involving *gharar* is prohibited in Islamic finance.

Fourth Principle The fourth principle of Islamic banking and finance is the guarantee of *halal*, i.e., permissible business, which means that Islamic banks are involved in business activities involving production and services that are *Shariah*-compliant. Business activities or investments that do not qualify under *Shariah* are not permitted in Islamic finance. Islam does not allow business activities that are injurious to human health and dangerous to humanity. For example, products such as tobacco, alcohol, narcotics, and opium are dangerous to human health. The Qur'an says that the harm in them exceeds their benefits. Similarly, destructive war materials are very deleterious to human welfare, as well as to plants and the environment. Islam prohibits their production and, thus, pork production. Islamic banking and financial institutions are forbidden to become involved in these activities.

12.3.2   Conceptual foundations of Islamic banking and finance

In addition to *riba*, *gharar*, and *maysir*, the following mechanisms represent important factors that laid the conceptual foundation of Islamic banking and finance.

First, Social Justice One of the core principles of Islamic banking and finance is to establish social justice. Islam always advocates and emphasizes the value of fairness, social justice, and equitable distribution of wealth. Islam stands for justice and is against any form of exploitation—socioeconomic or political exploitation. Any financial transaction leading to exploitation and injustice is forbidden. An Islamic financial system, Islamic banking and finance in particular, is built on the basic principles by which it provides equal access to financial access for all (rich and poor), stands ready to lend support to the needy and the poor, and addresses the needs of emerging entrepreneurs—Muslims and non-Muslims.

Islamic banking and finance stands against economic exploitation by providing equal access to loans for all and by sharing in risk profits and losses. Wealth accumulation by the rich through access to bank financing promotes social division and discontent and destroys social peace and harmony. Similarly, the charging of fixed interest irrespective of business outcome, failure in particular, represents oppression and exploitation. The PLS mechanism of Islamic banks aims to address the problem of the unfairness of inequitable distribution of risk and exploitation.

Islamic banks and financial institutions use other mechanisms to establish social justice. They are **Zakah** (alms giving), **sadaqa** (charity), and **qard hassan** (benevolent finance). The introduction of this mechanism has become an important foundation of Islamic banking and finance. The Holy Qur'an reiterates repeatedly the importance of helping the poor and the needy. The Qur'an emphasizes charity to the needy and poor, which is considered an investment as well as the source of forgiveness for believers. The Qur'an says:

>]If you lend Allâh a goodly loan (i.e. spend in Allâh's Cause) He will double it for you, and will forgive you. And Allâh is Most Ready to appreciate and to reward, Most Forbearing. (64:17)

"*Qard-al-hasan* (benevolent lending) is another mechanism. Islamic banking and finance provides "*Qard-al-hasan*, i.e., benevolent loans, to persons who are in need of financing to meet basic needs and obligations. It is a cornerstone of Islamic finance (Samad et al., 2005).

Zakah *Zakah*, or compulsory alms giving, is another mechanism of Islamic banking and finance and one of the five pillars of Islam. It is mandatory not only for individual Muslims but also for Islamic financial institutions (IFIs). Like individuals, IFIs are obligated to pay *Zakah* on profits to the poor. When Islamic banking was in its embryonic stage, it was expected that Islamic banks would be an instrument for ensuring a just and equitable society not only by paying *zakah* (alms) from their profits but also by financing small businesses, trades, and agriculture. The interests of small traders, businesses, and agriculture should not be neglected while serving the needs of big businesses, corporations, and industries. That is, placing an emphasis on microfinancing is one of the objectives of Islamic banks.

Second, *Shariah*-Approved Transaction The participation of *Shariah*-approved activities is an important foundation of Islamic banking and finance. All transactions of Islamic banking and finance are required to be followed by *Shariah*. Islamic banking and finance does not participate in any activity that is repugnant to *Shariah* law. For example, because activities like pornography, alcohol, and pork production are repugnant to *Shariah*, Islamic banking and finance does not participate in them irrespective of the prospect of profits.

Third, Money, Fiat/Paper Money in Particular, Is Not Commodity Money/ Capital Fiat money is one whose intrinsic (commodity) value is less than its face value. Money is simply a medium of exchange. It is used to facilitate transactions and is a unit of account. Under conditions of stable purchasing power, money is a good store of value and is not a commodity, and it cannot generate wealth. Since (paper) money is not a commodity, it cannot increase its purchasing power without real (physical) investment. Islamic finance believes that the generation of wealth is feasible through physical transactions of trade and commerce or investment. Wealth is produced only through investments.

Under stable purchasing power, money generates wealth when more than one dollar (or dinar or any other currency) is returned against the borrowing of one dollar. When money increases its value, it becomes a commodity. In such a case, money is no longer a medium of exchange because its value has increased. A borrower is hurt when more money is needed to purchase something than the original amount borrowed. This is unjust and exploitation. Islam is against it. By the same token, when the purchasing power of money declines due to inflation, returning the same amount of money that was originally borrowed would hurt the lender/financier. This is also unjust because the financier (lender) ends up buying fewer goods and services because their prices have increased.

12.4   Understanding basic operations of Islamic banking and finance

12.4.1   Islamic banking and finance

An Islamic bank is a firm whose aim is profit maximization through *Shariah* approved financial transactions and services. Understanding Islamic banking requires an understanding of the balance sheets of Islamic banks.

12.4.2   Balance sheet in Islamic banking and finance

The balance sheet is like an x-ray machine of any financial institution. The balance sheet is a statement of the assets, liabilities, and net worth of a bank. The liability side of the balance sheet of an Islamic bank shows the sources of funds, while the asset side shows the uses of funds. A prototype balance sheet of an Islamic bank or financial institution is presented below for demonstrating its basic function:

Uses of Funds (Assets)	Sources of Funds (Liabilities)
Cash or cash equivalent	*Al-Wadia* deposit (demand deposit)
Murabahah (cost-plus/mark-up)	*Al-Wadia* saving (saving deposit)
Mudarabah (Ownership/trust)	*Mudarabah* investment deposits
Musherakah (joint venture	Equity
Salam or *bai al-salam* (forward sale)	
Bai muajjal (deferred payment sale)	
Istisna (manufacturing contract)	
Ijarah (leasing)	
Quar hasan (benevolent loan)	

12.4.2.1   Assets (Uses of Funds of Islamic Bank)

The assets of an Islamic bank consist of the following financing contracts/assets.

Murabahah

This refers to a cost-plus/mark-up financial contract. Under this contract, an Islamic bank buys a certain product, for example a car, at a certain price (say, $10,000) and sells the product to borrowers/investors at cost-plus, i.e., at a price higher than the purchase price (say, $11,000). Because the cost-plus price ($11,000) is higher than the cost ($10,000), the difference between the purchase price and the selling price ($1,000) constitutes the profits of the bank. *Murabahah* is a type of debt contract. Under a *murabahah* financing contract, a client wishing to buy goods or assets (e.g., computers, jewelries, cattle) approaches an Islamic bank to buy them on his behalf. The Islamic bank then buys the product at the current market price, adds a profit margin to it, and then resells the product to the client. The key feature is that there is no fixed interest involved, although critics of Islamic banks do not acknowledge this. They call it a "back door for interest-based financing."

Although buying and selling are permitted (*halal*) in Islam, *Shariah* law requires that goods must be in the possession of a seller before they can be sold to a buyer. Whether the goods are, in fact, in the possession of the Islamic bank before they are sold is an important concern of critics of Islamic banks.

Musharakah

This is a partnership and joint venture financing contract. It is an equity type of contract. Under *musharakah* financing, an Islamic bank supplies funds to someone who wishes to invest in a project, like setting up a machine-and-tool factory, building an airport, or buying real estate. Under a *musharakah* financing contract, both parties (suppliers of funds, i.e., bank and investors) provide capital and manage the funds and projects. Profits or losses accruing from the venture are distributed based on the proportion of capital and predetermined agreement. The key features of this contract are as follows:

(1) PLS. Both parties share profits and losses. Unlike conventional banks' equity contracts, where banks do not bear the risk of financing investments, Islamic banks share the risk of investment.

(2) Unlike conventional banks' equity contracts, where banks enjoy a fixed rate of return on investments, even when there are losses, there is no predetermined rate of return for Islamic banks. The Islamic bank does not enjoy a fixed rate of return. Thus, PLS, avoiding fixed interest, is the key distinguishing feature of Islamic banking and finance. This is consistent with socioeconomic justice, which requires that both borrowers and investors share risk.

Mudarabah (Ownership/Trust)

Mudarabah is another innovative financing contract of the equity type. Under *mudarabah* contracts, Islamic banks provide all funds for a project, for example, building a T-shirt factory, and the person who wants to build the T-shirt factory provides all human capital (physical labor, and intellectual and management skills). Profits from the projects are distributed based on a pre-agreed ratio/arrangement. However, in case of loss, the bank that provided the funding (called *rab al maal*), will bear all losses of funds and the investor will bear the loss of his entire labor he or she put into the project. The key features of this contract are as follows: (1) the Islamic bank supplies the funding and the investor provides all necessary human capital, so clearly both bank and investor supply necessary ingredients of investment; (2) the supplier of financial capital (bank) and the supplier of human capital share the risk of investment in case of profits or losses; (3) there is no predetermined fixed rate of return for the bank.

Bai Baithaman Ajil' This is a variant of the *murabahah* (cost-plus) financing contract. In *bai baithaman* financing, the delivery of goods is immediate, i.e., at the time of contract, but payment for the goods is deferred. Payment may be made in installments. However, the price of the product is agreed by both parties at the time of the sale but should not include charges for deferred payment.

The difference with cost-plus pricing is that the delivery of goods is immediate but the payment of goods is deferred.

Salam or Bai Al-Salaam This is a forward sale contract where an entrepreneur sells specific goods to an Islamic bank at a price agreed upon and the purchase price is paid at the time of the contract but the delivery of goods is deferred. The key feature of this financing contract is that the payment for goods is paid at the time of the contract, whereas the goods will be delivered in the future.

Al-ijera is a lease financing contract and is similar to a conventional bank lease contract. *Al-ijera* is very popular in auto financing, such as cars, truck, Jeeps, and machines and tools. Under this type of contract, the Islamic bank purchases a car, truck, Jeep, or machines and tools for a customer and then leases them out for a fixed period and at a fixed rental charge agreed upon at the time of purchase.

There is little difference between an *al-ijara* contract of an Islamic bank and a conventional lease contract of an interest-based bank.

Istisna Istinsa is a financing contract under which a manufacturer /producer, a computer manufacturer, for example, borrows funds and agrees to future delivery of computers at a predetermined price.

Qard-hasan is a benevolent loan that Islamic banks extend to people in need of financing. The important feature of this type of loan is that the creditor, an Islamic bank, does not expect any return on this loan, even the principal, from the borrower. The Islamic bank remains the owner of the asset unless they are repaid in full.

12.4.2.2   *Comparison with conventional bank's assets*

First, irrespective of outcome (failure or success), a conventional bank's assets, i.e., loans, earn a fixed rate of return (interest), whereas an Islamic bank's returns on assets are not fixed. The returns of an Islamic bank are based on the outcome of the business. The bank earns profits if the investment succeeds but no profit or return if the investment fails.

Second, a conventional bank's financing is not securitized; loans are not asset-backed. On the other hand, the financing of Islamic banks is 100 percent asset-backed. All financings—auto financing, production (car) financing, and real estate financing—of Islamic banks are fully securitized. Third, Islamic banks have an ownership stake in assets until payments on financing are made in full. This feature that of conventional banks. When it comes to financing, both conventional and Islamic banks retain title of ownership of assets.

12.4.3   Liabilities (sources of funds of Islamic banks)

The most important liabilities of an Islamic bank are customer deposits. The deposit accounts of Islamic banks are grouped into three major categories: (1) current accounts, called *al amanah/wadiah* deposits; (2) savings deposits, called *mudarabah* saving deposits; and (3) investment deposits.

Current Account Deposits Current account deposits are similar to the demand deposits of conventional banks. Deposits in current accounts are based on two principles: *al amanah* and *al wadiah*. *Amanah* deposits are interest-free deposits of customers held by an Islamic bank in trust (*amanah*). Under an *amanah* arrangement, the

Islamic bank treats the funds as a trust; it does not guarantee the return of the deposit in case of any damage or loss to the *amanah* resulting from circumstances beyond its control. *Wadiah* deposits are safekeeping (w*adiah*) deposits. With *wadiah* deposits, the Islamic bank is a keeper and trustee of funds and has depositors' permission to use the funds for its operations in a *Shariah*-compliant activity. Deposits under *wadiah* take the form of loans from depositors to Islamic banks and the bank guarantees the return of entire amount of the deposit. While these deposits can be withdrawn at any time, depositors have no right to any return/profit on such deposits. Profits for depositors are at the bank's discretion.

Mudarabah Saving Deposits   Savings deposits at Islamic banks operate in a different way. Depositors at Islamic banks allow the banks to use their money, i.e., to invest in profitable business ventures that are legal and *Shariah*-compliant. Deposits in savings accounts are under the control of the Islamic banks, i.e., banks are fund managers of deposits (*mudarib*), Economic Studies, 25 (3), 223–240. whereas depositors are *rabb-ul-mal* (investors). Profits will be shared according to a predetermined ratio, while losses will be borne by the *rabb-ul-mal*, i.e., depositors. Savings deposits are generally placed in a joint investment pool with other deposits mobilized by the Islamic bank.

Mudarabah Investment Deposits   Deposits are similar to the fixed deposit accounts of a conventional bank. They are accepted for a fixed period of time or term and are governed by the *mudarabah* contract. When depositors agree to a fixed term, no withdrawal is normally allowed until the end of the term. However, some banks allow early withdrawals within an agreed notice period. Term deposits are by arrangement where depositors seek some return on their investments; they are taken on a *mudarabah* basis. These deposits are allocated to a number of investment pools, and Islamic banks invest the pooled amount in *Shariah*-compliant businesses. Profits from the assets are shared among depositors and bank according to a predetermined ratio agreed upon at the beginning of the contract. The weights of profit sharing are determined based on the various tenures and the amount invested under the arrangement. As required under *mudarabah*, depositors have to be informed in advance of the formula to be used for sharing the net earnings. In the case of an unlikely event, loss, depositors have to bear the loss on a *pro rata* basis and the bank goes uncompensated for its efforts. If a bank contributes its equity capital in a pool at the time of setting up an investment, the relationship will be a combination of *musharakah* and *mudarabah*, and the bank will be entitled to a proportionate profit on its own investment in relation to the total *mudarabah* investment pool. Islamic banks can also open a *murabahah* and leasing funds in which risk-averse investors may purchase units and be treated as *rabbul-mal* and earn the quasi-fixed return from profits or leases earned by the respective funds from the trading and leasing activities.[3]

12.4.3.1   *Characteristics of Islamic banks' deposits/liabilities*

First, there is no fixed rate of return on any type of deposit account of Islamic banks. The return to depositors at Islamic banks is linked to the return on the assets of the bank. If there are profits earned from using these funds in financing investments, depositors are entitled to a share of it. Unlike a fixed interest rate on conventional bank deposits, the return to depositors at Islamic banks on their deposits is not fixed. Because depositors take on the risk of their deposits under *mudarabah* savings deposits and *mudarabah* investment deposits, they earn money on their deposits as per a prearranged contract. The key feature of this liability contract is that Islamic banks neither guarantee the safety of depositors' capital nor any fixed return on deposits. In this sense, Islamic banks' *mudarabah* investment deposits are more risky than those of conventional banks' fixed deposits and as such deserve more earnings.

Second, profit and loss sharing on *mudarabah* investment deposits is not symmetric. Under this kind of contract, banks invest depositors' funds and share profits but not losses. If the project financed by the Islamic bank fails, depositors bear all losses, not the bank. In this sense, depositors at Islamic banks are more vulnerable than those at conventional banks.

Third, the comparative nature of the assets of conventional banks and Islamic banks is different. Islamic banks focus on asset-based financing investments. The credit risk of Islamic banks is minimal because credit is backed by real assets. On the other hand, the credit risk of conventional banks is high because the main focus of a conventional bank asset is the fixed income investment and the investments are non-assets based financing.

12.4.3.2   Summary of comparison between Islamic and conventional banks

Table 12.1 Summary of differences between Islamic banks and conventional banks

Islamic Bank	Conventional bank

A. Objective
(1) Constrained profit maximization, i.e., profit maximization of an Islamic bank is subject to *Shariah* law.
(2) Provides for social welfare, justice, and equitable distribution of wealth through
  (i) *zakah*,
  (ii) *qard hasana*
  (iii) Charitable contributions.
(3) As the objective of an Islamic bank is to ensure social welfare and justice, the production set of the bank is restricted (bounded). An Islamic bank is **prohibited**, even if it is highly profitable, to engage in the production of such goods and services as
  (i) pork,
  (ii) alcohol,
  (iii) pornography,
  (iv) prostitution,
  (v) war materials.
	A. Objective
	(1) Unconstrained profit maximization, i.e., there is no limit set by banking laws on profit maximization. The more profit, the better for shareholder income.
	(2) Social welfare is not the objective of banks but the function of government.
	(3) Because profit maximization is the main goal, the production set of conventional banks is unrestricted. Banks may engage in the production of any goods and services that maximize profits. As such, conventional banks do not hesitate to engage in the production of
	  (i) pork,
	  (ii) alcohol,
	  (iii) pornography,
	  (iv) prostitution,
	  (v) war materials.

(continued)

Table 12.1 (continued)

Islamic Bank	Conventional bank

B. Guiding principle
 	
(4) The Qur'an and *Sunnah* dictate the function and operation of an Islamic bank, i.e., divine principle guides the operation of Islamic banks.
 	
(5) Because the function and the operation of Islamic banks are guided by *Shariah*, Islamic banks are prohibited from engaging in
  (i) usury (exorbitantly high interest),
  (ii) *gharar* (uncertainty),
  (iii) *maisir*.
	B. Guiding principle
	
	(4) Manmade principles dictate the function and operation of conventional banks. It is not the divine rule/principle but entirely manmade wisdom/ doctrines, i.e., secular theory, that govern the operation of conventional banks.
	
	(5) Because the function of conventional banks is guided by human secular doctrine, there is no restriction on what banks can be involved in.

C. Characteristics of fund sources (deposits) (6) Mobilize household savings by offering deposit accounts. (7) However, depositors are not insured for all deposits. Banks provide guarantees of safety only for those deposits that are based on the principle of *al wadiah* (safety and trust). (8) Because there is no fixed interest rate, the income from savings deposits (*mudarabah* savings) and investment deposits (*musharkah* investment) is not insured. If there are profits or losses from investments out of saving and investment deposits, depositors share both profits and losses. (9) PLS is an important pillar of deposit mobilizations.	**C. Characteristics of fund sources (deposits)** (6) Mobilize household savings by offering deposit accounts. (7) All deposits at conventional banks are insured. In the USA deposits are insured up to $250,000. (8) Because the interest rate is fixed on all deposits, depositors' income from savings deposits, money market deposit accounts (MMDAs), money market mutual funds (MMMFs), and certificates of deposit (CDs) are guaranteed. (9) Fixed interest income is the life blood of conventional bank deposit mobilizations.
D. Characteristics of fund uses (assets) (10) In debt-type financing contracts, such as mark-up pricing, al-salam, *bai al-muajjil*, *al-ijara*, and *al istisna*, buying and selling are the basic principle. There is no interest involved. Both the financier and user of funds agree on buying and selling prices. (11) All financings are backed by assets (securitized) and the assets are in the position of the bank until the payment are is paid in full.	**D. Characteristics of fund uses (assets)** (10) In all debt-type financing contracts, short or long term, fixed interest is the key feature of all loans. (11) Debt financings are not securitized, i.e., loans are not backed by assets.

Table 12.1 (continued)

Islamic Bank	Conventional bank
(12) *Mudarabah* and *musharakah*, PLS, modes of financing are the most distinguishing characteristic of financing by Islamic banks. They are similar to equity financing of conventional banks. The key characteristics of these two modes of financing are as follows: (i) There is no guarantee of a fixed return. If a project financed by a bank makes profits, both the bank and the investor will share it as per the prior agreement. If the project incurs losses, both bank and investor will share the loss as per the agreement. Profit and loss sharing is the most distinguishing feature of Islamic bank financing. (ii) Banks share investment risk with investors. The risk of a project of failure or success is undertaken by both investors and bank. (iii) All equity financings (*mudarabah* and *musharakah*) are fully securitized. They are examples of asset-backed financing. Control over assets is in the possession of banks until payment is made in full.	(12) The key features of conventional bank equity financing are as follows: (i) Banks are guaranteed income. If an investment financed by a bank fails, the bank does not bear the risk. (ii) Banks do not share the risk of investments. Only one party, investors, bears the risk or earns the profit from an investment. (iii) Equity loans are not securitized. Such loans are not fully collateralized, and banks have no control over assets.
E. Moral hazard and adverse selection Moral hazard and adverse selection arise because of asymmetric information. (1) In Islamic banking and financing, because there is minimal asymmetric information between bank and investor, the potential of moral hazard and adverse selection is minimal.	**E. Moral hazard and adverse selection** (1) In conventional banking, there is asymmetric information between lender (bank) and borrower (investor). Because there is asymmetric information between banks and borrowers, the likelihood of moral hazard and adverse selection is high.

(continued)

Table 12.1 (continued)

Islamic Bank	Conventional bank
(2) Islamic banks, financiers, share all information about projects with investors. Banks not only share the same information but also jointly manage and supervise the venture with investors. Consequently, moral hazard and adverse selection are significantly minimized in Islamic banking and finance.	(2) Lenders (conventional banks) have no information about what investors do with loans. Investors do not have to share information and management with lenders (banks). The lack of symmetric information and absence of joint management gives rise to the highest probability of adverse selection and moral hazard. Consequently, moral hazard and adverse selection are significantly more likely in conventional banking and finance.

12.5   Contemporary experience of industry as alternative to conventional financial system and its merits, limitations, and constraints

12.5.1   Experience of Islamic banking industry

Those in the Western world have been aware of only one type of banking, interest-based banking, referred to here as conventional banking. Most Westerners are unaware of an alternative type of banking and finance, called interest-free banking and finance. Today Islamic banking and finance has emerged as a viable alternative to conventional interest-based banking and finance in global financial markets. According to a report of the General Council for Islamic Banks and Financial Institutions (IBFI), currently 275 institutions follow Islamic banking and financial principles. They operate in 53 countries around the world, including Europe and the US and manage $250 billion worth of assets (Samad et al., 2005).

According to a report published by the International Monetary Fund, the assets of Islamic finance have grown to an estimated $1.8 trillion in 2013. However, the growth in assets is concentrated mainly in Gulf Cooperation Countries (GCCs) and Malaysia, and those assets represent less than 1 percent of global financial assets. On the other hand, the Islamic Financial Services Board in its annual Stability Report in 2016 stated that the size of the Islamic financial market industry reached an overall total value of US$1.88 trillion as of 2015.

Participation banking assets with commercial banks in Qatar, Indonesia, Saudi Arabia, Malaysia, UAE, and Turkey (QISMUT) are set to US$801 billion in 2015 and will represent 80 percent of international participation banking assets.

The rapid growth of the Islamic banking and finance inspired its introduction in the Muslim countries as well as the non-Muslim countries.

The stability of these assets' performance is an important high-water mark of Islamic banking and finance. The global financial crisis of 2008–2009 had a serious impact on financial institutions. In 2009, 140 banks went bust, and 157 banks were wiped out in 2010 (*Time*: January 27, 2012). Whereas there was a large number of conventional bank failures in the Western world, there was not a single instance of an Islamic bank failure.

12.5.2   Limitations of Islamic banking

The growth in assets of Islamic banking and finance is not evenly spread over all Muslim countries. This growth is concentrated mainly in GCCs and Malaysia. Similarly, the development of Islamic financial institutions and the index of financial inclusion are uneven.

Mudarabah and Musharakah Financing Are Minimal

There are two key features of Islamic banking and finance are: (1) the *mudarabah* PLS contract and (2) *musharakah* PLS contract. PLS contracts are the key features of Islamic banking that distinguish it from conventional banking and finance. However, an evaluation of Islamic bank financing records shows that the *mudarabah* and *musharakah* financing of Islamic banking and finance account for less than 4 percent of the total. Samad et al. (2005) examined the Islamic banks of Bahrain and Malaysia and found that the combined average of *mudarabah* and *musharakah* financing for the two Islamic banks is less than 4 percent of the total finance and advances. The average financing under the *qard hassan* mode of financing is around 4 percent. *Istisna* financing does not yet exist in practice. *Murabahah* (trade financing) is found to be the most popular and prevalent of all modes of Islamic financing. The average *murabahah* financing for the two Islamic banks is over 54 percent.

Because *murabahah* financing by Islamic banks dominates over other modes of financing, it has posed a great challenge to Islamic banking and finance. Academic researchers and Islamic banks must find ways to establish and popularize the core mode of financing, i.e., *mudarabah* and *musharakah* financing, which is really the distinguishing feature of Islamic banking. We must consider the issue of whether the principal–agent problem in PLS under *mudarabah* and *musharakah* contracts are, in fact, more serious in practice than in theory.

Principal–Agent Problem in Islamic Banking

Islamic banking and financing suffers more than conventional banking because there are many players in Islamic banking and finance, namely, the *Shariah* board, Islamic financial institutions (lenders), depositors, regulators, and borrowers. When principals fail to monitor agents' activity, the principal agent problem becomes acute. In Islamic banking there are several principals such as depositors, IFIs, *Shariah* board, and regulators; at the same time there are several agents: IFIs (lenders) and client firms or individuals borrowing money.

Lack of a Single *Shariah* Board

There is no single *Shariah* board in any country except Malaysia. Different Islamic banks have their own *Shariah* board within a given country. The *Shariah* board of each Islamic bank consists of different levels of scholars and experts. Consequently, the judgment of a *Shariah* board over product innovation and interpretation is not uniform. Customers of Islamic banks have no standard of opinion. Similarly, there is no single *Shariah* board that supervises and monitors all Islamic banks and financial institutions operating across countries. Each country's *Shariah* board consults with scholars with different levels of knowledge of Islam and different cross-cultural backgrounds, which results in nonstandardized opinions on various issues of interest to Islamic banks. The time has come for all Islamic banks operating across countries to establish a standard *Shariah* board, like the Basel Accord, to supervise and monitor their activities.

Chapter Highlights

Banking and finance, including Islamic banking and finance, has played an important role in economic growth and development. Early economists supported the view that industrial development and economic growth were the direct result of financial development. The UK, US, and developing nations are examples of this.

There is little controversy over the origins of the emergence of Islamic banking. There are two opinions. According to one opinion, the first Islamic bank arose in the province of Punjab in Pakistan. The other account has the first Islamic bank being created in Egypt.

Today, Islamic banking and finance is a rapidly growing industry with a trillion dollars' worth of assets. The growth of Islamic banking and finance is phenomenal. The successful operation of Islamic banking and finance in the Muslim world inspired the establishment of Islamic banking in the Western world, including in the US, Canada, Switzerland, and the UK. There are 53 countries in the world where Islamic banks operate alongside conventional banks.

Islamic banking and finance represents a different breed of banking. Islamic banking and finance is an institution whose activities and governance are guided by *Shariah* law. According to *Shariah*, Islamic banks and financial institutions are prohibited from financing transactions involving *riba*, *gharar*, and *maisir* and the production of goods and services detrimental to humanity.

Islamic banking and finance stands against exploitation and in favor of social justice and the equitable distribution of wealth through the introduction of various mechanisms such as PLS, *zakah*, and *qard-hasan*.

The mode of operation and contractual character of Islamic banks differ from those of conventional banks. PLS contracts under *mudarabah* and *musharakah* financing are the most prominent features of Islamic banking. For a detailed comparison, see Table 12.1.

Although Islamic banking and finance has operated successfully side by side with conventional banks, Islamic banking and finance faces challenges and limitations. *Mudarabah* and *musharakah*, the key features that distinguish Islamic banking from conventional banking, are insignificant.

Although Islamic banking and finance has been quite successful, two main challenges remain. First, despite the PLS mode of production, *mudarabah* and *musharakah* are the most significant distinguishing features of Islamic banks, but they account for the lowest amount of financing of Islamic banks. It is about only 4 percent of its total assets (Samad et al., 2005). Most financing is done via debt-type contracts such as *al-salam*, *bai al-muajjil*, *al-ijara*, and *al istisna*. Second, although many Islamic banks may have operations in a given county, there is no single *Shariah* board to supervise and govern their activities on the basis of a standardized principle. Instead of a single *Shariah* board, each Islamic bank is guided and governed by its own *Shariah* board. The members of the *Shariah* board differ in their level of education, expertise, and understanding of the principles of Islamic banking and finance. Consequently, not only is there no standard policy for all Islamic banks across countries but there is also scope for questionable modes of production and operation. The absence of a single *Shariah* board in a country or across countries provides heterogeneous products and nonstandardized contract information.

Discussion Questions

1. What is the controversy between economic growth and the role of banking and finance?

2. Where did the idea of Islamic banking and finance originate?

3. Where did the first Islamic bank originate?

4. What does Islamic banking and finance mean?

5. Briefly discuss the development of Islamic banking and finance.

6. What are the key characteristics of Islamic banking and finance?

7. What are the main uses of assets and sources of funds in Islamic banking and finance?

8. Compare and contrast Islamic banking and conventional banking with respect to any three or four key aspects.

9. What are the main challenges and limitations of Islamic banking and finance?

References

Ahmed, A. (1993). *Contemporary Practices of Islamic Financing Techniques*. Jeddah: IRTI.

Alharbi, A. (2015). Development of the Islamic Banking System. *Journal of Islamic Banking and Finance*, 3(1), 12–25.

Bagehot, W. (1873). *Lombard Street, a Description of the Money Market*. Hammond: Richard D. Irwin.

Chachi, A. (2005). Origin and Development of Commercial and Islamic Banking Operations. *Journal of King Abdulaziz University: Islamic Economics*, 18(2), 3–25 (2005 A.D/1426 A.H).

Chapra, U. (1985). *Toward a Just Monetary System*. Leicester: The Islamic Foundation.

Goldsmith, R.W. (1969). *Financial Structure and Development*. New Haven: Yale University Press.

Hicks, J.R. (1969). *A Theory of Economic History*. Oxford: Clarendon Press.

Khan, M.S. and Mirahkor, A. (1986). The Framework and Practice of Islamic Banking. *Finance and Development*, September, pp. 1–32.

Mannan, M.A. (1998). Islam and Trend in Modern Banking: Theory and Practice of Interest-Free Banking. *Islamic Review and Arab Affairs*, November–December, pp. 73–95.

McKinnon, R. (1973). *Money and Capital in Economic Development*. Washington, DC: Brooking Institute.

Odedokun, M.O. (1998). Financial Intermediation and Economic Growth in Developing Countries. *Journal of Economic Studies*, 25(3), 223–240.

Redlich, F. (1968). *Modeling of American Banking: Men and Ideas*. New York: Hafner.

Samad, A. (2006). Development of Interest-Free Banking and Finance in the Global Financial Market. *Proceedings of the Seventh Annual Utah Valley State College*, pp. 153–163.

Samad, A., Gardner, N. and Cook, B.J. (2005). Islamic Banking and Finance in Theory and Practice: The Malaysian and Bahrain Experience. *American Journal of Islamic Social Sciences*, 22(2), 71–86.

Schumpeter, J. (1935). *Theories der Writschftlichen Entwicklung* [Theory of economic development]. Leipzig: Dunker & Humblot, 1912; Translated by Redvers Opie. Cambridge, MA: Harvard University Press.

Siddiqi, M.N. (1983). *Issues in Islamic Banking*. Leicester: The Islamic Foundation.

Wilson, R. (1983). *Banking and Finance in the Arab Middle East*. Surrey: Macmillan.

Notes

1. The dictionary meaning of usury is exorbitantly high rate of interest.
2. Umar b. al-Khattab, the second Caliph of Islam, said, "There are three things. If God's Messenger had explained them clearly, it would have been dearer to me than the world and what it contains: (These are) *kalalah*, *riba*, and *khilafah*." (*Sunan Ibn Majah*, Book of Inheritance, Vol. 4, #2727.
3. www.financislam.com/depositw.html

CORPORATE GOVERNANCE OF ISLAMIC FINANCIAL INSTITUTIONS

13

Shakir Ullah

Institutional Review Board (IRB), Stratford University,
Fairfax, VA, USA

Learning Outcomes

LO1: Describe the levels of conventional corporate governance structure as practiced in conventional financial institutions.

LO2: Understand the meaning of corporate governance within the *Shariah* framework as experienced in modern Islamic financial institutions.

LO3: Explain why Islamic financial institutions require a different governance structure.

LO4: Understand the levels of Islamic corporate governance structure as practiced in modern Islamic financial institutions.

LO5: Explain the distinct corporate governance structure and operation in Islamic financial institutions and conventional financial institutions.

Contents

13.1   Introduction to corporate governance

Corporate governance refers to a set of rules and processes that are used to direct and control an institution to balance the interests of all its stakeholders (Cadbury, 2000, p. 8). According to Cadbury (2000), firms exist not just to increase the value of their direct owners, but to create general social stability. Therefore, corporate governance ensures that managers will run their businesses for the benefit of their institutions' stakeholders, including shareholders, management, customers, suppliers, creditors, the community, government agencies, and nonprofit entities. Corporate governance involves all aspects of management, which includes strategic orientation, setting goals and objectives, incorporating action plans, and ensuring internal controls and external reporting.

To formulate and implement corporate governance rules, processes, and practices, companies need to have a corporate governance structure in place. This system includes company management and is strengthened by regulatory authorities, rating agencies, and governments to protect the interests of all stakeholders. The primary stakeholders of a for-profit company are the shareholders and their primary interest is the company's market value (Shleifer and Vishny, 1997). Therefore, the governance structure is set up in such a way as to maximize shareholder wealth. However, the governance structure of an Islamic financial institution (IFI) is slightly different because such institutions are trusted by all stakeholders to ensure that shareholder wealth maximization will be achieved in a *Shariah*-compliant way. Achieving *Shariah* compliance and maximization of shareholder wealth may, at times, be in conflict, requiring a trade-off. Therefore, a parallel corporate governance structure, called *Shariah* governance, is needed in corporations in order to cater to *Shariah's* strictures on compliance with the processes and products of institutions. Because IFIs are governed by two parallel governance structures, it can be rightly said that they work under a dual governance system, and this distinguishes IFIs from conventional corporations.

This chapter explores the levels of management involved in conventional corporate governance as well as *Shariah* governance. A comparative analysis is presented, followed by a chapter summary.

13.2   Levels of conventional corporate governance structure

The role of the governance structure in any organization is to determine the organization's strategic direction, develop its mission and vision, and then devise goals, objectives, and strategies to steer the organization toward the chosen strategic direction. Three main levels of conventional governance/management, top, middle, and lower, can be found in a typical organization. Because IFIs are also corporate entities, they also possess a conventional structure. Managers are also classified into three categories based on the level of management they work at, i.e., top-, middle-, and lower-level managers. Let us discuss these managerial levels in more detail.

13.2.1   Top management

This is the managerial level that sets the strategic direction of the company. It includes the board of directors (BOD), president, vice-president, and chief executive officer (CEO). The members of the BOD are elected or appointed by the shareholders, who in turn nominate one member as the chairman of the board. This cadre of management controls and oversees the entire organization. It develops goals, strategic plans, and company policies and makes decisions on the direction of the business. It plays a key role in mobilizing external resources, including financing.

13.2.2   Middle management

Managers in this cadre are responsible for translating the strategic direction of the company into strategies and action plans. These managers include general managers, branch managers, and department managers. They report to the top management about the performance of their respective departments. As against the top management, whose job is to provide a strategic direction to the organization, middle managers spend most of their time on directional and organizational functions. They execute plans in accordance with company policies and strategic direction. They also translate the company's policies, which are set by the top management, into actionable plans and communicate them to the lower management for implementation. They provide guidance to, inspire, and lead lower management to achieve optimal organizational performance. They also set performance indicators and are involved in the hiring, training, evaluation, and promotion of lower management and employees.

13.2.3   Lower management

This managerial level is the actual implementation organ of the company. Managers in this cadre are responsible for implementing and executing the plans set forth by middle management. They report to middle management and are responsible for solving routine managerial issues. The managers in this category include, for example, supervisors, section leaders, and foremen. They assign tasks to employees, supervise routine activities, ensure product quality and quantity, resolve employee problems, and motivate them to achieve business targets.

13.3   Corporate governance for Islamic financial institutions (IFIs)

Corporate governance (CG) in IFIs differs from corporate governance in conventional financial institutions mainly as a result of the purposes served by these types of FIs. Corporate governance of IFIs is treated as a system that ensures fairness to all its stakeholders through a huge degree of transparency and accountability with respect to Islamic law. The CG system of IFIs at the first stage of analysis consists of a transactional structure to ensure that it is free of any sort of element abhorrent in Islamic law with respect to business because *Shariah* law is not just concerned with the substance but with the form of business as well. According to Akhtar (2007), CG in IFIs emerges with two basic elements: first, a belief-based perspective that dictates that business activities should be conducted in accordance with Islamic law and, second, with the aim of earning profits, which acknowledges the existence of investment and business transactions and the growth of shareholder wealth, for example.

This makes it quite clear that the key focus of an IFI is to ensure *Shariah* compliance (SC), so Islamic banks (IBs) are governed under a complex system of CG. It can be rightly inferred that IFIs are governed under two internal structures of CG, as stated by Lewis (2007): maximization: the BOD, and the *Shariah* Supervisory Board (SSB). According to Siagh (2004) the BOD ensures the protection of shareholders' interests and strives to maximize their value, the while the SSB focuses on the Islamic community and customers and to abide by *Shariah* law.

13.4   Profit versus interest

According to Ozsoy (2010), as far as the connection between interest and profit is concerned, profit is an excess of assets, distributed among capital and entrepreneur, as a result of money invested in an economic pursuit such as industry, agriculture, and commerce, which is then realized whether in a greater sum (when profit is earned) or a minor sum (in the case of loss). Thus, profit and loss are twins.

When the owner of capital creates a business, he has to bear the risk of loss in that business to earn a profit. Therefore, profit can be viewed as the return for assuming risk. For, after all, businesses can fail; thus, when it comes to profit, the rule is "Nothing ventured, nothing gained."

One of the key factors that allows profits is that it represents the ratio of a realized positive outcome at the end of some business activity, unlike the rate of return earned over a liability, which is predetermined in the case of interest (Ozsoy, 2010).

As stated earlier, profit is the outcome of an actual economic activity, but interest itself is not earned as a result of an actual economic activity.

With regard to profit, the owner of capital is directly affected if the investment ends up in a loss, and the community is affected indirectly. On the other hand, interest is the known income of the lender, regardless of profit or loss be incurred by the borrower. This is to highlight the fact that the rate of interest can be set at the cost of all others in the community. Interest can be taken without any sacrifice, while profit can only be earned if capital is contributed to the community in terms of producing a positive outcome of the investment.

13.5   The role of regulations in the governance of a company, including financial institutions

Islamic banks perform the same functions as conventional banks. These are companies established by shareholders for the purpose of wealth maximization, but with a pledge to achieve this objective in a *Shariah*-compliant way. Thus, they are regulated by the same broader set of governmental regulations that apply to all banks. In fact, banks are subject to rather stricter regulations compared to other corporations because any failure in the banking sector can have a drastic spillover effect on the whole economy. Banking regulations serve a number of purposes. First, they are prudential in nature, targeted at reducing banks' risk and protecting depositors. Second, they reduce banks' systematic risk to avoid bank runs. Third, regulations are targeted at minimizing or preventing the misuse of banks, for example, for criminal purposes. Lastly, banking regulations direct the flow of credit to desired sectors. To conduct routine banking activities, Islamic banks are subject to governmental regulations to achieve the aforementioned purposes. The specific banking regulations applicable to Islamic banks regard capital, reserves, governance, reporting, and disclosure.

To comply with regulatory requirements and carry out normal banking activities, Islamic banks should have, like their conventional counterparts, a sound governance system in place (Islamic Financial Services Board [IFSB], 2006) as endorsed by the Basel Committee on Banking Supervision. Islamic banks are required to "establish a comprehensive governance policy framework which sets out the strategic roles and functions of each organ of governance and mechanisms for balancing the IIFS's accountabilities to various stakeholders" (IFSB, 2006, Part 1, Principles 1.1). Therefore, Islamic banks also have three management levels, top, middle, and lower, in their conventional corporate governance structure. The purpose of conventional governance is to ensure that banks remain financially viable and profitable business entities within the regulatory constraints.

13.6   Need for a parallel governance structure for IFIs

IFIs need an additional governance layer, called the *Shariah* governance structure (SGS), because their appeal is their *Shariah*-based business proposition, which often requires certain financial sacrifices, e.g., being ethical, responsible, and philanthropic. It also requires that they refrain from investments in tobacco, alcohol, pornography, or earning interest. This additional governance layer ensures that *Shariah* principles are upheld rigorously and that the business objectives of the conventional management do not supersede *Shariah* compliance. The reason for having this additional layer is that IFIs' sponsors and managers may be inclined to exploit the holistic business model to advance their business interests because Muslim customers are often willing to pay a premium for the *Shariah* compliance label. In order for IFIs to be accepted by the market, they need to be certified by *Shariah* scholars, who are integral to the SGS. Let us explore the SGS in more detail.

13.7   Pillars of *Shariah* governance structure

IFIs are financial entities that are required to comply with *Shariah* principles in addition to having conventional governance mechanisms in place. Such mechanisms include compliance with standards set out by international bodies and local *Shariah* regulatory frameworks prepared and enforced in different countries. In fact, the first few IFIs established in the 1970s and 1980s did not have a proper SGS in place, which raised questions about their *Shariah* compliance. To increase their acceptability in the market, some of the early IFIs started to consult *Shariah* scholars for guidance on *Shariah* issues. However, the existence of a formal SGS later on became a necessary legitimization tool for IFIs. Without any such formal structure, today's IFIs would have little legitimacy and credibility. Rammal (2006, p. 205) mentioned that the presence of a *Shariah* board in Islamic banks was determined to be a prerequisite for admission into the International Association of Islamic Banks (IAIB), which compelled IFIs to have a formal *Shariah* supervision body in place. Modern IFIs are also required/expected to have *Shariah* audit and compliance divisions in addition to having *Shariah* boards/advisors within the banks. These mechanisms are discussed below.

13.8   International standard-setting bodies

There are three main international bodies that set *Shariah* compliance standards for IFIs. Perhaps the most prominent of these bodies is the industry-sponsored Accounting and Auditing Organization for Islamic Financial Institutions (AAOIFI), based in Manama, Bahrain. The standards issued by this body are called AAOIFI standards. One such set of standards issued by AAOIFI is the Accounting, Auditing and Governance Standards containing 23 accounting standards, 5 auditing standards, 6 governance standards, and 2 codes of ethics. Another set of AAOIFI standards is called the *Shariah* standards that contain 41 standards on *Shariah* compliance. Though AAOIFI standards are comprehensive, they are not mandatory in all jurisdictions (Wilson, 2009). For example, they are mandatory in Bahrain, enforced by the State Bank of Pakistan (SBP) after some amendments, and not mandatory in UAE. However, Islamic banks are increasingly adopting AAOIFI standards because of their impact on the banks' credibility and legitimacy.

The IFSB is another such body that sets standards and guidelines for IFIs. This body is based in Kuala Lumpur and is sponsored by Bank Negara, the central bank of Malaysia. It has issued a number of standards/guidelines related to governance, *Shariah* governance, and ethical practices of IFIs. Again, these standards are not mandatory for IFIs, but different countries and banks have adopted them voluntarily (Wilson, 2009). The third and last credible standard-setting body for IFIs is the Organization of Islamic Countries (OIC)-sponsored Fiqh Academy based in Saudi Arabia. Though the objective of this academy is to issue *fatwas* on all *Shariah* issues, most of its *fatwas* so far relate to the Islamic finance industry.

13.8.1   Local regulatory frameworks

Local regulatory frameworks refer to the country-specific regulatory control mechanisms designed for IFIs. Wilson (2009) made a comprehensive comparison of such frameworks, which vary across countries. For example, Malaysia, Sudan, and Pakistan have *Shariah* boards at the central banks that issue *fatwas* related to emerging issues. The central boards also amend AAOIFI and IFSB standards/guidelines, if necessary, and then impose them on Islamic banks within their jurisdictions. Central *Shariah* boards not only facilitate *Shariah* compliance across Islamic banks in their respective countries, they also serve as a stage for the settlement of disputes between Islamic banks' managers and *Shariah* scholars. Bahrain, on the other hand, does not have any central *Shariah* governance mechanism. However, it is mandatory for Islamic banks in the country to adhere to AAOIFI standards. On the other extreme, UAE neither has central *Shariah* governance mechanisms nor makes AAOIFI and IFSB standards mandatory for Islamic banks within the country. Islamic banks are free to determine their own *Shariah* governance mechanisms. Such frameworks give enough leeway for some Islamic banks to shop for *fatwas* that give them more and easier financial gains rather than better *Shariah* compliance.

13.8.1.1   *Organizational-level* Shariah *governance systems*

Within the communities of academics and practitioners, *Shariah* governance normally refers to all the mechanisms and systems within IFIs that ensure an organization's compliance with *Shariah* principles. The IFSB (2009) defines a *Shariah* governance system as "the set of institutional and organizational arrangements through which [IFI] ensures that there is an effective independent oversight of *Shariah* compliance ..." This definition clearly does not encompass *Shariah* compliance mechanisms at the country or international level. An organizational-level *Shariah* compliance system consists of a *Shariah* board or *Shariah* advisor, a *Shariah* compliance unit, and a *Shariah* control and audit unit. These are discussed below.

13.8.1.2   Shariah *board/advisor*

The *Shariah* board/advisor is the first and most important pillar in an IFI's SGS. It has a number of duties, but the most important is the issuance of relevant *Shariah* resolutions/*fatwas* on *Shariah*-related issues of IFIs. Though such *fatwas* are issued at the request of bank management, *Shariah* boards/advisors can issue resolutions on matters they realize are important and related to *Shariah*. A *Shariah* board is a highly recommended vehicle for *Shariah* governance (IFSB, 2006; AAOIFI, 2010), which consists of three or more *Shariah* scholars. The board issues *Shariah* pronouncements based on a consensus, which reduces the chances of undue influence of management. However, the IFSB recommends that the establishment of a full *Shariah* board depends on the size and complexity of the organization (IFSB, 2009). It also leaves it to the discretion of local regulatory authorities to decide whether Islamic banks should set up full-fledged *Shariah* boards or appoint single *Shariah* advisors as part of their *Shariah* governance system. In Pakistan, for example, the central bank requires IFIs to appoint at least one *Shariah* advisor while the matter of setting up a *Shariah* board is left to the discretion of the individual banks. *Shariah* boards/advisors have the authority to access the confidential information of banks. Management is also obliged not only to provide all relevant details to the *Shariah* board/advisor but also to assist them in seeking further clarifications/information if needed (IFSB, 2009). This body has the authority to reject any proposed structure if found to be not in compliance with *Shariah*. It can also nullify transactions after their execution and allocate the corresponding profits to charity. The pronouncements of the *Shariah* board/advisor are considered unchallengeable; however, exceptional disputes with managers could be referred to regulators or central *Shariah* boards.

13.8.1.3   *Internal* Shariah *compliance unit*

Obtaining *Shariah* pronouncements from a *Shariah* board/advisor is the first part of a *Shariah* governance system. Proper implementation of such pronouncements should ultimately follow. Therefore, part of the SGS's role is to disseminate pronouncements to all relevant parties for implementation. The IFSB (2009) recommends the appointment of an internal *Shariah* compliance unit (ISCU) or a *Shariah* compliance officer to carry out this task. Though the ISCU is part of management, it also has to report to the *Shariah* board/advisor to ensure the pronouncements are properly implemented.

13.8.1.4   *Internal* Shariah *audit unit*

The internal *Shariah* audit unit (ISAU) is probably the last—but still a very important—pillar in the SGS. Its purpose is to evaluate transactions' compliance with the pronouncements of the *Shariah* board/advisor after execution. Transactions are inspected for any breach of *Shariah* pronouncements during implementation. The functions performed by an ISAU are similar to those of an internal auditor. However, the difference is that the ISAU identifies loopholes in *Shariah* compliance and reports them to the *Shariah* board/advisor instead of the audit committee (IFSB, 2009).

13.8.1.5   *External* Shariah *audit*

In addition to internal *Shariah* compliance and audit units, as discussed earlier, the IFSB (2009) recommends an annual *Shariah* audit to verify that *Shariah* compliance has been properly implemented and audited. This audit is ideally carried out by the *Shariah* board/advisor that issued the initial *Shariah* pronouncements/*fatwas*. This audit could be facilitated by the central bank. Alternatively, the IFI can appoint an external *Shariah* auditing firm to carry out this task.

In summary, IFIs are subject to dual governance systems, i.e., the traditional governance and *Shariah* governance, as illustrated in Table 13.1 below.

Table 13.1 Comparison of *Shariah* and traditional governance in IFIs

Traditional governance tool	Role	Shariah governance tool
Board of Directors	Governance Body	*Shariah* Board/ Advisor
Internal audit department	Compliance body	Internal *Shariah* review unit
External audit firm		Internal *Shariah* audit office/department
Regulatory financial compliance officer/ unit/department	Control Body	Internal *Shariah* audit unit
		External *Shariah* audit

Case Study

Please read the IFSB's governance guidelines and comment on the independence of the SGS. This activity should be completed in class, with students divided into groups.

13.9   Lines of authority in dual governance structures

The SGS embedded in traditional for-profit corporate entities is unique to IFIs. However, it can be established in any company whose leadership is determined to embed a *Shariah* compliance component in the company's strategic orientation.

The organizational structure of an IFI with a dual governance structure may vary from company to company and country to country. The final reporting authority for the conventional governance part are the shareholders, whose primary interest in the company is their wealth maximization, though they may want to achieve this objective in a *Shariah*-compliant way. On the other hand, the final reporting authority for the SGS is the *Shariah* board. However, there is an informal line of authority to a central *Shariah* board (CSB), which is a board maintained by central banks in some countries like Pakistan, Sudan, and Malaysia. It is also clear that the *Shariah* compliance department has a formal line of authority running through the SGS, but it also reports to the CEO, chairman of the board, and the BOD through an informal line of authority. This means the department keeps the conventional management informed of its activities but will receive directives only from the SGS. Similarly, the *Shariah* board (SB) also has an informal reporting responsibility to the BOD and shareholders. However, the BOD and shareholders cannot issue orders to the SB on matters related to *Shariah* compliance.

Interestingly, the SGS has a religious responsibility and is answerable to God. In other words, it will be accountable for the *fatwa* and *Shariah* pronouncements to God. This is the strongest check on the SGS.

Case Study

Please read Ullah et al. (2016)[1] and then answer the following questions related to the corporate governance structure of IFIs:

a) Who determines and defines *Shariah* compliance? In other words, is it the *Shariah* scholars who dictate *Shariah* compliance or managers, or an alliance between the two?

b) What are the various levels of *Shariah* compliance within IFIs?

c) What causal and intervening factors determine the level of *Shariah* compliance within IFIs?

d) What strategies are adopted by *Shariah* scholars and managers to deal with this phenomenon?

e) As per your own understanding and research on the topic, how effective is the *Shariah* governance system?

Case Study

Managing the Working Capital Finance Service of Islamic Banks: A Narrative Case Study of *Murabahah* Finance.

Directions: Please study the case study and then answer the following questions. It is all right if you not understand everything in this case study; the contents are mainly from Islamic finance, and some of the terms may be difficult to understand, but that is where your learning begins. Please do some online research on *murabahah* finance before attempting the case study.

1. Identify and discuss the roles of various stakeholders involved in the *murabahah* case. Do the current theoretical *murabahah* models define the roles of these stakeholders well?

2. What is the actual need of the company in the case? What should the bank look for related to the *Shariah* compliance of the need?

3. What alternative Islamic finance model, in your opinion, could the bank and company use to fulfill the same need of the company? Conduct a comparative viability analysis of the *murabahah* and your proposed model.

4. Identify and discuss the supporting services that are considered essential for the actual implementation of the *murabahah* service.

5. Discuss the role of client and market research in the successful management of the application of *murabahah* finance.

6. Does the application of *murabahah* presented in the case study support and strengthen the current evolutionary framework of the state bank? Suggest any improvements.

Chapter Highlights

IFIs are expected to maximize the wealth of shareholders in a *Shariah*-compliant way, which may be in conflict at times. Therefore, a single governance structure composed of the top, middle, and lower levels of management may not suffice to achieve these two-pronged objectives at the same time. Hence, a parallel governance system is needed to keep a check on the wealth maximization greed of conventional management. The parallel governance structure is called *Shariah* governance, and it consists of a *Shariah* board, *Shariah* supervisor, international *Shariah* compliance unit, and internal *Shariah* audit unit.

Abbreviations

AAOIFI	Accounting and Auditing Organization for Islamic Financial Institutions
BOD	Board of directors
CEO	Chief executive officer
IAIB	International Association of Islamic Banks
IFI	Islamic financial institution
IFSB	Islamic Financial Services Board
ISAU	Internal *Shariah* audit unit
ISCU	Internal *Shariah* compliance unit
OIC	Organization of Islamic Countries
SB	*Shariah* board
SBP	State Bank of Pakistan
SGS	*Shariah* governance structure

Key Terms

Cadre	*Fiqh*	Profit
Comply	For-profit	Philanthropic
Corporation	Holistic	Prudential
Consensus	Interest	Risk
Depositor	Investment	Reporting
Disclosure	Jurisdiction	Stakeholders
Devise	Legitimization	*Shariah* scholars
Entrepreneur	Managerial	*Shariah* law
Execute	Management	*Shariah*
Framework	Proposition	pronouncements
Fatwa	Proprietor	*Shariah* compliance

Online Resources

http://time.com/4121/why-shareholder-value-should-not-be-the-only-goal-of-public-companies/

http://www.businessdictionary.com/article/601/the-role-of-stakeholders-in-your-business/

http://www.businessdictionary.com/article/618/why-is-corporate-governance-important/

https://www.imoney.my/articles/all-about-that-base-how-does-base-rate-work

https://papers.ssrn.com/sol3/papers.cfm?abstract_id=795548

http://erf.org.eg/wp-content/uploads/2014/07/734.pdf

References

Akhtar, S. (2007). Islamic Finance: Emerging Challenges of Supervision. 4th Islamic Services Board Summit held at Dubai, United Arab Emirates on May, 15.

Cadbury, S.A. (2000). The Corporate Governance Agenda. *Corporate Governance: An International Review*, 8(1), 7–15.

Lewis, M.K. (2007). Islamic Banking in Theory and Practice. *Monash Business Review*, 3(1), 1–8.

Ozsoy, I. (2010). Islamic Banking: Conceptual Fundamentals and Basic Features. *Экономический вестник Донбасса*, 4(22).

Shleifer, A. and Vishny, R.W. (1997). A Survey of Corporate Governance. *The Journal of Finance*, 52(2), 737–783.

Siagh, L. (2004). Environnement Intense et Choix Stratégiques: Le Cas des Banques Islamiques. Cahier de recherche N, 20, 06.

Wilson, R. (2009). *Shariah Governance for Islamic Financial Institutions*. Lumpur: ISRA.

Note

1. Ullah, Shakir, Ian A. Harwood, and Dima Jamali. "'Fatwa Repositioning': The Hidden Struggle for *Shariah* Compliance Within Islamic Financial Institutions." *Journal of Business Ethics* (2012): 1–23.

ISLAMIC ACCOUNTING: PRINCIPLES AND PRACTICES

14

Sutan Emir Hidayat and Alfatih Gessan

University College Bahrain, Janabiyah, Bahrain

Bahrain Institute of Banking and Finance,
Manama, Bahrain

Learning Outcomes

LO1: Describe the purpose and main principles of Islamic accounting.

LO2: Describe the similarities and differences between Islamic and conventional accounting.

LO3: Explain the relevance of the IFRS and AAOIFI in international accounting regulations and standards for the industry.

LO4: Understand the main financial statements of Islamic banks.

Contents

Does Islamic Accounting Really Exist?

In China, from the 1950s until 40+ years later, even after the launch of the economic reforms in 1978, accountants were among hundreds of thousands of professionals and intellectuals who were condemned and banished. Accounting education at university was largely shut down. As a replacement, the Soviet bookkeeping system, designed for a centrally planned economy, was used throughout. This system was very different from the traditional and Western type of accounting, and as a result there was a significant period during the early millennium where China was desperate for senior accountants with the right level of experience and oversight relevant to the modern economy it now has. It isn't just for the accounting sector but also for other sectors, such as banks, businesses, and the legal profession, where there is a dearth of senior people with proper education and experience. At that time, the situation could have caused a slowdown in China's efforts at integrating into global capital markets.

This piece of history reveals that there are in fact other types of accounting philosophies besides the one we are all accustomed to, and this is a result of the underlying ideology that is the main essence of an accounting system. This confirms the rightful existence of Islamic accounting, which is accounting based on the ideology found in the sources of Islamic law, or *Shariah*. It is not just a label that is added for its own sake; it really does exist.

This chapter consists of two sections: accounting from an Islamic perspective and accounting standards for Islamic financial institutions (IFIs). It is important to note that there is a clear distinction between Islamic accounting and accounting standards for IFIs. Therefore, the two sections of this chapter discuss the aforementioned areas separately. In the section on accounting from an Islamic perspective, the discussion starts with the history of accounting and then accounting and Islam. Referring to the history of Islam, we find that during the early days of Islam, there was a kind of accounting system practiced by the Holy Prophet in the management of *bait al-mal* (the government treasury). However, the current form of accounting from an Islamic perspective has been evolving in parallel with the development of the Islamic financial industry. In terms of the main principles and foundations of Islamic accounting, in general there are several similarities between the principles of Islamic and conventional accounting. However, since Islamic accounting takes into account revelation as one of the main sources of knowledge, there are differences between Islamic and conventional accounting that must be clearly understood. The first two subsections of this chapter elaborate on these two topics.

In the second section of this chapter, the discussion starts with the identification of benefits and challenges of applying conventional accounting standards by IFIs. Because of the main challenges of applying conventional accounting standards by Islamic financial institutions (IFI), there is a need for a separate accounting framework for IFIs that adequately cater to *Shariah* compliance requirements. Thus, the establishment of the Accounting and Auditing Organization for Islamic Financial Institutions (AAOIFI) aims to fill that need. In the later part of the section, further discussion is presented on the required financial statements for an Islamic bank to prepare as per the AAOIFI accounting standards.

14.1   Accounting from an Islamic perspective

This section provides an overview of the history of accounting, the main principles and foundations of Islamic accounting, and how Islamic accounting differs from its conventional counterpart of today.

14.1.1   Evolution and historical development of international financial reporting standards (IFRS) and practices

The development of the practice of accounting and reporting has evolved from one era to another, customizing itself to oft-changing needs, conditions, and systems related to economic, social, cultural, and political aspects. The word *account* in everyday language can be used as a substitute for an explanation or report of certain actions and events. If you are a fund manager, for example, you have to report to shareholders or fund owners how your investments are performing. To explain or report, you will have to remember past incidents in order to report what had happened. Because it is not always easy to recall information in detail, you will need to keep some form of written record, as stated in the Qur'an, Chapter Al Baqarah verse 282, which will be discussed in more detail in the next subsection. In effect, such records provide the foundation of a system of rudimentary accounting. In a primitive sense, humankind has always been practicing or been involved in some form of accounting. It can be illustrated when a ranch owner counts how many horses or cattle he owns and then translates it to how much wealth he has in total. This further evolved with the growth of a monetary system that enables a more sophisticated method to be developed.

It took a very long time, however, for formal documentary systems to become commonplace, with possible traces of modern bookkeeping dating back to as far as the fifteenth century when the double-entry bookkeeping system was prevalent in the West. It is universally acknowledged that the origins of an organized and systematic method of accounting come from the Italian mathematician Luca Pacioli, considered the father of accounting. He authored a book focused mainly on mathematics titled *Summa de Arithmetica, Geometria, Proportioni et Propotionalita*, published in 1494; it had sections on accounting, specifically elaborating on double-entry bookkeeping, trial balances, balance sheets, and a variety of other tools used in accounting to this day. Credit for inventing the first accounting system goes not to Pacioli, though he was one of the first individuals to codify and publish a system (Napier, 2007). As will be discussed later, merchants have been using a certain methodology for accounting activities used in trade and commerce since the Middle Ages. It also has been found that Islamic accounting has been practiced from as early as the 600s (Zaid, 2004).

Political and economic changes had an effect on the economic system where the conversion from a feudal to a mercantile and later to a capitalist economic system occurred. This had an effect on the types of institutions that conducted economic activities and on the accounting and financial reporting that was applied (CIMA, 2008). Furthermore, with the Industrial Revolution in the 1800s, the large-scale mobilization of funds emphasized the importance of corporate entities and banking institutions. The capitalistic spirit was highlighted as the principal motivation behind the economic system, and because accounting is also shaped by the economic environment in which it operates, it also had an effect on the accounting system. In more specific circumstances, the economic environment also differs from one region or country to another, hence very diverse national financial accounting systems have also been developed. However, due to the expansion of the global economy where institutions are progressively making cross-border decisions, comparability of international financial information is essential without ignoring the fact that these corporations have to prepare financial statements according to unique local standards too. Uniqueness here is also linked to compatibility with the principles of Islamic law, which will be discussed in a subsequent section.

Substantial efforts to standardize and harmonize accounting practices globally have taken place since the 1970s, which include statements of financial accounting and the financial reporting framework. Among the reasons cited for the evolutionary process was the need to gain investors' confidence through the provision of relevant and reliable information based on specific reporting standards formulated by a board that represents the interests of various stakeholders. The primary purpose of the financial reporting framework was to enable coherent and consistent accounting and reporting standards to be promulgated so as to guide reporting practices. In 1973 the International Accounting Standards Committee (IASC) was founded in

London resulting from an agreement between 10 accounting bodies based in the United Stated of America, the United Kingdom, the Republic of Ireland, Australia, Canada, France, Germany, Mexico, and the Netherlands. In 2001 it was changed to the International Accounting Standards Board and is the body responsible for the development of the International Financial Reporting Standards (IFRS). It is a global language widely applied in business affairs so that financial statements of corporations are understandable and comparable internationally.

14.1.2   History and principles of Islamic accounting

Accounting is generally defined as the process of identifying, measuring, and communicating economic information of economic entities that is used by external and internal users to make specific decisions. The American Accounting Association, one of the oldest accounting bodies, was established in 1916 to promote all-round excellence in accounting-related education, research, and practice, and it defines accounting very similarly, emphasizing only information that is related to economic events (Hameed, 2003). This has always been the focus of accounting in general, resulting in a deficient focus on socioeconomic information that has a greater effect. The definition of Islamic accounting, on the other hand, has a more broad and holistic scope. It can be defined as the process of identifying, measuring, and communicating economic and other relevant information inspired by the Islamic worldview, ensuring compliance with Islamic law, to permit informed judgments and decisions by potential and expected users, with an objective to enhance social welfare (Iqbal and Mirakhor, 2011). In addition, Islamic accounting aims to reflect the implementation of *maqasid al Shariah* (objectives of *Shariah*) by IFIs in their activities.

The difference in definition stems from the different principles and philosophies that underpin Islamic accounting, which dates back farther than conventional accounting history. People living on the Arabian peninsula during the time of the Prophet Muhammad PBUH was one whose entire economic system was more or less reliant on trade and commerce, so they applied the basics of accounting or bookkeeping to keep records, resulting in the inevitable need to create an accounting system to deal with economic transactions of the time. Historical records indicate that Muslims had a comprehensive accounting, reporting, and auditing system, even adopting a double-entry bookkeeping system. This is evident from the documented works of two Muslim scholars, Al-Khawarizmi and Al-Mazendarani. Al-Khawarizmi in particular was an Islamic scholar who mastered numerous areas of science and made contributions to them, such as mathematics, astronomy, geography, cartography, and, of course, accounting.

The motivation for developing an accounting system during that period was initially religiously motivated and associated with the imposition of *zakah*. This is obviously different from the capitalistic motivation discussed earlier. Accounting was initiated together with the establishment of centralized finance authorities or *diwans* for the recording of revenues and expenses of the public treasury that existed at that time (*bayt al maal*). According to Napier (2007), the precise date of the emergence of accounting systems is unknown, but it appears that these systems were first documented by Al-Khawarizmi in 976 A.D. The systems were designed to portray the various types of projects that had been carried out, for example, industrial, agricultural, financial, housing, and service projects. Such projects would have been recorded by a specific individual referred to as *al kaateb* (bookkeeper). A set of books and recording procedures were developed, some of which were general in nature and applied to all accounting systems, while others were prescribed specifically for a particular accounting system. These accounting systems were livestock accounting, construction accounting, agricultural accounting, warehouse accounting, mint (currency) accounting, sheep grazing accounting, and treasury accounting.

Islam's emergence, manifested through the Qur'an's revelation, provided guidance and instructions on multifaceted aspects of life, including economic transactions. The Qur'an even provided explicit guidance on conducting accounting-related activities. It is because of this religious motivation that Muslims are obliged to follow certain rules and regulations, including what has been laid down in Chapter Al Baqarah verse 282[1]:

"O you who have believed, when you contract a debt for a specified term, write it down. And let a scribe write [it] between you in justice. Let no scribe refuse to write as Allah has taught him. So let him write and let the one who has the obligation dictate. And let him fear Allah, his Lord, and not leave anything out of it. But if the one who has the obligation is of limited understanding or weak or unable to dictate himself, then let his guardian dictate in justice. And bring to witness two witnesses from among your men. And if there are not two men [available], then a man and two women from those whom you accept as witnesses - so that if one of the women errs, then the other can remind her. And let not the witnesses refuse when they are called upon. And do not be [too] weary to write it, whether it is small or large, for its [specified] term. That is more just in the sight of Allah and stronger as evidence and more likely to prevent doubt between you, except when it is an immediate transaction which you conduct among yourselves. For [then] there is no blame upon you if you do not write it. And take witnesses when you conclude a contract. Let no scribe be harmed or any witness. For if you do so, indeed, it is [grave] disobedience in you. And fear Allah. And Allah teaches you. And Allah is Knowing of all things."

From the foregoing Qur'anic verse, several key concepts emerge in the context of the theory of Islamic accounting. The command to have a scribe write things down when it involves a future obligation clearly signifies the importance of keeping records in financial transactions, which is a part of the accounting process. This is required to avoid possible negative implications in the future that could cause conflicts between the involved parties. Another moral that can be taken from the verse is an emphasis on the mandatory nature of accounting as mentioned through the sentence *"Let no scribe refuse to write as Allah has taught him,"* so appointing someone to record a company's financial transactions is considered to be a *fardhu kifaayah*, which translates as communal obligation where if one fulfills the obligation, others are relieved of the duty to do so. The concept of materiality in Islam is also mentioned in the verse, where even if it involves small or large amounts, it is still recommended to put it in writing. The concept of materiality in traditional accounting is the principle whereby inconsequential matters are to be unheeded, but all important matters need to be considered and disclosed.

One of the underlying principles of Islamic accounting is that absolute ownership belongs to God and that man has a twofold role according to the Islamic worldview, which is that he is a servant of God and that he is a trustee of God. These ideas are mentioned in the Qur'an multiple times, for example, in Chapter Ad Dhariyat verse 56: "And I did not create jinn and mankind except to worship me" (al-Qur'an, 51:56) and in Chapter Al Baqarah verse 30: "I will create a vicege-rent on earth". All of the mentioned duties translate as the religious accountability of man toward God, which is a fundamental principle of Islamic accounting sub-suming other responsibilities toward other stakeholders. Another term that can be interchangeably used for religious accountability is Islamic accountability. This includes both horizontal accountability toward society and vertical accountability to God. Islam's worldview, which is one of the components of Islamic accounting and what sets it apart from traditional or conventional accounting, aims to attain success both in this world and in the extended time horizon of the Hereafter. It encompasses a dual aspect of the world and of religion, which are treated as two elements that are inseparable. The worldly aspect is regarded as a tool to achieve desired goals contained in the religious aspect. Islam's primary focus is on the religious aspect, but without implying any neglect toward the worldly aspect since they are interdependent on each other.

14.1.3   Objectives of Islamic accounting

The standardization of Islamic accounting is needed not only by the Islamic finance industry due to the incessant growth and internationalization of Islamic finance. Another reason why it is needed is due to the limitations of the standards that exist in conventional accounting. Conventional standards focus more on economic events and transactions than social, environmental, and religious aspects. The capitalist principle that underlies conventional accounting also impedes concerns for social welfare, which is imperative in Islamic accounting. The inability to provide assurance that all activities will be within the bounds of Islamic law is another point of concern. As a solution, AAOIFI was established to serve as a standard-setting body for Islamic finance, with a mandate to issue relevant standards that address the aforementioned deficiencies.

There are fundamental differences between Islamic and conventional accounting, so a unique Islamic accounting approach is needed, including in terms of its objectives. There are, of course, many similarities between the two, for example in terms of the technicalities of the accounting process, such as the usage of the double-entry system, but outlined below are Islamic accounting's unique features:

- Clear distinction of accounting objectives, i.e., religious obligation vs. commercial obligation, which will have an impact on the different aspects of financial statements.

- A different view of the need for accounting information by users, i.e., legitimate and equitable transactions and wealth vs. maximization of wealth.

- Compliance with the principles and rules of Islamic law.

- Different Islamic contractual relationships exemplified in the various Islamic nominate contracts in Islamic finance.

- A distinct accountability of relationships that covers both accountability toward God and toward society.

- An emphasis on the determination of *zakah*.

These differences have also resulted in the formulation of different objectives that are specific to Islamic accounting. Experience has shown that human effort that does not start with clear aims and objectives will eventually cause problems, run into limitations, and lack clarity regarding what needs to be achieved. Therefore, the establishment of accounting standards without determining a set of clear objectives will most likely lead to inconsistent standards that may not be suitable for the entities being accounted for. Just as conventional financial institutions need to set clear objectives for setting accounting standards, IFIs need to as well because these objectives will be used as guidelines by accounting standards boards and IFIs in setting standards, so they need to assure consistency. These objectives will also aid IFIs in making choices from among alternative accounting treatments in the absence of accepted accounting standards. In the end it will increase users' confidence in accounting information.

In terms of the objectives of financial accounting for IFIs, their shareholders, investors, and customers have a primary objective of ensuring compliance with the precepts of Islamic *Shariah* law in financial activities. In addition to this factor, IFIs have unique features that require different accounting objectives because they must comply with the precepts of *Shariah* in all of their financial and nonfinancial activities. IFIs have different contractual relationships with their investors, depositors, and customers compared to the relationships that exist between conventional financial institutions and their investors, customers, and depositors. For example, IFIs use a profit-sharing contract (*mudarabah*) in the case of deposit mobilization and other instruments such as *murabahah*, *ijarah*, *istisna*, *salam*, and *musharakah* in the case of consumer financing.

This does not mean that IFIs reject all of the objectives and principles of conventional accounting. Islam indeed recognizes human efforts made by non-Muslims as long as such efforts do not contradict the precepts of Islamic law. It is also recognized that there are common objectives between users of accounting information in IFIs and conventional financial institutions, such as the desire to maximize profit and increase wealth. This is an objective well recognized by Islam, so any accounting standards based on such common objectives would be relevant and acceptable for IFIs.

As a result of shared accounting objectives, numerous accounting principles, accounting concepts, accounting methods, financial reports, and disclosure requirements are common across accounting systems. For example, the historical cost principle, economic entity principle, monetary measurement, and accrual accounting and the concepts of assets, liabilities, equity, revenues, expenses, and fixed asset depreciation methods are all acceptable and relevant for IFIs.

An approach that has been chosen to establish accounting objectives is to start with contemporary conventional accounting objectives and then test them against the precepts of Islamic law. The result is to accept objectives that are consistent with *Shariah* and reject those that are not. Based on this approach, the objectives of Islamic accounting have been established as follows:

- Determine the rights and obligations of all parties in an IFI in accordance with the principles of *Shariah* and its concepts of fairness, charity, and compliance with Islamic business values.

- Contribute to the safeguarding of an IFI's assets, its rights, and the rights of others in an adequate manner.

- Contribute to the enhancement of the managerial and productive capabilities of the IFI and enhance compliance with its established goals and benefits.

- Provide thorough periodic reports and financial information to the users of these reports to enable them to make legitimate decisions.

Because of the aforementioned objectives and some unique objectives of the users of accounting information in IFIs and some different functions of these institutions, many unique accounting methods, financial reports, and disclosure requirements have been created in the financial accounting standards promulgated by AAOIFI. For example, per Financial Accounting Standard (FAS) No. 1, an IFI must prepare and publish a Statement of Changes in Restricted Investment and a Statement of Sources and Uses of *Zakah* and Charity Funds and a Statement of Sources and Uses of Funds in *Qard*. This same standard also requires the presentation of two types of equity in the Statement of Financial Position: equity of shareholders and equity of holders of unrestricted investment accounts. Moreover, numerous unique disclosure requirements are emphasized in Islamic accounting standards, such as the disclosure of income/expenses prohibited by *Shariah*, disclosure of the method used for the distribution of income between shareholders and holders of profit-sharing *mudarabah* accounts, and disclosure of the *zakah* per share.

14.2   Accounting standards for Islamic financial institutions

This section discusses the accounting standards for IFIs. The section consists of two subsections: the first is "Application of International Financial Reporting Standards for Islamic Financial Institutions: Benefits and Challenges," and the second is "Financial Statements of an Islamic Bank."

14.2.1   Application of international financial reporting standards for Islamic financial institutions: Benefits and challenges

As the Islamic financial industry has gone through an incredible phase of evolution since the 1970s, the spread of Islamic finance all over the world has generated the necessity of having a common accounting standard for IFIs. The turning point was in the 1990s, when the AAOIFI was established as a standard-setting body of accounting, auditing, ethics, governance, and *Shariah* for IFIs.

At the present time, almost all segments of conventional finance have been covered by Islamic finance (PwC, 2010). As a result, it is essential to have an accounting framework that is equivalent to a conventional finance framework and amenable to *Shariah* teachings. This requirement is very important, especially for multinational and global financial institutions that have significant Islamic finance activities such as Citi Group (PWC, 2010). As a consequence, there is a proposal within the Islamic financial industry to apply International Financial Reporting Standards (IFRS) to IFIs in order to align them with existing accounting practices. The proponents of this idea argue that the application of the IFRS to IFIs obviously has some benefits. The main benefits are as follows (PwC, 2010; Hidayat, 2011):

1. improvement in transparency and international comparability;

2. international recognition and usage; and

3. better efficiency.

For the first benefit, application of a single accounting framework to both Islamic and conventional products and transactions will enhance the level of transparency and international comparability of financial reporting for IFIs and, hence, cause an important boost to further investment in and development of the Islamic financial industry. Once a universal accounting standard is in place, the users of accounting information will be able to make an accurate appraisal of financial institutions (Islamic and conventional) with minimum accounting risks, which are risks created as a result of using different accounting frameworks.

As for the second benefit, applying IFRS will offer the advantages of international recognition and usage and make it the most appropriate framework for global institutions and compatible with Islamic and non-Islamic products, which will appeal to multinational stakeholders. The application of the IFRS is also expected to increase the willingness of more market players to take part in Islamic finance. This is due to their familiarity with the IFRS, which will enable them to make effective decisions.

With respect to the third benefit, the IFRS emphasizes the economic substance of a product or transaction rather than its legal form, so the standard can easily be applied in any jurisdiction. These will result in lower costs of financial reporting for global financial institutions that have Islamic and conventional products. The cost efficiency will be achievable through IFRS principles rather than an Islamic legal structure, which will ultimately determine the accounting treatment. As a result, there is no need for global financial institutions to prepare separate sections or statements for their Islamic financial activities.

However, not everyone agrees with the preceding arguments. In fact, many oppose the proposal. Its opponents have identified two major issues in applying the IFRS to IFIs:

1. The users of accounting information from IFIs and conventional financial institutions (FIs) have different objectives (Hameed, 2009).

2. IFIs have contractual relationships with their clients that differ from those of conventional FIs with their clients (Hidayat, 2011).

The differences in the objectives between the users of IFIs' accounting information and the users of conventional FIs' accounting information stem from differences in their worldviews. SFA1 (Para 21) of the AAOIFI accounting standards states that those who deal with Islamic banks are primarily concerned with submitting to and satisfying Allah in their financial and other dealings. As a result, in the case of IFIs, shareholders, investors, and other users of accounting information have as their primary objective to comply with *Shariah* in all their financial activities while at the same time accomplishing the objectives of the organizations (Hameed, 2009). This is also the original wisdom behind the establishment of IFIs, which is to achieve *maqasid al-Shariah* or the objectives of *Shariah* (Hidayat, 2010a, b). On the other hand, the ultimate purpose of conventional financial accounting users is to efficiently allocate scarce resources to their most efficient and profitable uses based on informed decisions (Hidayat, 2011).

These differences have some consequences. The first consequence has to do with the types of information identified. A conventional accounting framework concentrates only on identifying economic events and transactions (financial information). On the other hand, the users of IFI information are interested not only in financial information but also nonfinancial information, such as *Shariah* compliance, specific religious requirements, and fulfilling social responsibilities (Hameed, 2009). The second consequence is seen in the way in which assets, liabilities, and equity are measured, valued, recorded, and communicated. Conventional accounting mainly uses historical cost (or lower) to measure and value assets and liabilities. Although the idea of introducing fair value measurements has been proposed, its implementation would be quite difficult owing to the complexity of measuring fair value and its presumed lack of verifiability. On the other hand, from an Islamic point of view, at least for the computation of *zakah*, current valuation of total assets is obligatory (Hameed, 2009).

Another major issue are the differences in contractual relationships. IFIs have different contractual relationships with their investors, depositors, and customers compared to the relationships that exist between conventional financial institutions and their investors, customers, and depositors. Conventional FIs mostly use loans with interest in their contracts with clients. On the other hand, IFIs use various forms of Islamic commercial contracts when dealing with clients. For example, IFIs use a profit-sharing contract (*mudarabah*) in the case of deposit mobilization and other instruments such as *murabahah, ijarah, istisna, salam,* and *musharakah* in the case of customer financing (Hidayat, 2011).

Besides the issues identified in the preceding discussion, there are certain accounting issues that an IFI needs to disclose not addressed by IFRS. These including the following items (Hidayat, 2011):

1. Benevolent loans (*qard hasan*) are not addressed by conventional accounting standards. One of the important functions of IFIs is to provide social services based on the Statement of Financial Accounting 2 of the AAOIFI (AAOIFI, 2010). Failure to perform this function reduces IFIs to capitalist financing institutions.

2. Funds paid out as *zakah* or charity: The users of IFI accounting information may be interested in additional analysis of the sources of *zakah* funds, the methods of its collection, and its uses.

3. Revenues incidentally earned from transactions or relationships that are not compliant with *Shariah* such as income from late penalties. The users of IFI accounting information may be interested in more details about the causes of such earnings, their sources, how they are used, and procedures in place to prevent IFIs from entering into transactions prohibited by *Shariah*.

4. Restricted investment accounts: Islamic banks raise deposits through restricted profit-sharing contracts (*mudarabah muqayyodah*). In this kind of contract, Islamic banks do not acquire full control over funds as depositors (*rabbul mal*) place restrictions on where the money can be invested. As a result, the funds from this contract cannot be treated as an on-balance-sheet item. A separate statement to disclose transactions using this contract becomes necessary.

The IFRS may require disclosure of such transactions in additional notes. However, the additional notes will not provide details of those transactions as required by IFI accounting information users. Therefore, the AAOIFI requires a different set of financial statements from IFIs. The discussion on the required financial statements for IFIs such as Islamic banks will be discussed in detail in the next subsection.

Before proceeding to the next section, it is important to note that, even though the application of IFRS by IFIs poses challenges, harmonization between AAOIFI accounting standards and the IFRS is still possible. In fact, the approach used by the AAOIFI in developing its accounting standards is not a procedure started from scratch. The approach used by the AAOIFI in developing its standards can be divided into three steps (Hameed, 2009):

1. Accept conventional procedures such as the IFRS accounting principles that don't contradict *Shariah* principles.

2. Reject conventional processes such as IFRS accounting principles that are not in line with *Shariah* principles. In this step, if amendments can be made, this would be preferable.

3. Develop new concepts that are unique to Islamic financial transactions.

Based on this approach, it is clear that Islamic banks that follow AAOIFI standards in practice are still applying IFRS, especially in connection with those principles that do not contradict *Shariah*. In addition, continuous dialogue and consultation between the International Accounting Standard Board (IASB) and the AAOIFI take place regularly in an effort to harmonize and minimize the differences between the two accounting frameworks. The next subsection discusses the financial statements of Islamic banks as per the requirements of AAOIFI standards.

14.2.2 Financial statements of an Islamic bank

FAS No. 1 of the AAOIFI, "Presentation and Disclosure in the Financial Statements of Islamic Banks," states that an Islamic bank must prepare the following seven financial statements (AAOIFI, 2010):

1. Statement of Financial Position (Balance Sheet);

2. Income Statement;

3. Statement of Cash Flows;

4. Statement of Retained Earnings, or Statement of Changes in Owners' Equity;

5. Statement of Changes in Restricted Investments;

6. Statement of Sources and Uses of Funds in *Zakah* and Charity Funds; and

7. Statement of Sources and Uses of *Qard* Fund.

FAS No. 1 further explains that these seven financial statements actually reflect several roles that an Islamic bank must perform in their operations. First, the Statement of Financial Position, Income Statement, Statement of Cash Flows, and Statement of Changes in Owners' Equity reflect the role of an Islamic bank as an investor. Second, the Statement of Changes in Restricted Investments reflects the Islamic bank's role as an agent. Lastly, the Statement of Sources and Uses of Funds in *Zakah* and Charity Funds and the Statement of Sources and Uses of Funds in the *Qard* Fund reflect the social and religious roles of an Islamic bank (AAOIFI, 2010).

These seven statements can also be divided into ones that are similar to conventional banks and ones that are unique to Islamic banks. The Statement of Financial Position, Income Statement, Statement of Cash Flows, and Statement of Changes in Owners' Equity are categorized as statements similar to those of conventional banks, while the Statement of Changes in Restricted Investments, Statement of Sources and Uses of Funds in *Zakah* and Charity Funds, and the Statement of Sources and Uses of Funds in the *Qard* Fund are unique to Islamic banks (AAOIFI, 2010). The following subsubsections elaborate on each statement further.

14.2.2.1 *Statement of financial position (balance sheet)*

FAS No. 1 of the AAOIFI requires earning assets of an Islamic bank to be classified on the asset side of the Statement of Financial Position as sales/receivables, financing, or investments. Unlike conventional banks that record most of their earning assets as "loans and advances," Islamic banks classify their earning assets based on the underlying Islamic commercial contracts of each transaction. For example, any transactions that use *murabahah*, *salam*, *istisna*, and other sales contracts will be disclosed as "receivables" on Islamic banks' books (AAOIFI, 2010).

Table 14.1 Components of an Islamic bank's statement of financial position

Assets		Liabilities/investment A/Cs/equity	
Earning assets	• Cash and equivalents • Short-term instruments	• Current accounts (based on *qard*, *wadia*, or *amanah* contract) • Payables • Accruals	**Liabilities**
	• **Sales receivable** • *Murabahah* receivables • *Istisna* receivables • *Salam* receivables • *Ijarah* rent receivables • **Financing** • *Mudarabah* • *Musharakah* • **Investments** • *Ijarah* (leasing) assets • Real estate • Equity • *Sukuk*	• Equity of unrestricted investment account holders (based on *mudarabah* profit-sharing contract)	**Profit-sharing deposits**
Fixed assets	• Fixed assets • Other assets	• Paid-up capital • Equity reserves • Prudential reserves	**Owner's equity**

On the liability side, FAS No. 1 of the AAOIFI requires unrestricted investment accounts' funds (*mudarabah mutlaqah* deposits) to be presented on the right-hand side of the statement of financial position in a separate section, not as liability or equity, but under "Unrestricted investment accounts." Unrestricted investment accounts refer to funds received by an Islamic bank from individuals and others on the basis that the Islamic bank will have the right to use and invest those funds without restrictions (*mutlaqah*), which includes the Islamic bank's right to commingle those invested funds with its own investments in exchange for proportional participation in profits and losses after the Islamic bank receives its share of profits as a *mudarib* (AAOIFI, 2010). Table 14.1 summarizes the components of an Islamic bank's statement of financial position.

In addition, Figure 14.1 provides an example of an Islamic bank's statement of financial position prepared according to the AAOIFI accounting standard.

14.2.2.2   Income Statement

An Income Statement represents a measurement of revenue and expense performance of an entity over a defined accounting period. The Income Statement of an Islamic bank discloses income from Islamic sales transactions, financing transactions and investments, the allocation of income to unrestricted investment accountholders, share of profits to the bank as *mudarib*, fee income from services, expenses, provisions, and tax deductions. The unique feature of an Income Statement of an Islamic bank is the amount allocated out of income to investment accountholders (AAOIFI, 2010). It is unique because this account is neither an expense (in the case

Albaraka Islamic Bank B.S.C. (c)
BALANCE SHEET
At 31 December 2008

	2008 US $	2007 US $
ASSETS		
Cash and balances with banks	216,028,978	176,360,747
Sales receivables	508,913,704	531,764,090
Mudaraba financing	12,989,281	22,800,961
Ijara Muntahia Bittamleek	44,207,291	70,705,679
Musharaka financing	23,900,235	19,469,240
Investments	140,858,730	155,879,593
Investment properties	1,636,061	5,402,171
Ijara income receivables	22,184,818	24,673,365
Premises and equipment	11,818,214	7,368,622
Other assets	18,924,098	24,405,896
TOTAL ASSETS	1,001,461,410	1,038,830,364
LIABILITIES		
Due to banks and other financial institutions	12,692,962	33,315,885
Current accounts	66,537,321	60,668,407
Other liabilities	29,731,525	24,284,388
TOTAL LIABILITIES	108,961,808	118,268,680
UNRESTRICTED INVESTMENT ACCOUNTS	706,842,162	731,419,482
EQUITY		
Share capital	122,457,800	122,457,800
Reserves	27,673,124	33,273,767
Retained earnings	35,526,516	33,410,635
TOTAL EQUITY	185,657,440	189,142,202
TOTAL LIABILITIES, UNRESTRICTED INVESTMENT ACCOUNTS AND EQUITY	1,001,461,410	1,038,830,364
RESTRICTED INVESTMENT ACCOUNTS	166,983,914	143,530,415
CONTINGENCIES AND COMMITMENTS	132,658,770	125,668,276

Figure 14.1 Example of an Islamic bank's statement of financial position (balance sheet)

of profit) nor revenue (in the case of loss) to shareholders. It is an allocation or distribution of profits to unrestricted investment accountholders for a joint participation scheme in the financing and investment activities of the IFI, just like dividends for shareholders. All deductions above the profit line are expenses. Expenses are ex-ante performance (before profits or losses are determined). Distribution is made after profits are determined (ex-post performance). Therefore, the return on unrestricted investment accounts and their equivalent cannot be classified as an expense like an interest expense in a conventional bank.

In a conventional bank, interest expense is subtracted from interest income to arrive at net interest income. This is not the case for the amount allocated out of income to investment accountholders. This amount is determined based on a profit-sharing ratio mutually agreed upon by the investment account holders and the Islamic bank. Even though this account shares similarities with dividends for shareholders in the sense that both are ex-post performance, it is important to note that the dividends paid to investment account holders are based on an agreed profit-sharing ratio, not at the discretion of the board of directors, as in the case of dividends paid to shareholders. As a result, more disclosures are required with regard to

Consolidated Statement of Income
For the year ended 31 December 2008

	Notes	**2008** **BD 000s**	2007 BD 000s
Income from retail and corporate banking activities	22	**38,664**	26,304
Income from investment activities	23	**30,428**	29,467
Share of income of associates	11	**21,034**	14,173
Other income		**8,386**	2,049
		98,512	71,993
Less: Profit on Murabaha due to banks and non-banks		**14,870**	14,639
		83,642	57,354
Staff costs	25	**10,848**	8,106
Depreciation		**3,519**	1,871
Provisions	26	**8,453**	3,233
Other operating expenses	27	**12,523**	9,812
		35,343	23,022
NET INCOME BEFORE PROFIT ON UNRESTRICTED **INVESTMENT ACCOUNTS**		**48,299**	34,332
Less: Profit on unrestricted investment accounts		**9,865**	1,662
NET INCOME FOR THE YEAR		**38,434**	32,670
Attributable to:			
Shareholders of the Parent		**35,686**	31,399
Minority interest		**2,748**	1,271
		38,434	32,670

Figure 14.2   Example of an Islamic bank's income statement

this item's determination and distribution (AAOIFI, 2010). Two disclosure methods are recommended by the AAOIFI with regard to income determination:

1. Pooling method
2. Separate investment account method

The pooling method distributes the net profit between investment account holders and the bank only after all revenues earned are deducted with both direct and indirect expenses. On the other hand, the separate investment account method distributes gross profits between account holders as the capital providers (*rabul mal*) and the bank as the *mudarib* after deducting the cost of financing and related costs of the use of the funds. Figure 14.2 provides an example of an Islamic bank's income statement.

14.2.2.3   Statement of cash flows and statement of owners' equity
There is no feature of these statements that is specific to Islamic banks. Both statements are exactly the same as that required by IAS/IFRS, as per IAS No. 30.

14.2.2.4   Statement of changes in restricted investments
Restricted investment accounts are based on the restricted *mudarabah* (*mudarabah muqayyadah*) contract. In this contract, the Islamic bank restricts itself or is restricted by investors to investing funds in a specified asset class/investment, a specified geographic region, or with a specified counterparty (AAOIFI, 2010). Funds raised

Consolidated Statement of Restricted Investment Accounts

For the year ended 31 December 2008

	Balance at 1 January 2007 BD 000s	Deposits BD 000s	Gross Income BD 000s	Mudarib Share BD 000s	Withdrawals/ distributions BD 000s	Balance at 31 December 2007 BD 000s
Murabaha receivables	5,363	59,800	1,766	(380)	(8,680)	57,869
Istisna'a	13,746	-	973	(237)	(6,285)	8,197
	19,109	59,800	2,739	(617)	(14,965)	66,066

	Balance at 1 January 2008 BD 000s	Deposits BD 000s	Gross Income BD 000s	Mudarib Share BD 000s	Withdrawals/ distributions BD 000s	Balance at 31 December 2008 BD 000s
Murabaha receivables	57,869	50,704	4,225	(837)	(25,294)	86,667
Istisna'a/Ijarah Muntahia Bittamleek contracts*	8,197	-	614	(150)	(2,059)	6,602
	66,066	50,704	4,839	(987)	(27,353)	93,269

* Istisna'a reported in prior year has become Ijarah Muntahia Bttamleek due to completion of construction.

Figure 14.3 Example of an Islamic bank's Statement of Changes in restricted investments

through these accounts are required to be reported off balance sheet in the Statement of Changes in Restricted Investments since the money is not qualified to be reported on the balance sheet. This is because an Islamic bank doesn't have the right to commingle these funds with other funds as in the case of unrestricted *mudarabah*. In other words, the bank doesn't have full control over how to use the funds, making the funds unqualified to be reported on the balance sheet.

In this statement, the Islamic bank should present all types of restricted funds it is managing (examples are real estate funds, equity funds, commodity funds, and fixed income funds) showing the balances of the restricted funds in the beginning, additions/withdrawals during the period, administrative expenses, bank fee as agent or share of profits as *mudarib*, income for the period, and balances at the end of the period. The statement should also show the units or shares in each fund and the unit value at the beginning and end of the period. Figure 14.3 provides an example of an Islamic bank's Statement of Changes in Restricted Investments.

14.2.2.5   *Statement of Sources and Uses of* Zakah *and Charity Funds*

The Statement of Sources and Uses of *Zakah* and Charity Funds shows the sources of funds from *zakah* paid by the bank as well as investment accountholders, in addition to any donations for charitable purposes received by the bank. The statement should also disclose the distribution of these funds to various recipients. In AAOIFI accounting standards, *zakah* is discussed in FAS No. 9. *Zakah* is one of the pillars of Islam. It is an obligation related to the redistribution of wealth when it has fulfilled certain conditions. Islamic banks may either advise shareholders on the amount payable or pay *zakah* on behalf of shareholders. For the computation of *zakah*, the AAOIFI recommends two methods:

1. Net assets method
2. Net invested funds method.

STATEMENT OF SOURCES AND USES
OF CHARITY AND ZAKAH FUND

FOR THE YEAR ENDED 31 DECEMBER 2007

	2007	BD 000's 2006
Sources of charity and zakah fund		
Contributions by the Bank	150	-
Non-Islamic income	3	3
Total sources	**153**	**3**
Uses of charity fund and zakah fund		
Contributions to charitable organisations	-	-
Total uses	**-**	**-**
Excess of sources over uses	153	3
Balance at the beginning of the year	3	-
Undistributed charity and zakah fund at 31 December (note 14)	**156**	**3**

Figure 14.4   Example of an Islamic bank's Statement of Sources and Uses of Zakah and Charity Funds

Under the net assets method, the *zakah* base is computed as follows:

Zakah base = assets [subject to *zakah*] − (liabilities due in current period + equity of unrestricted investment account + equity held on behalf of government, endowment, charities, and not-for-profit organizations).

Assets subject to *zakah* are cash and cash equivalents, receivables net of provision for doubtful debts, trading assets, and net financing assets.

Under the net invested funds method, the *zakah* base is computed as follows:

Zakah base = paid-up capital + reserves + provisions not deducted from assets + retained earnings + net income + liabilities (noncurrent) − net fixed assets − investments (not for trading) − accumulated losses.

Using either of the two methods, the amount of the *zakah* base must be identical. At the end, the *zakah* base will be multiplied by 2.5 percent to determine the *zakah* obligation. Figure 14.4 provides an example of an Islamic bank's Statement of Sources and Uses of *Zakah* and Charity Funds.

14.2.2.6   Statement of Sources and Uses of Qard Fund

The Statement of Sources and Uses of *Qard* Fund presents the opening balance of funds available for *qard*, sources of funds during the period available for *qard*, and uses of funds for the period. Funds available for *qard* can come from external or internal sources, including current accounts, shareholders' funds, and income prohibited by *Shariah* that is coincidentally earned. Uses of *qard* funds represent the amount of gross decreases in funds available for lending during the financial period and may include loans to students, craftsmen, low-paid bank employees, and recovery of loans from current accounts. The *qard* fund is established for the purpose of satisfying the requirements of the corporate social responsibility of banks (AAOIFI, 2010). Figure 14.5 below provides an example of an Islamic bank's Statement of Sources and Uses of *Qard* Fund.

Consolidated Statement of Sources and Uses of Good Faith *Qard* Fund

For the year ended 31 December 2008

	Qard hasan receivables BD'000	Funds available for *Qard* hasan BD'000	Total BD'000
At 1 January 2008	27	101	128
Uses of qard fund:			
Marriage	17	(17)	–
Refurbishment	16	(16)	–
Medical treatment	14	(14)	–
Others	11	(11)	–
Total uses during the year	58	(58)	–
Repayments	(75)	75	–
At 31 December 2008	10	118	128
At 1 January 2007	35	93	128
Uses of qard fund:			
Marriage	20	(20)	–
Refurbishment	16	(16)	–
Medical treatment	17	(17)	–
Others	12	(12)	–
Total uses during the year	65	(65)	–
Repayments	(73)	73	–
At 31 December 2007	27	101	128

	2008 BD'000	2007 BD'000
Sources of Qard Fund		
Contribution by the Bank	125	125
Donation	3	3
Total of sources during the year	128	128

Figure 14.5   Example of an Islamic bank's Statement of Sources and Uses *Qard* Fund

14.2.2.7   *Notes to financial statements*

As in conventional accounting, the AAOIFI also includes notes to financial statements as an integral part of financial statements. They should be made available immediately after the disclosures of the last financial statement. At the bottom of every page of a statement should be written "Notes to financial statements from page X to page X are an integral part of financial statements" (AAOIFI, 2010).

14.3   Conclusion

This chapter has achieved its intended learning outcomes. In the early sections of the chapter, the purpose and main principles of Islamic accounting are clearly defined. The chapter also critically discussed the similarities and differences between Islamic and conventional accounting, which led to the existence of two accounting frameworks, the IFRS and the AAOIFI. With reference to AAOIFI standards, IFIs such as Islamic banks and *takaful* companies are required to prepare additional financial statements that are not required for their conventional counterparts. This chapter, like other studies, has at least two limitations that could be addressed by future studies. First, this chapter uses a library-based method, which is a qualitative research approach. Future studies could provide empirical evidence of the differences between Islamic and conventional accounting. Second, this chapter focuses on Islamic banks, leaving other segments of Islamic finance unexplored. Therefore, future studies could extend this study by covering other aspects such as *sukuk*, mutual funds, and *takaful* companies.

It was not the aim of this chapter to ignore all aspects of conventional accounting. However, some unique characteristics of Islamic finance that are not covered by conventional accounting need to be addressed. In many aspects, it is possible to harmonize international accounting standards/international financial reporting standards with AAOIFI standards. This is work that needs to be continuously done by all accounting stakeholders.

Discussion Questions

1. AAOIFI FAS 2 – Murabahah and Murabahah to the Purchase Orderer

World Islamic Bank is doing a murabahah transaction with Ebrahim. The asset involved costs BD10,000. The mark up at World Islamic bank is 4 percent per year. Ebrahim chose a period of financing of 5 years. Payment is made at a yearly basis.

a) Do the yearly journal entries in year 0 and year 1–5. Do not forget to provide all calculation processes!

b) Do the yearly extract of the Balance Sheet and Income Statement

c) What are the journal entry changes if a Hamish Jiddiyah was introduced? For example, the bank requiring Ebrahim to pay a 20 percent Hamish Jiddiyah.

d) What are the journal entry changes if Ebrahim pays 2 months late from the due date in year 5? Penalty is fixed at BD100, with no time related conditions.

e) What are the journal entry changes if Ebrahim accelerates payment in the last year by a full year thus earning him a rebate of 75 percent from the yearly profit?

2. AAOIFI FAS 4 – Musharakah Financing

ABC Islamic Bank has entered into a Musharakah with XYZ Company for the development of a project and gradual sale of its commercial land. The bank is participating in the Musharakah by contributing land of which the book value in the Bank's book is USD 1.2 million. XYZ Company is contributing USD 0.5 million in cash.

The cost to the bank of the feasibility study for the Musharakah was USD 50,000 and for an independent professional valuation of the land amounting to USD 25,000. According to the professional valuation, the land has a fair value of USD2.1 million.

It has been agreed between the bank and XYZ that the gradual transfer of the land title from the Musharakah books to XYZ books will be made on a yearly basis that will be completed in 3 years. Each year the bank will transfer 1/3 of the land to XYZ.

Every year a valuation is done towards the project. The cost of the valuation will be borne by the bank in accordance with the Musharakah agreement.

The details of the Musharakah are as follows:

	Project Fair Value	Valuation Cost
Year 1	3,000,000	20,000
Year 2	3,200,000	24,000
Year 3	3,800,000	28,000

Required
   a) The journal entries to record the above transactions in the books of the bank
   b) The notes to the financial statements of the bank for all 3 years

3. AAOIFI FAS 8 – Ijarah & Ijarah Muntahia Bittamleek

Bank Ihsan signed an ijarah contract deal with a client to lease a piece of heavy duty equipment for a period of 5 years. The bank purchased the equipment from another party on the 1st of January for RM500,000, not including the custom duty of RM40,000, and the installment of the machine of RM10,000. The bank also incurred legal fees of RM15,000 which is considered to be material.

According to the contract agreement, installments should be paid at an annual basis, of RM11,000 per month. The net realizable value of the equipment in the end of the contract is estimated to be RM30,000.

In the 1st year the client found technical difficulty in the equipment and incurred RM20,000 to retain its full working order. The machine broke down again in the last year due to a mistake done by one of the workers. The cost incurred for that incident totaled to another RM20,000. Every year, routine maintenance costs were rounded up to RM600.

The transaction is an ijarah muntahia bit tamleek in which the lessor agreed that the customer pay only 40 percent of the estimated residual value at the end of the useful life.

You are required to:
Prepare the journal entries only for the following periods:

   a) At the beginning
   b) At the end of a 1st year
   c) At the end of the ijarah term (year 5)

4. AAOIFI FAS 7 – Salam and Parallel Salam

On 1st February, 2018, the Islamic Bank of America entered into a salam financing contract with Rubber Growers Cooperative to supply 100 metric tons of RSS1 (superior grade) rubber on the 1st week of June 2018 at $1,000 a metric ton. The amount was paid to the muslam ileihi on the same day. On 25th of May, 2018, the bank entered into a parallel salam contract to supply the same to Nike at $1,200 a metric ton on 1st week of June 2018.

On the 1st week of June 2018, the cooperative delivered only half the promised quantity of RSS1 rubber. It also delivered 50 tons of RSS2 (lower grade) rubber which the bank accepted to take costing only AT$800 a metric ton. The cooperative informed the bank that since it is insolvent, it cannot afford to pay the difference to the bank.

Meanwhile, Nike refused to take delivery of the RSS2 rubber and only accepted delivery of the 50 tons of RSS1. The bank was forced to buy RSS1 from the market at $1,250 per metric ton to deliver to fulfil its commitment to Nike.

Answer the following questions:

a) Prepare the journal entries for the whole transaction.

b) Determine whether the business was profitable or not.

Selected Bibliography

AAOIFI (2010). *Accounting, Auditing and Governance Standards*. Manama: AAOIFI.

AOSSG (2010). *Financial Reporting Issues Relating to Islamic Finance*. Kuala Lumpur: AOSSG.

CIMA (2008). *Accounting for Islamic Financial Institutions*. London: Chartered Institute of Management Accountants.

Hameed, S. (2003). Islamic Accounting – A Primer. *Accountants Today Journal*, January–February 2003 Edition.

Hameed, S. (2009). *Accounting for Islamic Financial Institutions*. Kuala Lumpur: INCEIF.

Hidayat, S.E. (2010a). Islamic Finance: The Original Wisdom Behind Its Establishment. *Islamic Finance News*, 7(31), 23.

Hidayat, S.E. (2010b). Takaful: Establishing a Caring Society. *Islamic Finance News*, 7(17), 20–21.

Hidayat, S.E. (2011). International Financial Reporting Standards for Islamic Finance: Benefits and Challenges. *Islamic Finance News*, 8(48), 24–26.

Iqbal, Z. and Mirakhor, A. (2011). *An Introduction to Islamic Finance*. Singapore: John Wiley & Sons (Asia).

Napier, C. (2007). Defining Islamic Accounting: Current Issues, Past Roots. *Accounting History*, 14(1–2), 121–144.

PWC (2010). *Open to Comparison: Islamic Finance and IFRS*. London: PricewaterhouseCoopers.

SII (2006). *Financial Statements for Islamic Banks*. SII.

Zaid, O. (2004). Accounting Systems and Recording Procedures in the Early Islamic State. *Accounting Historians Journal*, 31(2), 149–170.

Note

1. Translation of Saheeh International, 1997.

GLOSSARY

Aakhira (hereafter)
Islamic belief that there is life after death and human beings will be accountable before God for their deeds in this life

AAOIFI
Accounting and Auditing Organization for Islamic Financial Institutions, the leading standard-setting organization for the Islamic finance industry, headquartered in Bahrain

Abd
Servant; adherent of Islam who submits to Allah to worship and obey Him

Accidental opportunity discovery
Identifying and recognizing an opportunity serendipitously, which occurs when recognition of the value and relevance of new information leads to a specific transformation

Accountability
Answerability, blameworthiness, or liability in connection with stakeholders as part of governance

Accounting
The discipline of comprehensive and systematic recording of financial transactions pertaining to a business

Adālah
Justice or fairness

Adverse selection
Situation where there is information asymmetry between buyers and sellers

Akhlaqul karimah
Good morals or a spontaneous act according to both reason and religion. For example, honesty, fairness, humility

Al-falah
Situation where an individual is adequately provided for in terms of basic needs, enjoys necessary freedom, leisure to work for spiritual and material advancement

Al-khuluq
Behavior or power of the soul that drives action easily and spontaneously without thought

Al-muhsineen
A *muhsin* (male, plural *muhsineen*) and a *muhsina* (female, plural *muhsinaat*) are those who do good

Amanah
Reliability; trustworthiness; loyalty; honesty; A value of Islamic society in mutual dealings also refers to deposits in trust. A person may hold property in trust for another, sometimes based on the terms of a contract

Anchoring bias
Judging or deciding based on a familiar reference point that is incomplete, inadequate, or irrelevant to the problem being solved or issue being addressed

Aqd
Contract delineating the terms of transactions or the rights and duties of the transacting parties

Balance sheet
One of the key financial statements pertaining to a company's financial condition and showing its assets, liabilities, and net worth

Banker's acceptance
Commercial contract, commonly in international trade, establishing that payment of a bill upon maturity or an agreed date is guaranteed by the endorsing bank

Bottom line
Net income, calculated by subtracting all expenses from gross sales

Bounded rationality model
Model based on the assumption that when individuals make decisions, rationality is limited or bounded by a number of factors

Business environment
Dynamics resulting from the interaction of all internal and external factors related to a business

Business ethics
Organizational principles, norms, standards, and sets of values governing actions and behaviors in a business organization

Cadre	Group of people trained for a particular profession
Capital	Assets, tangible and intangible, that help create or add to the long-term net worth of a business
Capital formation	Process of accumulating capital stock in an economy by investing in productive assets
Capital market	Market where long-term debt and equity securities are traded
Casualty insurance company	Financial institution that sells insurance policies against loss of property from accidents, fire, theft, and so forth
Certificate of deposit	Bank-issued short-term time deposit that is traded and specifies an interest rate and maturity date
Charitable contract	Unilateral contract to facilitate giving or transferring wealth to another party without any return or advantage to the giver
Clean environment	Environment that is safe and free from pollution and other forms of degradation
Climate change	Long-term or permanent changes in earth's climate system resulting in new weather and environmental patterns
Cohesion	State of sticking together, especially in a group or organizational setting
Collective responsibility	Beyond individual level, responsibilities at the level of organizations, groups, societies, and nations
Commercial bank	Depository institution that accepts deposits, makes loans, and offers check-writing accounts
Commercial paper	Unsecured, short-term promissory note issued by a corporation
Common stock	Security representing equity ownership in a publicly traded corporation
Community engagement	Collective involvement of communities and organizations to build sustained relationships for the common good
Community welfare	Programs providing a minimum level of benefits or services for disadvantaged peoples
Commutative contract	Contract of reciprocity where each party to the transaction receives an equivalent benefit
Comply	Act in accordance with a particular set of rules
Conscious reasoning	Deliberate use of recognized logical principles and tools to arrive at judgments or decisions
Consensus	General agreement or harmony
Contagion of financial crises	Examples are herd behavior, commercial ties, and financial ties
Cooperation	Working together for a common pursuit
Corporate bond	Long-term debt instrument issued by a corporation
Corporate governance	Framework of processes and relations by which corporations are managed
Corporate structure	Organization of various departments or units within a firm or business
Corporation	Company or group of companies authorized to carry out business as a single entity
Creative decision making	Critical skill in business operations to study a problem, identify options, and make informed, effective decisions
Creativity	Capacity to come up with something new
Creditor	Lender, individual, or institution
Customer satisfaction	Degree to which a customer is satisfied with a product, service, or experience
Debt-creating contract	Contract that causes a client to end up with debt obligations
Deceit	Practice designed or meant to mislead others

Demographic factors	Traits or characteristics of individuals that are used to gather and assess data on people in a given population
Depositor	Person who keeps money in a financial institution
Derivative market	Market where derivative securities such as futures and options are traded
Disclosure	Unknown fact that is made known, here corporate facts revealed in the annual report of a company
Distribution of risk	Function that reduces risk through alternative financial assets
Dividends	Distribution of profit in the form of payment made by a corporation to its shareholders
E-commerce	Commerce conducted online or in digital space
Economic environment	Economic factors or determinants affecting the behavior of individuals and businesses
Efficiency	Ability to do things effectively and without waste
EFTA	European Free Trade Association, a regional trade organization and free trade area consisting of four European states: Iceland, Liechtenstein, Norway, and Switzerland
Enabling factor	Factor or force that facilitates or impedes change in various contexts
Entrepreneur	Person who creates a business and takes financial risk to earn a profit
Entrepreneurial activity	Human endeavors in pursuit of the creation of value by identifying, exploiting, and addressing new opportunities
Entrepreneurial culture	A culture or environment that encourages, facilitates, and rewards the mindset of bringing positive changes in a business or socioeconomic context
Entrepreneurial opportunity	Situation where entrepreneurs can take action or undertake activities to make or augment profit
Entrepreneurial process	Methods and decision-making styles for entrepreneural pursuits
Entrepreneurship	Willingness and ability to successfully identify and exploit opportunities in business and manage risk
Escalation commitment	Continuing to channel resources and time to a failing cause or approach
Ethical codes	Principles and norms designed to assist professionals and organizations to conduct business with integrity
Euro-currency markets	Money held in overseas banks
Execute	Put a plan into effect
Exploitation	Taking advantage of parties who are in a weaker or vulnerable position for one's selfish goals
Extrinsic motivation	Behavior shaped or driven by external factors, such as positive or negative incentives
Factors of production (resources)	Economic term relating to four categories of resources or inputs used in the production process
Falah (success, prosperity)	Believer's pursuit of success in this world and salvation in the hereafter
Fard (obligatory)	Obligation or duty categorized as compulsory in Islam
Fard kefayah	Obligatory duty considered rendered if done by some people on behalf of society
Fatwa	Ruling on a matter of Islamic law handed down by a recognized authority
Fee-based contract	Contract based on agreed upon fixed fees rather than being open-ended

Finance	Ways to mobilize and allocate funds for business activities, making purchases, or investing
Finance company	Financial institution that obtains its funds from the market to make loans to individuals and small businesses
Financial intermediary	Financial institution that helps connect deficit units (borrowers or capital seekers) with surplus units (savers or lenders)
Financialization	Contemporary phenomenon where financial sector increases in size and threatens to overwhelm the real economy
***Fiqh* (Islamic law)**	Theory or philosophy of Islamic law based on teachings of Qur'an and of the Prophet Muhammad (PBUH)
Firm	Commercial entity that produces or sells goods and services to consumers for profit
FOREX market	International market for trading foreign currencies
For-profit	Denoting an organization operated to earn profits
Framework	Important support structure
Framing bias	Allowing factors other than facts to influence decision making
Gharar	One of three key prohibitions in Islamic law, involving avoidable uncertainties that have major consequences
Global business	Economic or corporate activities that take place globally or across different countries
Global connectivity	Potential opportunities for seamless global communication through the Internet
Global finance	Financial system comprising regulators and financial markets and institutions conducting business internationally
Global warming	Trend and pattern of long-term rise in average temperature of earth's climate system, upsetting ecological sustainability
Goodwill	Established reputation of a brand or business, treated as an intangible but quantifiable asset
GRI	Global Reporting Initiative, an international standard-setting organization to assist public and private sectors in dealing with global issues such as human rights, climate change, exploitation, and corruption
Ḥadīth	Records of narrations covering particular sayings and actions of Prophet Muhammad (PBUH)
***Halal* (permissible)**	That which is allowed according to Islamic law
***Haram* (prohibited)**	Unlawful or that which is against Islamic law
Hindsight bias	Based on past experience, tendency people have to view occurrences as more predictable and reliable than they really are
Holistic	Marked by belief that the elements of something are closely unified and justifiable only by reference to the whole
Homo economicus	Figurative, imaginary, or even mythical human being characterized by its unbounded capacity to act and make decisions rationally
Homo Islamicus	An alternative to *homo economicus*, where human beings act and make decisions based on Islamic parameters
HRM	Human resource management, the approach to effectively and efficiently managing an organization's human capital to gain competitive edge
Human resources	Human capital to staff and operate a business entity or other organization
Human resource crisis	Brain drain from Muslim-majority countries to developed world
IASB	International Accounting Standards Board: an independent, international accounting standard-setting body of the IFRS Foundation

Ibadah	Worshipping, obeying, and serving Allah; living a life shown by Allah through Islam
IFRS	International Financial Reporting Standards: internationally recognized accounting standard used in 110+ countries
Iḥsān	Benevolence; act or behavior shaped by compassion and care above and beyond fairness or justice
Ijma`	Names of two kinds of consensus: 1. *Ijma` al-ummah*: consensus of a whole community. 2. *Ijma` al-aimmah*: consensus by religious authorities
Ijtihad	In Islamic law, for those matters not categorically established by the Qur'an or *sunnah*, using independent reasoning to derive rulings on knowledge of truth in religious matters
Iman	True faith or believer's faith in metaphysical aspects of Islam
Income statement	One of the main financial statements pertaining to a business's operations and the relationship between revenue, expense, and net profit
Information technology	Technology-related sector that deals with communication or transmission of data or information using computers and telecommunication
Information transmission	Function that increases information efficiency
Inhibiting factor	Factor that inhibits or impedes achievement of an outcome
Innovation	Introduction of something new or improved
Inside story	Pertinent or valuable information to which only some people closely associated with something are privy
Institution	Pattern of behavior or activities, governed by custom or law, reflected in various organizations or entities
Institutional factors	Range of social institutions within which organizations operate or which they must take into consideration
Integrity	Quality of being honest and upholding persistent adherence to strong moral and ethical principles, norms, and values
Intention	State of mind reflecting an interest in or commitment to undertaking and carrying out an action in the future
Interest	Amount of money paid on a regular basis at a certain rate for the use of money lent or to postpone the settlement of a liability
International bond markets and eurobonds	Markets where bonds issued outside their domestic market are traded
International trade	Trade of goods and services, importing and exporting, among countries
Intrinsic motivation	Something that comes from within, where people's actions are due to some special personal satisfaction obtained
Intuitive decision making	Instead of fact or learning based, decision making based primarily on intuition
Invalid contract	Contract that does not meet Islamic legal requirements
Investment	Action of dedicating time, effort, or energy to a particular economic activity with the expectation of earning a profit
Islamic accounting	Accounting process and standards in compliance with Islamic legal rulings and meeting the needs of the Islamic finance industry
Islamic banking	Banking that complies with the prohibitions in Islamic law
Islamic entrepreneurship	Entrepreneurial pursuits guided by Islamic values, principles, and norms
Islamic finance	Financial services that comply with the prohibitions of Islamic law

Islamic values	Norms and principles, apart from legalities, that underlie the Islamic way of life
Isthikhara	Contemplative Islamic prayers seeking inspirational guidance in making choices and decisions
Jurisdiction	Official power to make legal decisions and judgments
Khalifah (**vicegerent**)	Islamic belief that human beings are vicegerents of Allah on this earth and thus are accountable to Allah for their life in this world and are to serve as trustees in this world
Legal environment	Laws and regulations subject to which businesses operate in a jurisdiction
Legal framework	System of rules by which business decisions and activities are governed and regulated
Legitimize	Make something legal
Lenient	Being easy, flexible, or kind in dealing with a situation
Life insurance company	Financial institution that sells insurance policies to protect individuals against loss of income from premature death, illness, or retirement
Liquidity	Function that increases the convertibility of least liquid assets into liquid assets
Locus of control	Degree to which people believe that have control over the outcome of events in their lives
Logical sequence	Sensible order of things or events
Management	Organizing and coordinating activities of a business or entity to achieve certain objectives
Manager	One who is responsible for controlling or directing an institution or business entity
Managerial	Pertaining to the role and function of management
Maqaāṣid al-shariah	The field of study of higher objectives of various Islamic laws and rulings
Market competitiveness	Pursuit of excellence relative to others in a market or industry
Marketing	Act of promoting the buying and selling of a product or service
Maṣlahah	Islamic legal doctrine of determining the permissibility or nonpermissibility of something based on public interest
Maysir	Gambling, one of the three key prohibitions in Islamic commercial law, involving outcomes based purely on chance where often one person's benefit comes at the expense of others
Mercy	Compassion, kindness
Merger and acquisition	Combining two companies into one through absorption or takeover
Minimum criterion	Least requirement for something to be decided upon
MNC	Multinational corporation with operations, facilities, or assets beyond the home countries
Money market	Market where short-term financial instruments are traded
Money market mutual fund	Mutual fund that invests in money market instruments
Moral hazard	Risk that the borrower may use the money in unethical investments
Mortgage	Debt instrument secured by collateral of specified real property
Motivation	Reason or factor to act or behave in a certain way
Mudharabah (**silent partnership**)	Islamic partnership where capital provider (*rabb al-maal*) and entrepreneur partner (*mudharib*) join as partners

Mudharib	Entrepreneur partner in Islamic partnership known as *mudarabah* (silent partnership)
Musharakah (partnership financing)	Islamic partnership where partners share in capital contribution and risk
Muslim-majority country	Country where Muslims constitute a majority of the population
Mutual fund	Portfolio of securities purchased in the name of a group of investors and managed by a professional fund manager
NAFTA	North American Free Trade Agreement, composed of the USA, Canada, and Mexico
National factors	Factors at national level affecting business environment or a business
Natural resource	Naturally occurring input for production, e.g., land, water, air
Nonprofit organization	Noncommercial organization that carries out its activities without seeking profit
Nonprogrammed decision	Unstructured, unique decisions, often based on intuition or creativity, for example
Opportunity creation	Allocation of resources to find or create new opportunities
Opportunity discovery	Systematic approach and effort to identify new (start-up) opportunities
Opportunity recognition	Alert, proactive, and competitive effort to recognize ideas for new business ventures or expanding existing ones
Over-the-counter market	Market where participants trade with one another through global computer and telecommunication networks
Overconfidence bias	Egotistical tendency to hold a false and unreasonable assessment of one's abilities
Participatory decision making	Decision-making process where pertinent stakeholders participate in various ways
Partnership	Arrangement or agreement among parties to cooperate in a defined pursuit of mutual interests
partnership-based contract	Islamic commercial contracts are based on participation of various parties as owners and risk takers
Pension fund	Fund that receives contributions from employers and/or employees that are invested on behalf of the employees to provide retirement cash flows
Philanthropic	This term is used to describe organization seeking to promote the welfare of the community.
Political environment	Regulatory and policy-related decisions and actions taken by the government with potential impact on a business
Political stability	Absence of disruptions or violence, enhancing durability of a current government or regime
Population explosion	Rapid increase in population, due to accelerating birth rate, declining infant mortality, and increase in life expectancy
Primary market	Market where new issues of securities are first sold and provide a direct cash flow to issuing entity
Private ownership	Ownership of assets by individuals or businesses other than the state
Procrastinating	Habit of delaying the start or completion of a task in a reasonable time frame
Professional ethics	Principles or codes that govern the behavior of a person or group in a business or organizational environment
Profit	Financial gain, especially the difference between the amount earned and the amount spent in buying, operating, or producing something

Profit maximization	Assumption of modern economics that the ultimate goal of a business is to earn as much profit as possible
Prognosis	Forecasting the probable course and outcome of a particular event or undertaking
Programmed decision	Decision made as part of a standard process, guided by commonly identifiable factors
Prohibition	Islamic ruling regarding nonpermissibility of something
Property rights	Rights associated with ownership of property, including right to use, sell, or give it away
Proposition	Statement or assertion expressing a judgment or opinion
Proprietor	Owner of a business or holder of property
Proprietorship	Ownership of a business
Prudential	Showing care to abide by laws
Public ownership	Majority or controlling shareholding (51 percent) of a firm by a government
Qana`ah	Feeling of contentment
Qard	Loan commonly understood in Islamic commercial law as being free of interest or without any return to lender
Qard hasan	Benevolent or charitable loan without any worldly return to lender
Qiyas	Analogical reasoning, a method of Islamic jurisprudence to derive rulings from what is known to apply to what is a new situation
Qur'an	Verbatim and preserved divine revelation from Allah, as believed by Muslims to have been received by Prophet Muhammad (PBUH)
R&D initiative	Ongoing and systematic effort in research to come up with new product or service or improve existing ones
Rabb al-mal mudarabah	Capital provider in Islamic form of partnership, known as
Rational decision making	Systematic, multistep process for identifying and selecting from a set of alternatives
Real economy	Part of economy involving production, distribution, and consumption of goods and services, as contrasted with financial sector activities
Reasonable profit	Profit target or benchmark that is not disconnected from cost and competitive factors
Regulations	Examples are limiting entry, transparency, supervision of bank balance sheet, and deposit insurance
Regulatory body	Government agency exercising authority in a regulatory or supervisory capacity
Reporting	Making a formal statement about something to the necessary authority
Repurchase agreement	Agreement between a borrower and a lender to sell and repurchase a government security
Reputation risk	Potential loss or vulnerability due to unfavorable exposure leading to negative public perception
Resource mobilization	Undertakings to secure new and additional resources for a business or organization
Restricted *mudarabah*	Type of Islamic partnership where capital provider restricts the entrepreneur partner's freedom of choice regarding where to invest
Return policy	Process of granting a customer the right to return merchandise to the seller and receive a refund, an exchange, or other adjustment
Riba	Commonly equated with interest, or any preagreed excess paid or received over and above the principal in a loan contract

Risalah (prophethood/ messengership)	Belief that God has sent a message (revelation) to humanity through various prophets and messengers
Risk	Potential for the occurrence of an unfavorable outcome or event
Rizq	Provisions that God designates or allocates for a person in this world
Secondary market	Market where existing, previously issued securities are traded among investors
Service-based contract	Islamic commercial contract involving the provision of services, for example, banker's acceptance or safekeeping
Shareholder	Owner of a business or entity, especially a corporation
Shariah	Divine guidance in Islam as enshrined in the Qur'an and the life of Prophet Muhammad (PBUH)
Shariah **law**	Body of legal rulings emerging from the interpretation of *Shariah*, commonly referred to as Islamic law or *fiqh*
Shariah **pronouncement**	Jurist opinion on any matter related to *Shariah* law
Shariah **scholars**	Scholars who are well versed in *Shariah* law
Shariah **compliance**	Banking or banking activity that complies with Islamic law
Shariah-**compliant**	Agreeing with *Shariah*, but more specifically meaning avoidance of prohibitions
Shura	Consultation involving pertinent stakeholders in decision making
Shura-**style decision making**	Decision making based on participation of the relevant stakeholders
Small business	Privately owned business with fewer employees and smaller-scale activities than a regular-sized business or corporation
Small business sector	Sector comprising small businesses
Social accountability	The ways citizens and government engage positively to monitor and assess public officials or institutions
Social activism	Mobilizing resources and acting as an organized factor to bring about desired changes in practices and policies of business or government
Social business	Nonprofit business established and designed to address some major or broad socioeconomic problems, such as poverty or healthcare, for example
Social consciousness	Collective self-awareness shared by individuals within a society
Social responsibility	Obligation to do good for society at large beyond selfish motives
Sociocultural factors	Values, customs, mores, and lifestyles characterizing or shaping a society or group
Stakeholder	A person, group, or institution related to an organization that is affected by and can affect the organization
Sunnah	Sayings and acts of the Prophet Muhammad (PBUH) as well as reports of companions' acts or sayings with which the Prophet agreed
Supply chain	Complete sequence of business processes enabling satisfaction of customer demand for a product or service
Supporting contract	Contract that generally serves the purpose of strengthening or facilitating other Islamic commercial law contract
Sustainable community	Community planned, built, or modified based on the vision and aspiration of sustainable living
Taqwa (**God-consciousness**)	Consciousness of Allah (fear and love) that motivates and guides an individual to act morally and uprightly
Tawakkul	Reliance on Allah or trusting in God's plan, followed by one's due diligence

Tawhid (monotheism)	Belief in oneness of Allah; unified paradigm emanating from that belief
Technological innovation	Introduction of something new or improved through technology
Thrift institution	Depository institution in the form of savings and loans, savings bank, or credit union
Tolerance	Allowable departure or deviation from a specification or standard or a fair and accommodating attitude toward differing opinions, beliefs, and practices
Top line	Gross sales or revenue, displayed at the top of a company's income statement
Transformational leadership	Style of leadership where leaders and followers work as a team to help and motivate each other to achieve higher levels of success
Transparency	Characteristic of institutions and individuals being open in the proper disclosure of information relevant to stakeholders
Treasury bills	Short-term obligations issued by a government
Treasury bond	Long-term debt obligation issued by a government
Trust	Quality of deserving of reliance on the character or truth of someone or something
Trustworthiness	Quality of deserving confidence and trust
Truthfulness	Habitual trait of telling or upholding the truth
Ummah	Community; people; group; nation
Uncertainty	Outcome or consequence of not having accurate or adequate knowledge of a situation
Universal brotherhood	View that the global Muslim community is one fraternity
Usul al-fiqh	Islamic legal theory or principles of Islamic jurisprudence
Valid contract	Contract that meets Islamic legal requirements
Wasta	One's connections or influence to get things done or achieve goals
Zakah	Compulsory levy on each Muslim who has wealth equal to or more than a minimum called *nisab;* it is one of the five pillars of Islam. There are eight categories of those who receive *zakah*, including the poor and needy
Zikr	A kind of devotional act through remembrance or invocation of Allah

INDEX

Printed in the USA
CPSIA information can be obtained
at www.ICGtesting.com
LVHW080158140624
783111LV00003B/353